Iwan Baan BRASILIA–CHANDIGARH Living with Modernity

Cees Nooteboom
EX NIHILO: A Tale of Two Cities

Martino Stierli
Monuments to Modernity,
a Historical Epilogue

Lars Müller Publishers

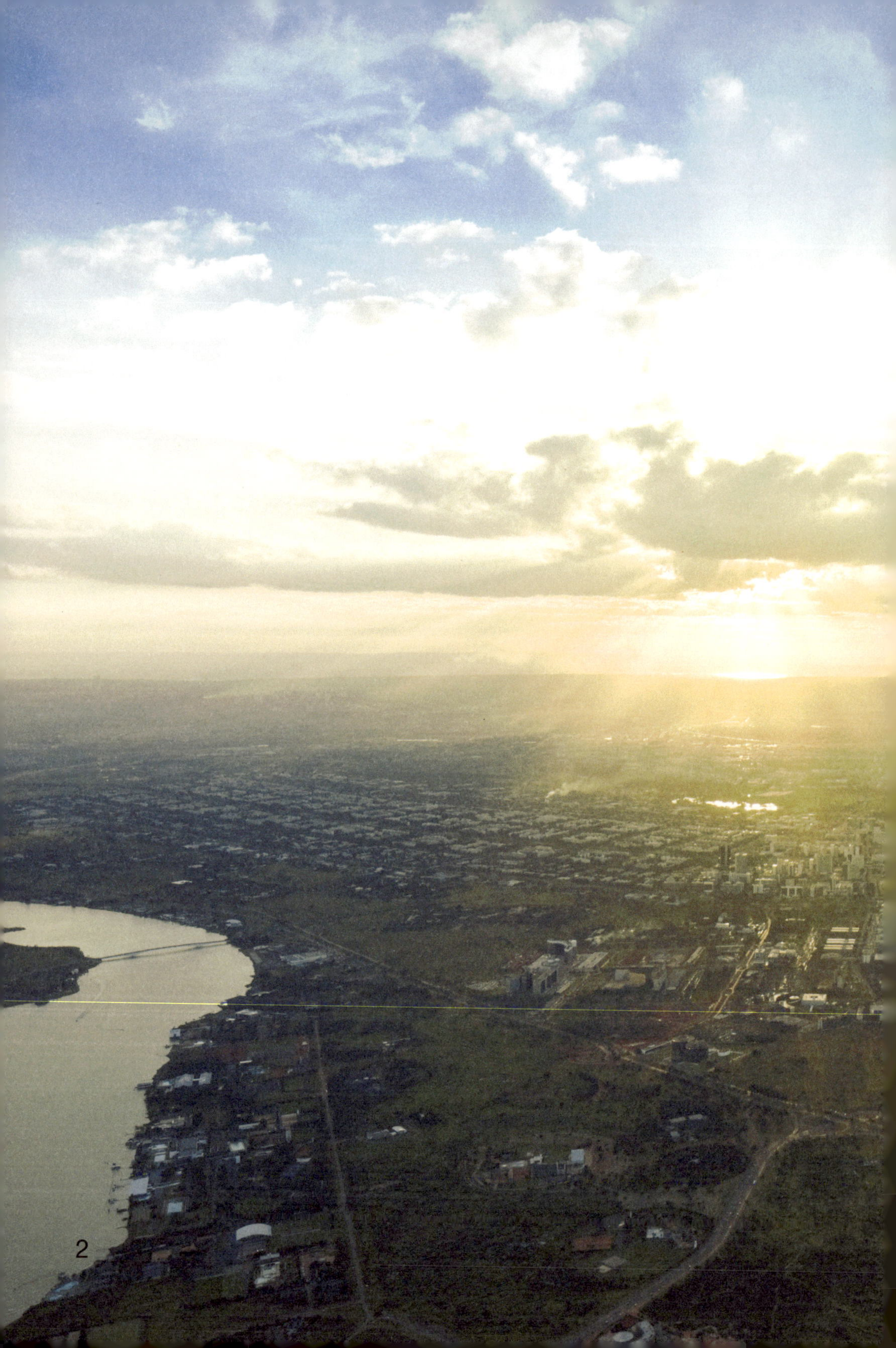

2

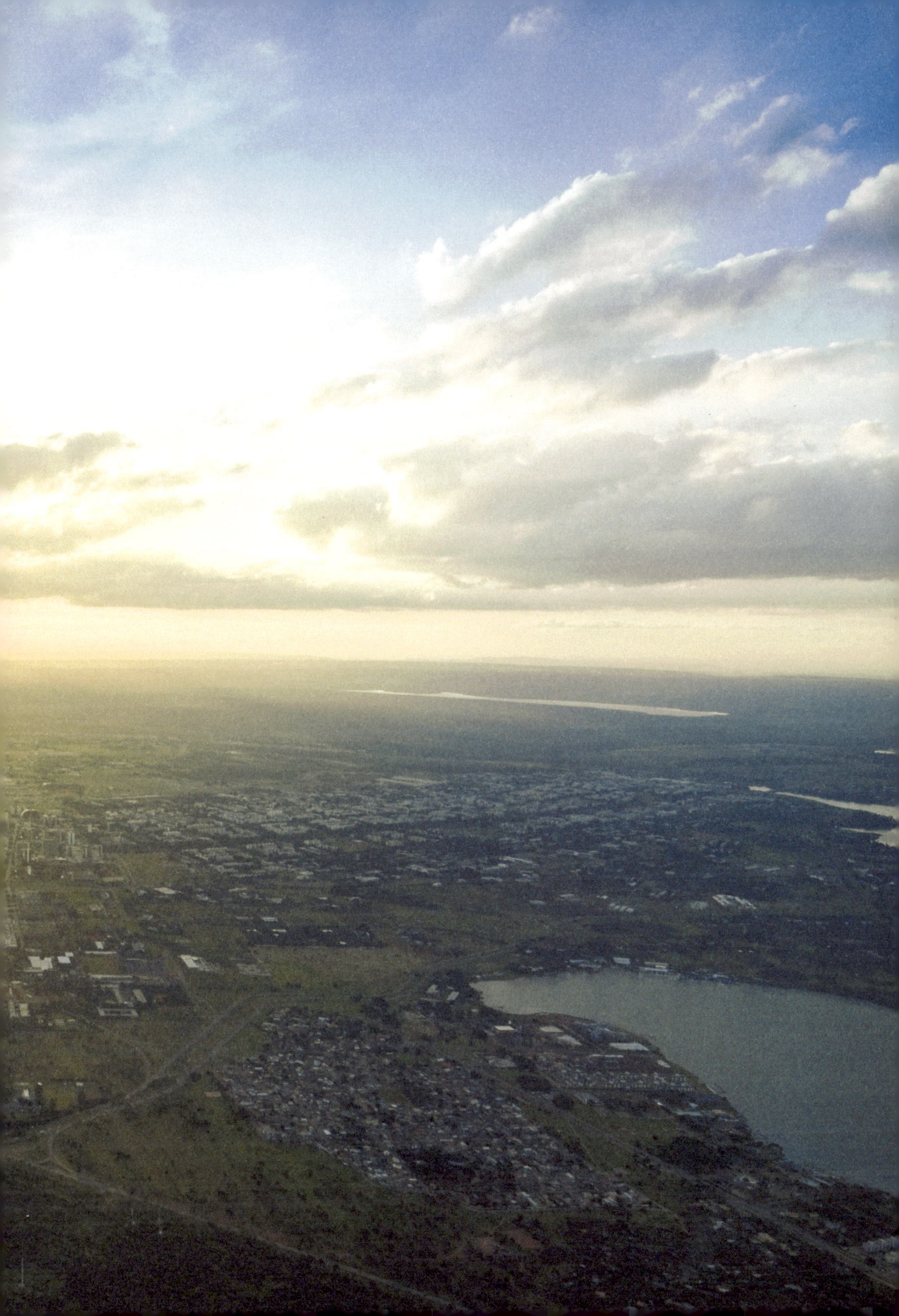

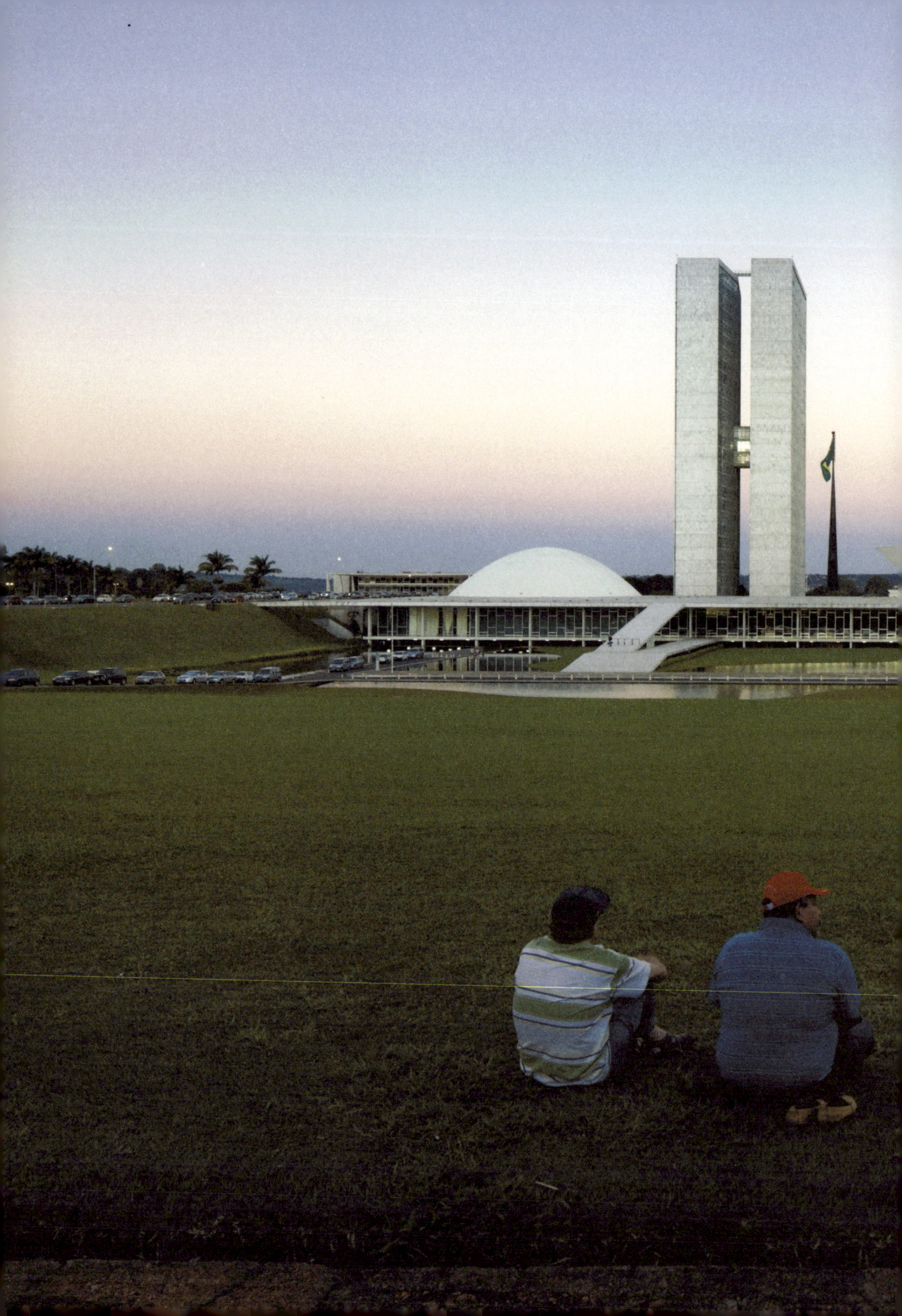

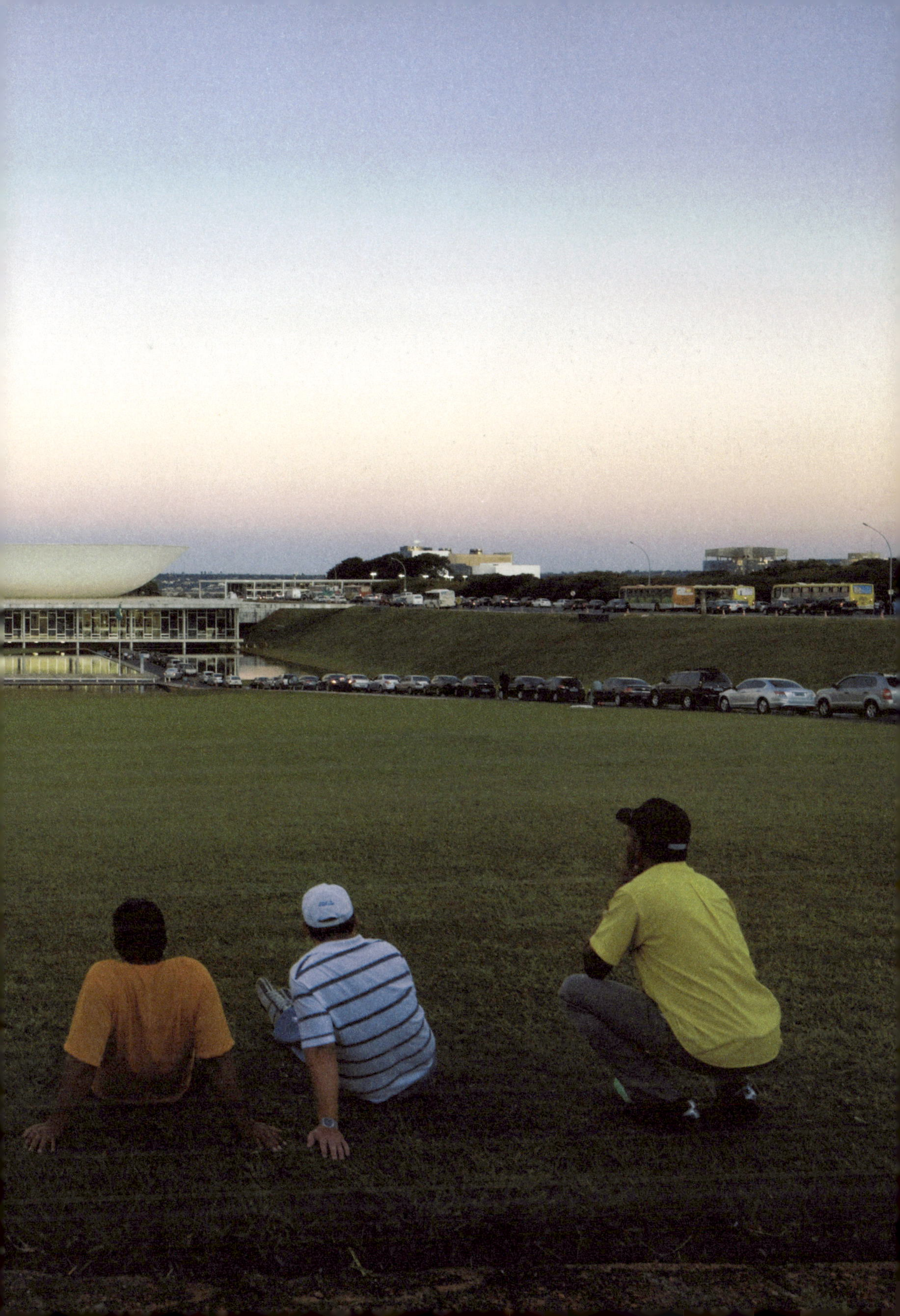

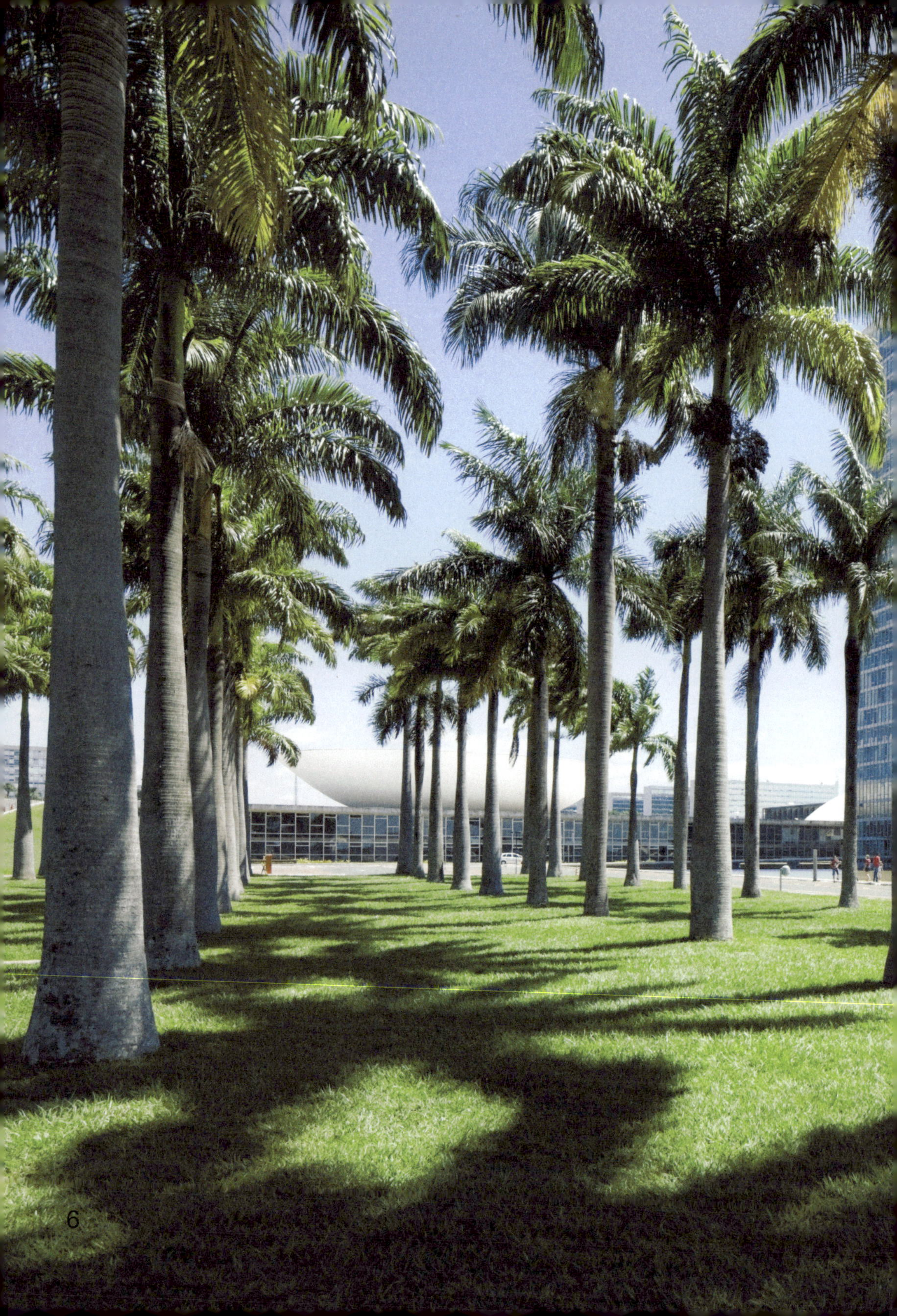

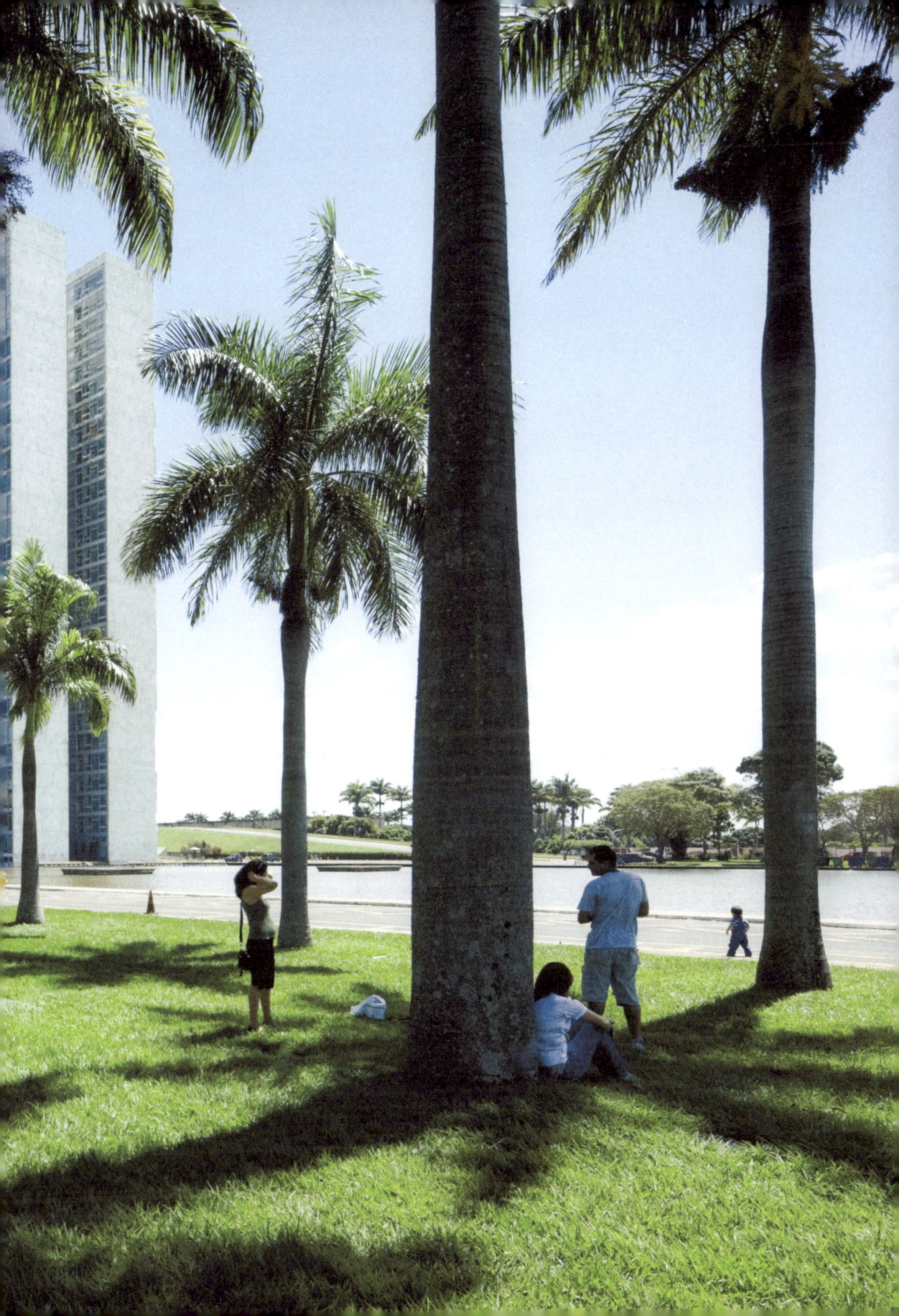

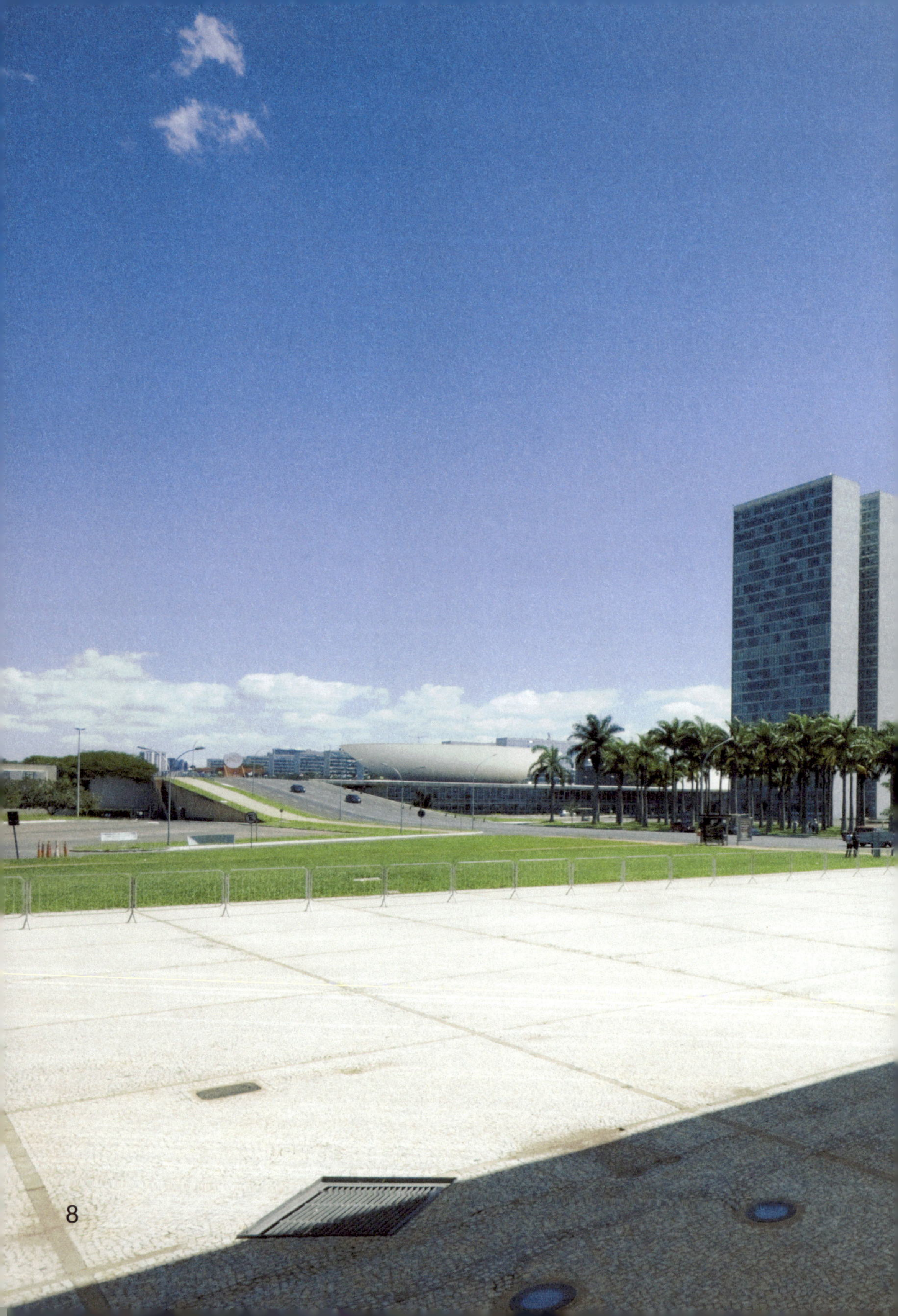

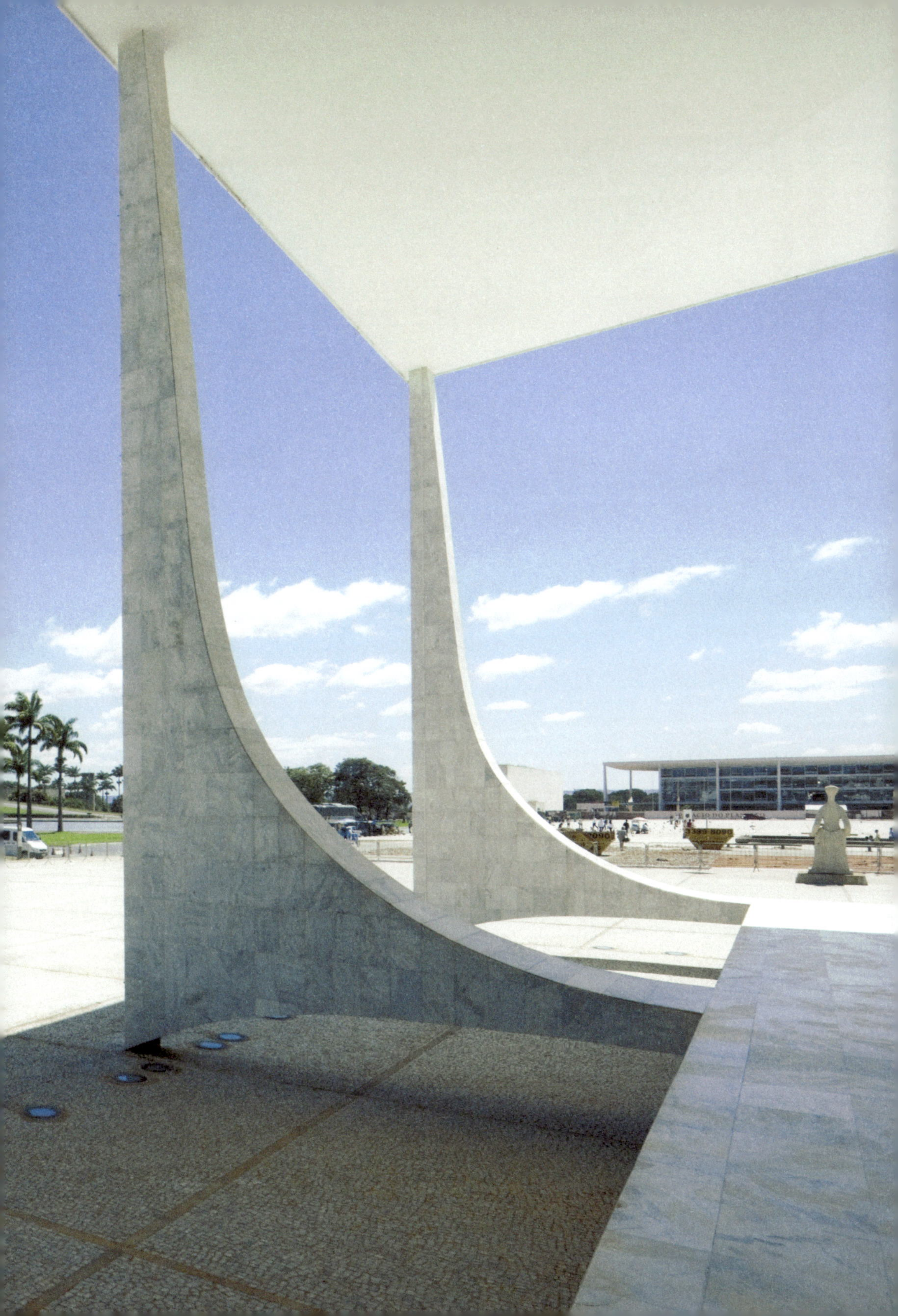

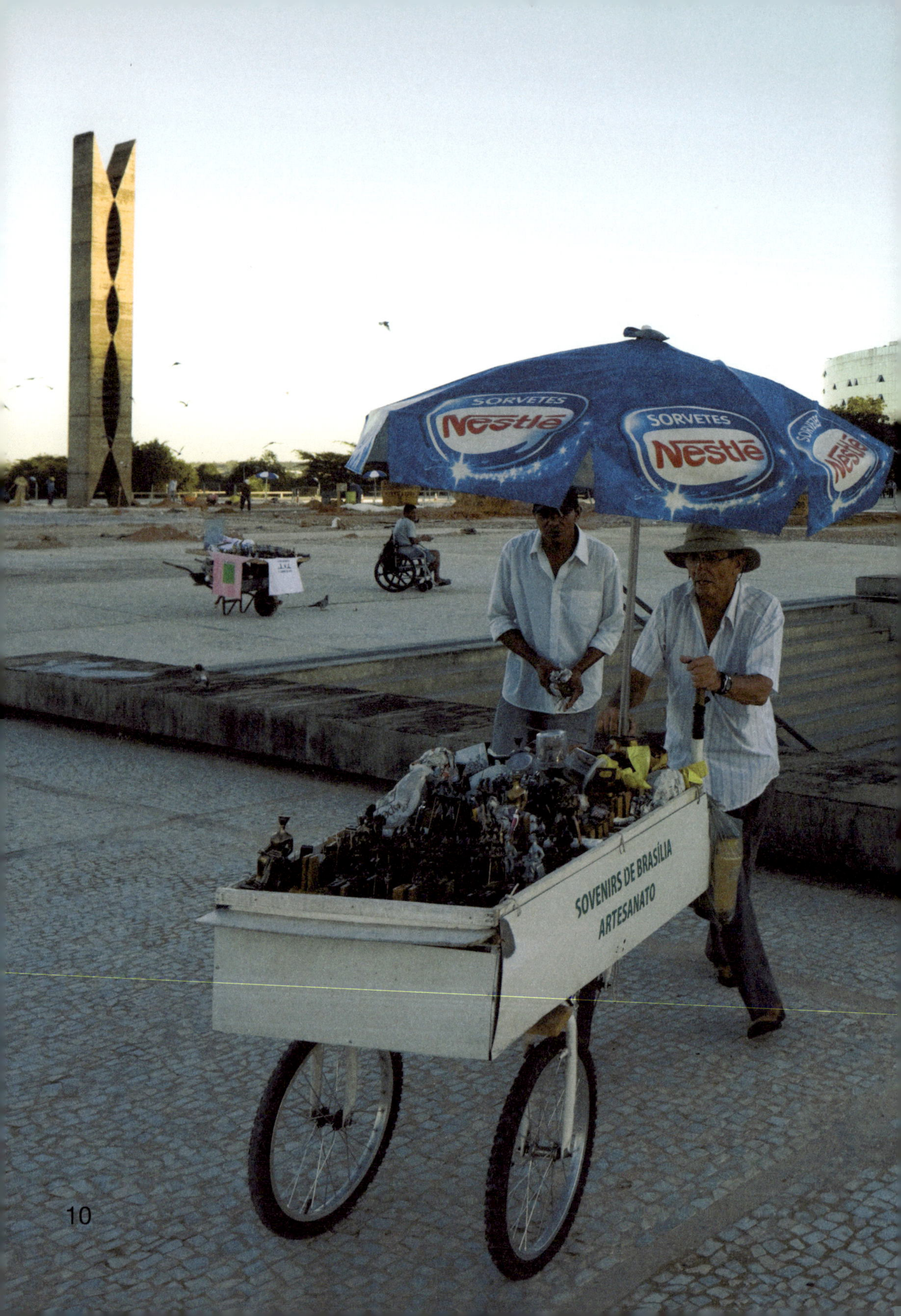
SORVETES
Nestlé
SORVETES
Nestlé
SOVENIRS DE BRASÍLIA
ARTESANATO

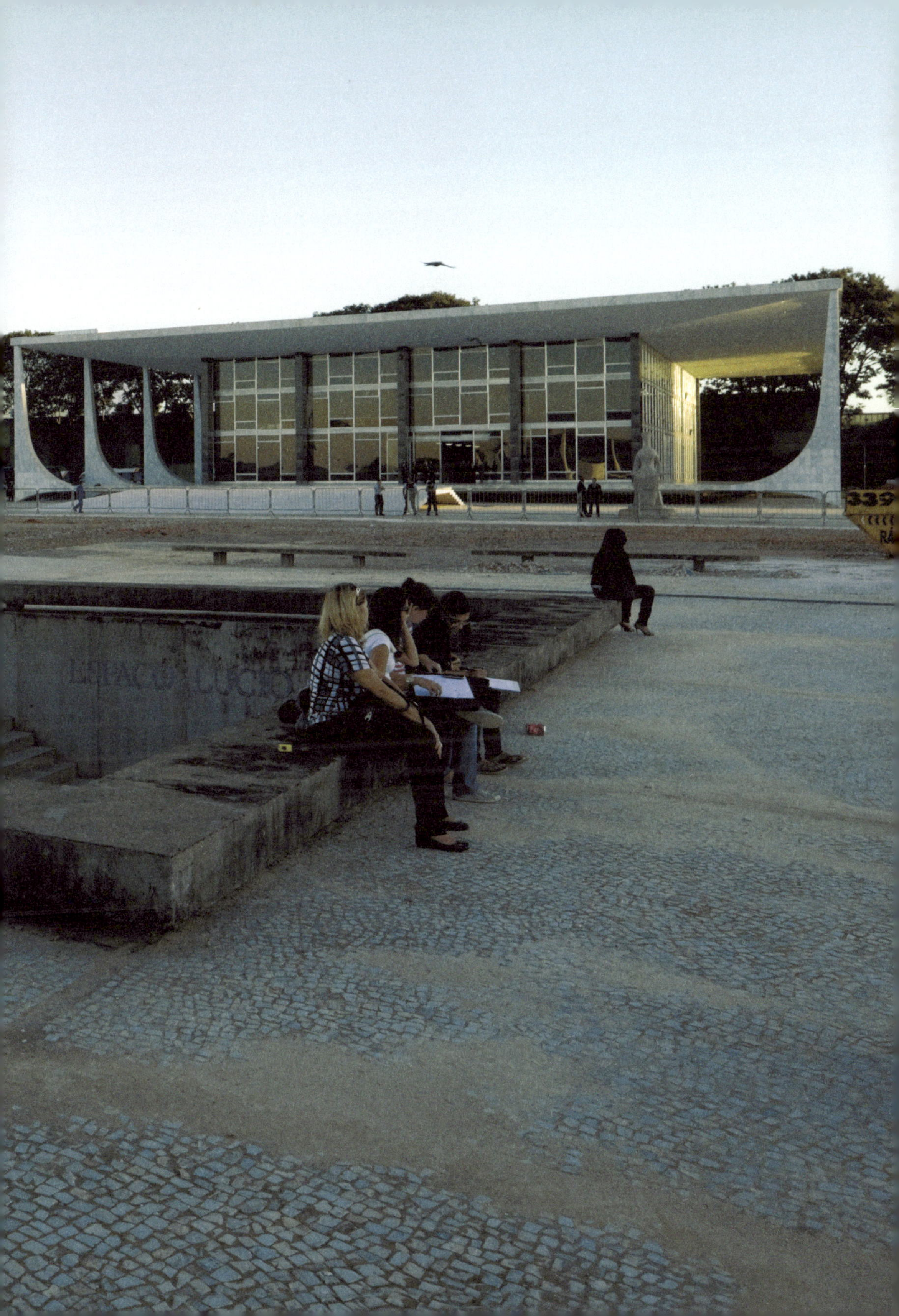

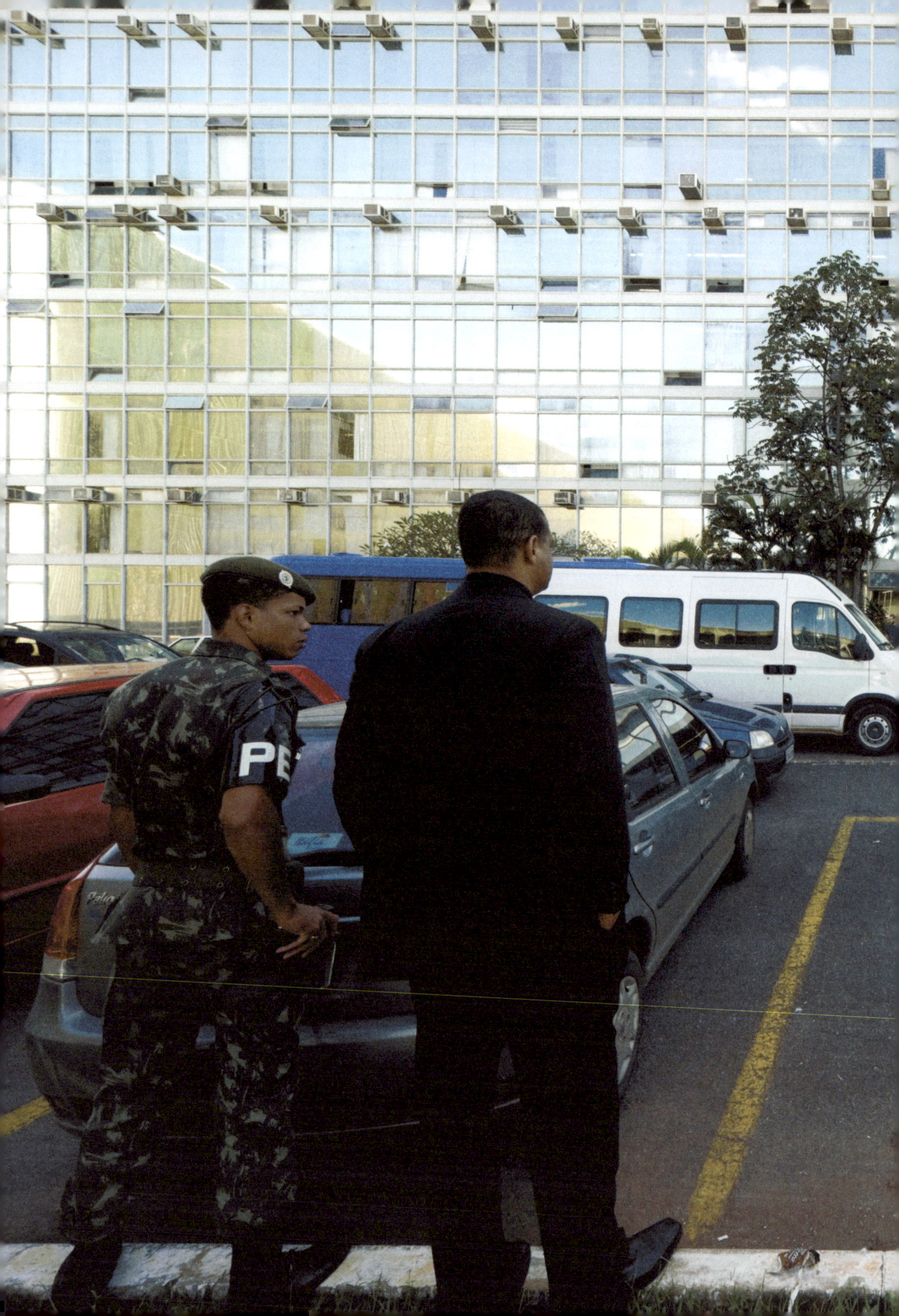

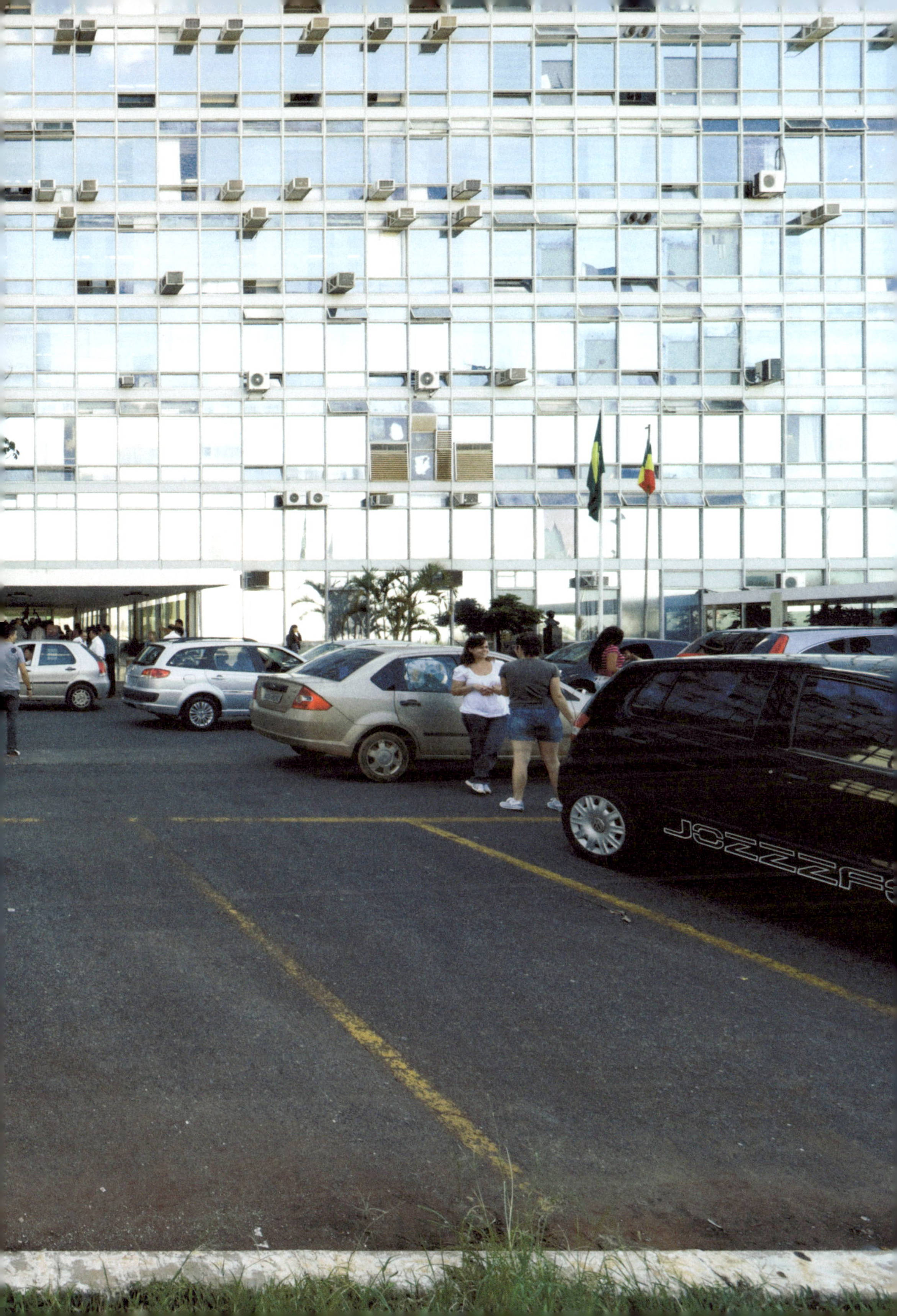

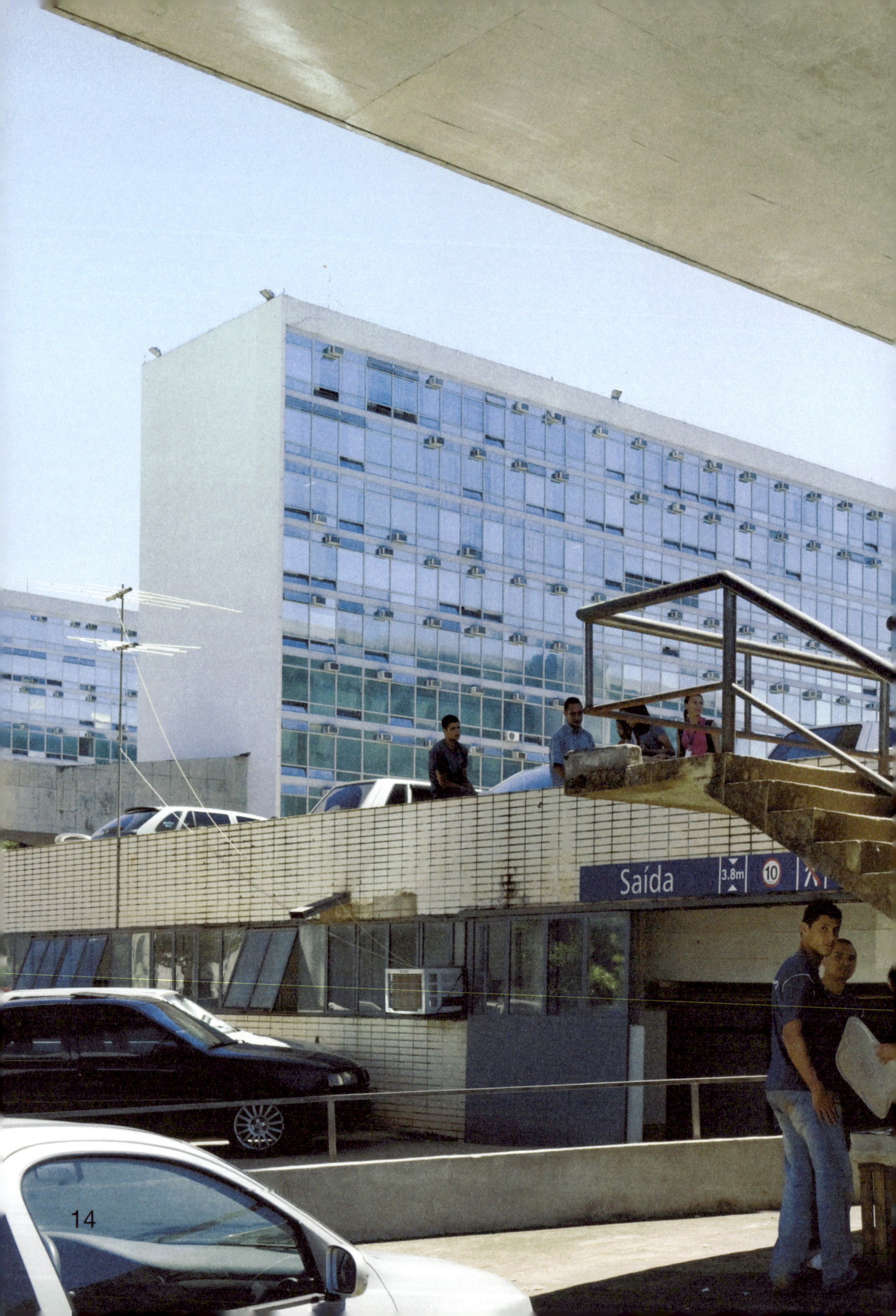
Saída
3.8m
10

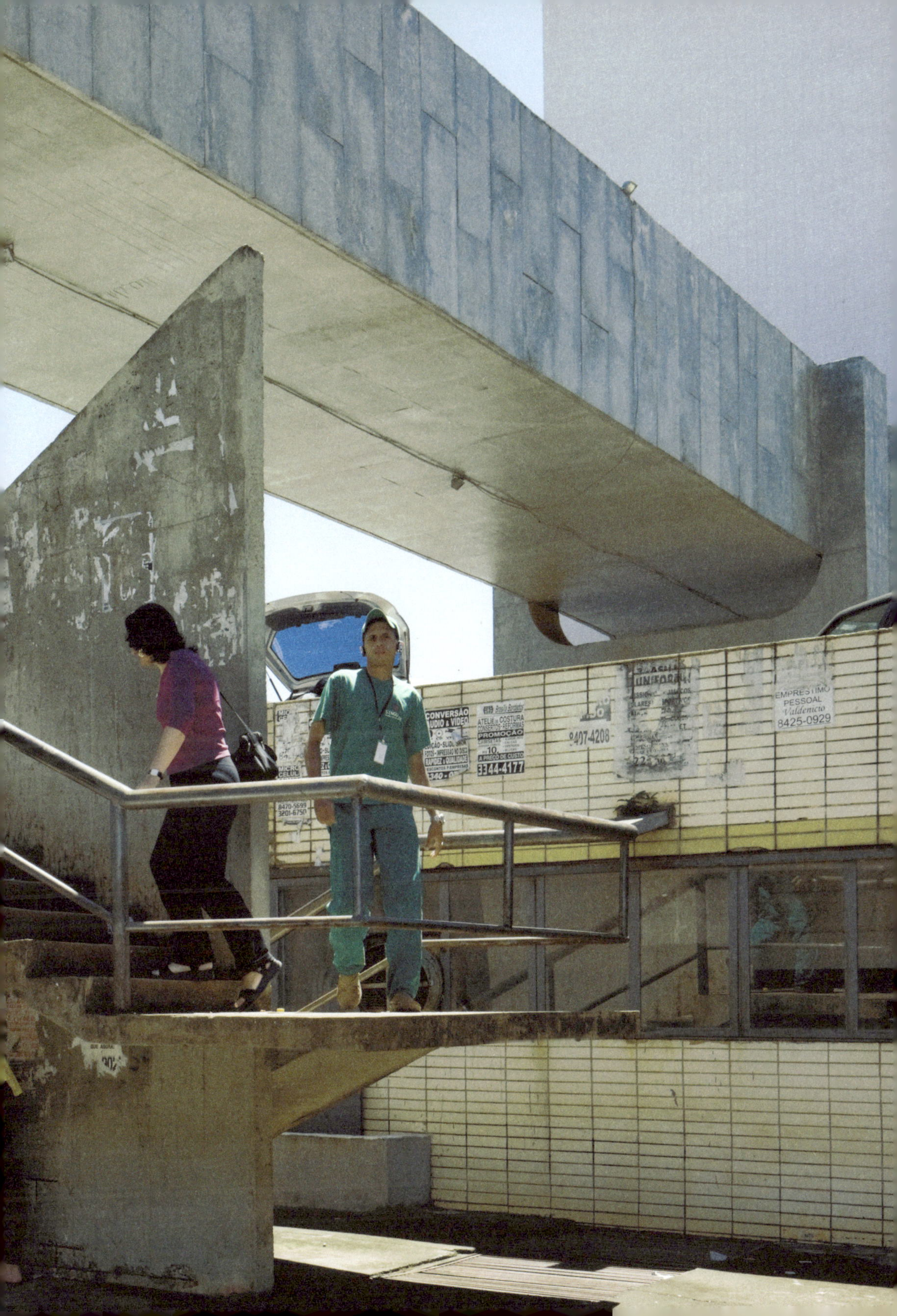
CONVERSÃO
ÁUDIO & VÍDEO
ATELIÊ de COSTURA
PROMOÇÃO
A PREÇO DE CUSTO
3344-4177
8407-4208
8470-5699
3201-6750
EMPRESTIMO
PESSOAL
Valdenicio
8425-0929

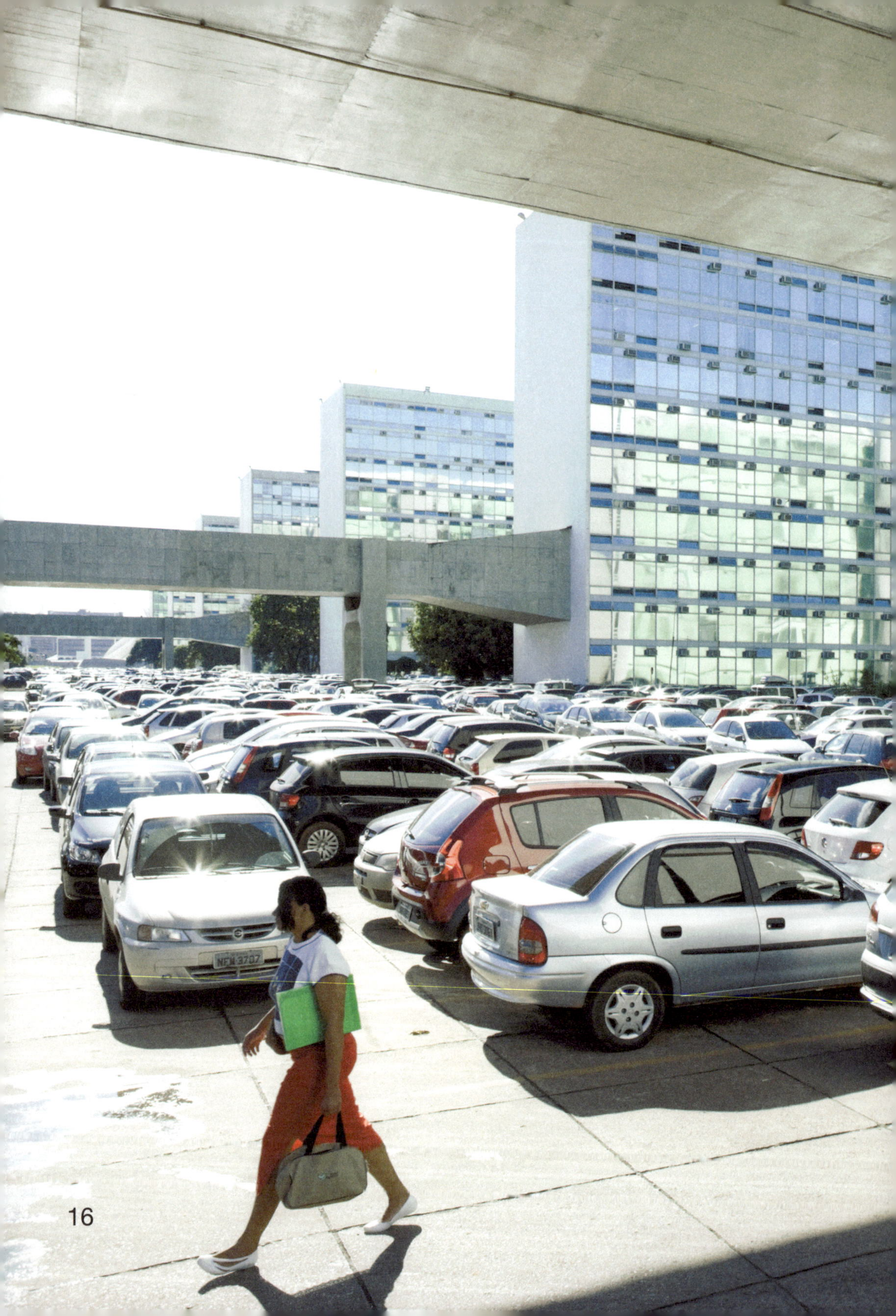
NFW 3707

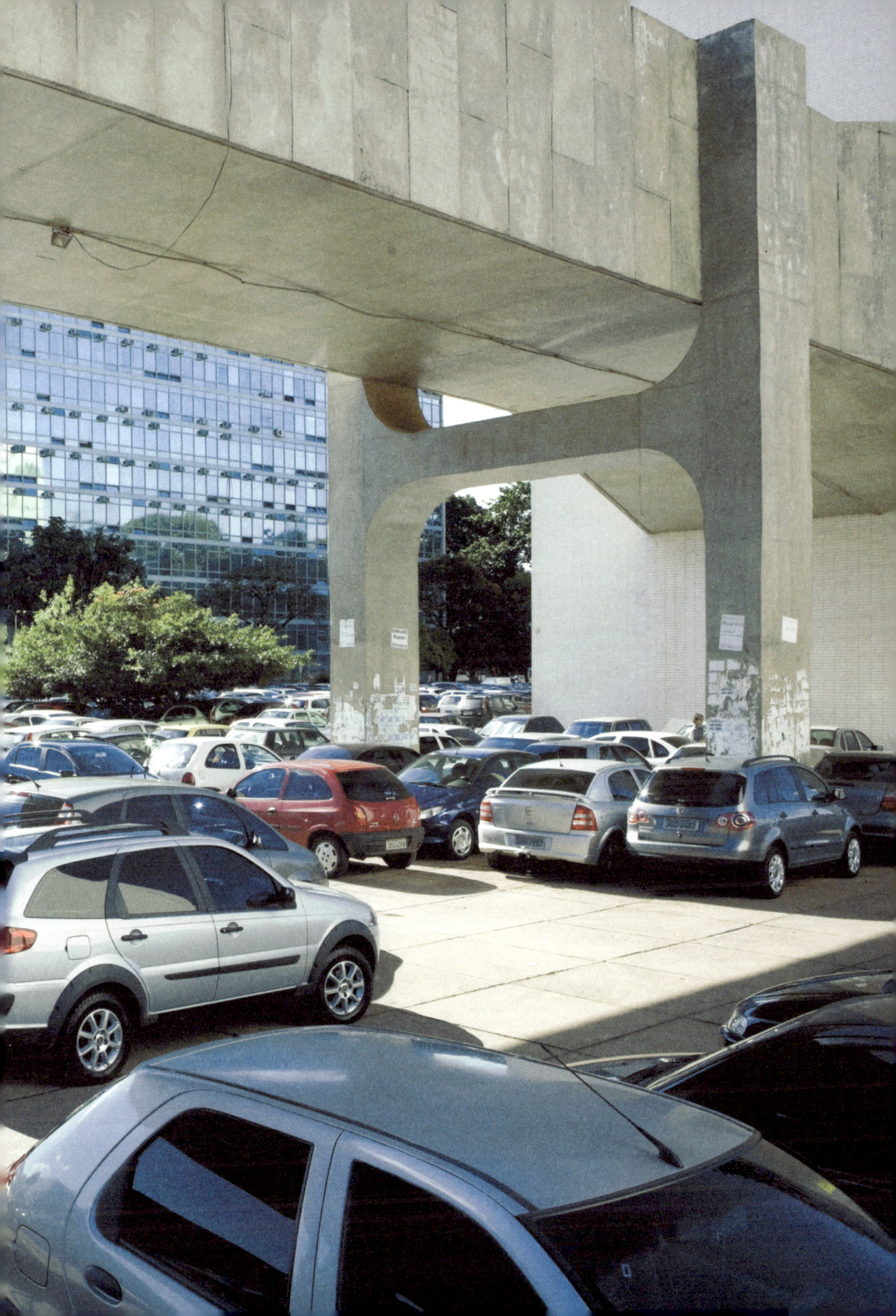

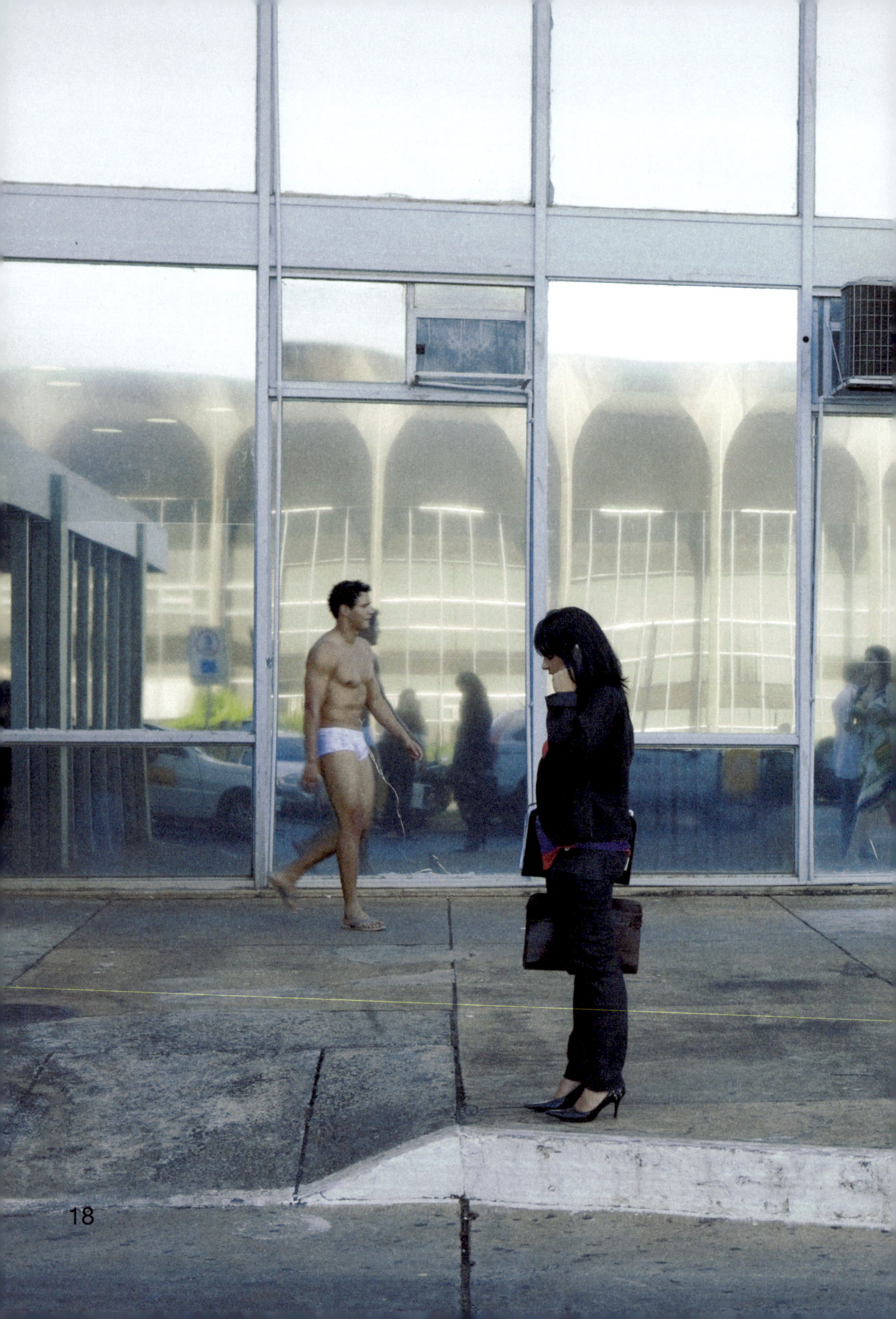

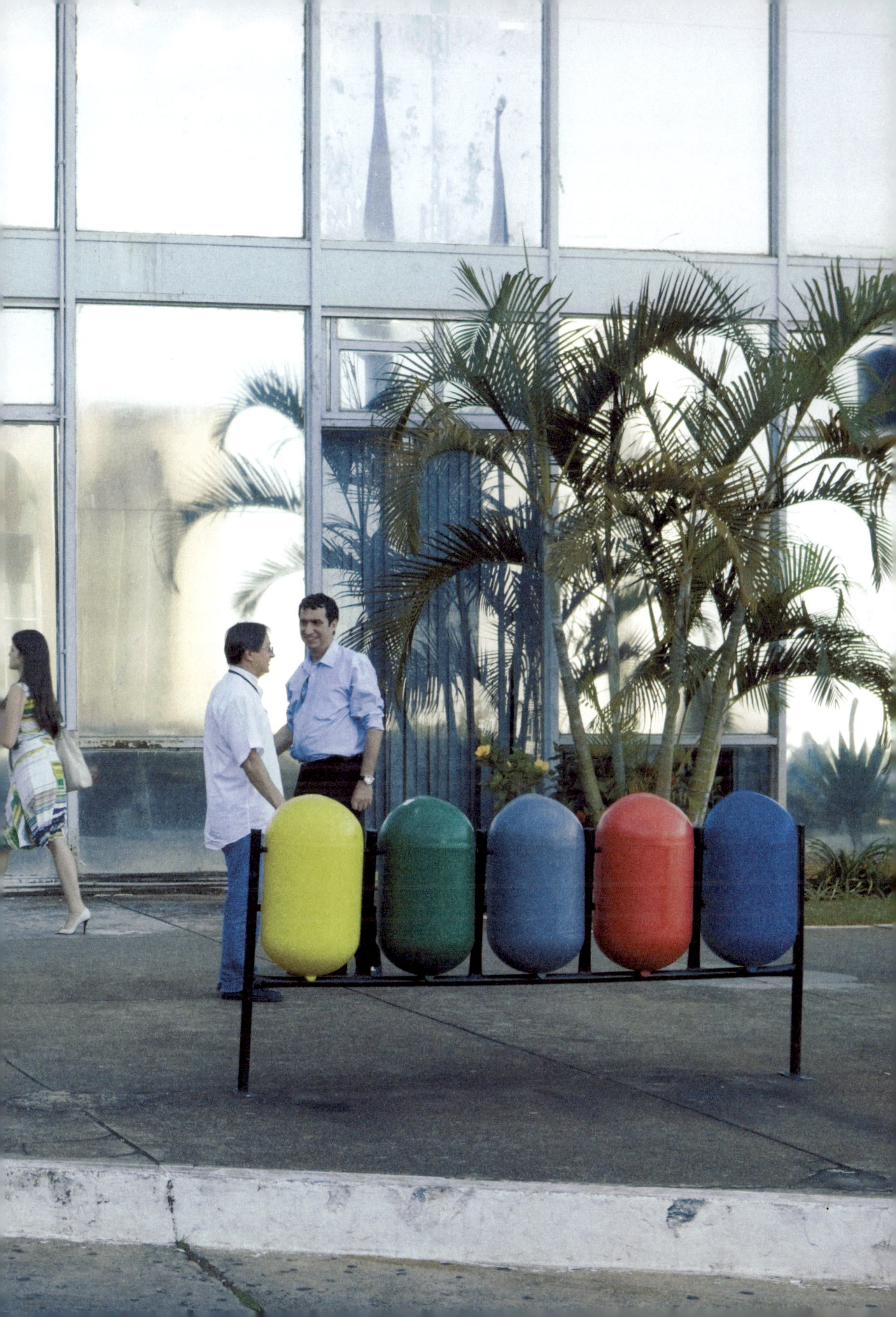

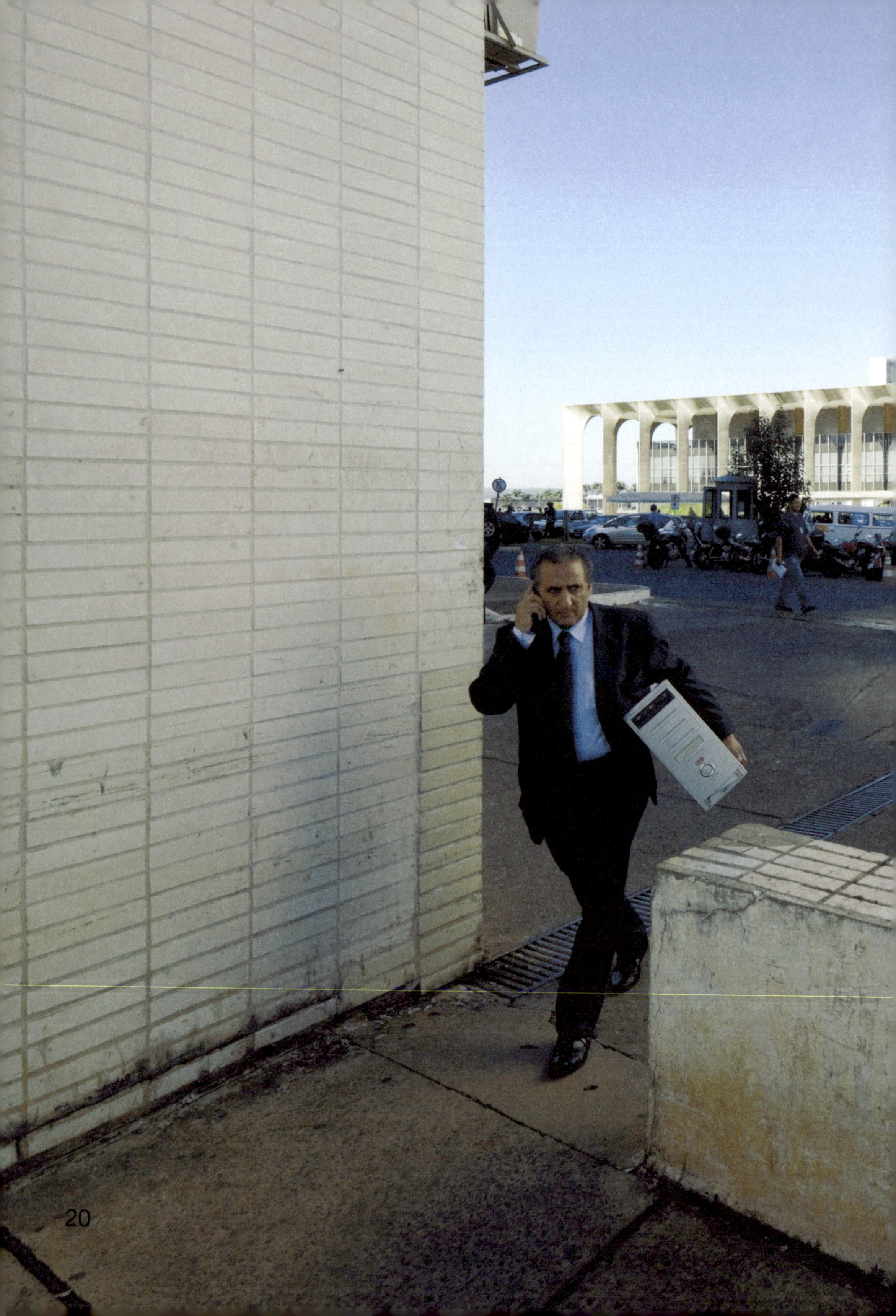

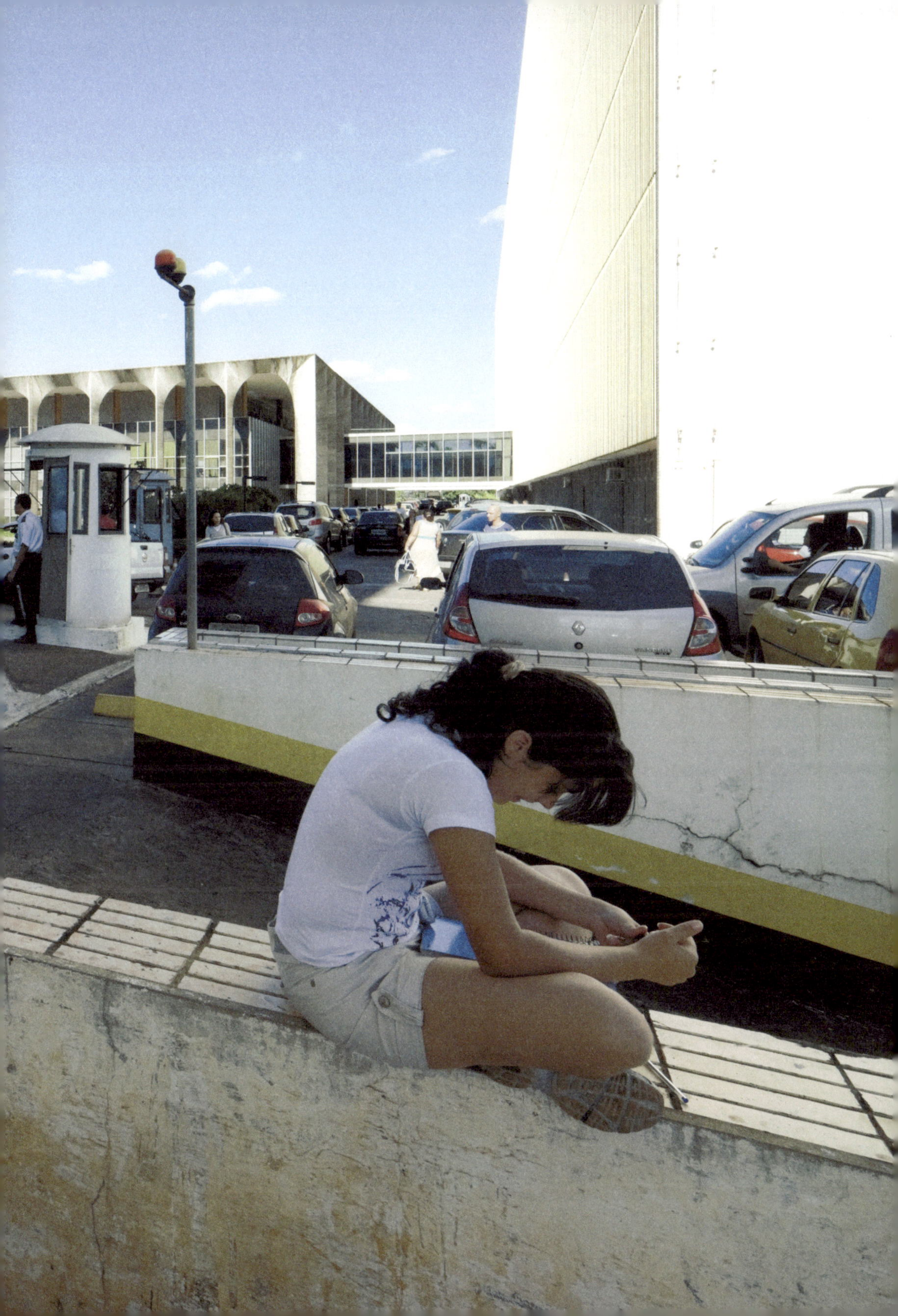

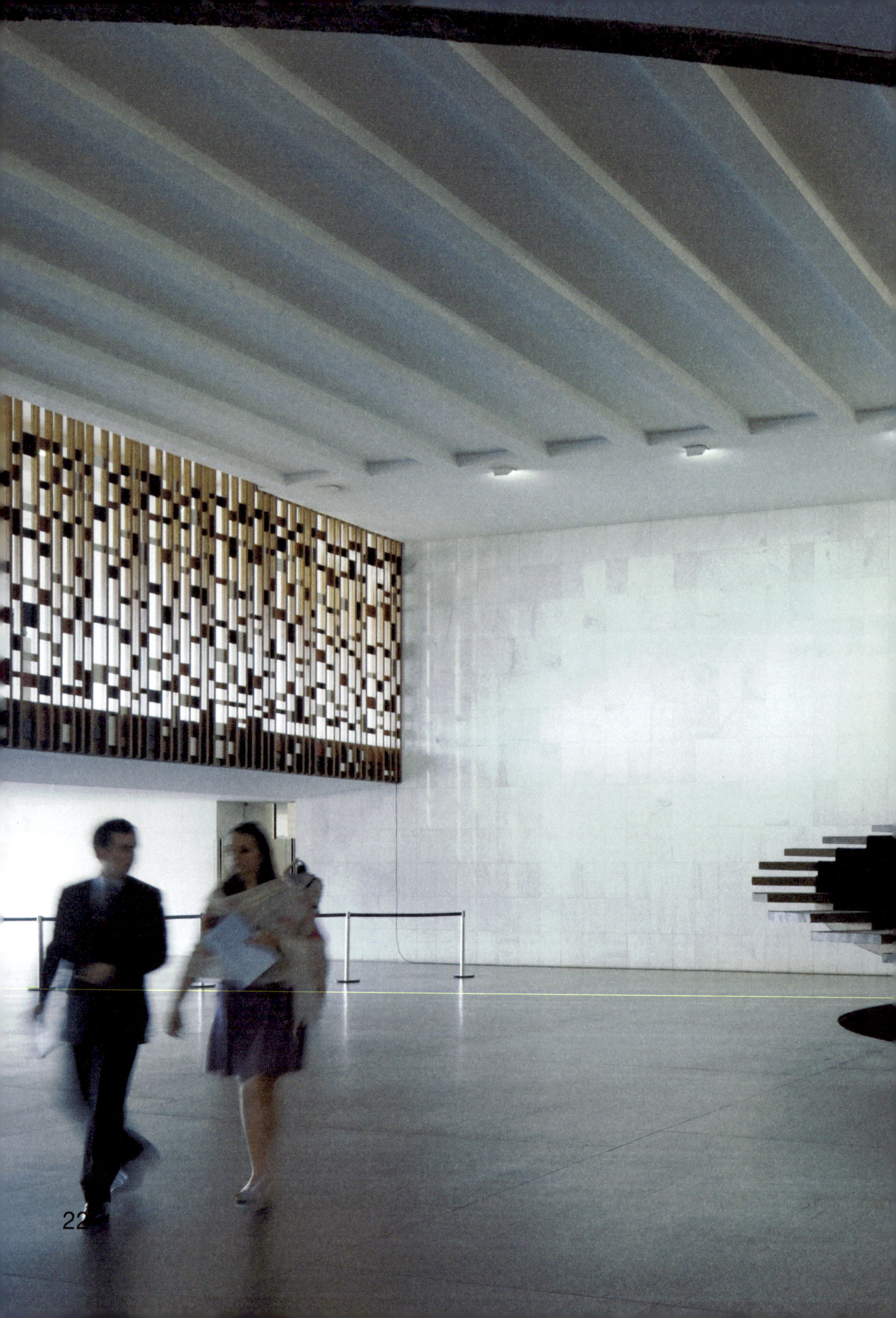

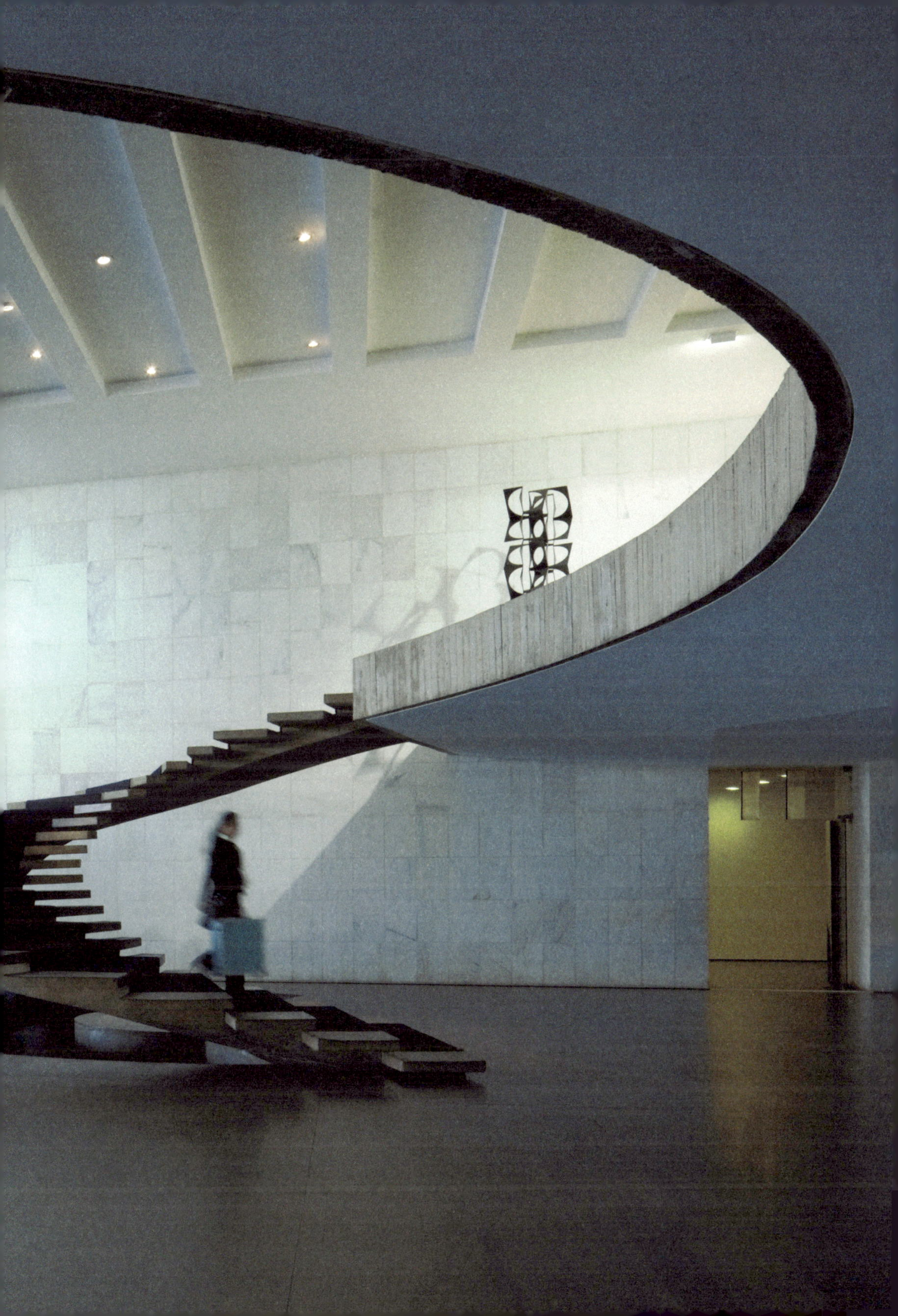

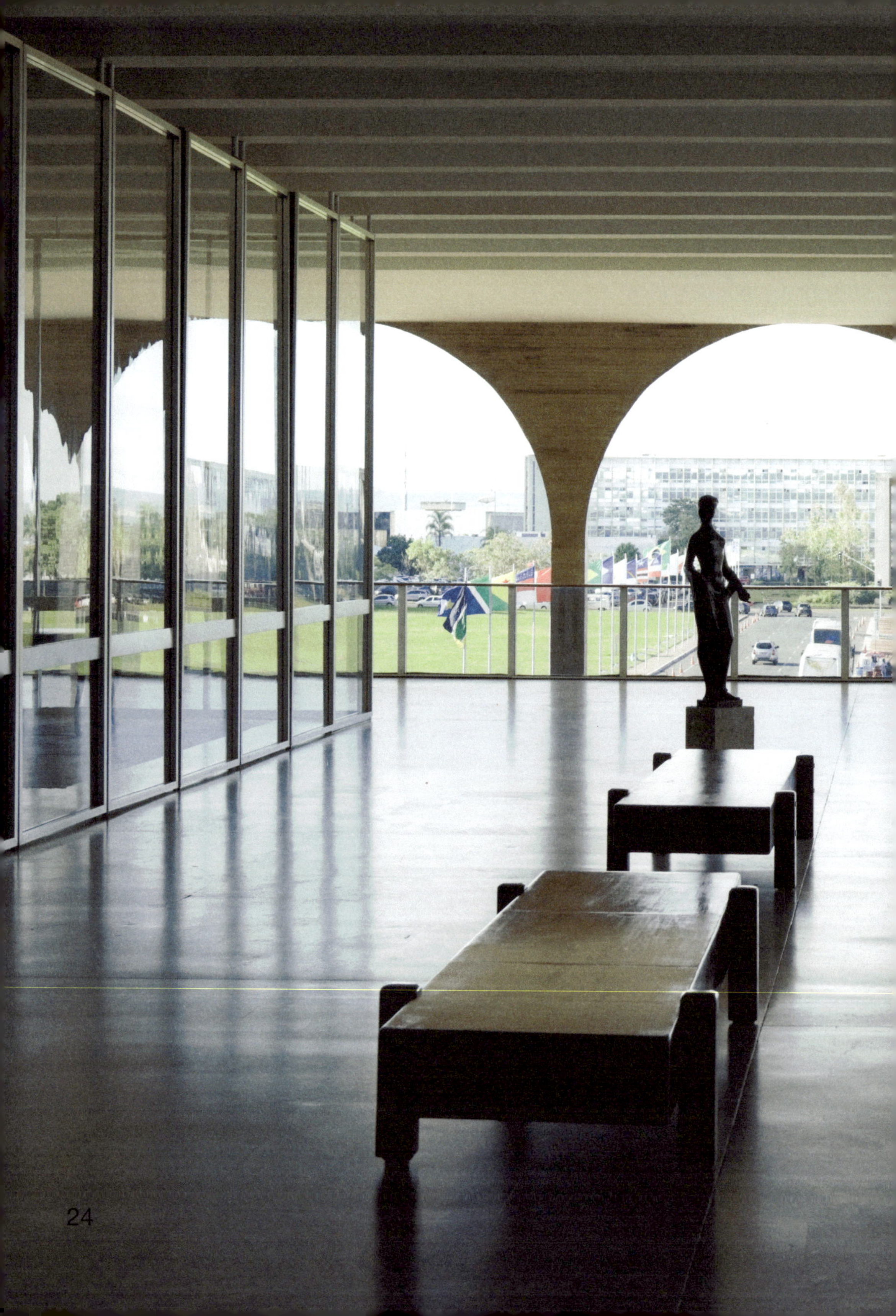

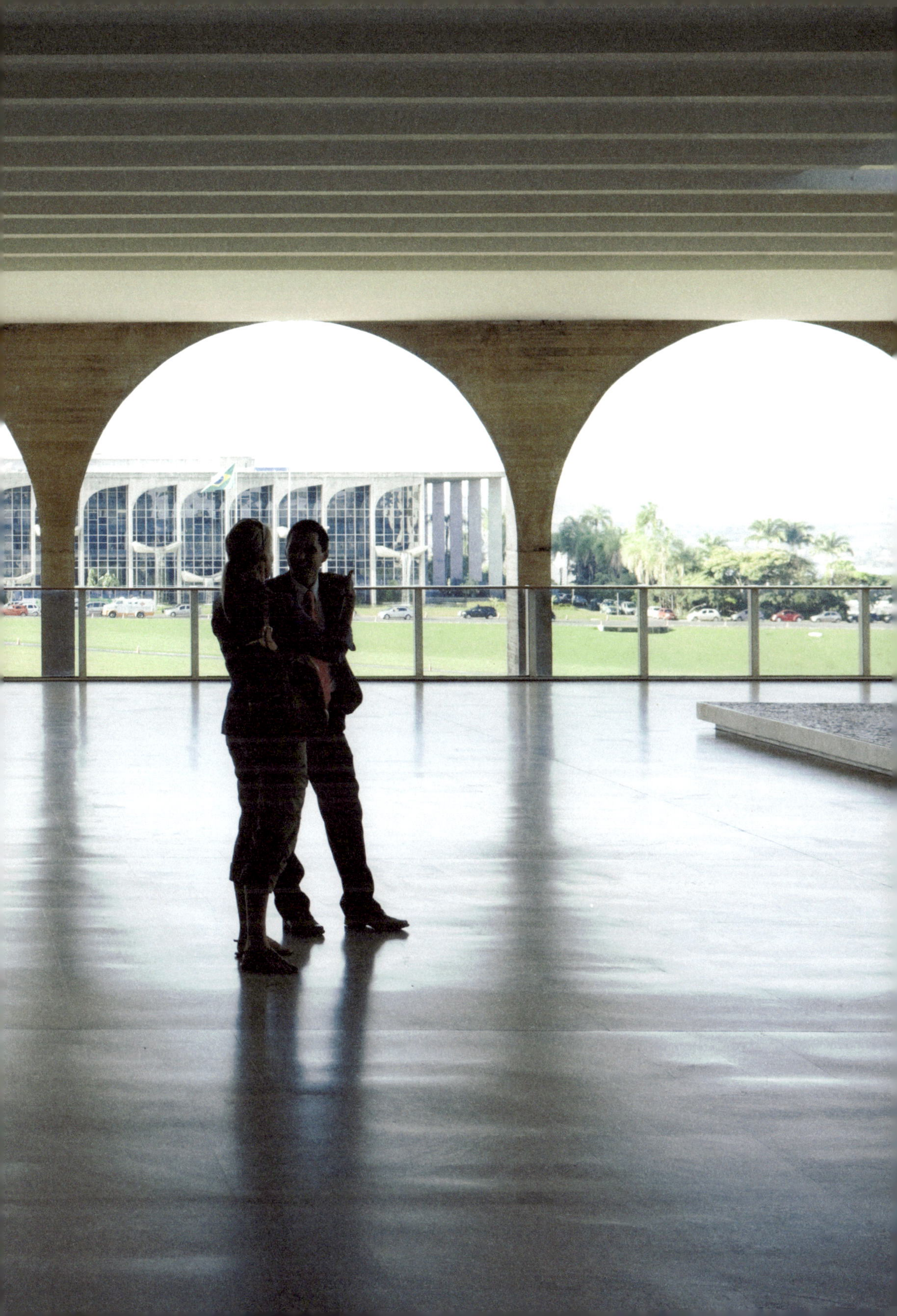

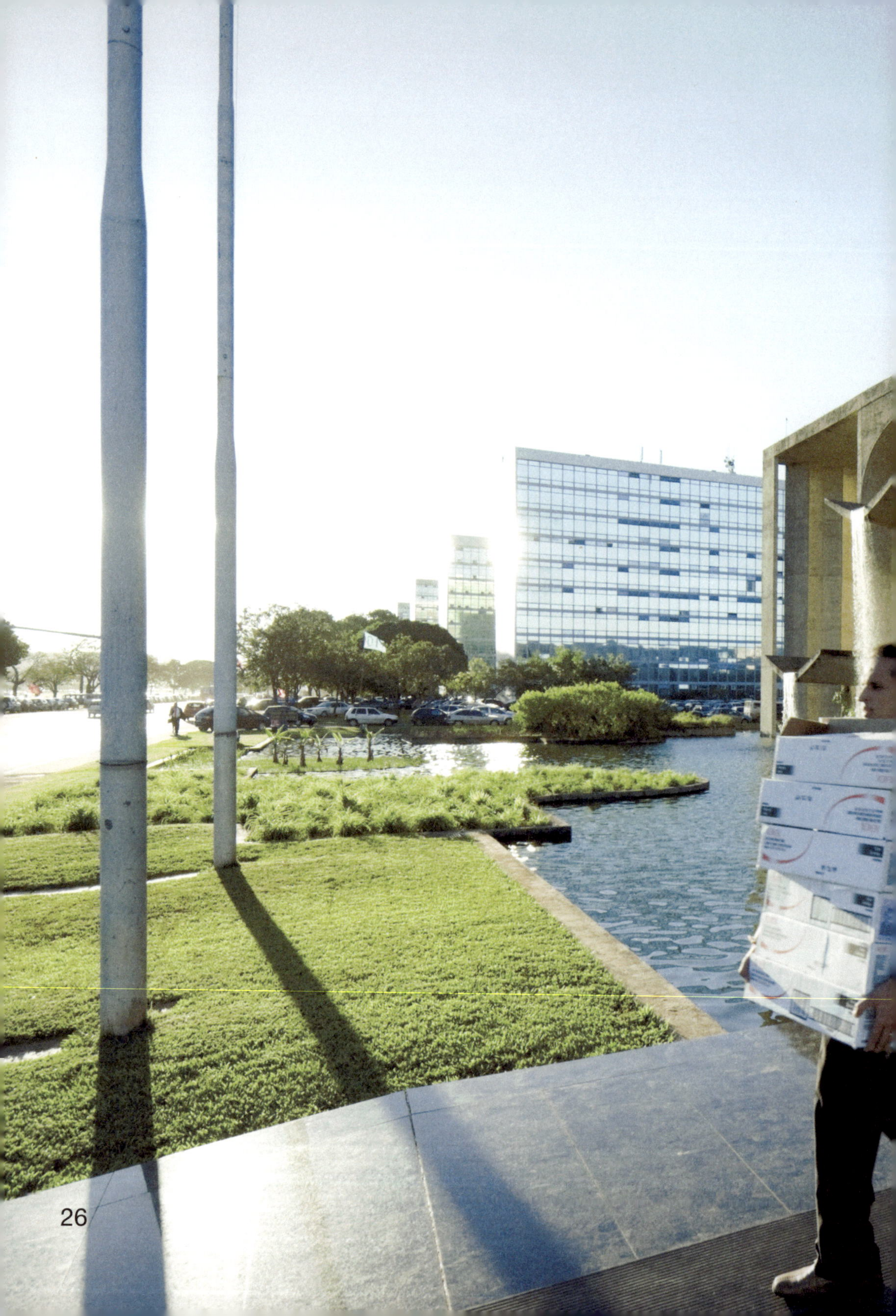

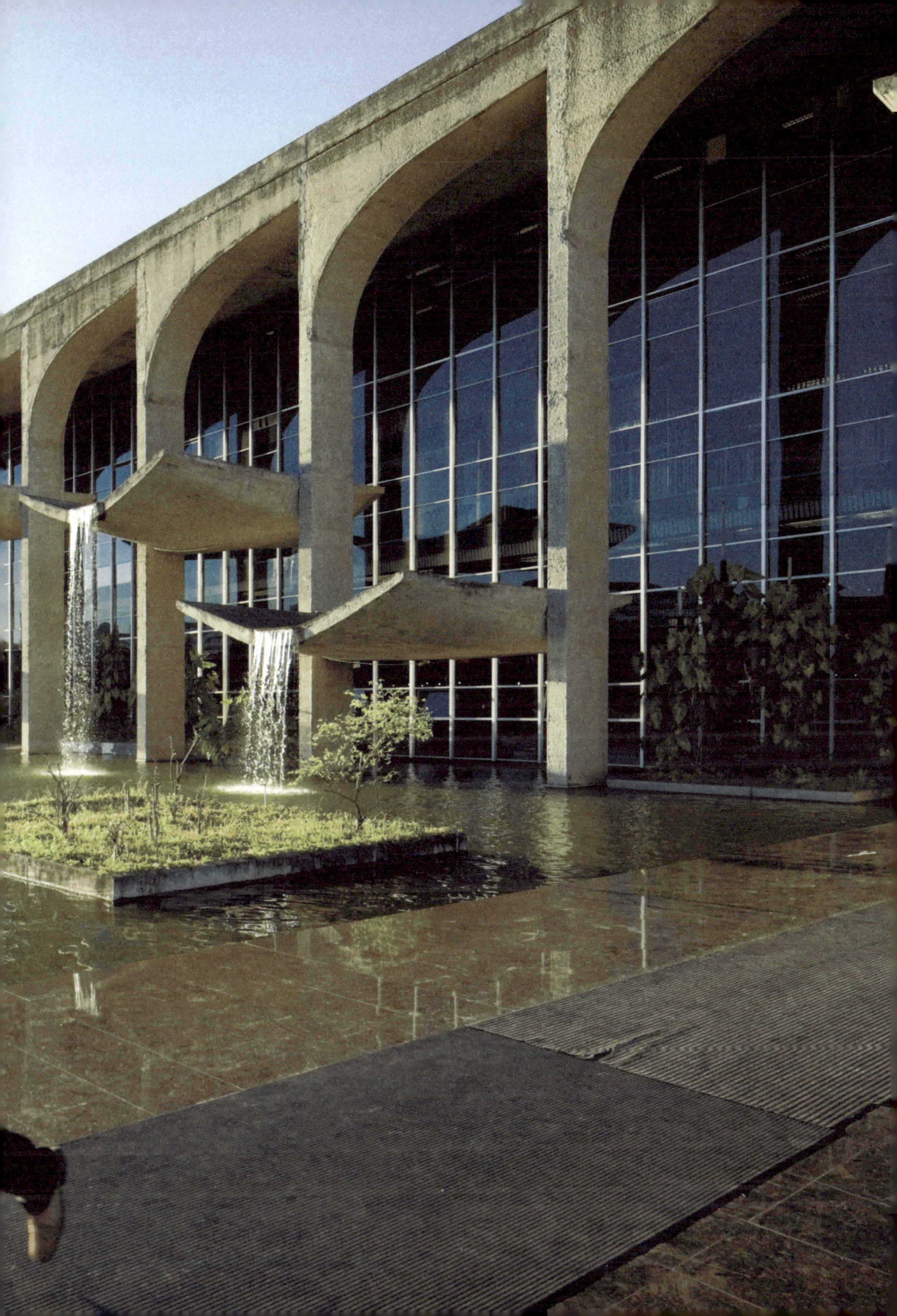

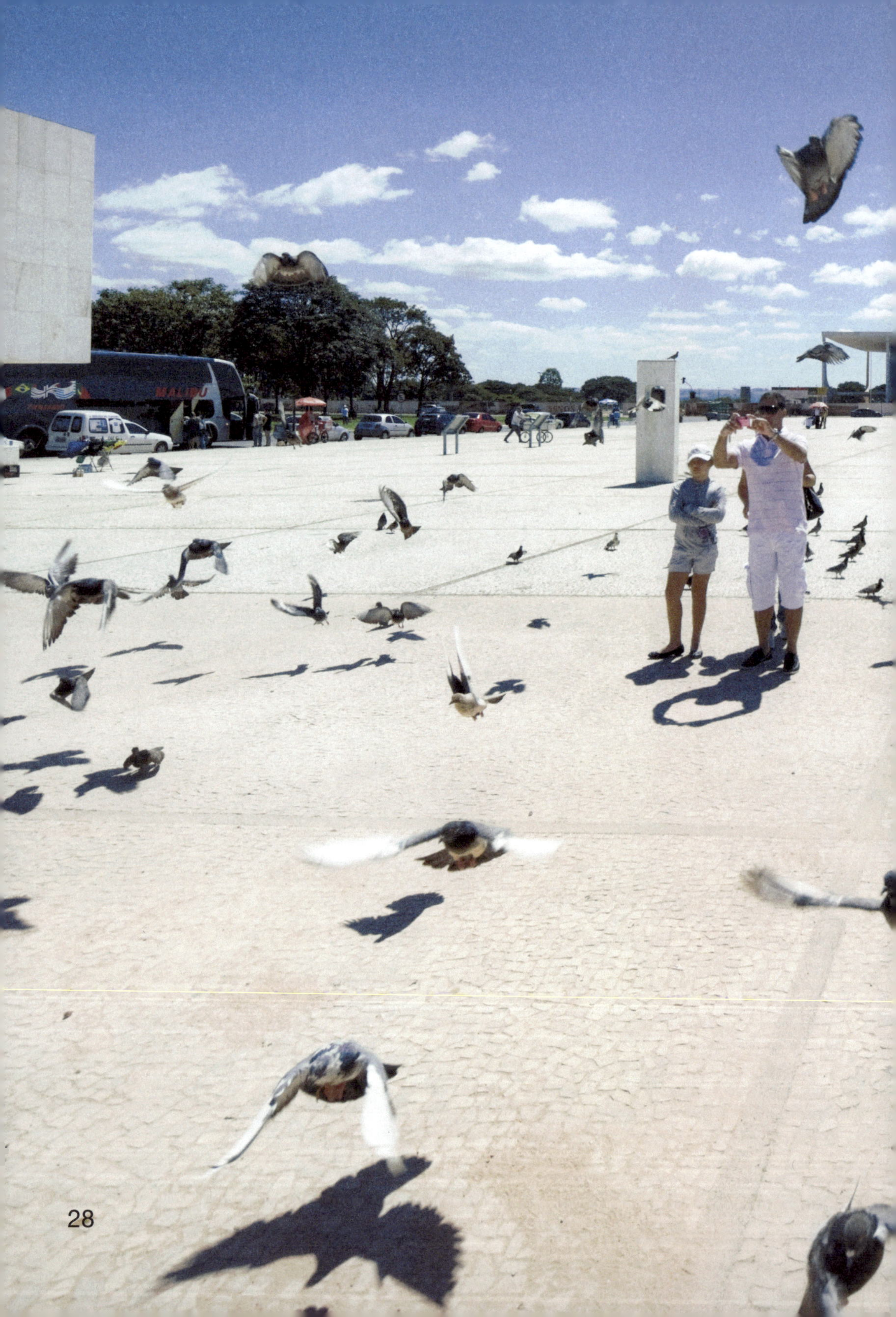
MALIBU

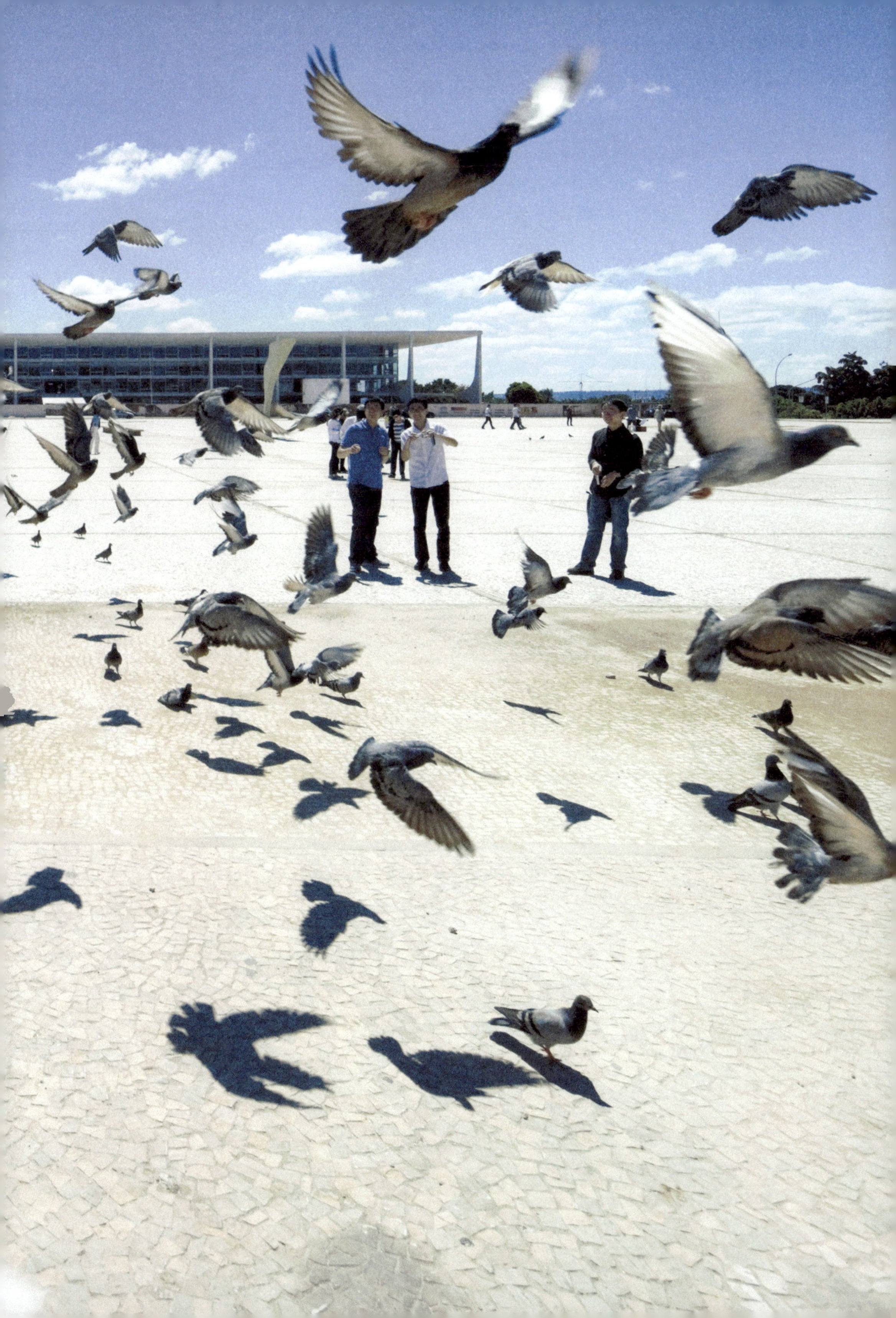

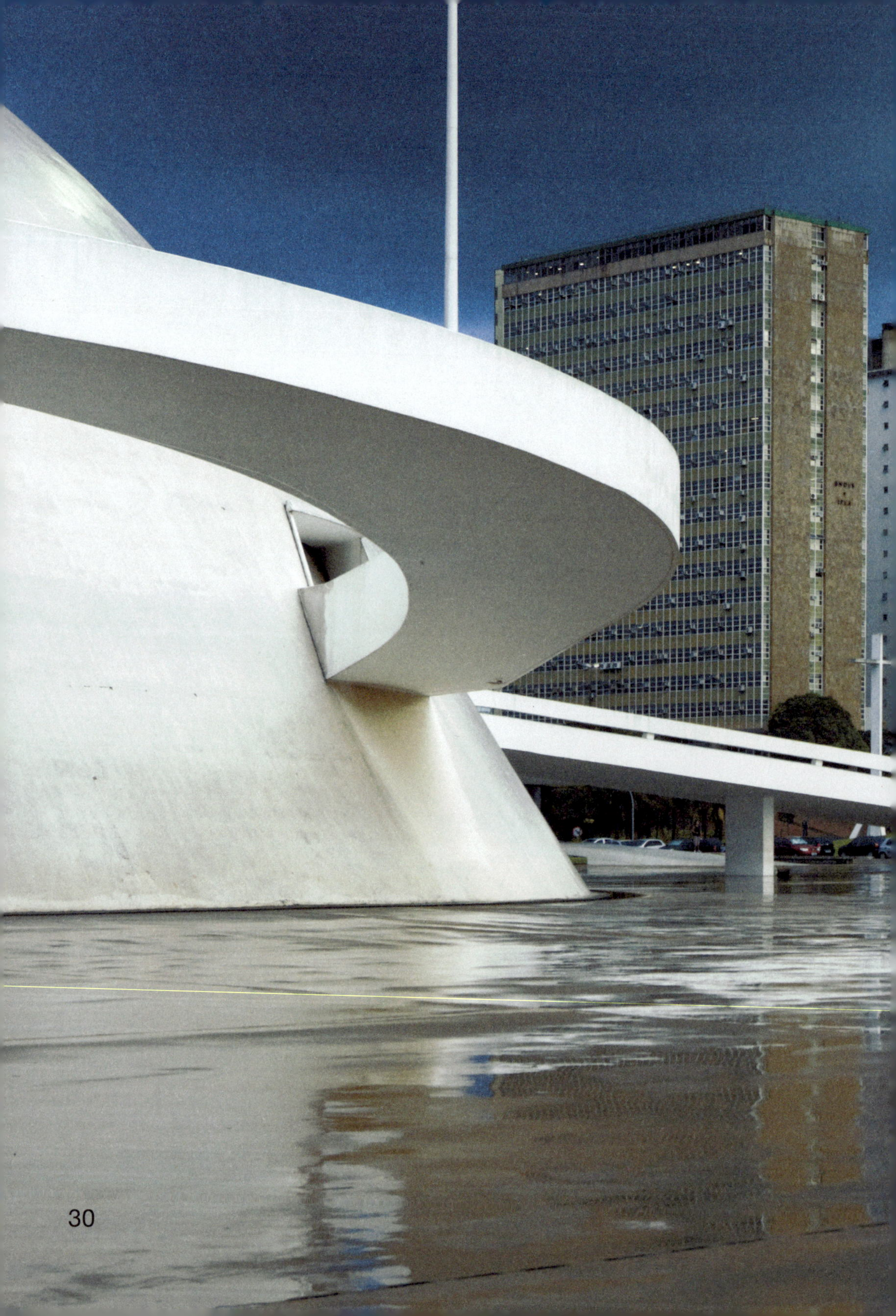

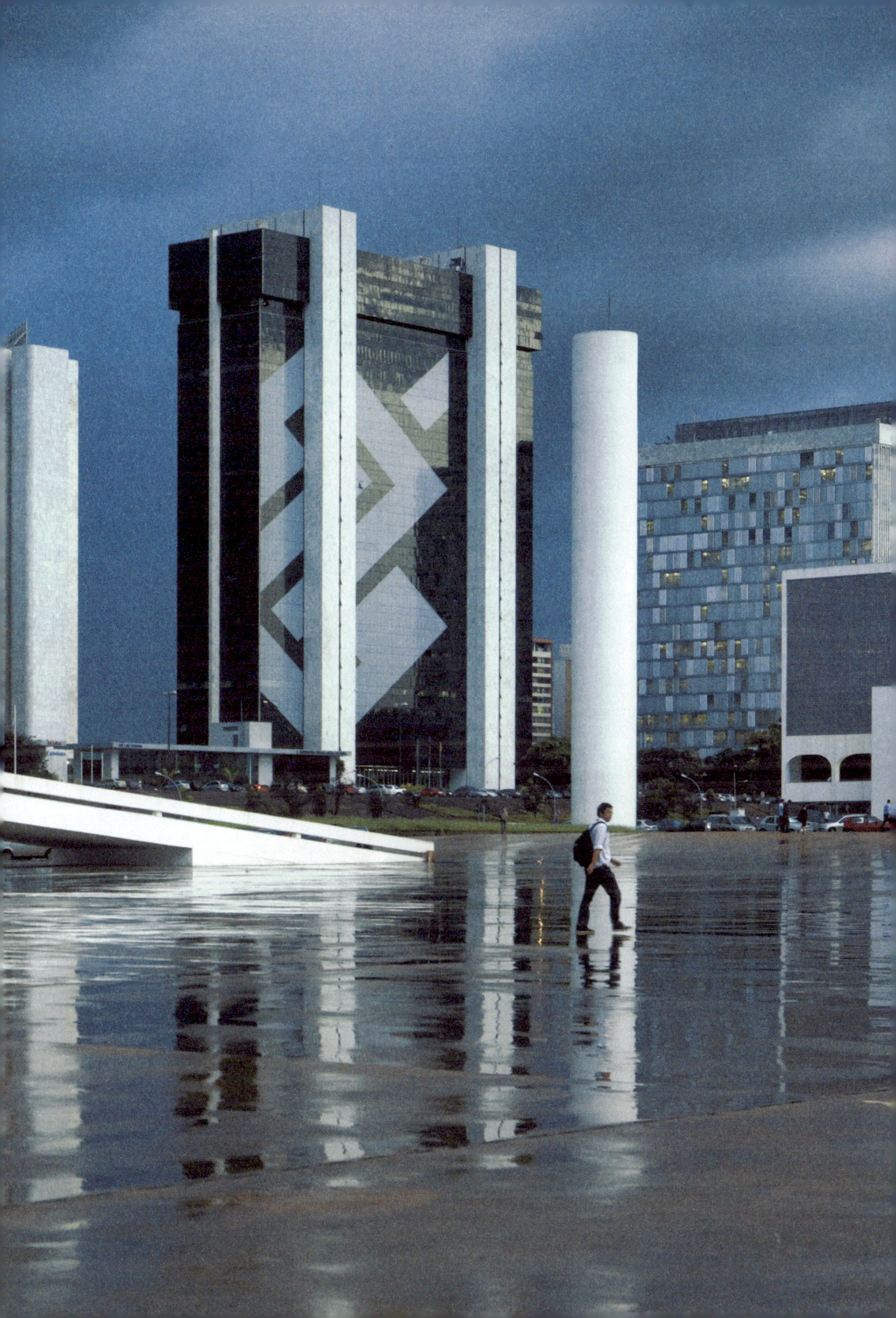

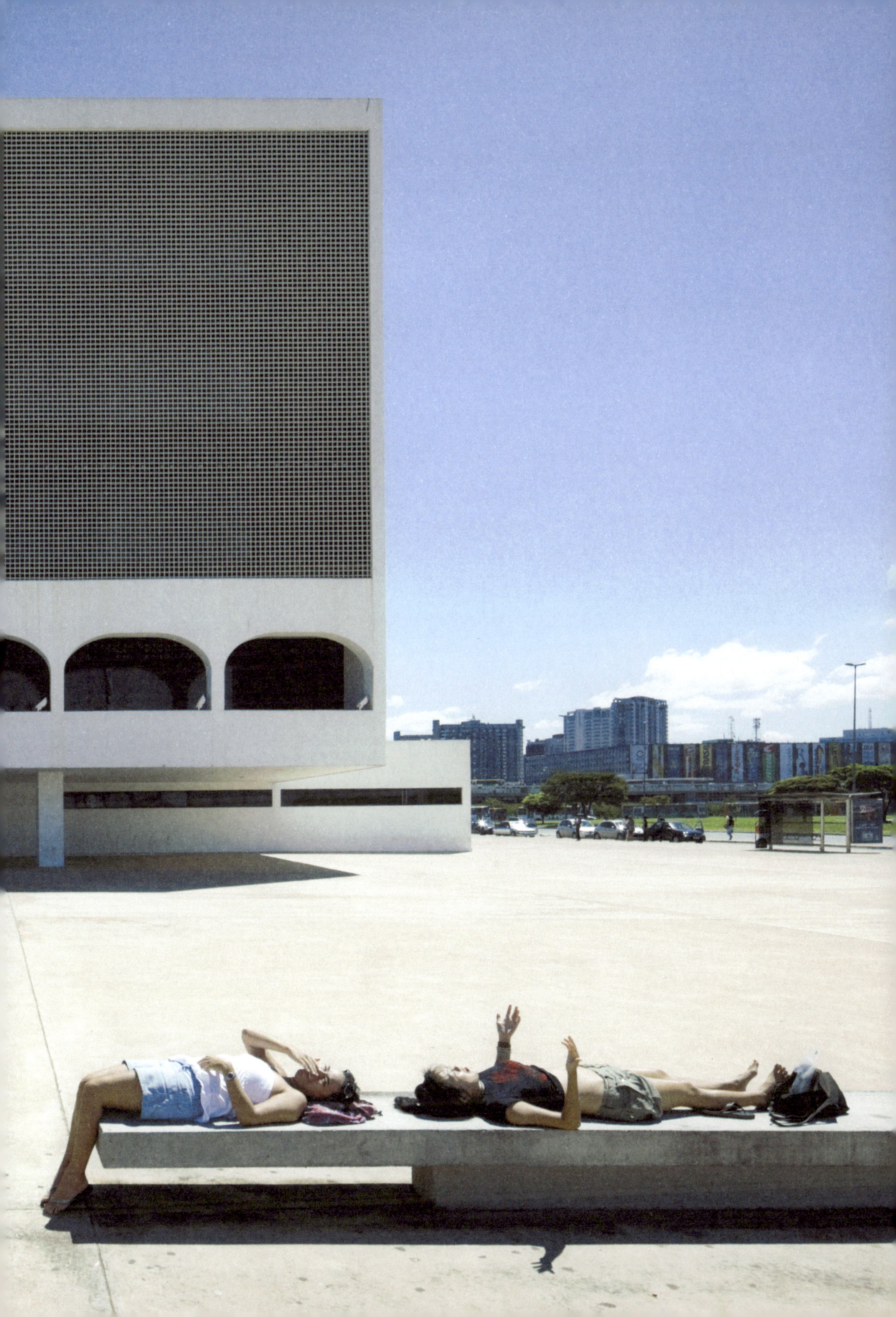

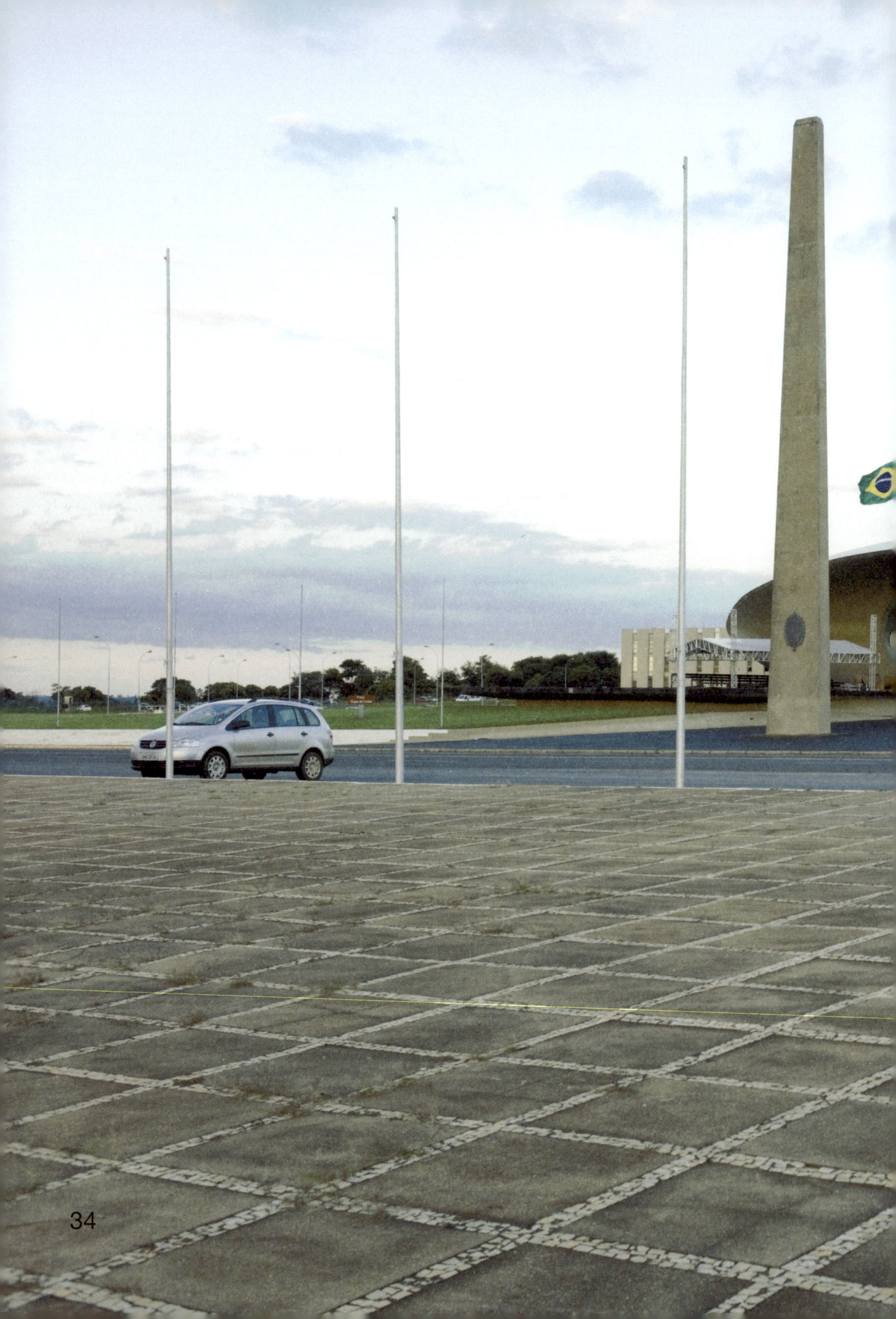

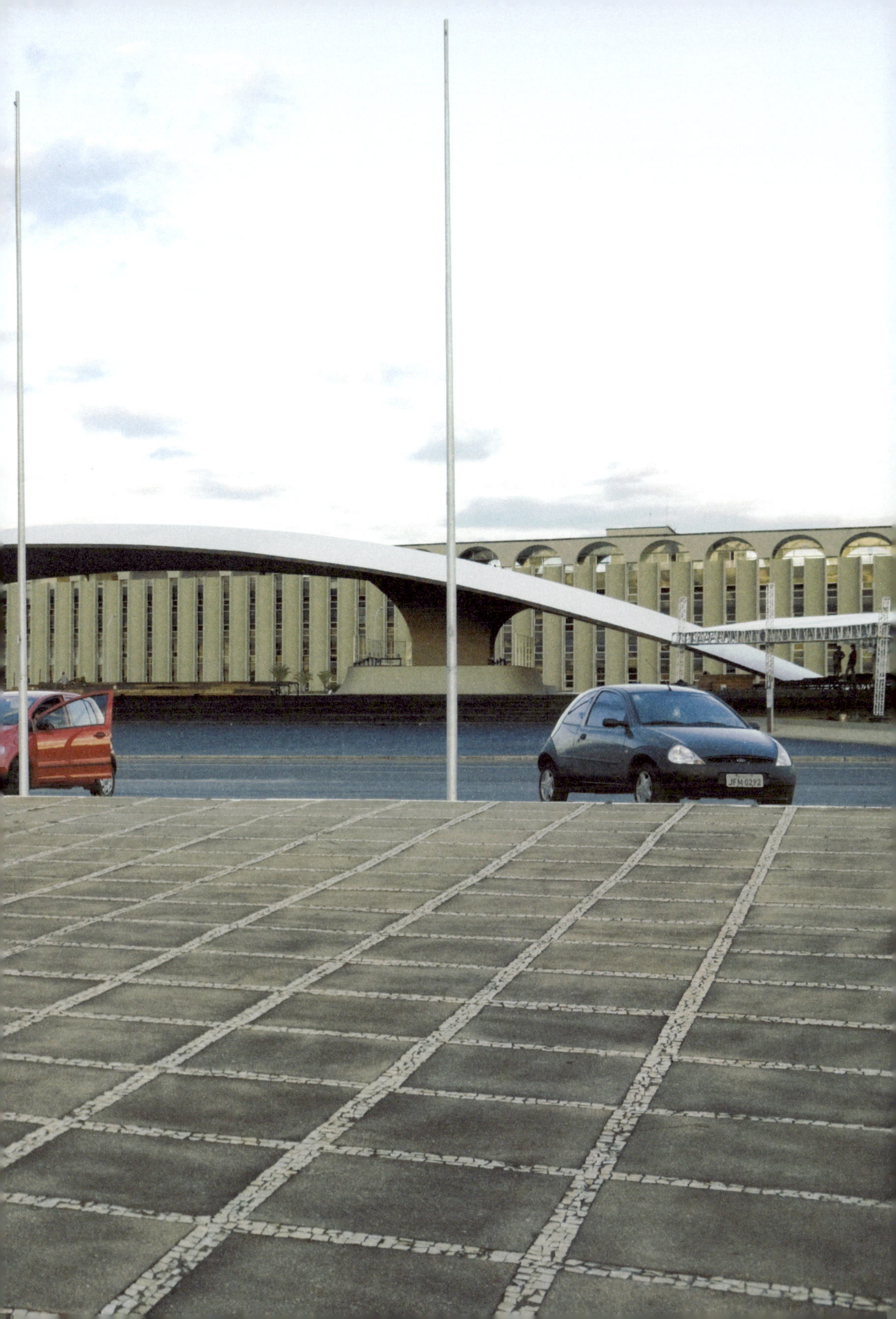

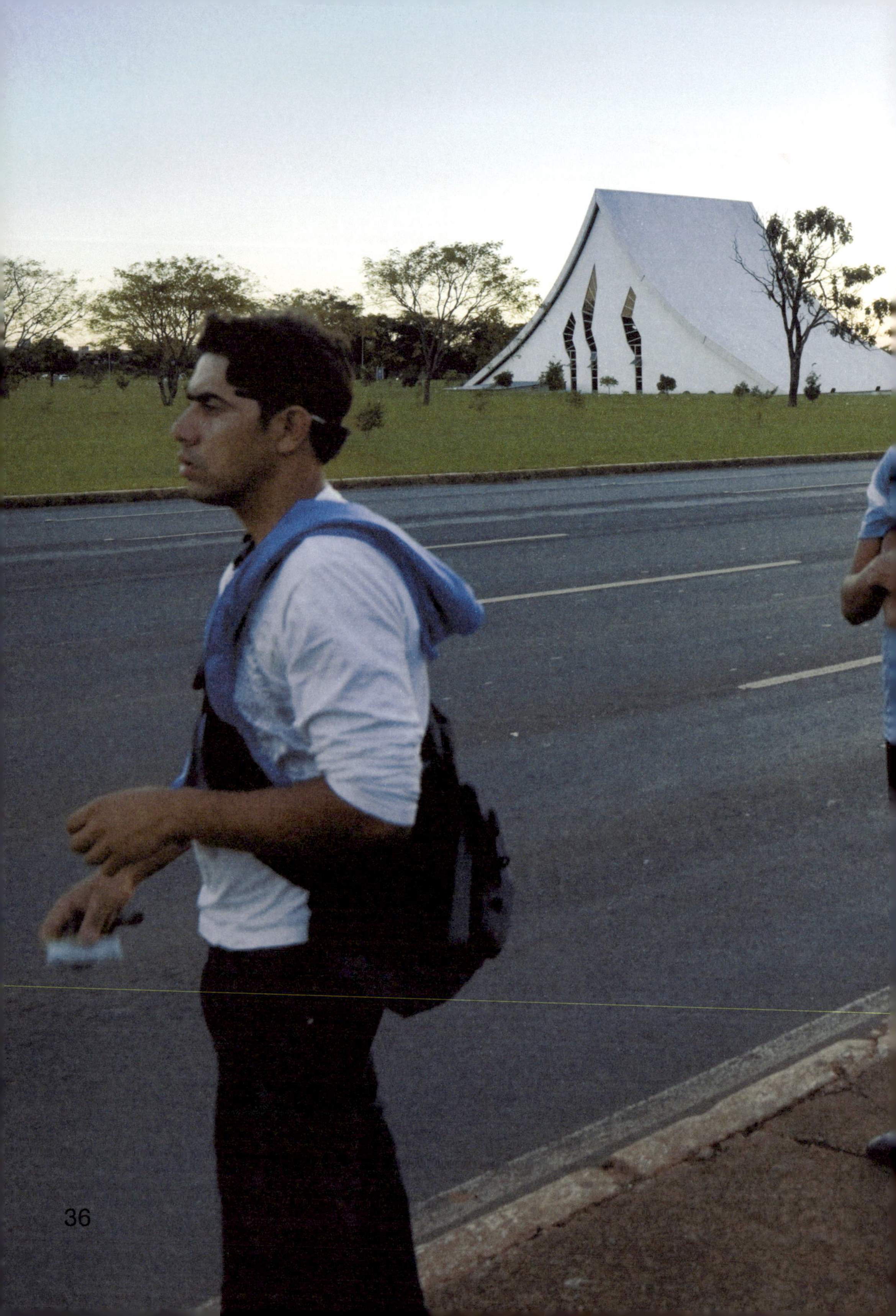

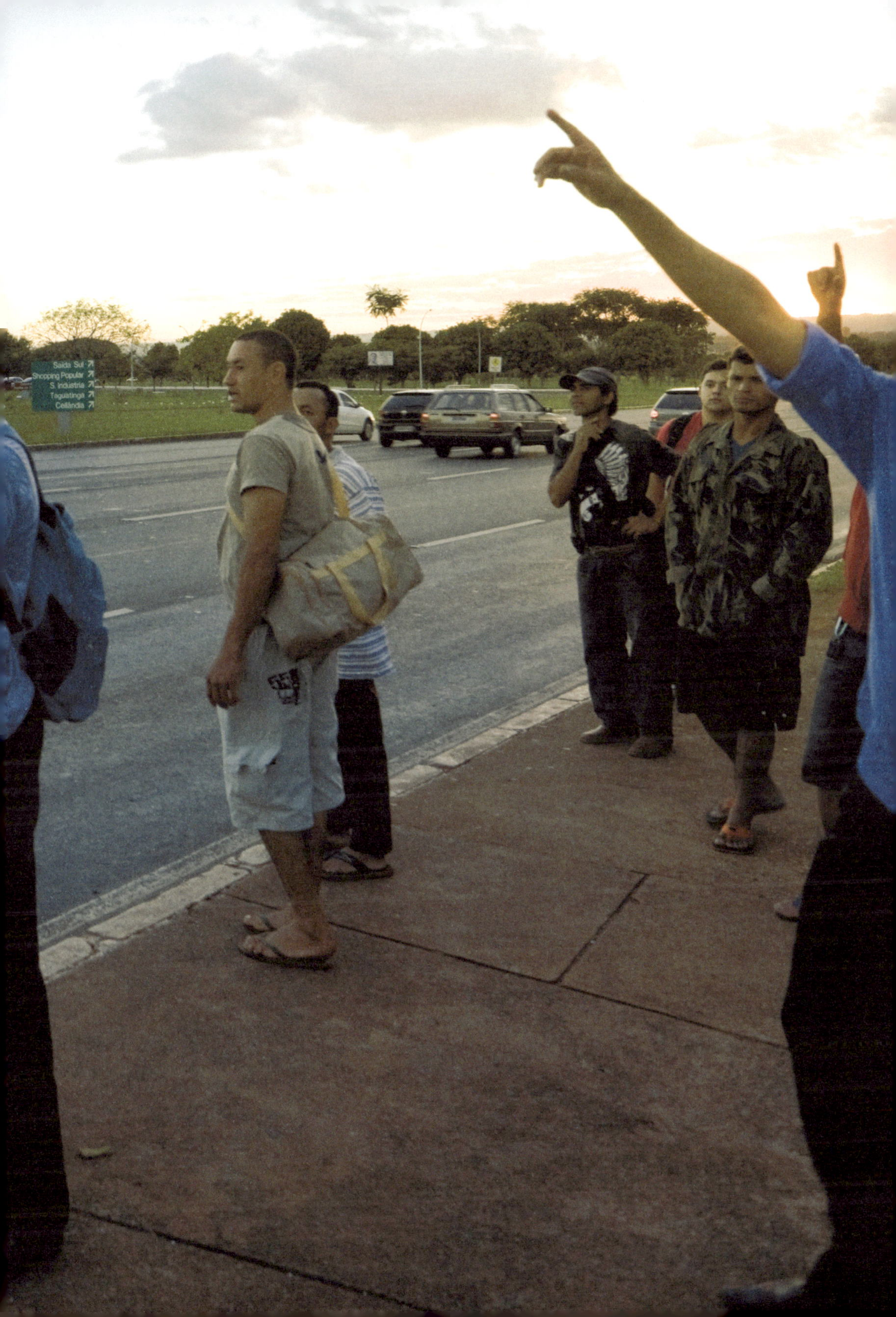
Saida Sul
Shopping Popular
S. Industria
Taguatinga
Ceilândia

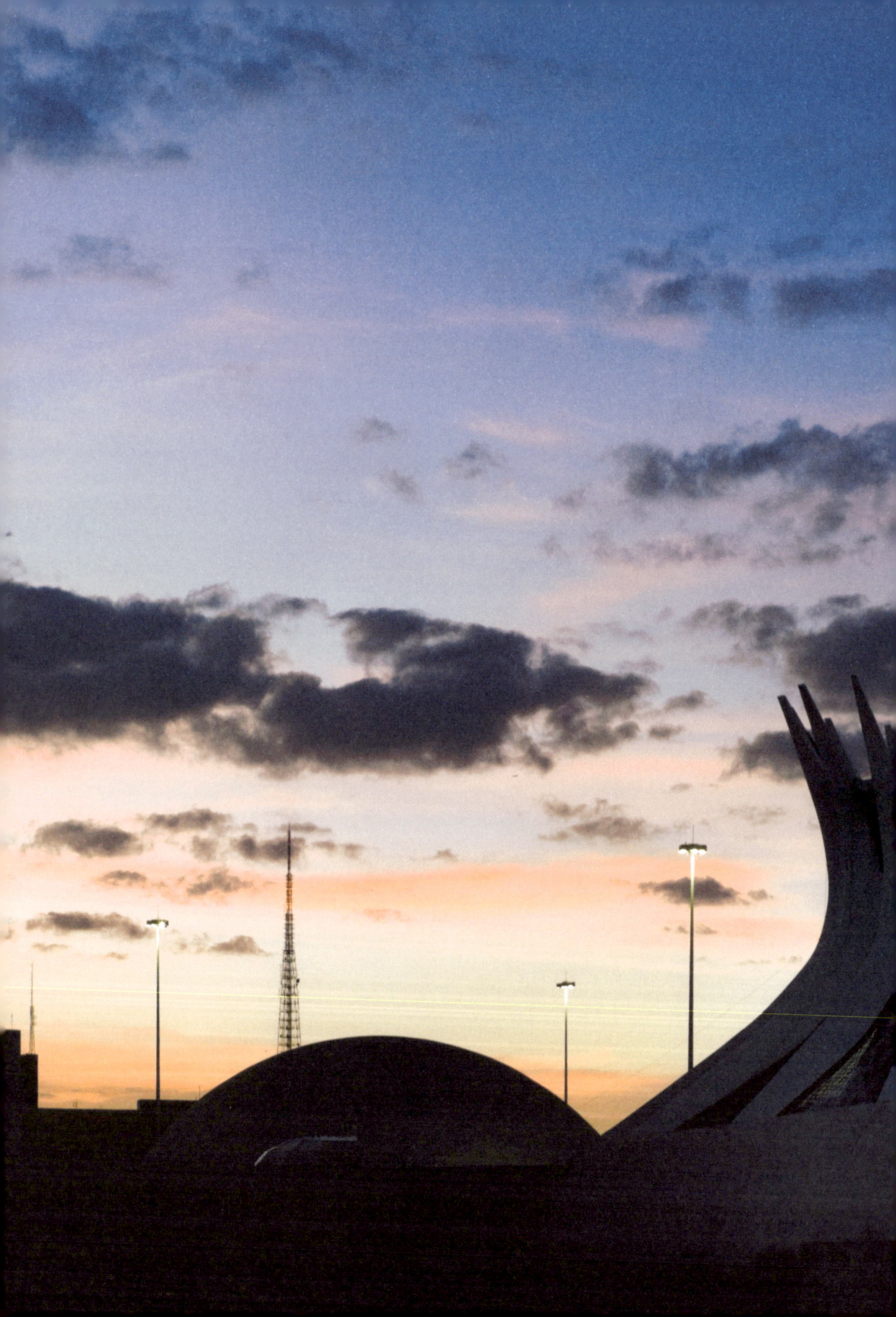

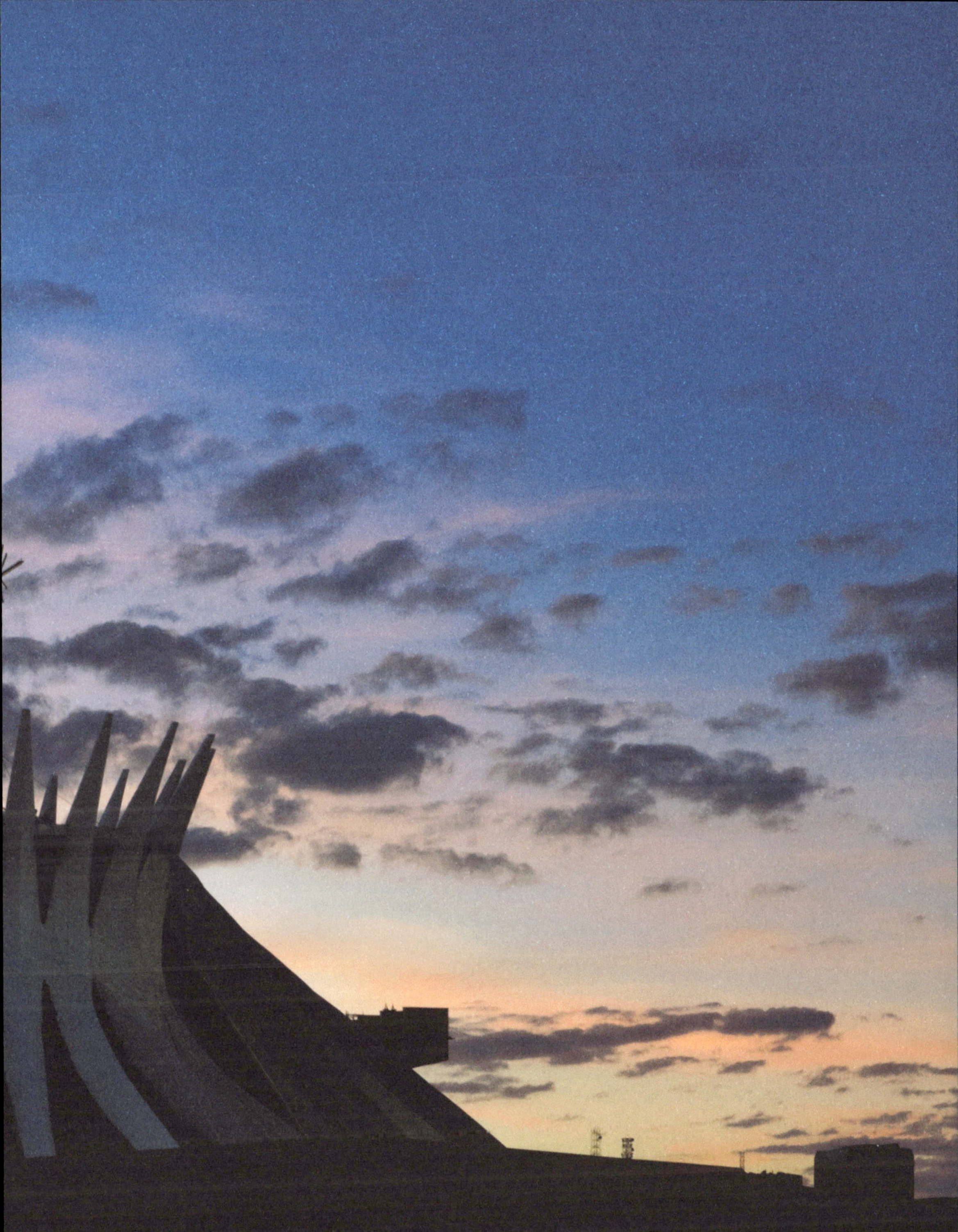

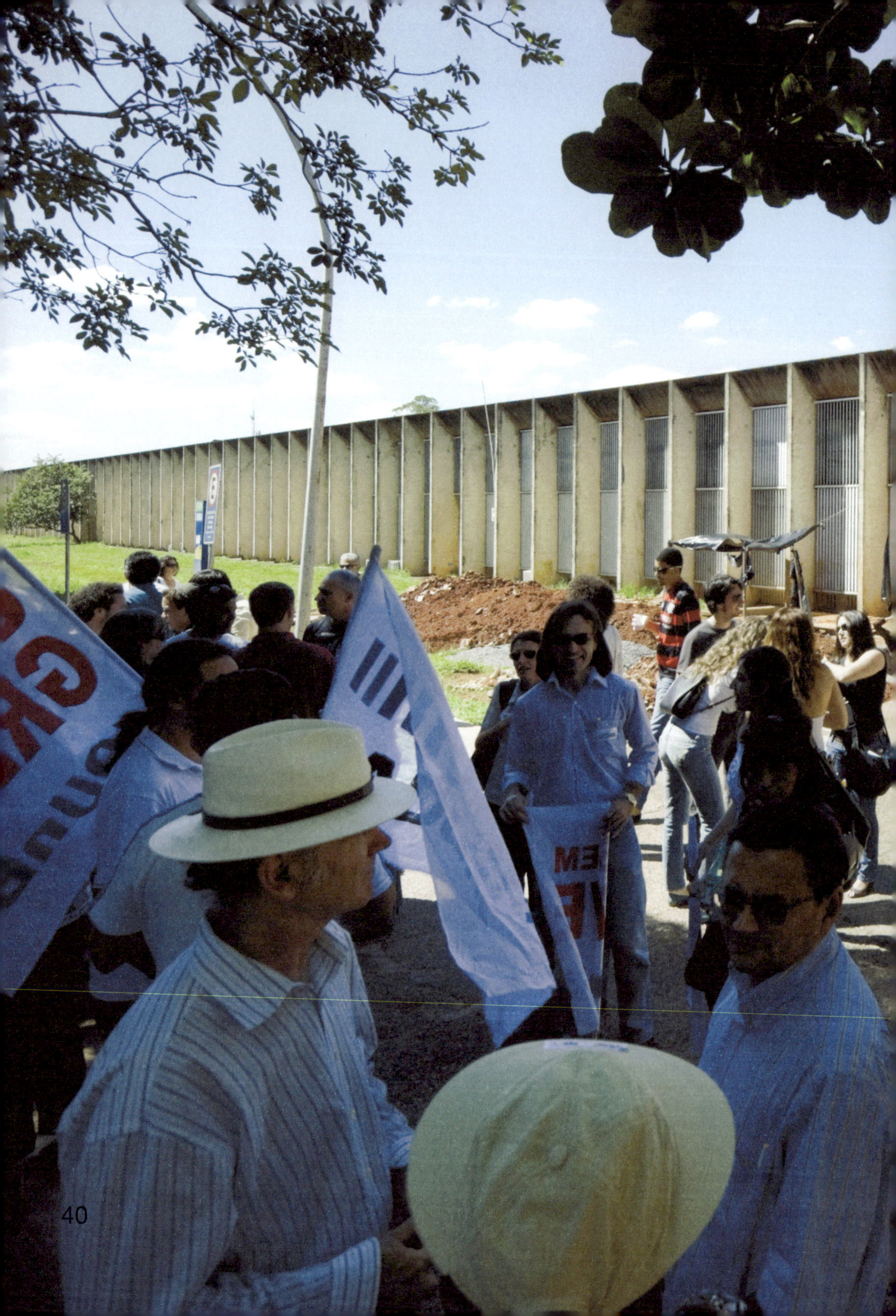

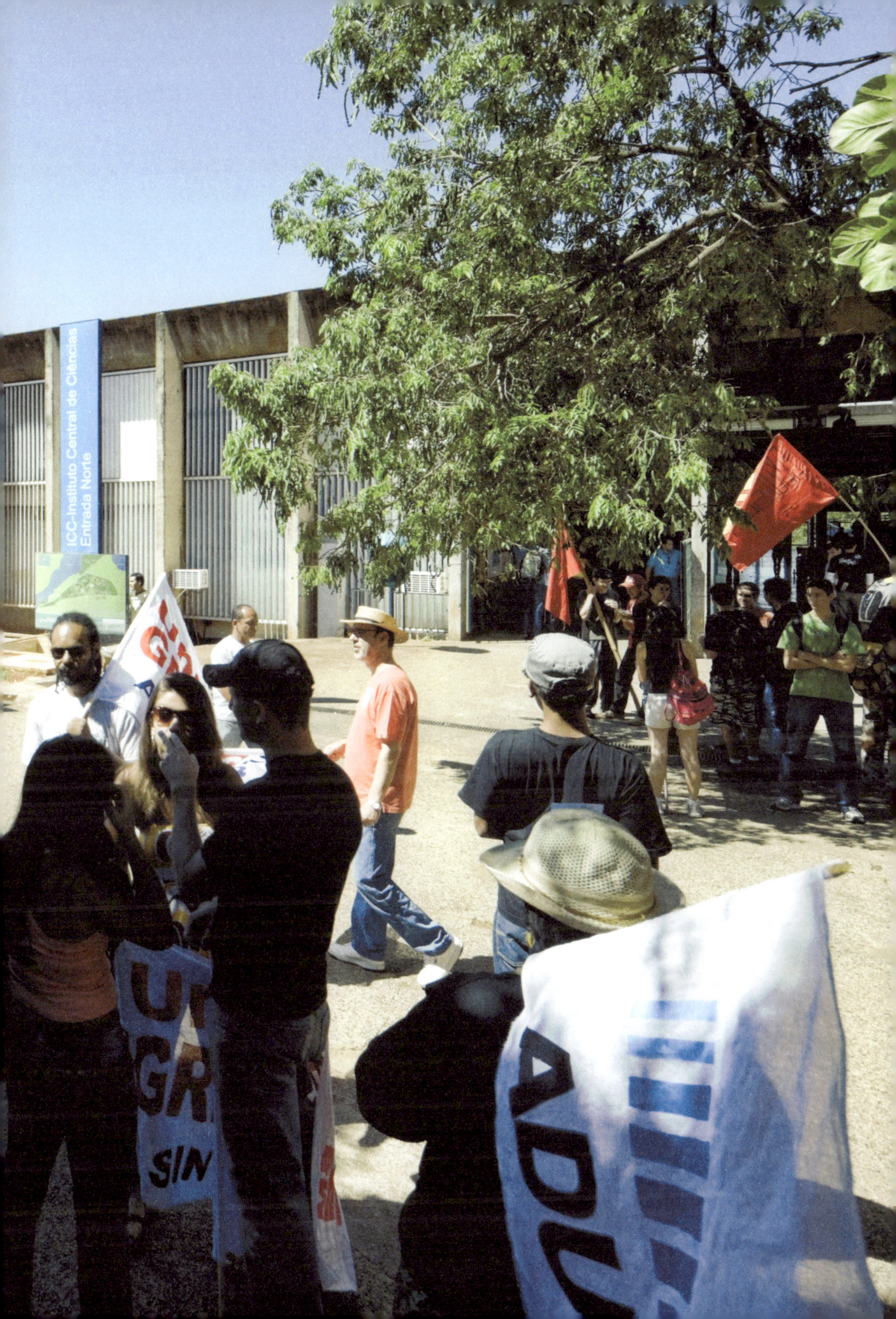
ICC-Instituto Central de Ciências
Entrada Norte

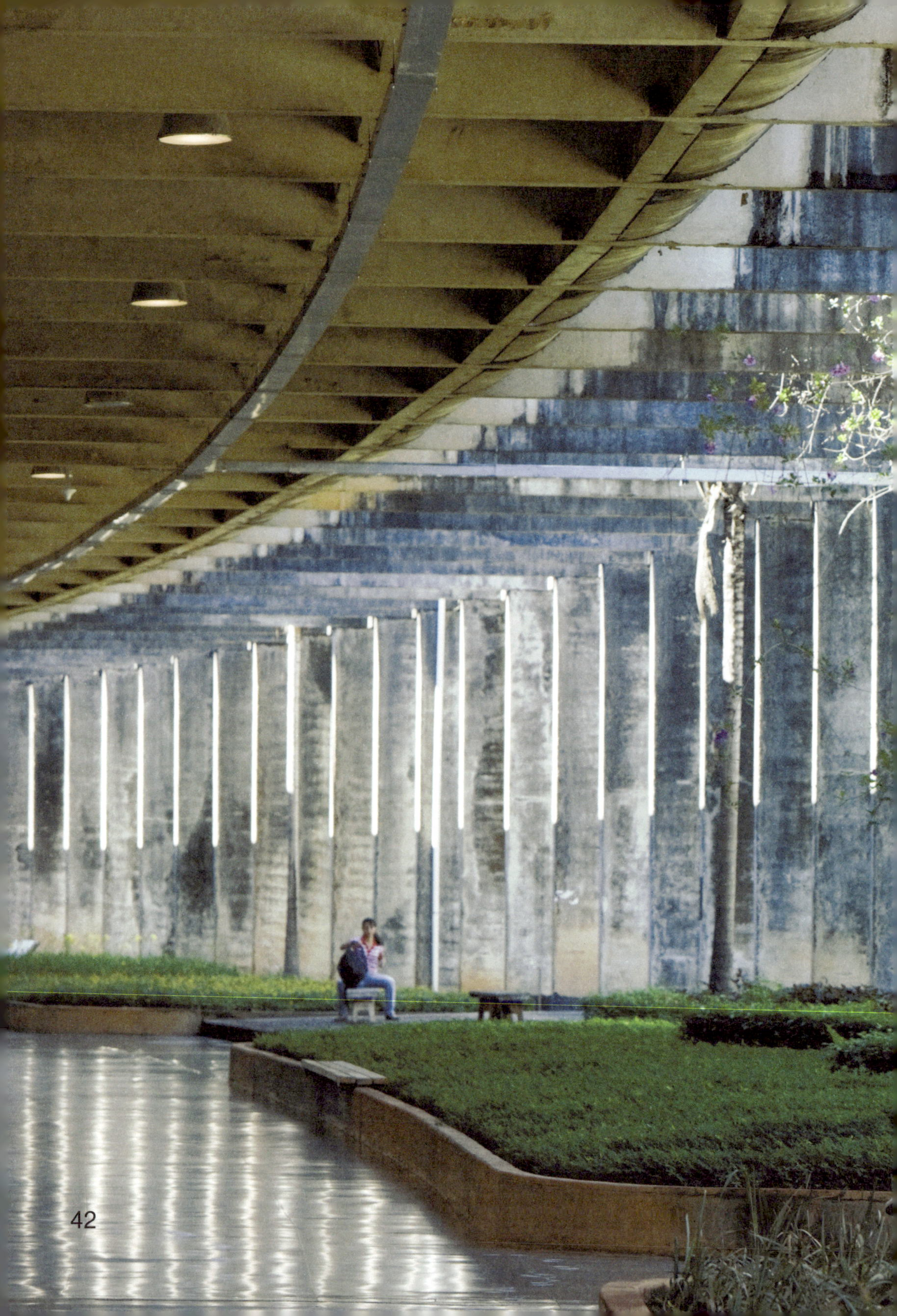

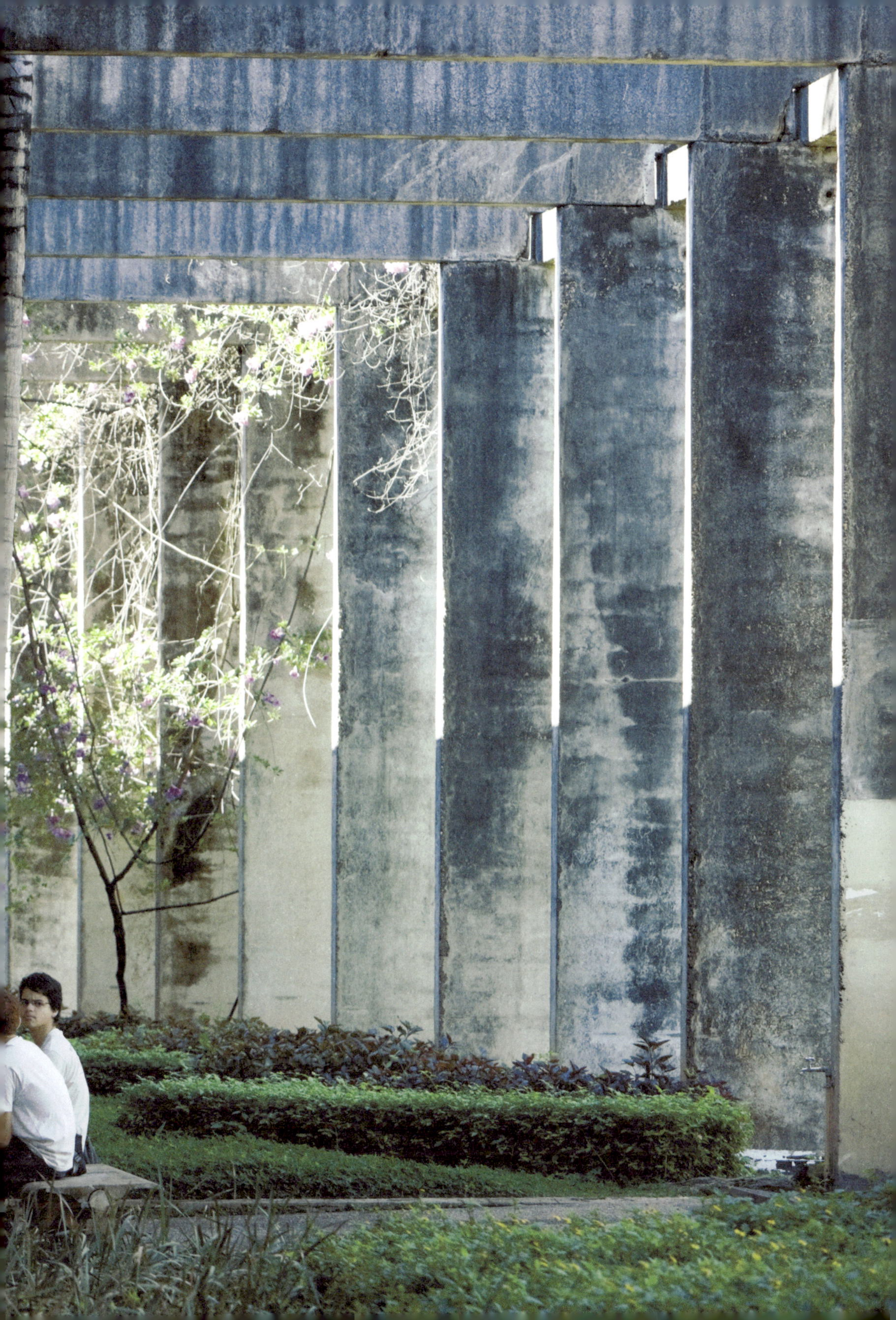

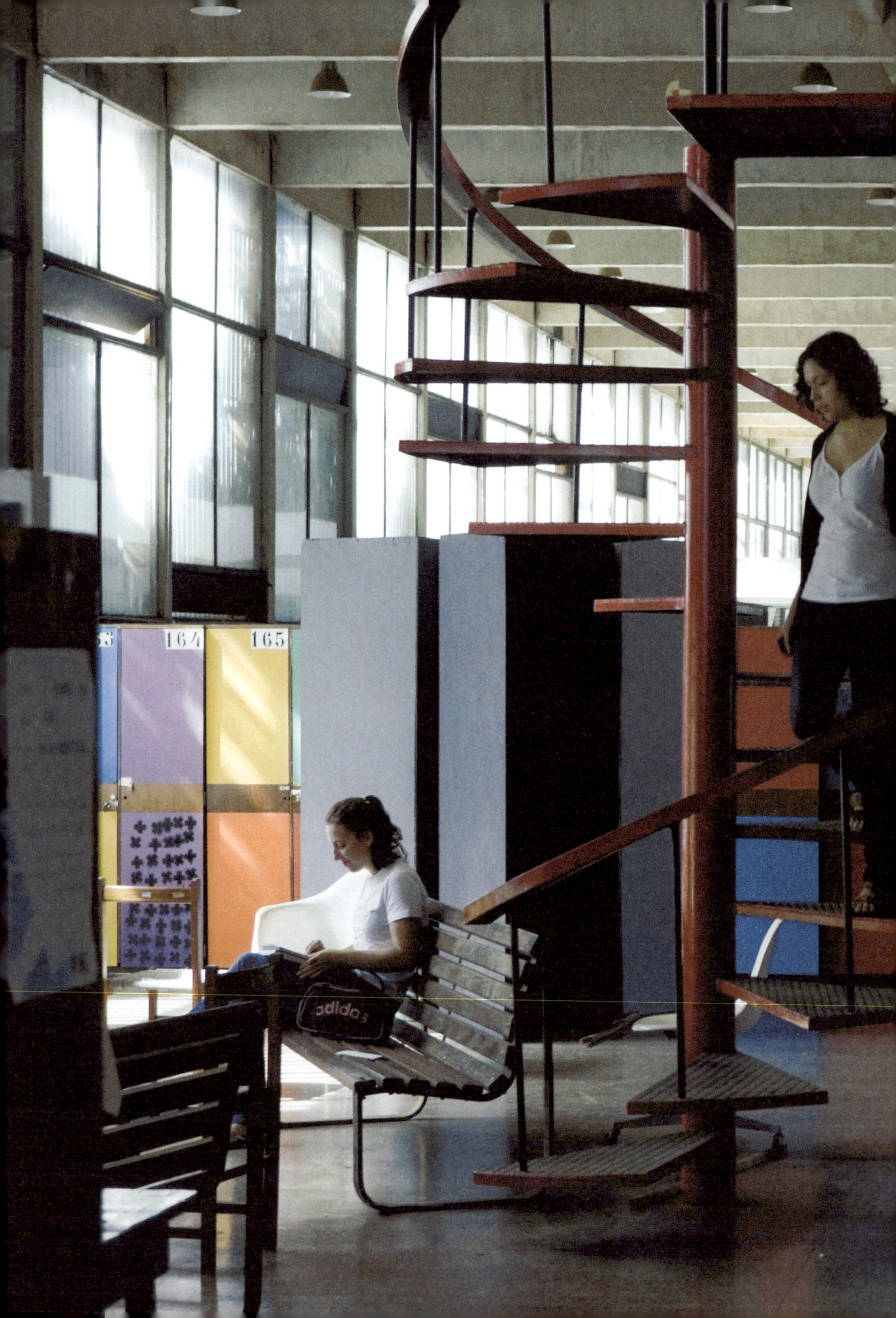
164
165
adidas

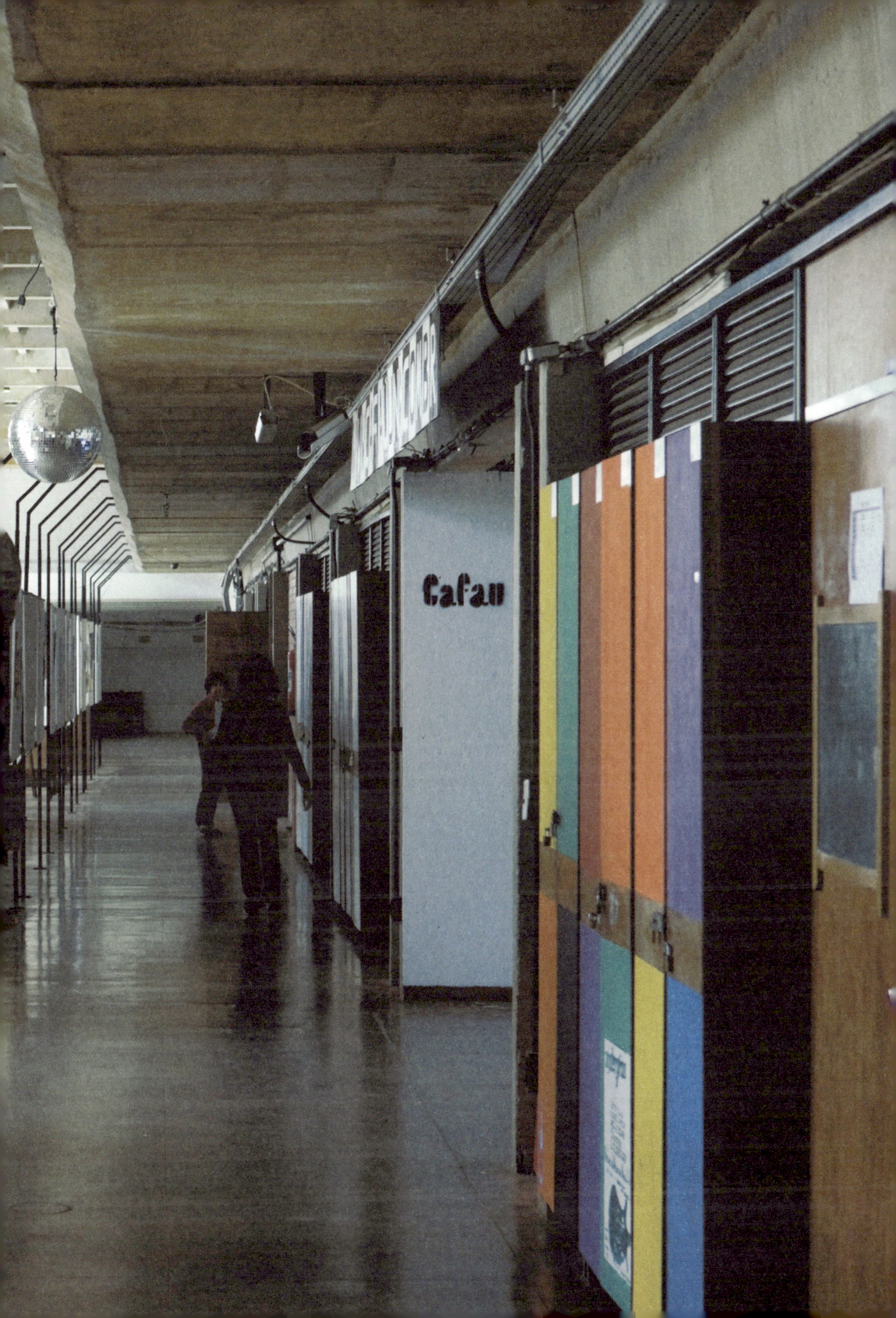
Cafau

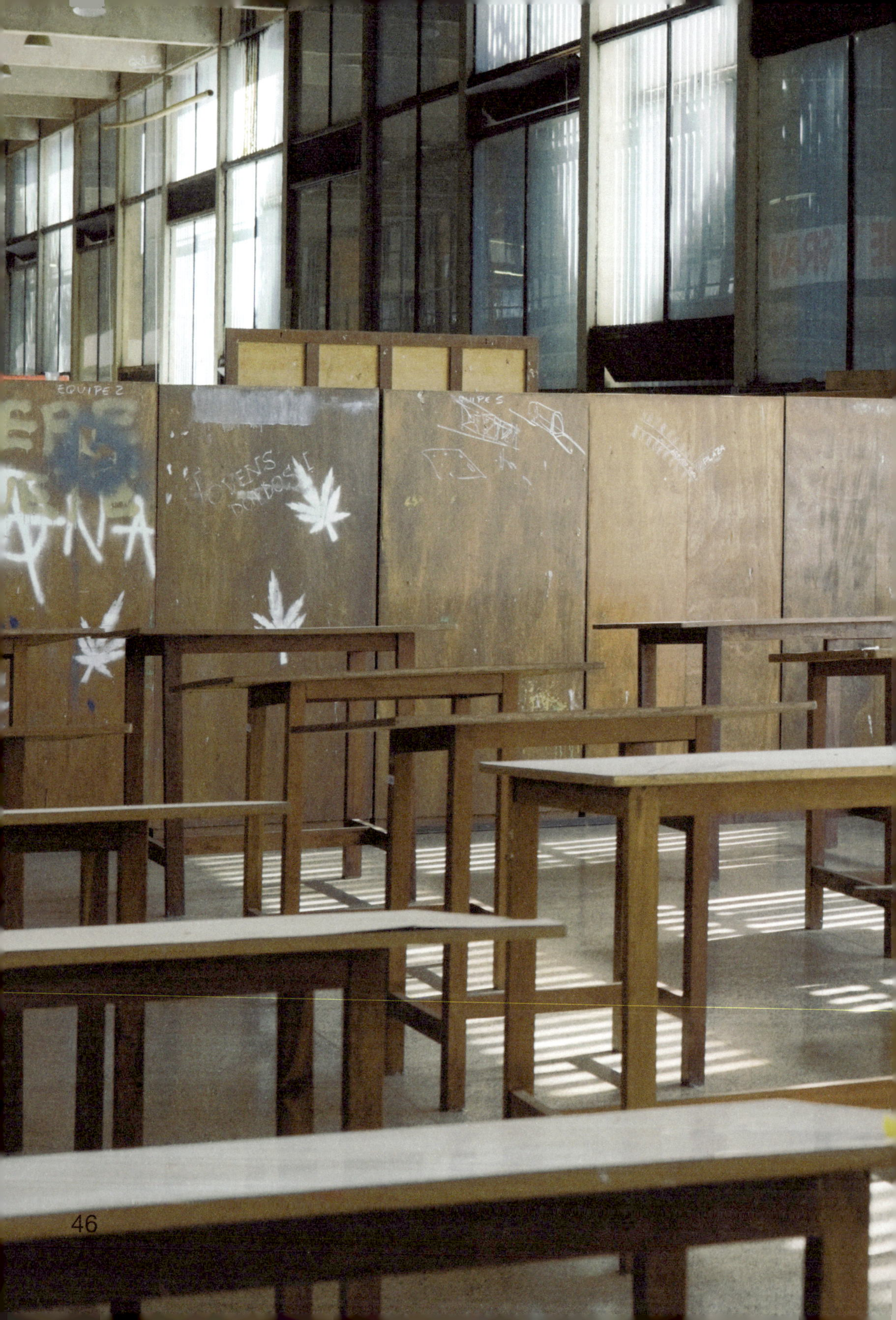
EQUIPE 2

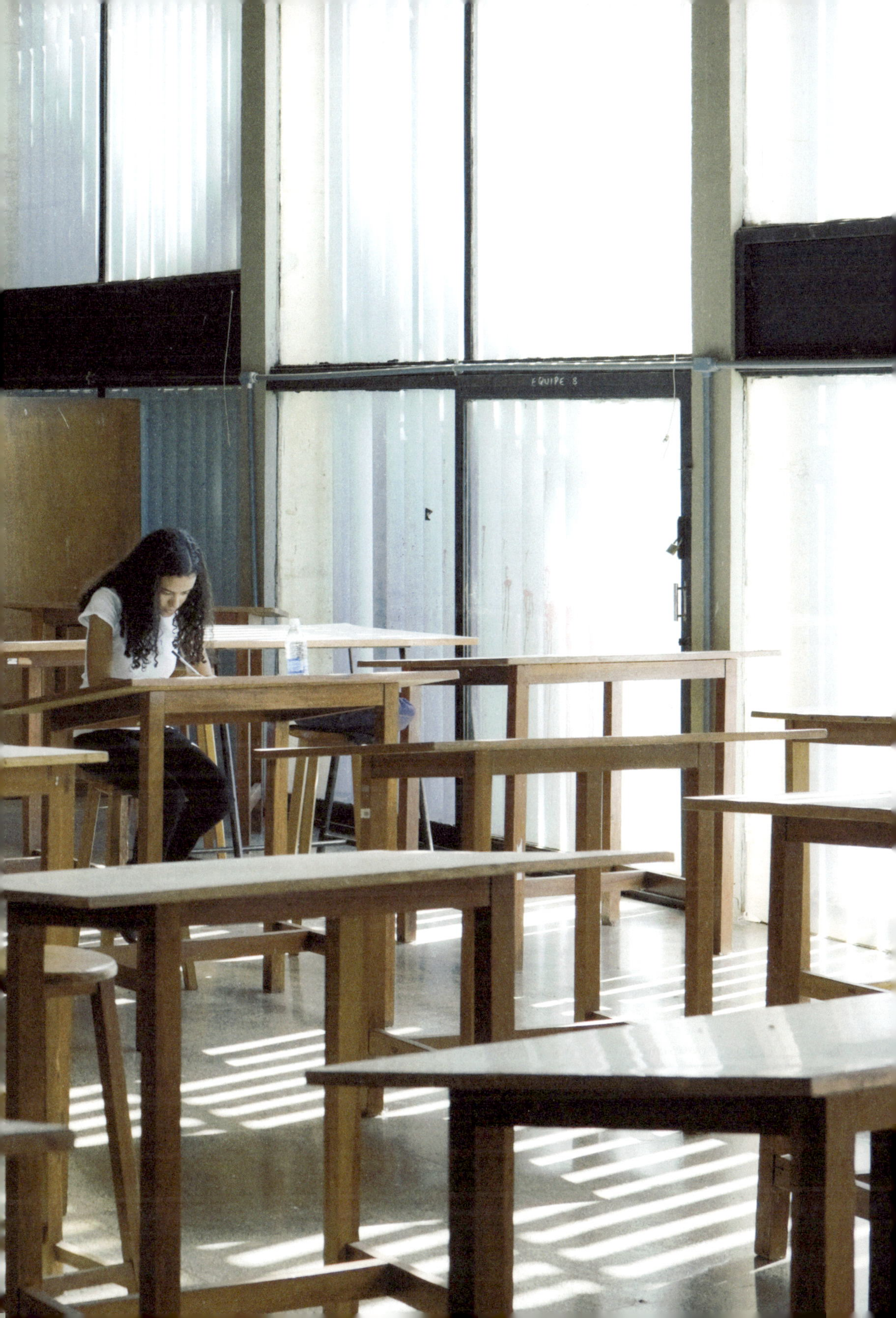
EQUIPE 8

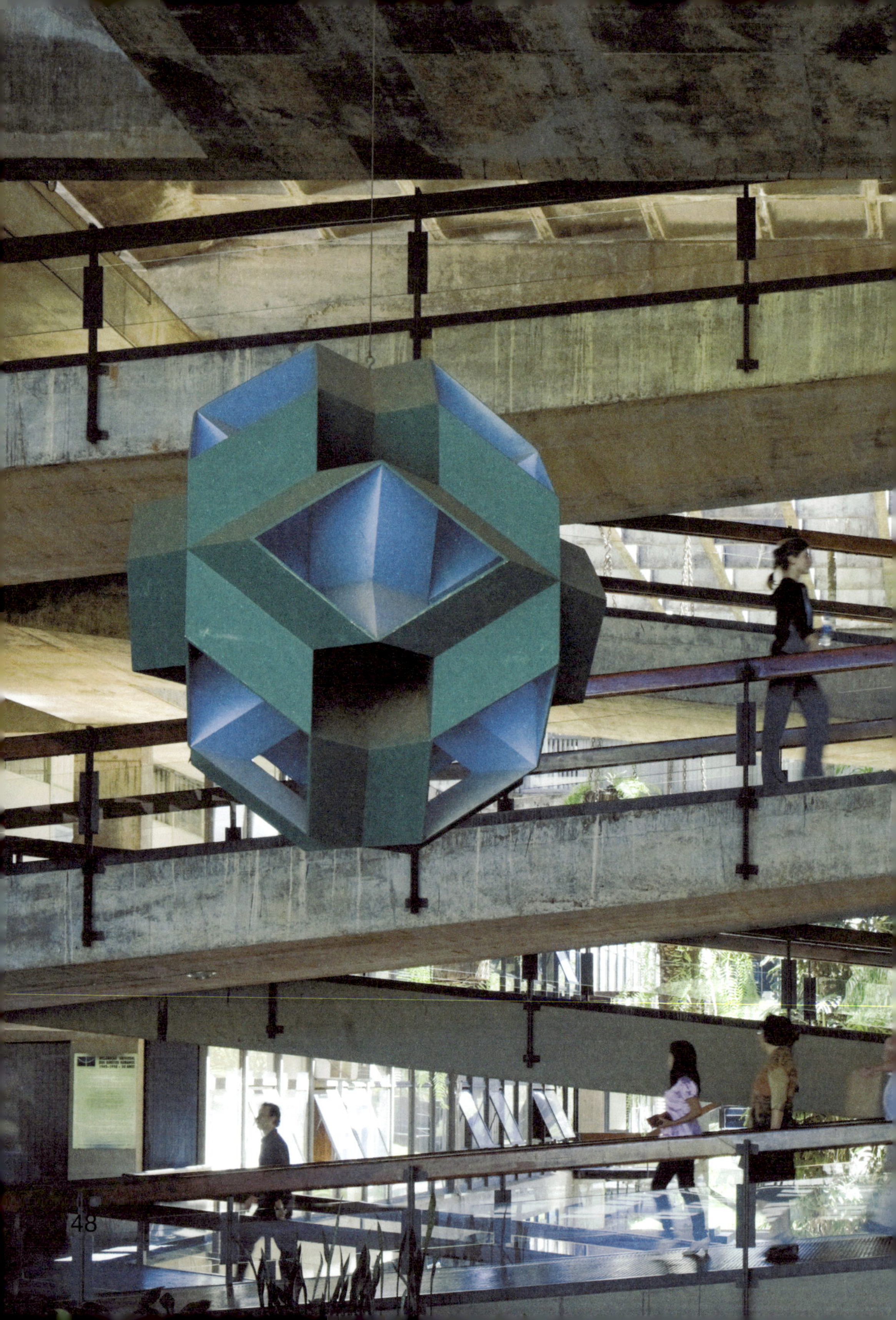

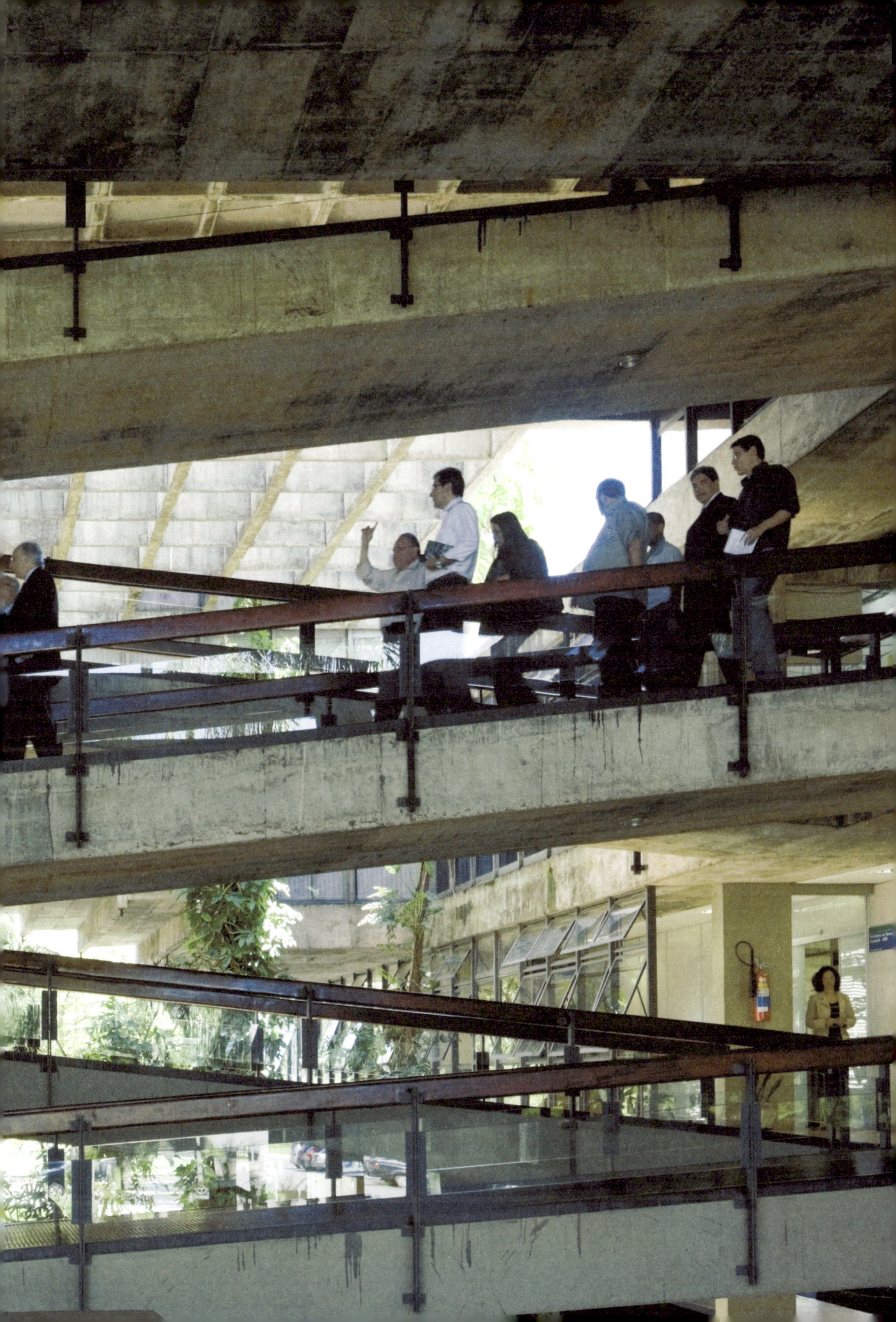

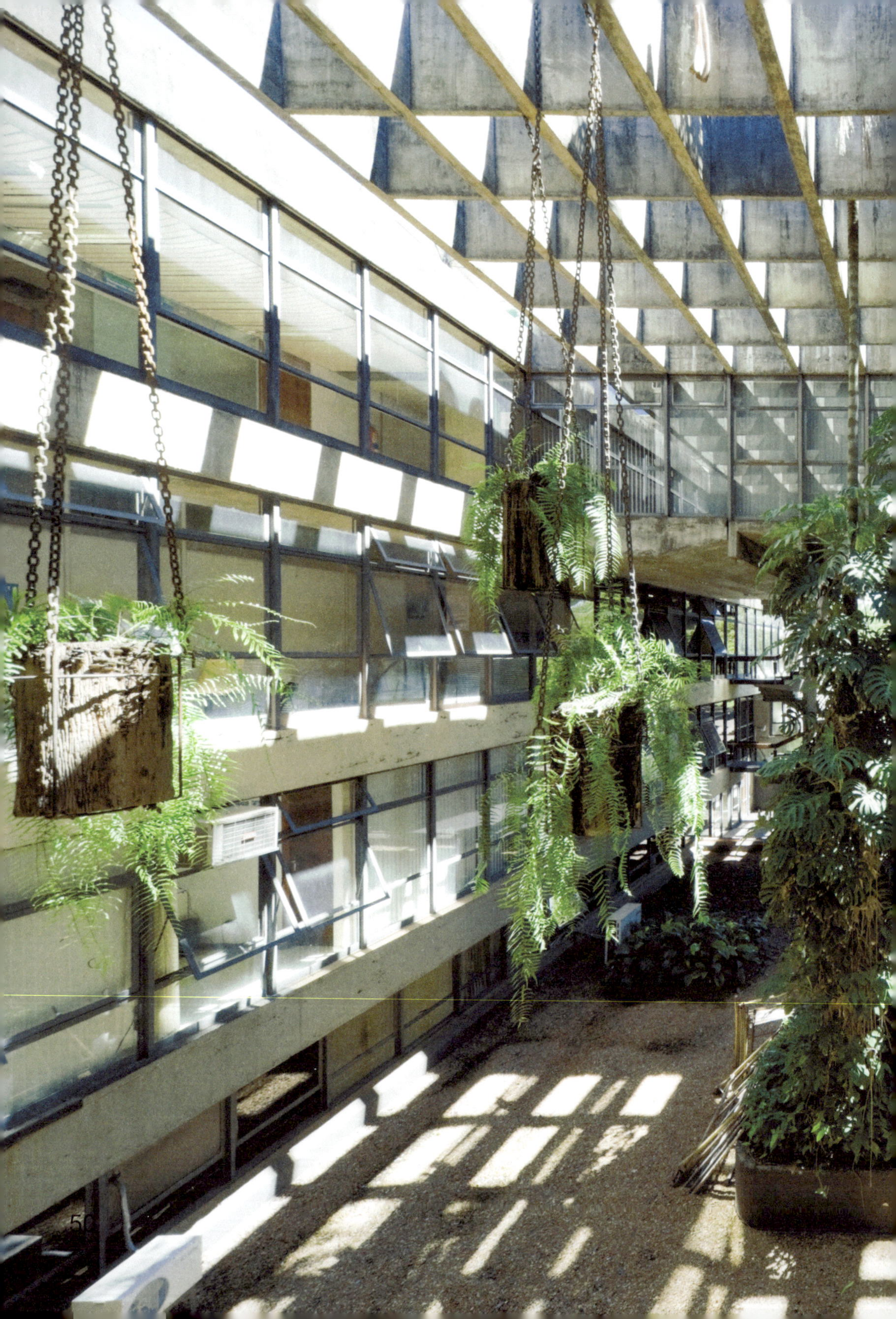

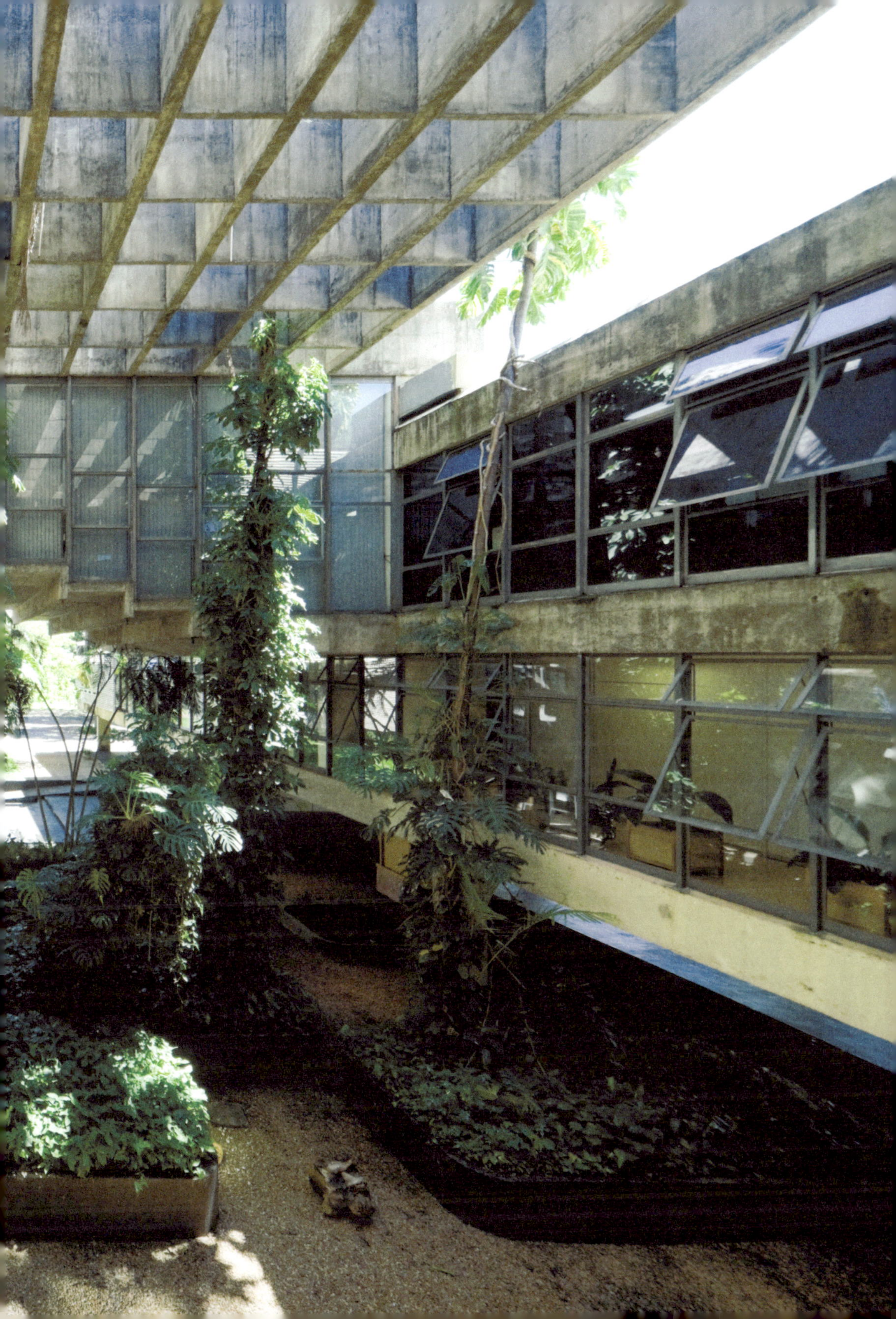

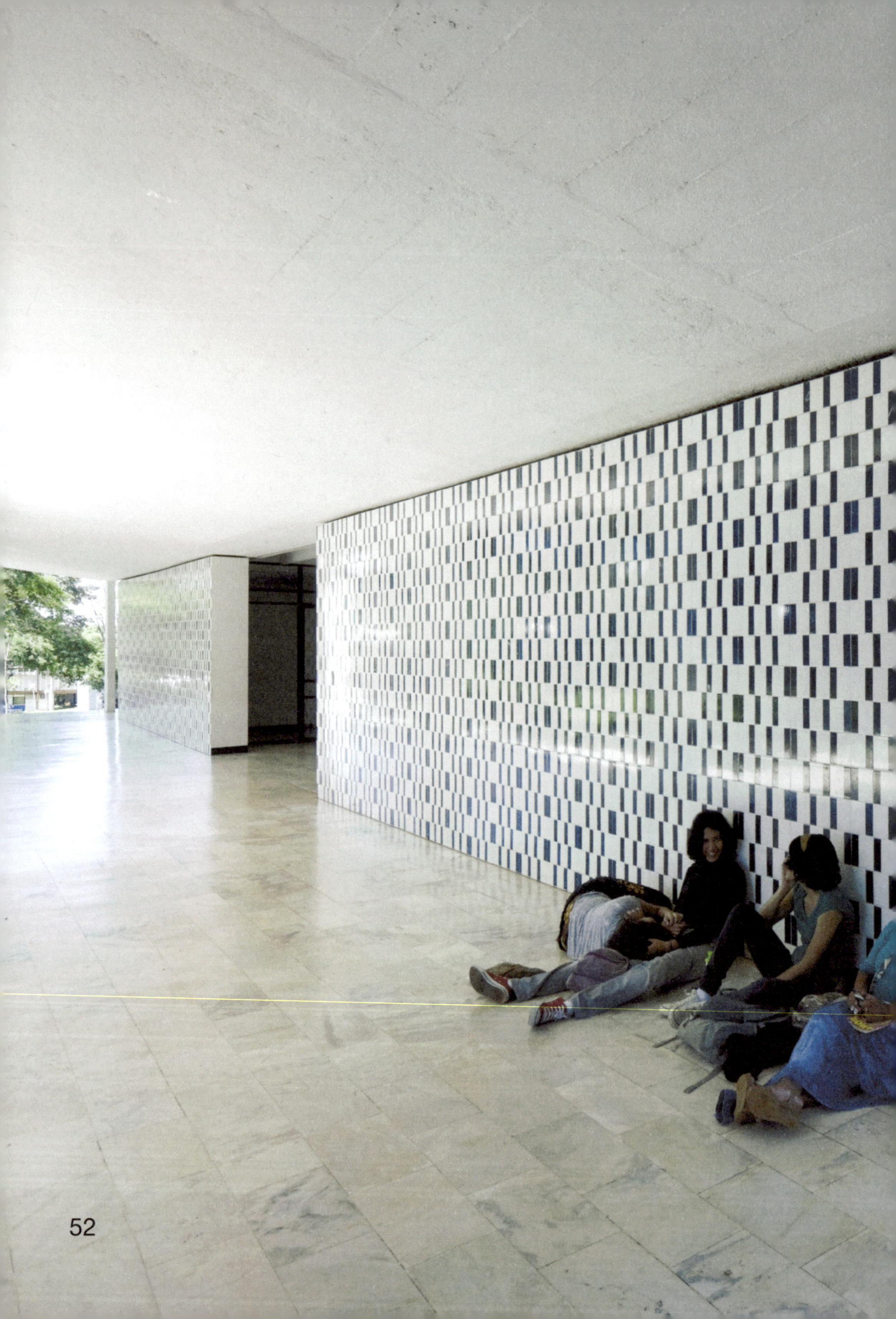

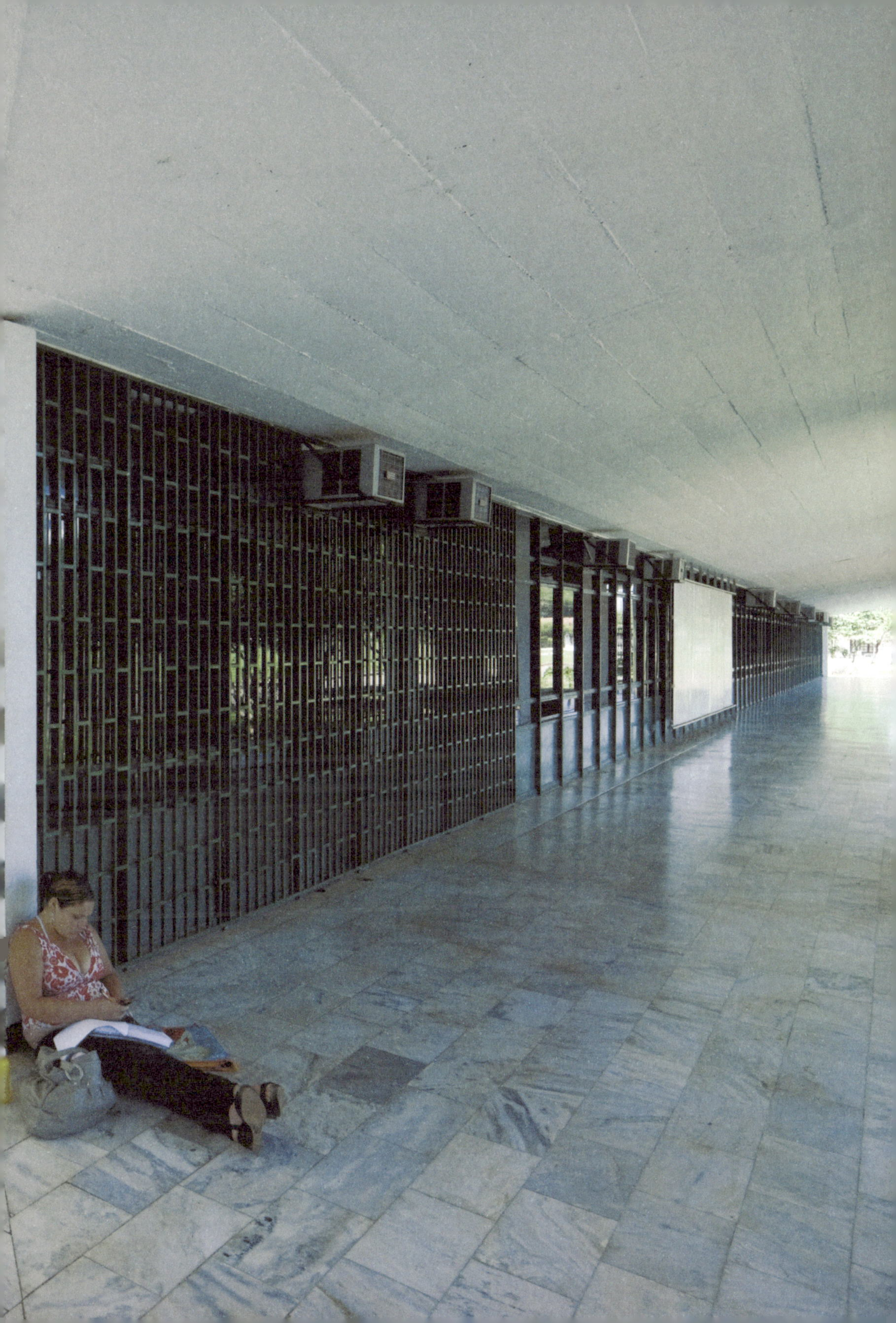

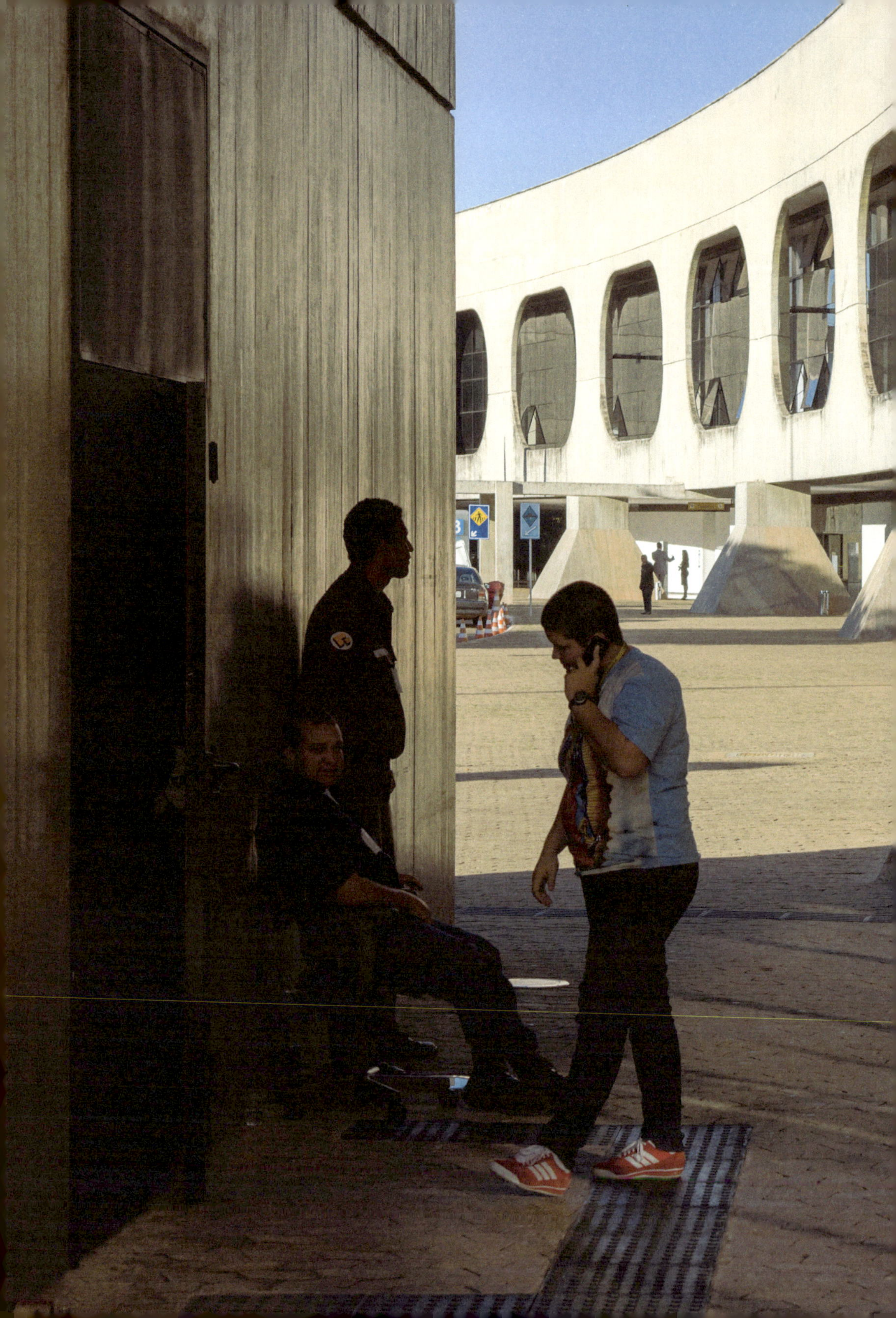

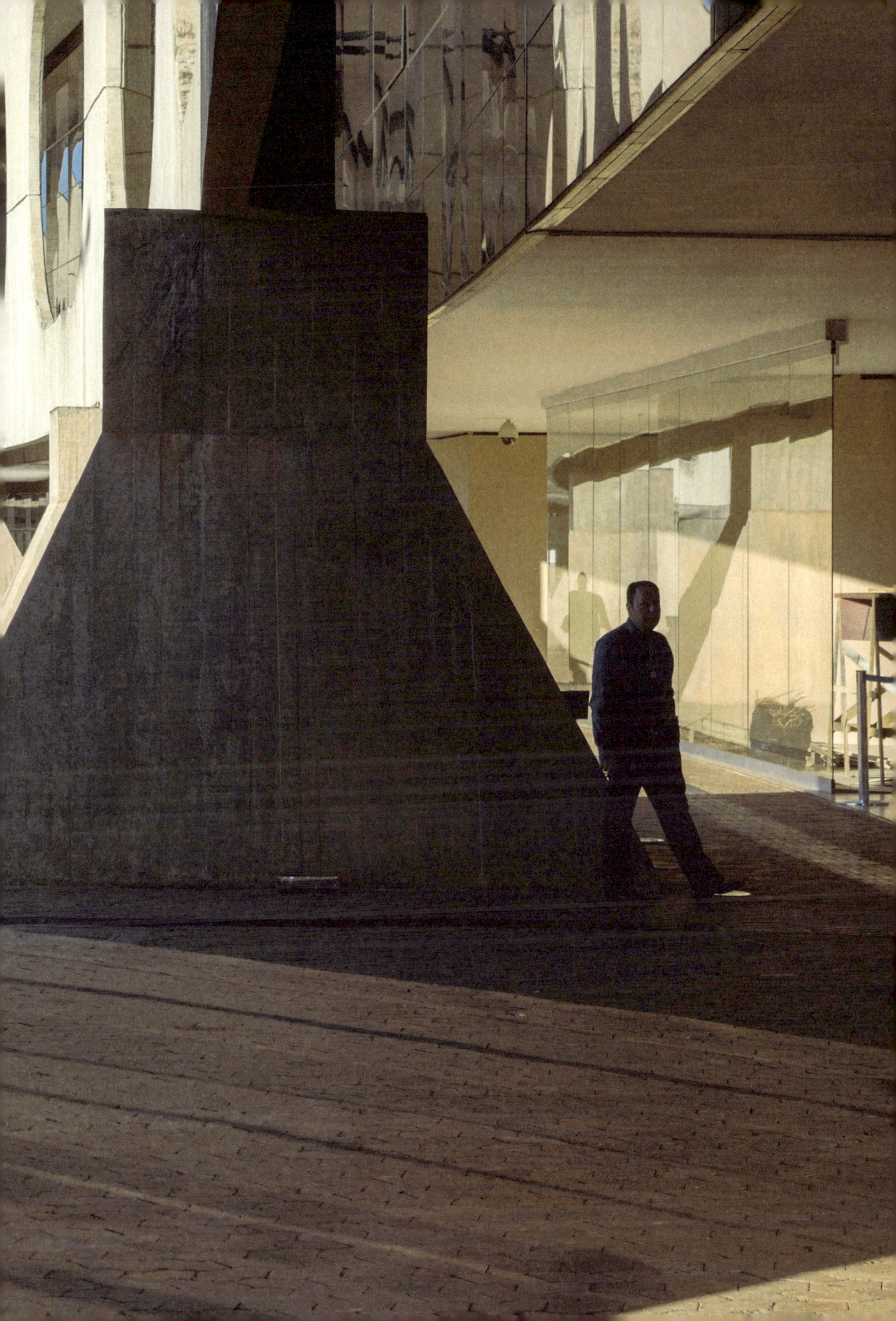

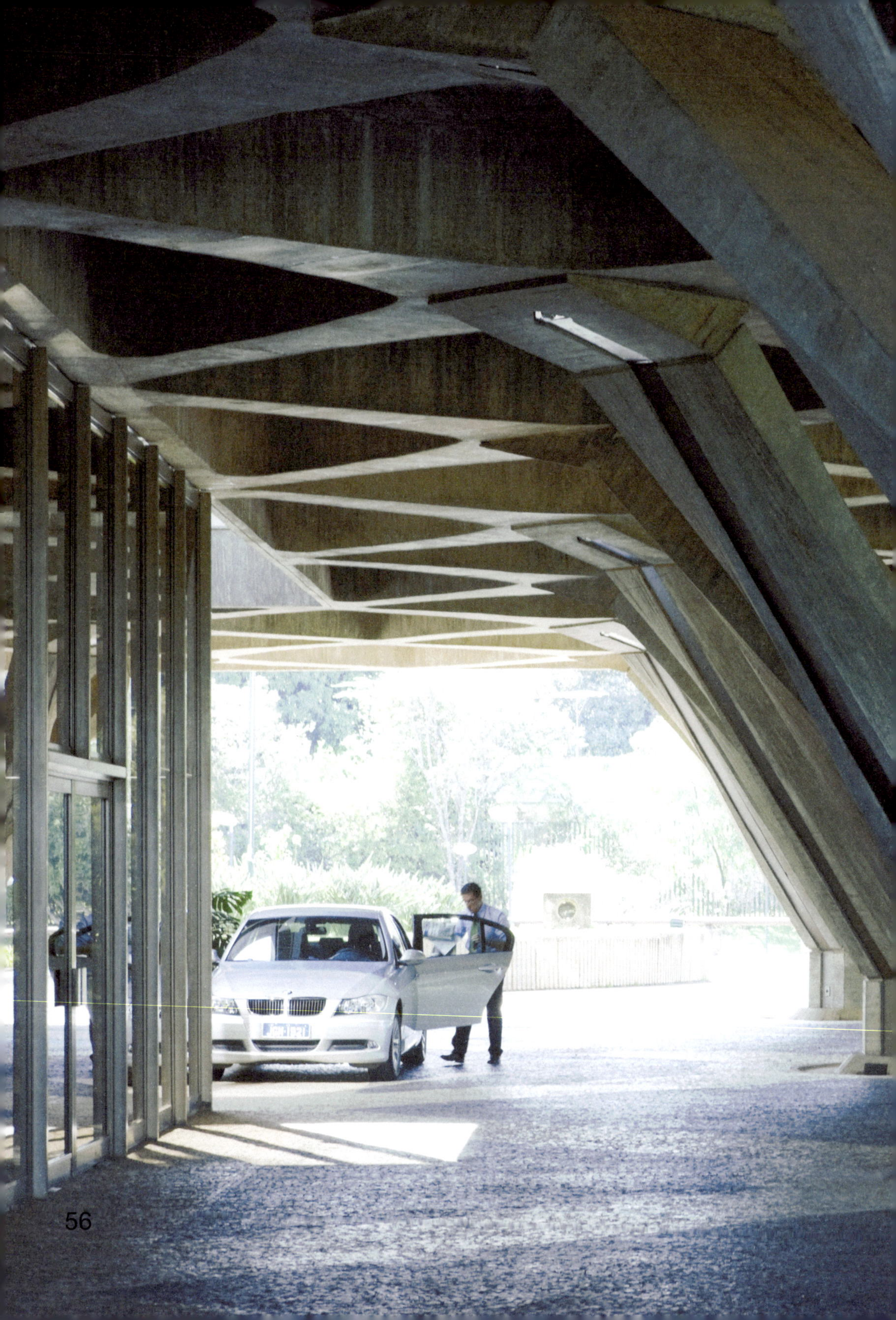

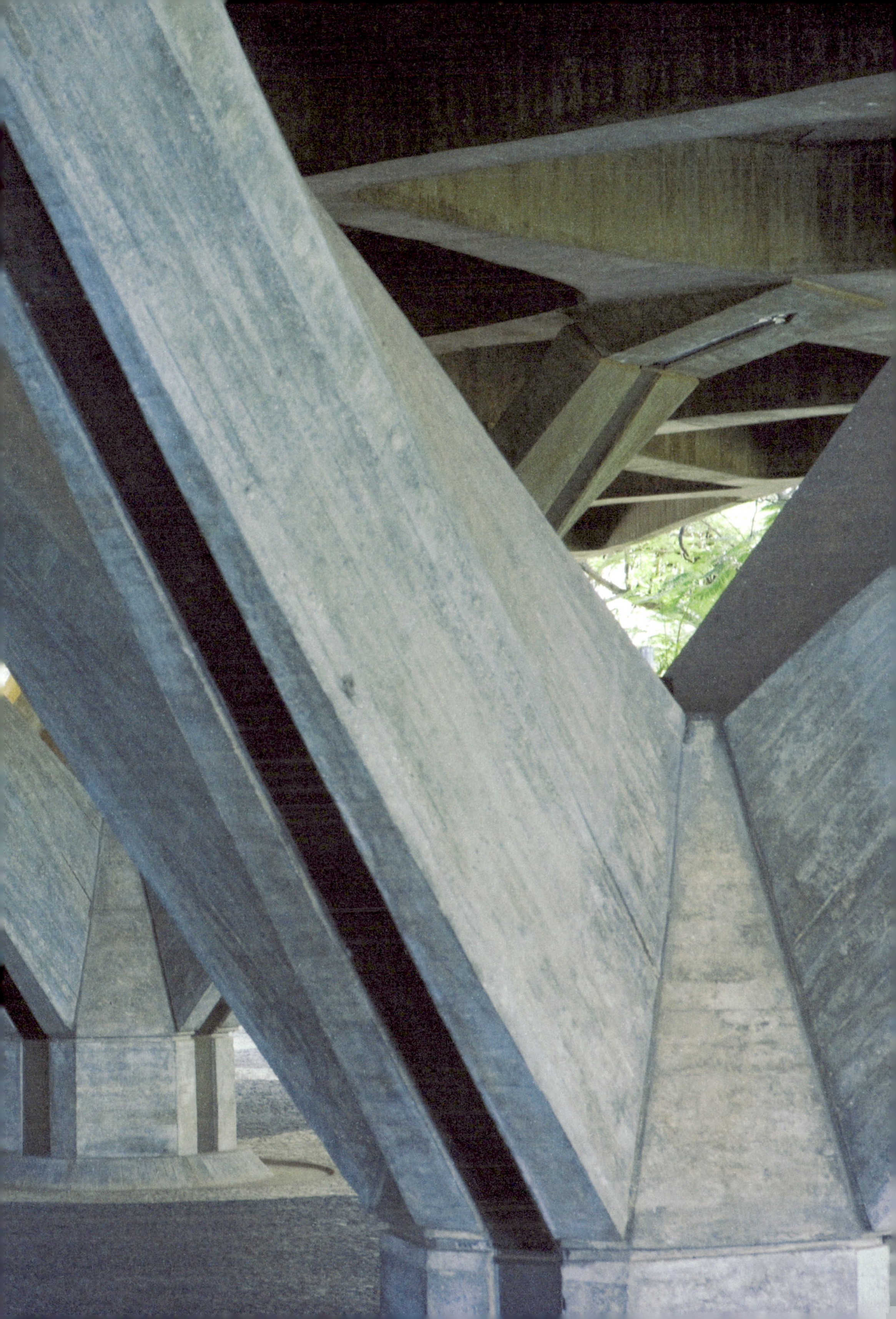

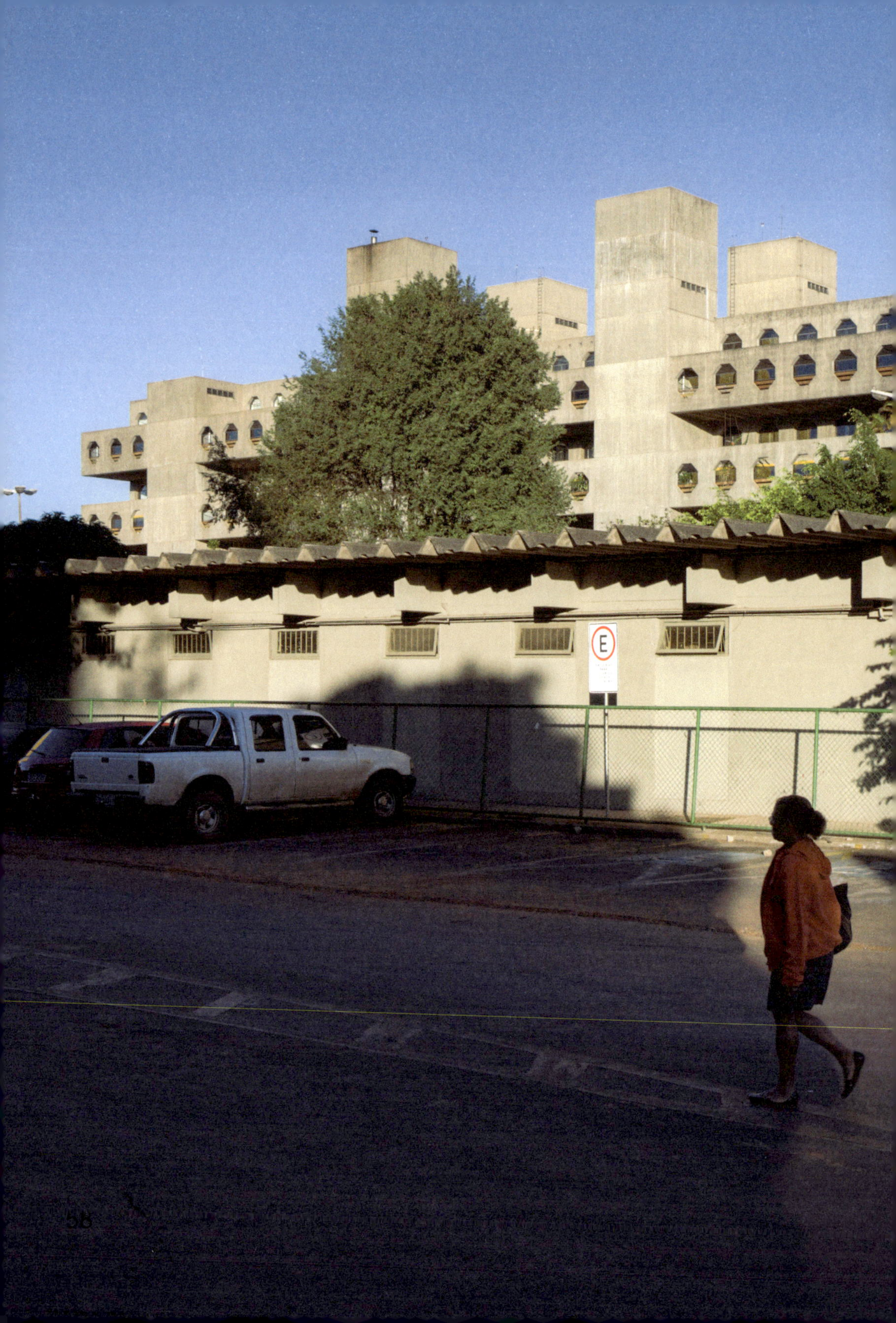
E

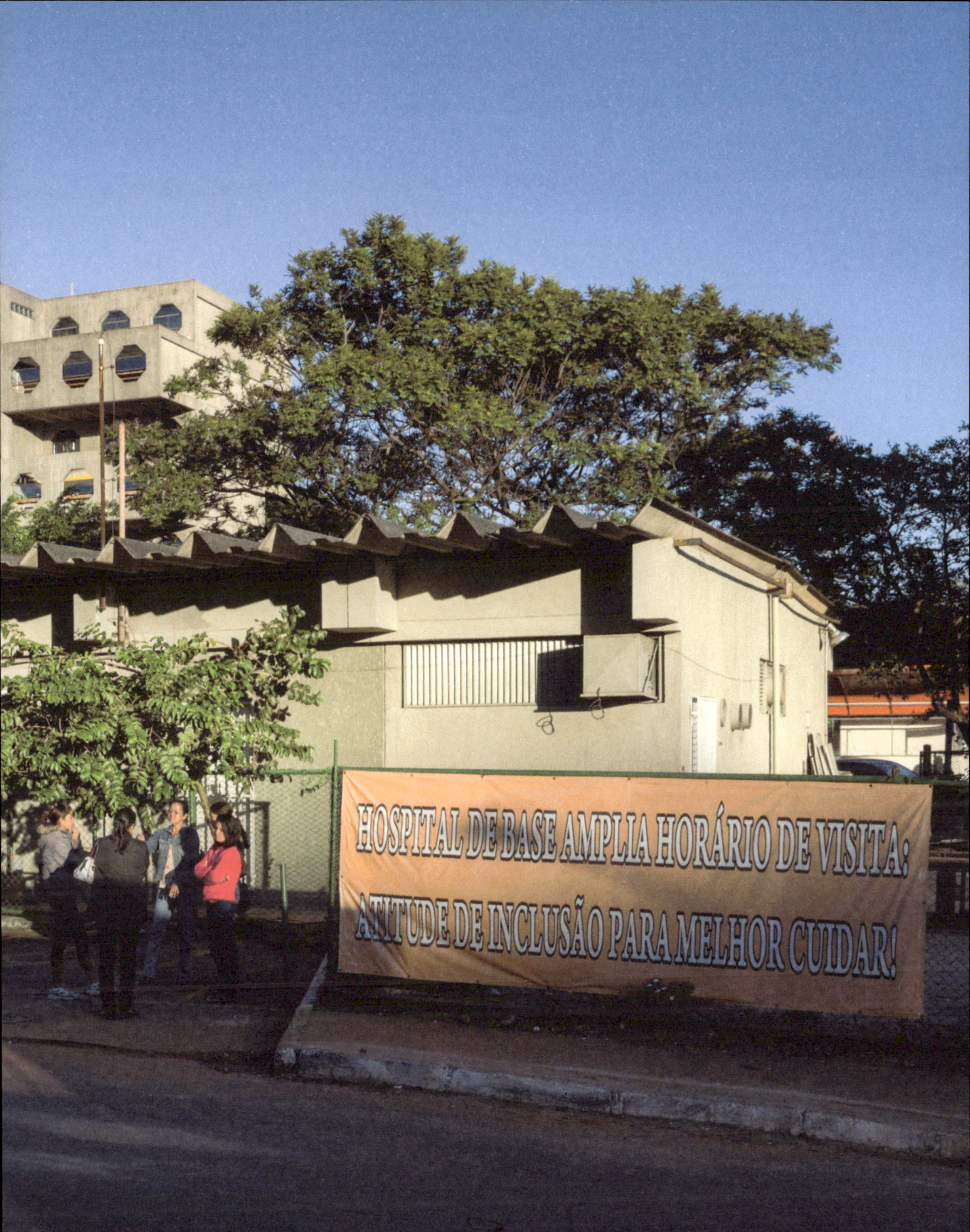
HOSPITAL DE BASE AMPLIA HORÁRIO DE VISITA:
ATITUDE DE INCLUSÃO PARA MELHOR CUIDAR!

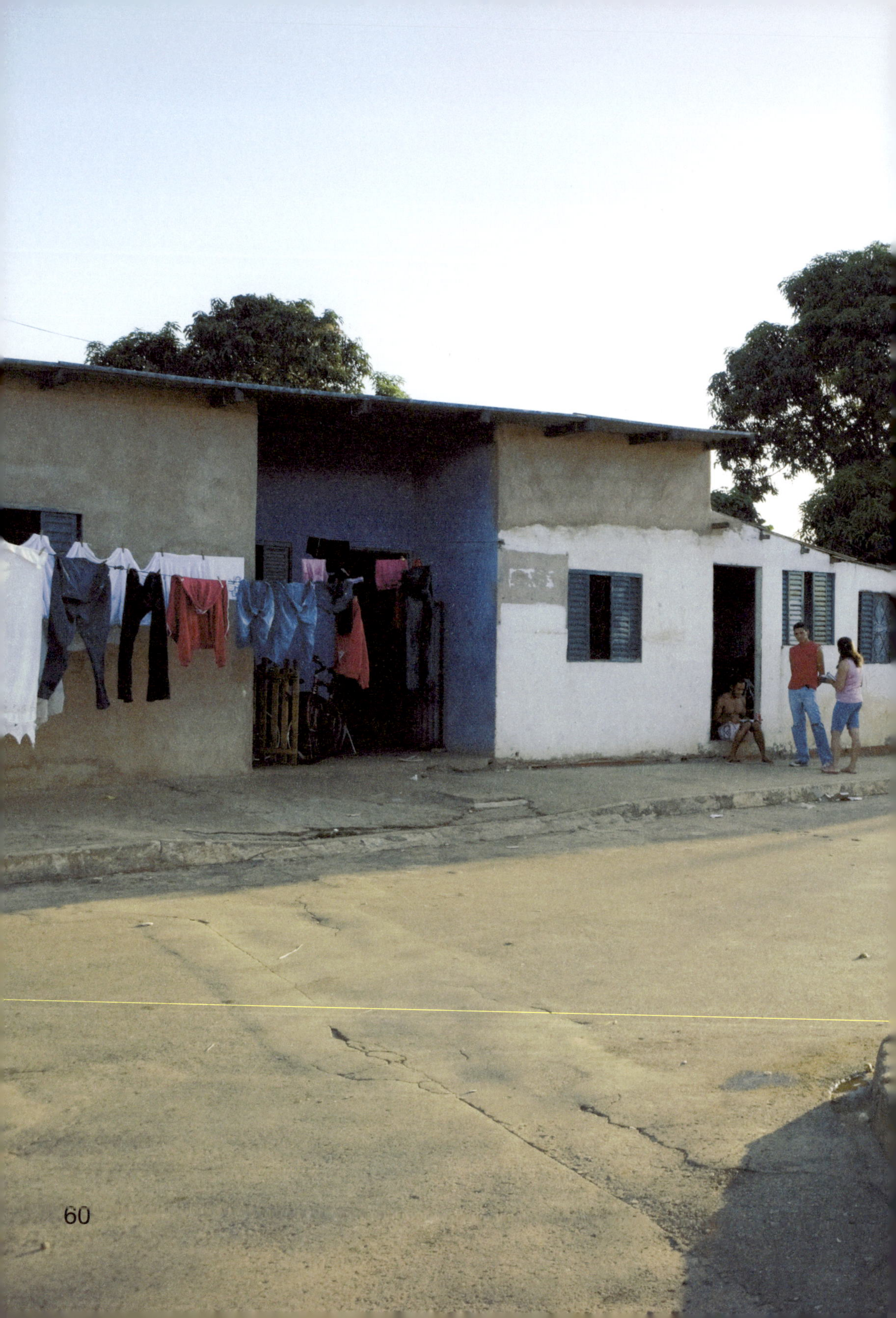

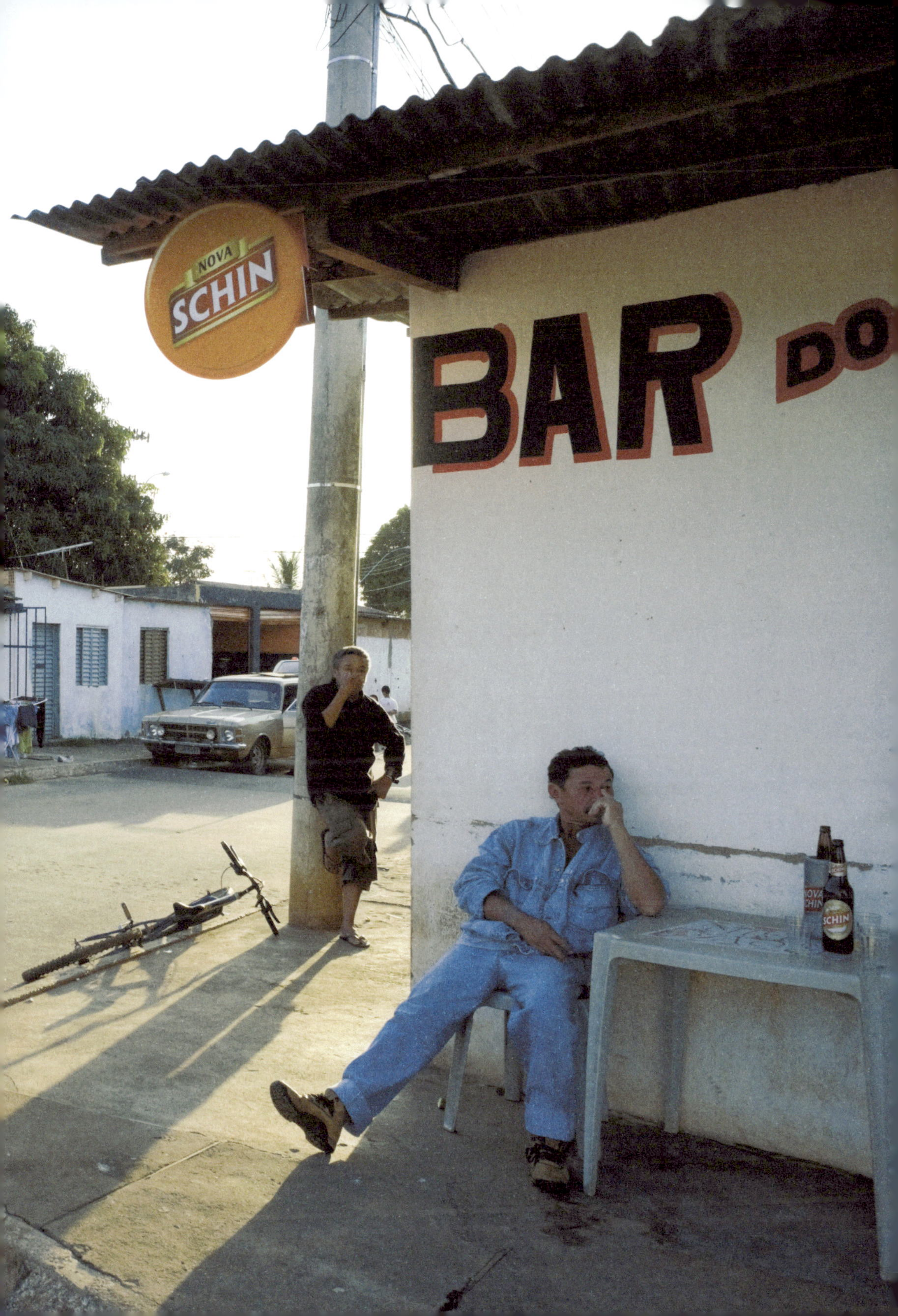
NOVA
SCHIN
BAR DO

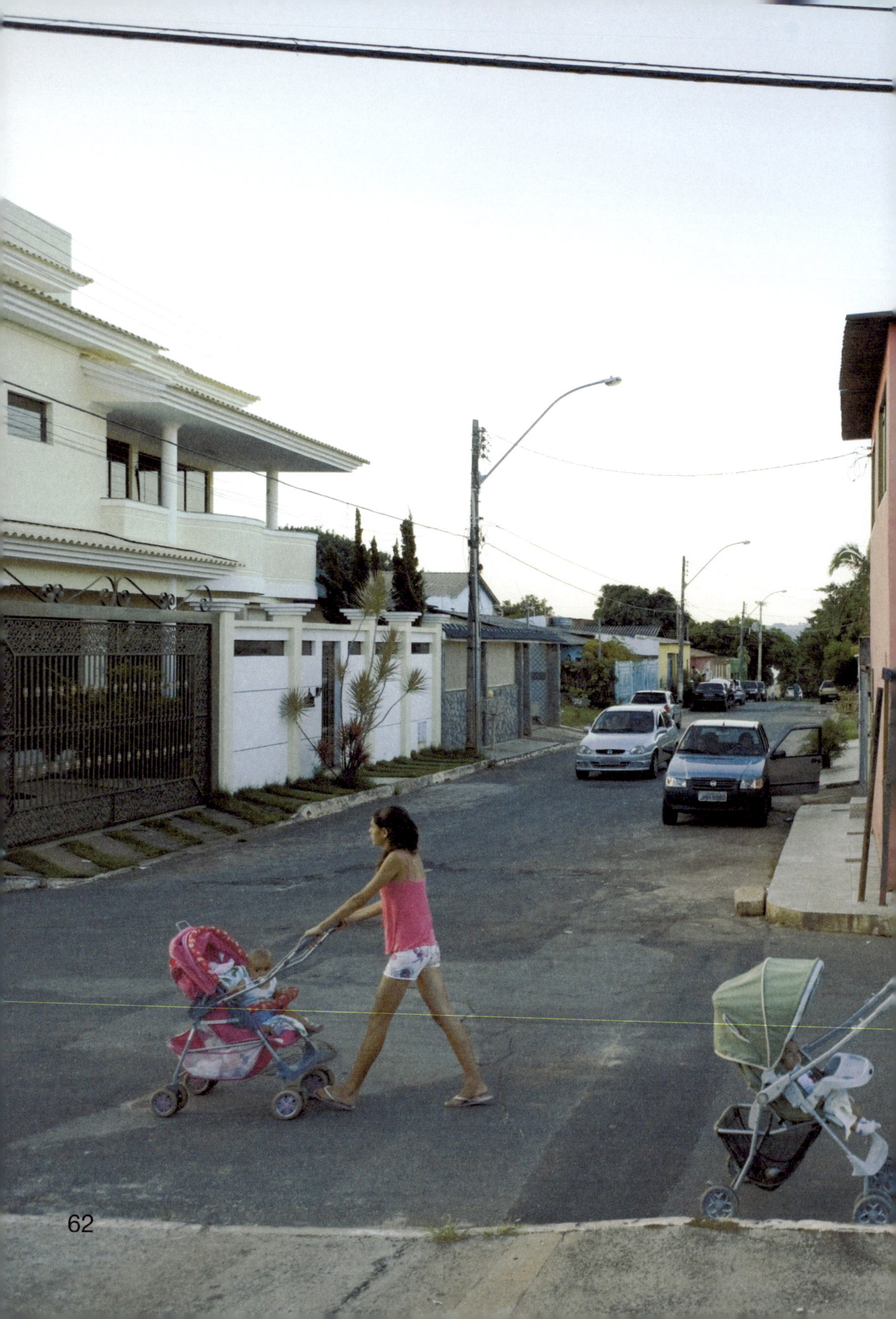

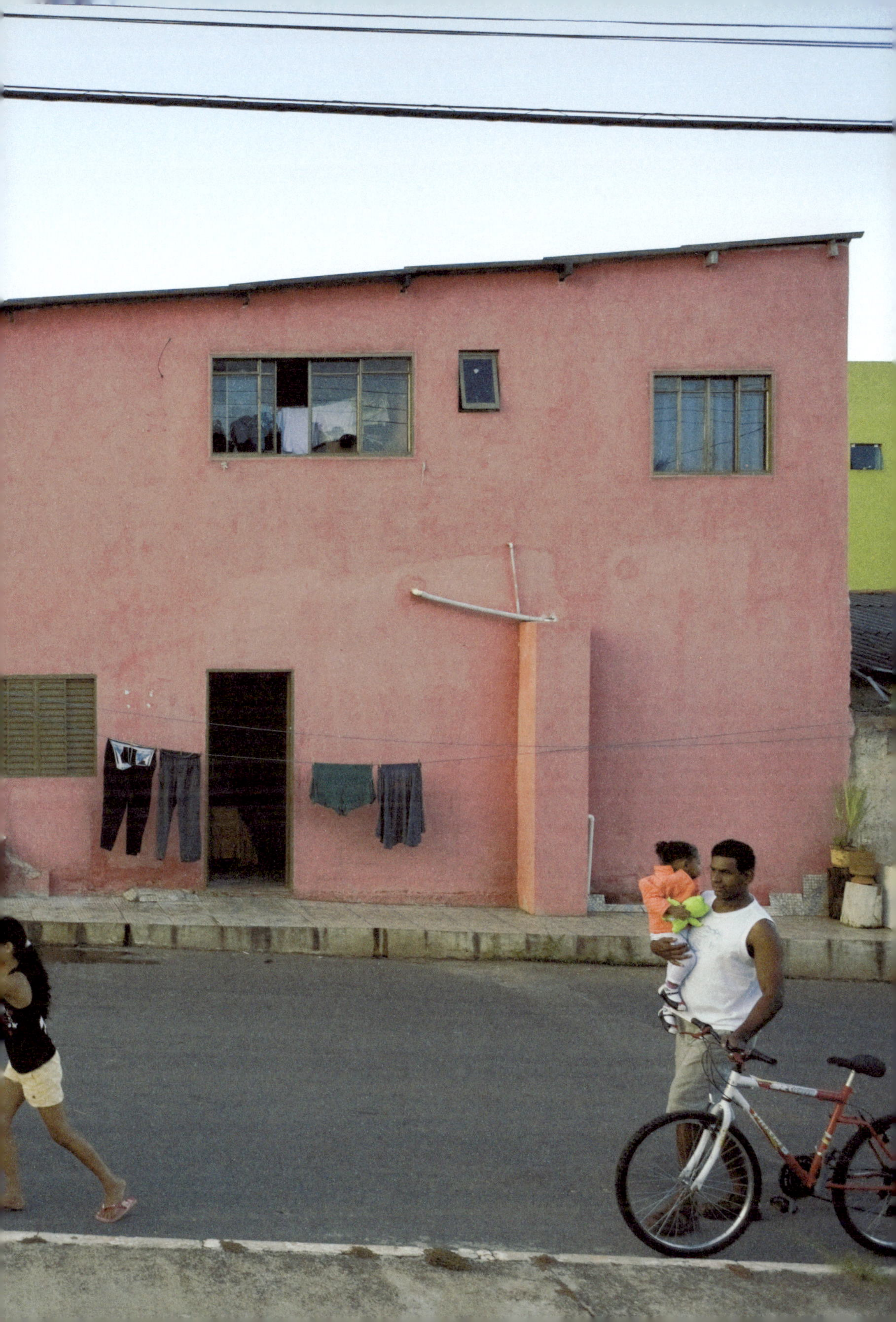

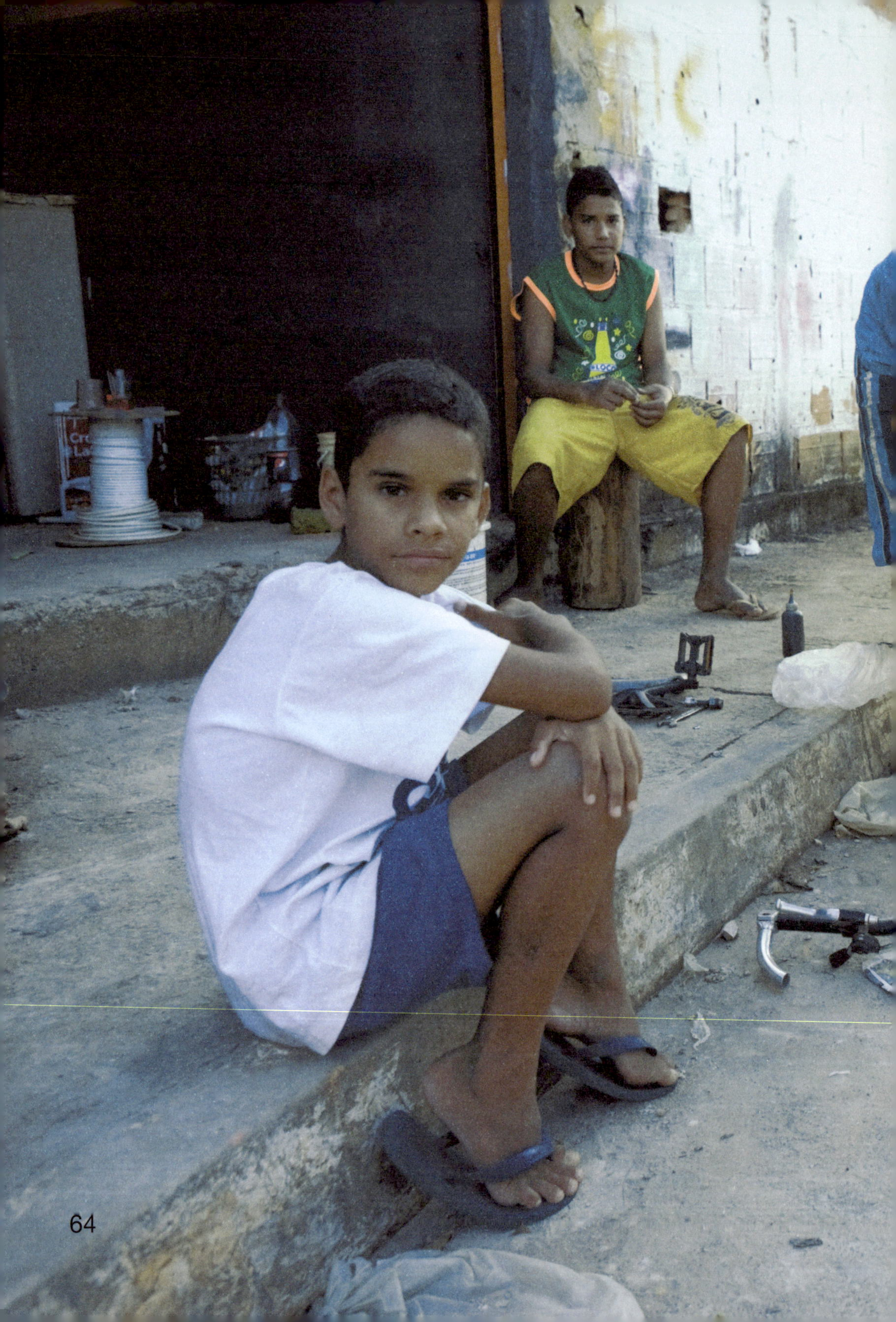

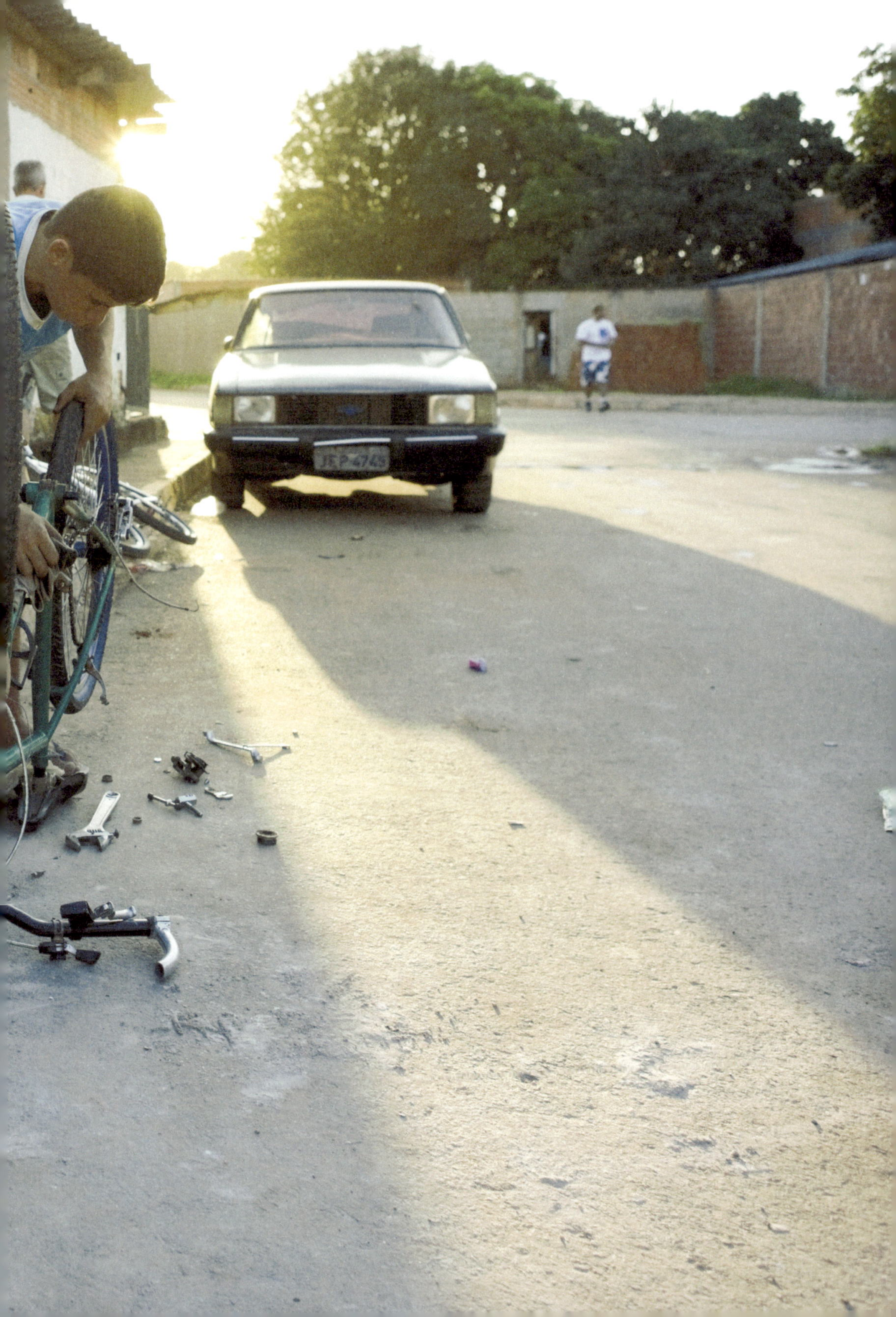

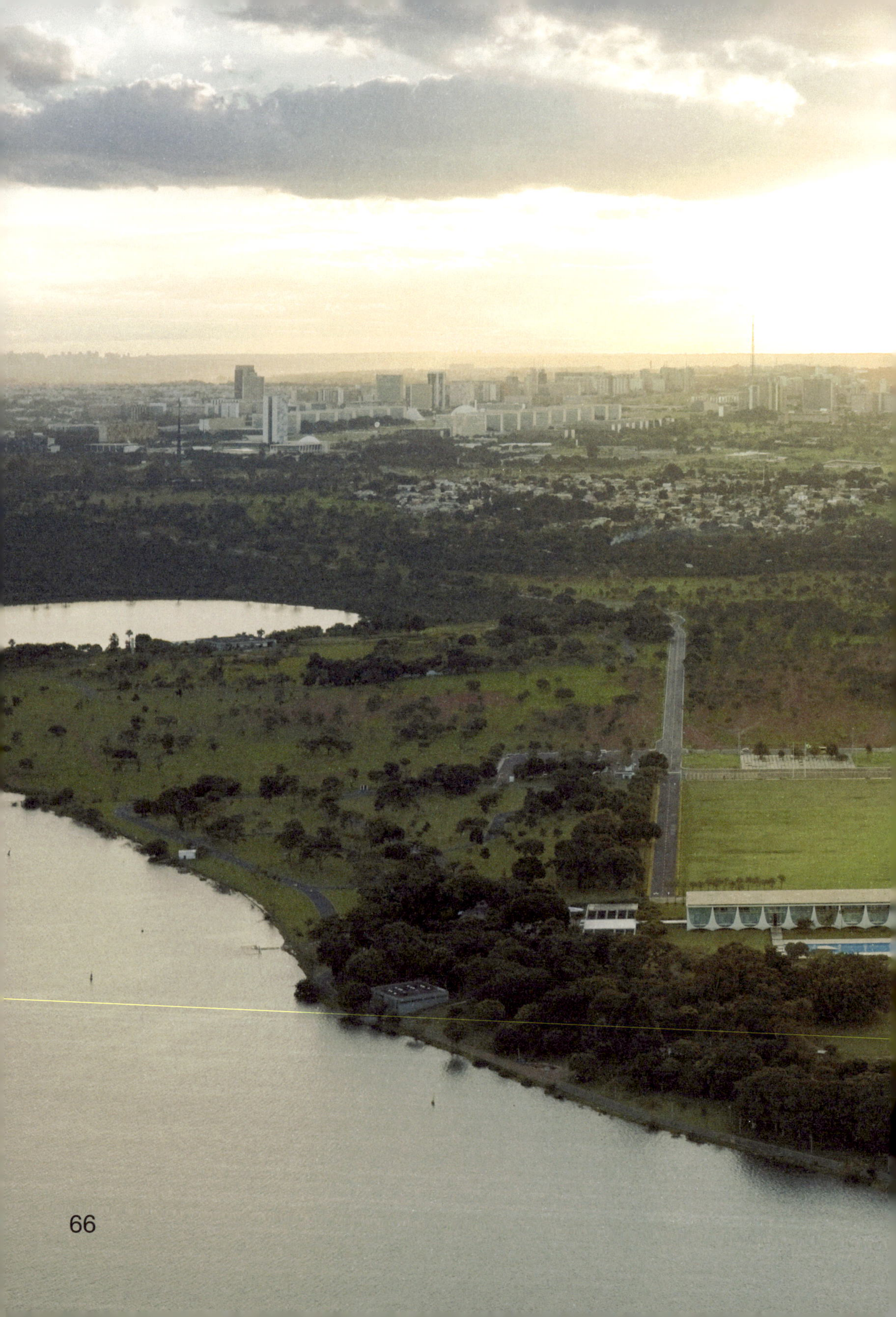

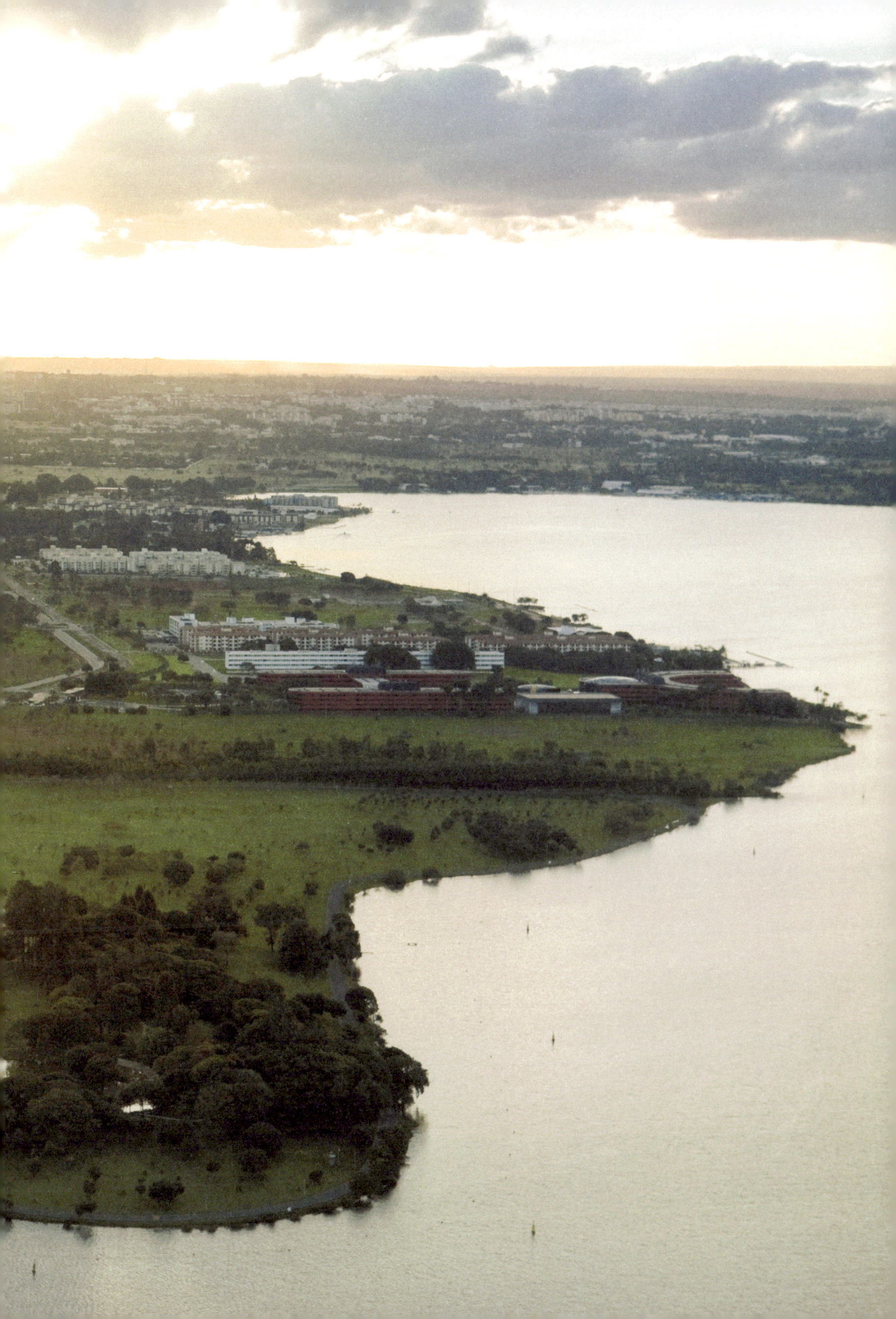

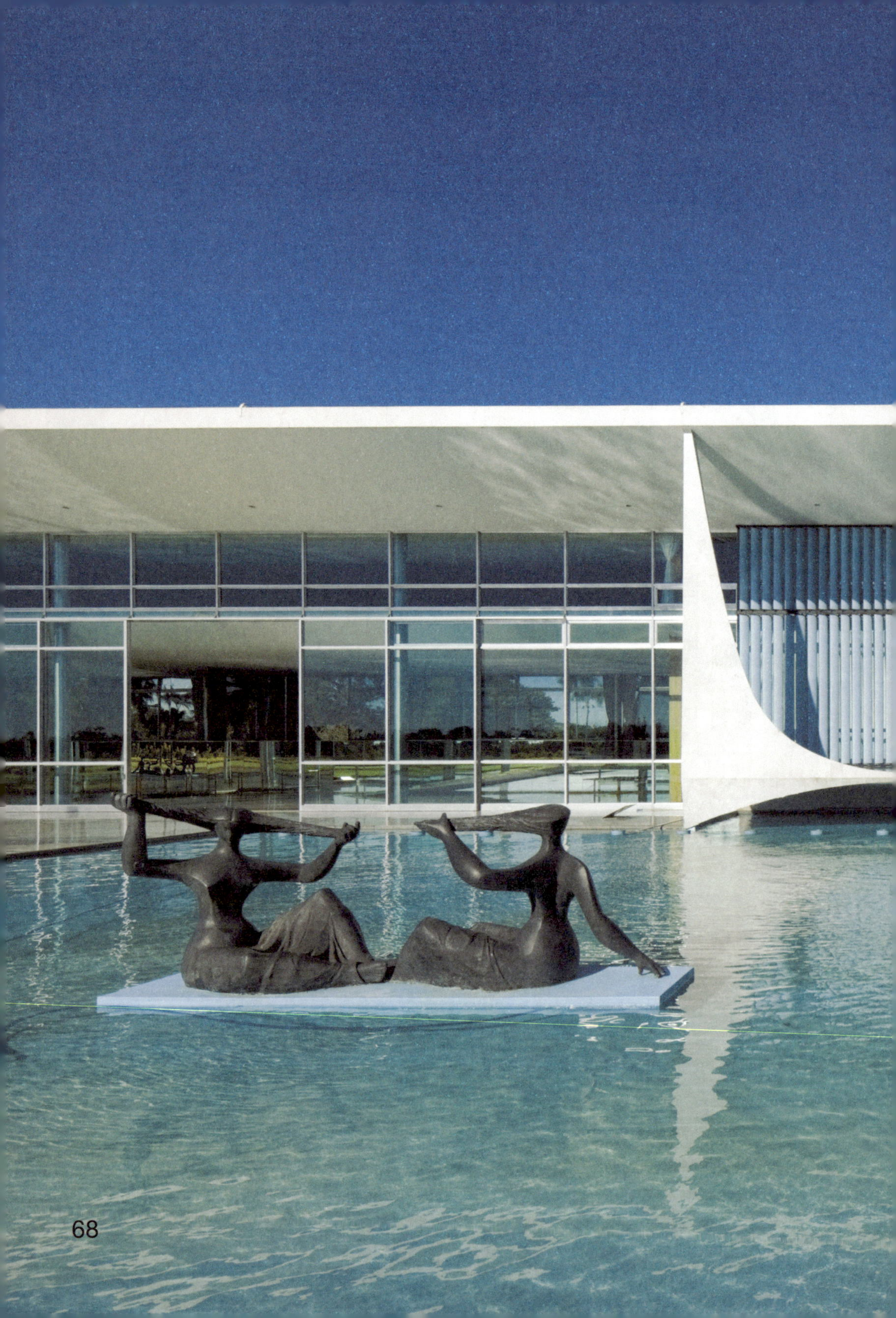

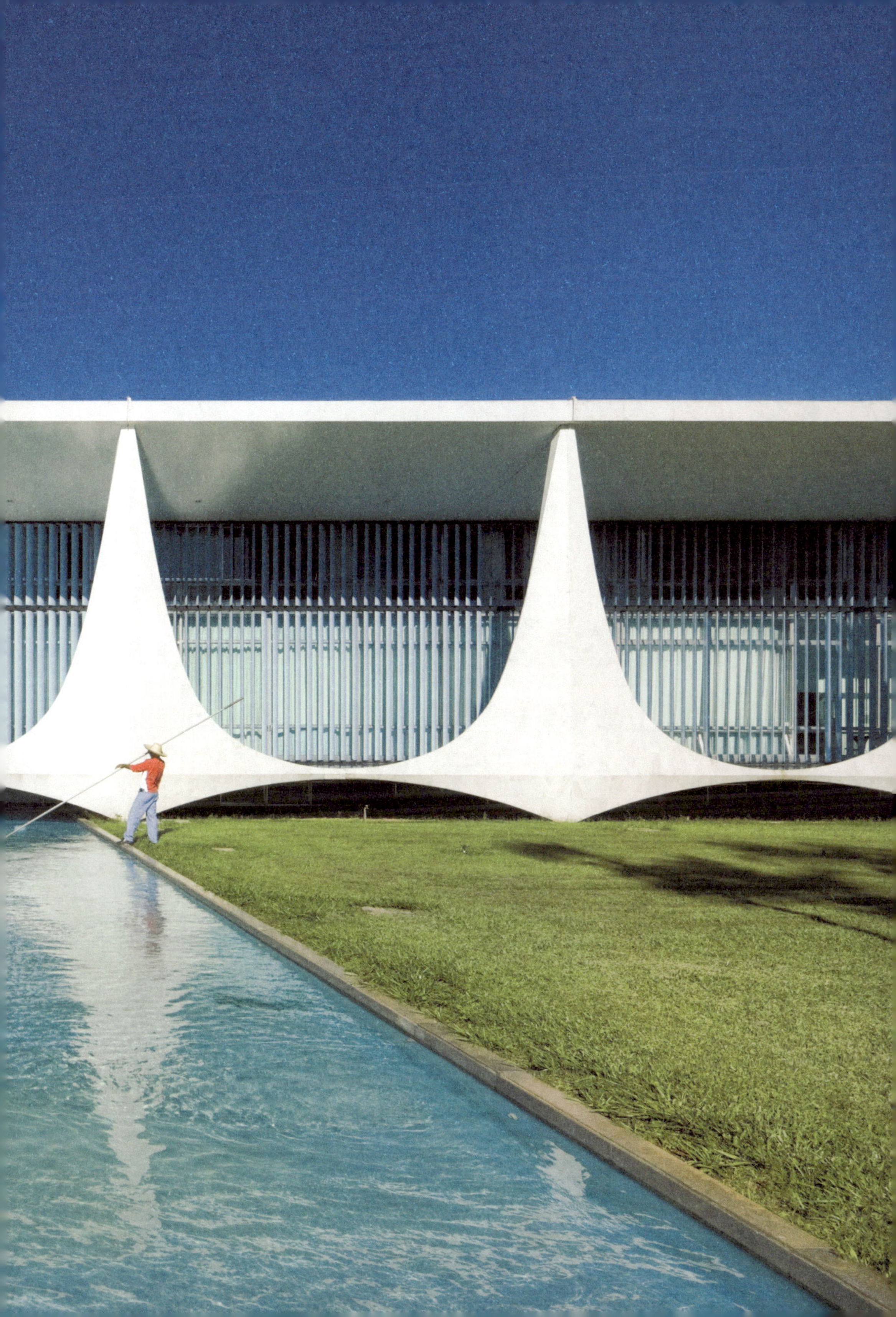

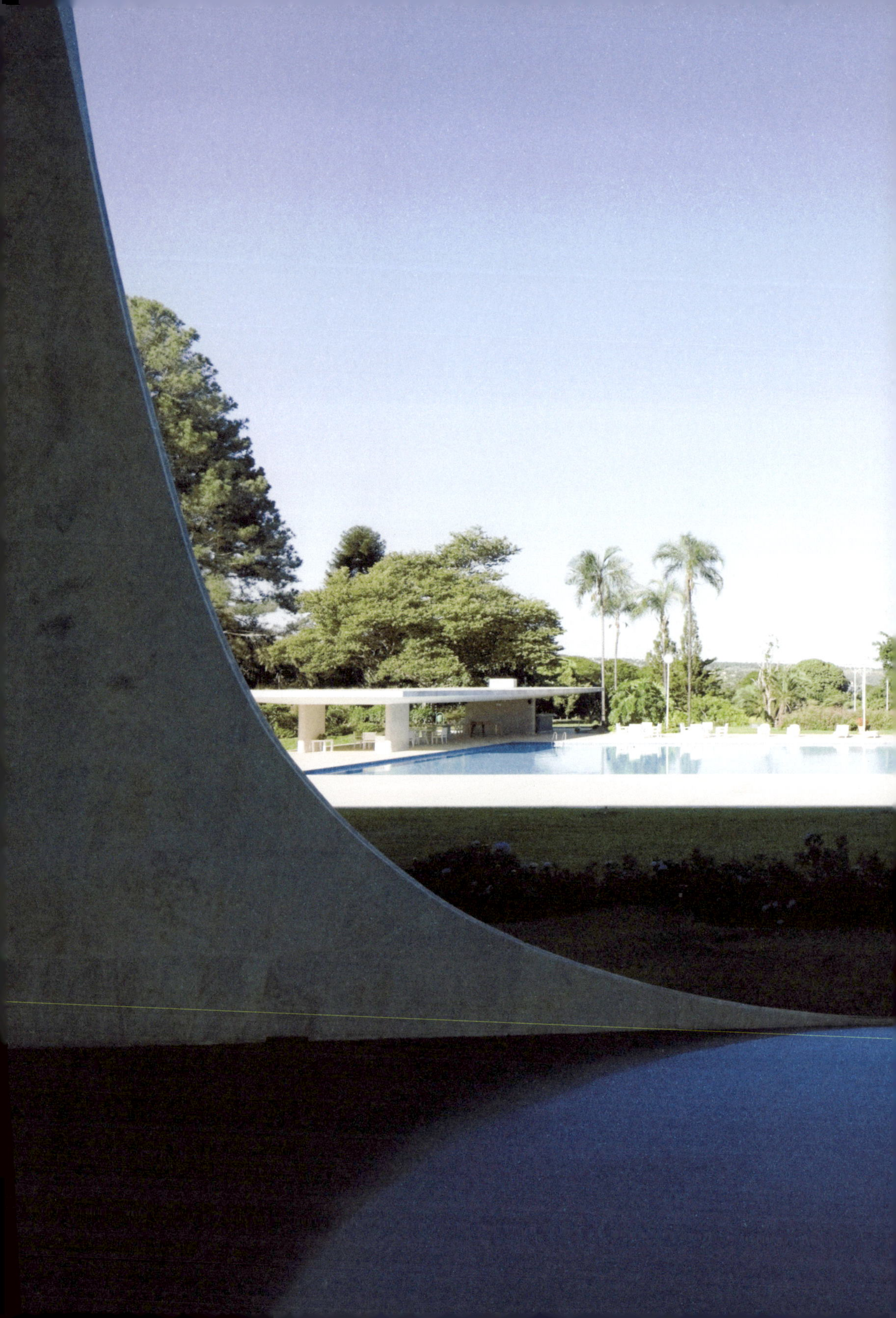

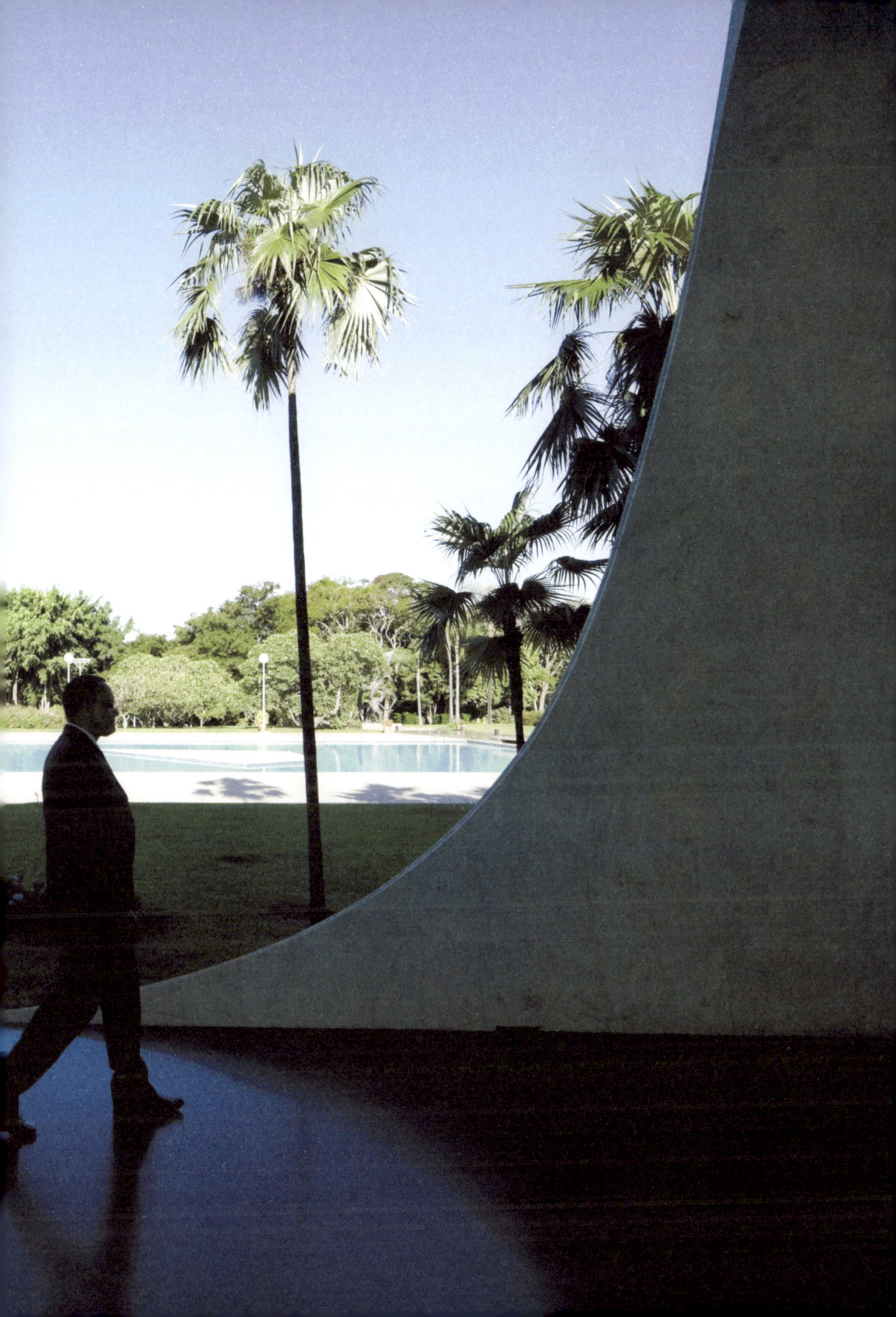

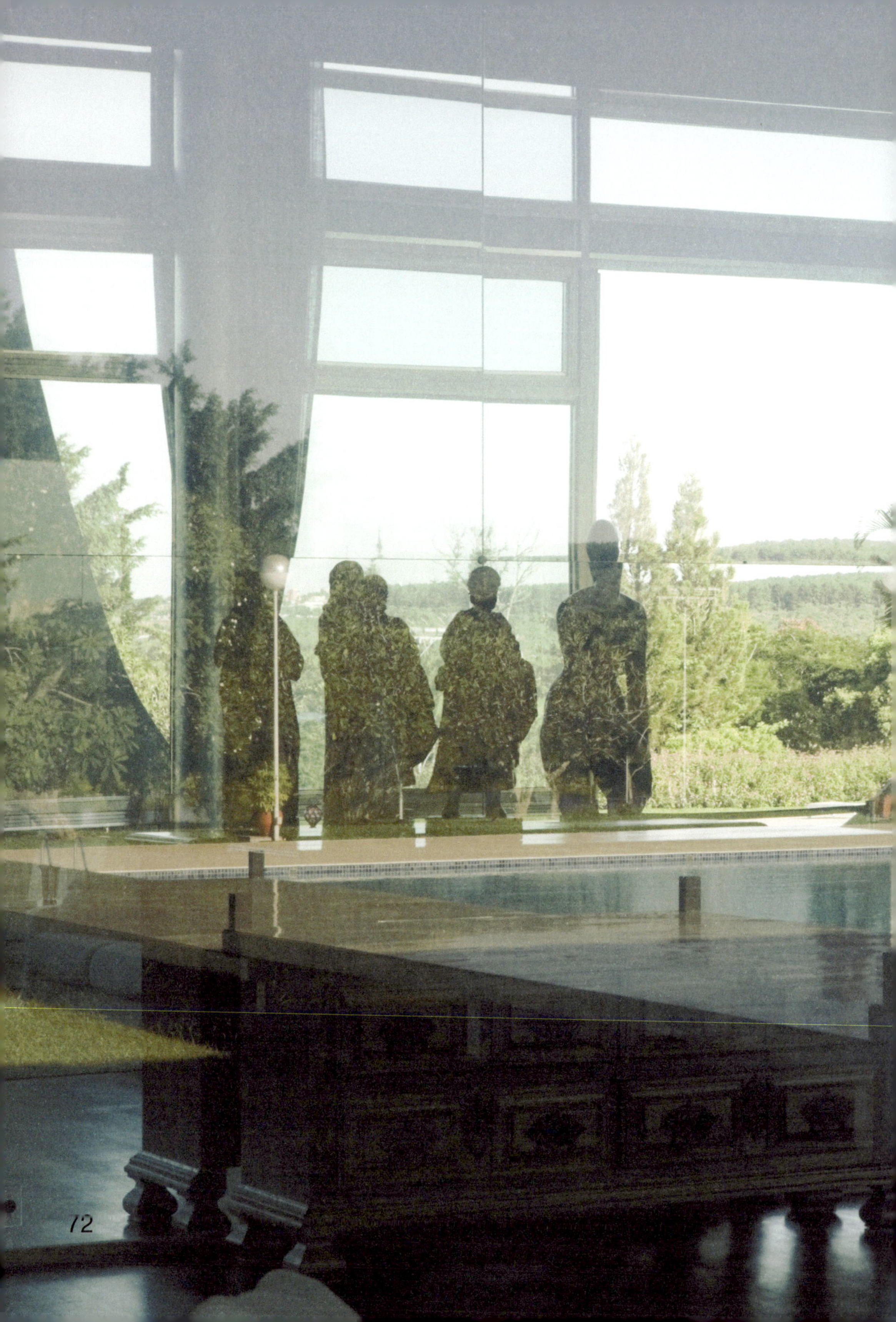

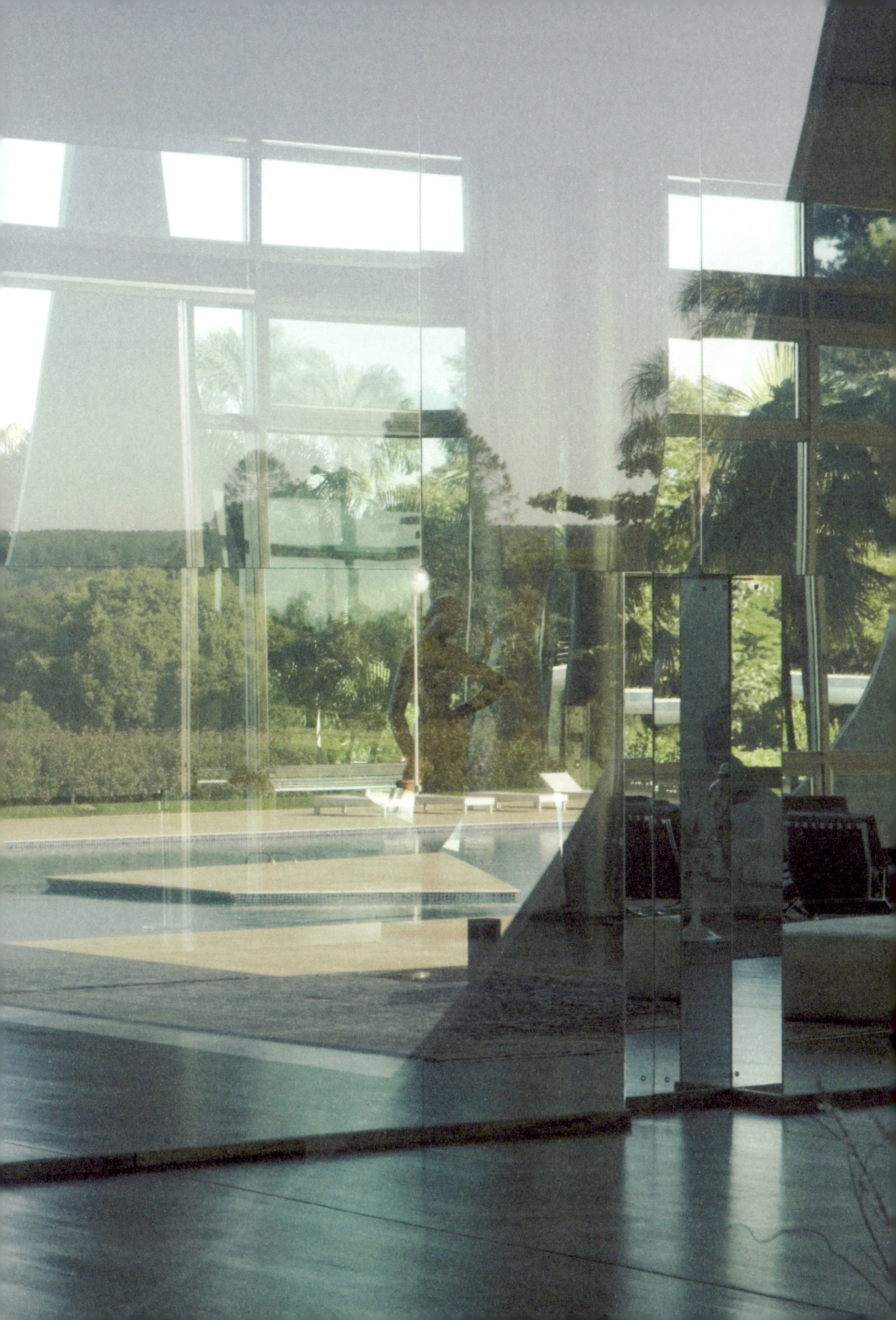

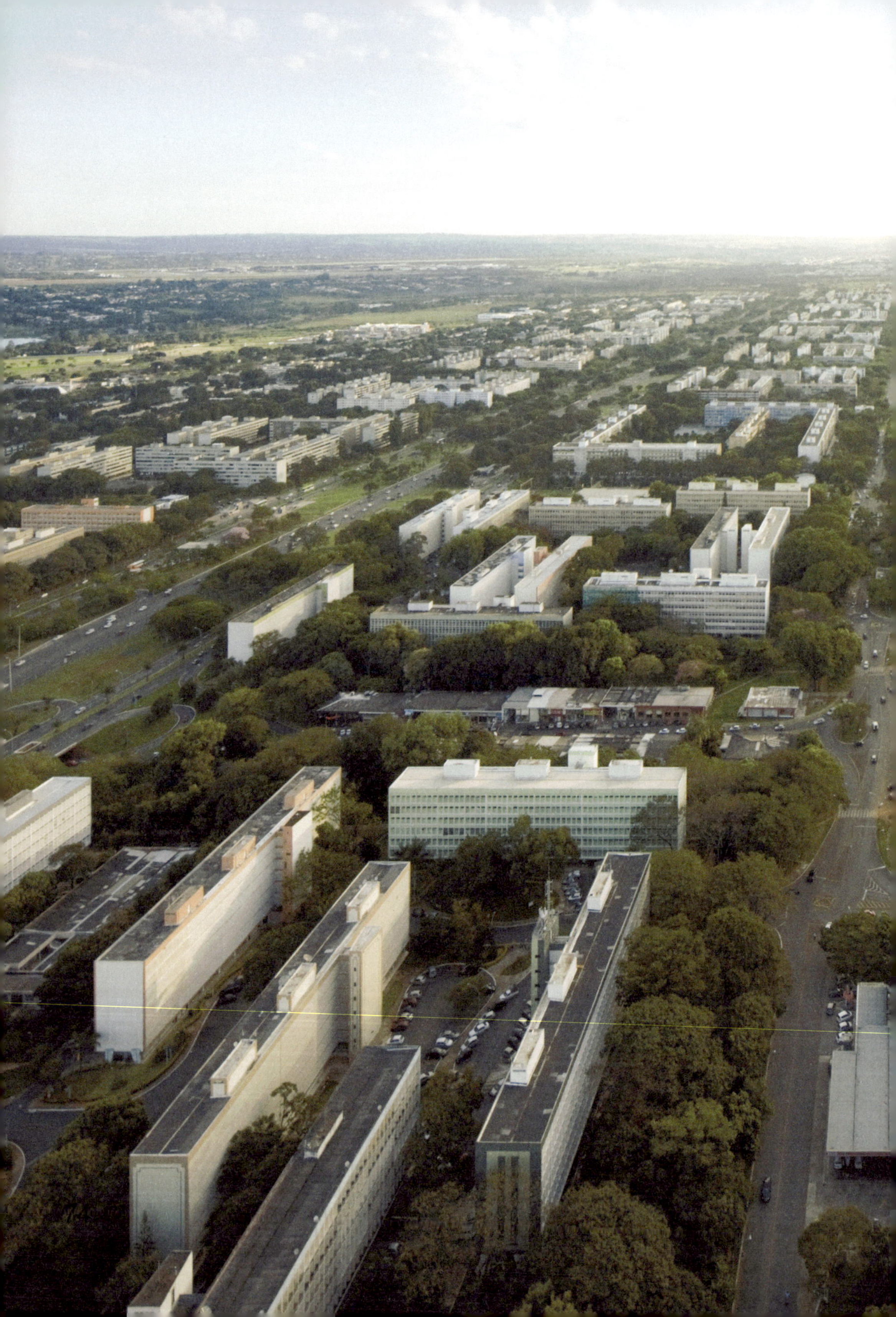

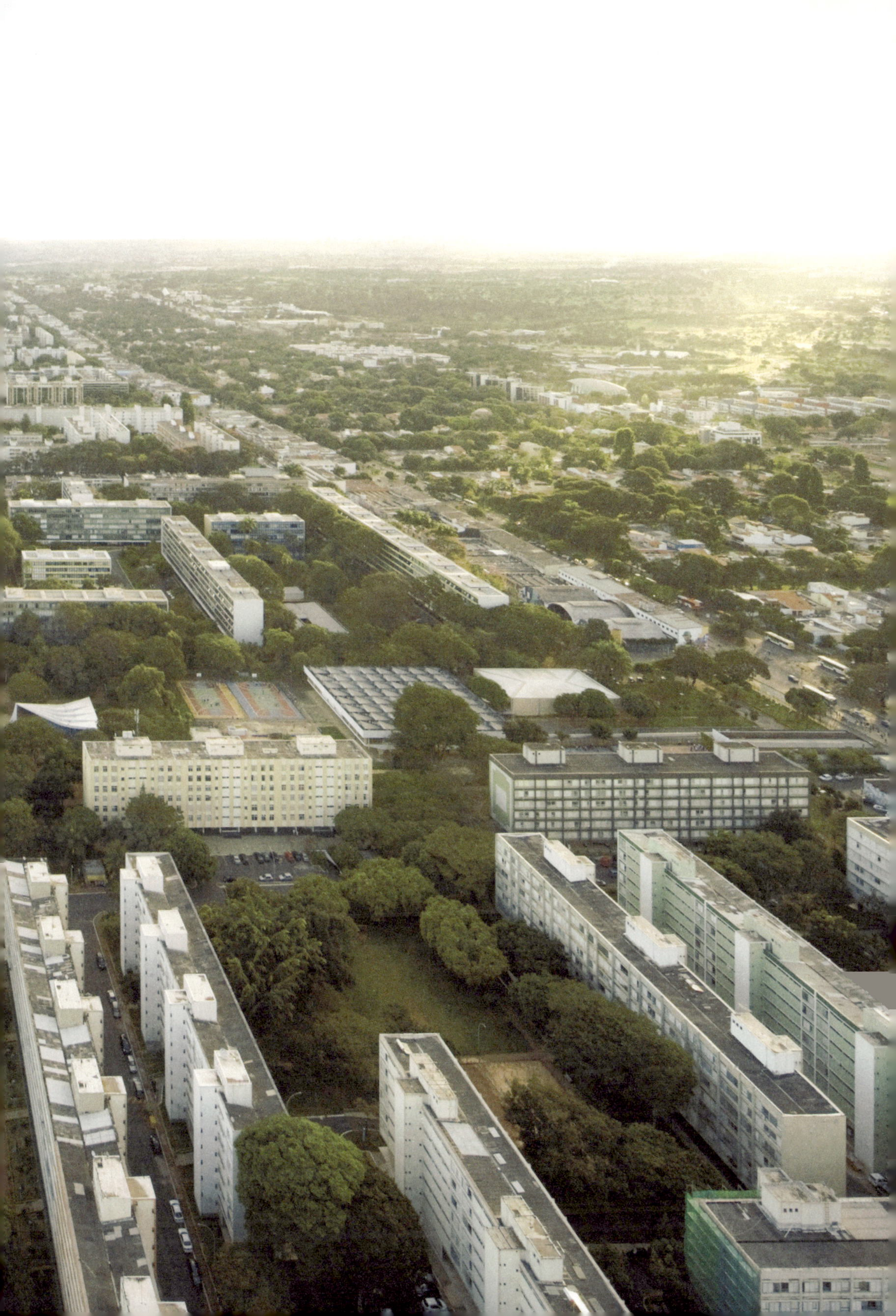

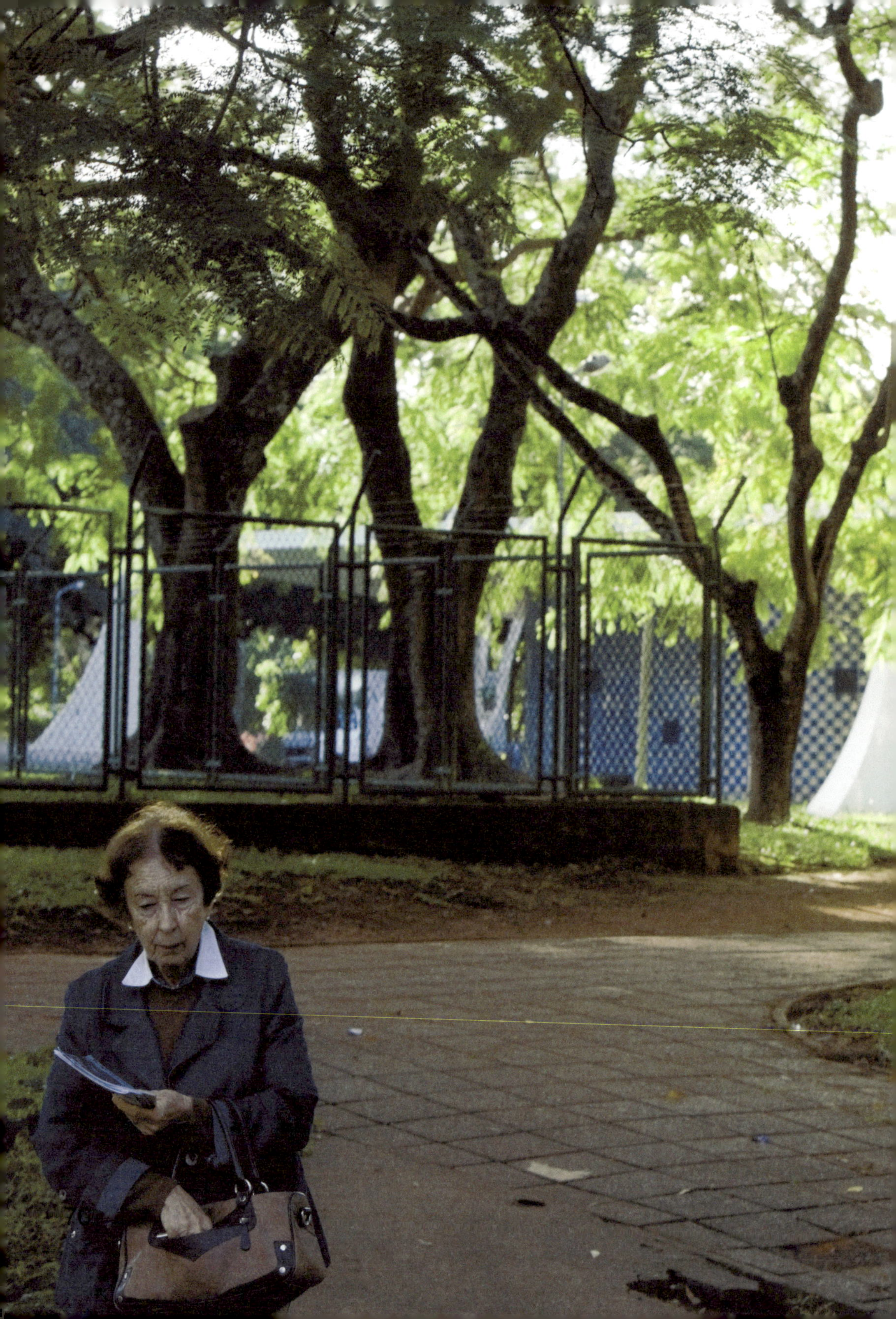

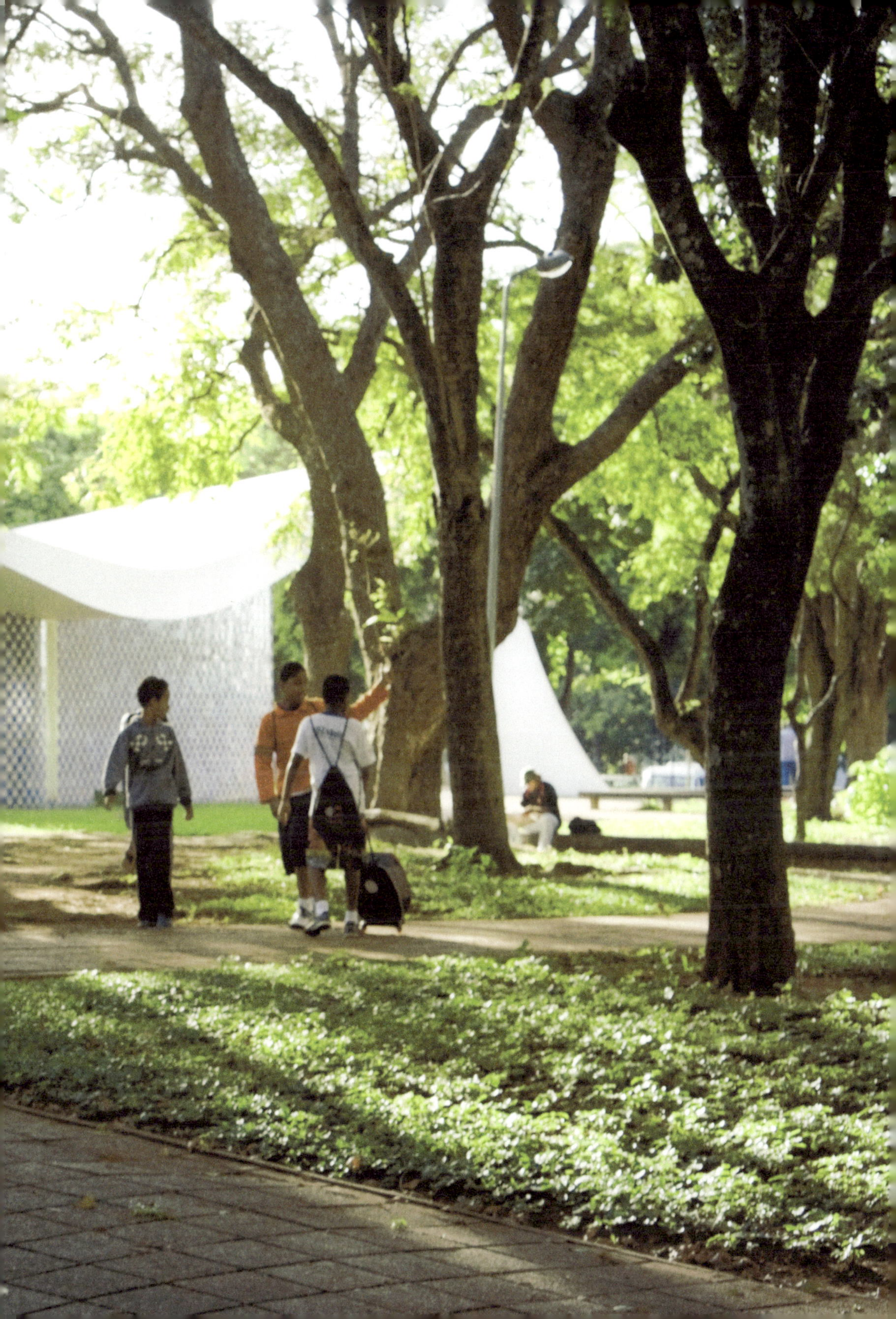

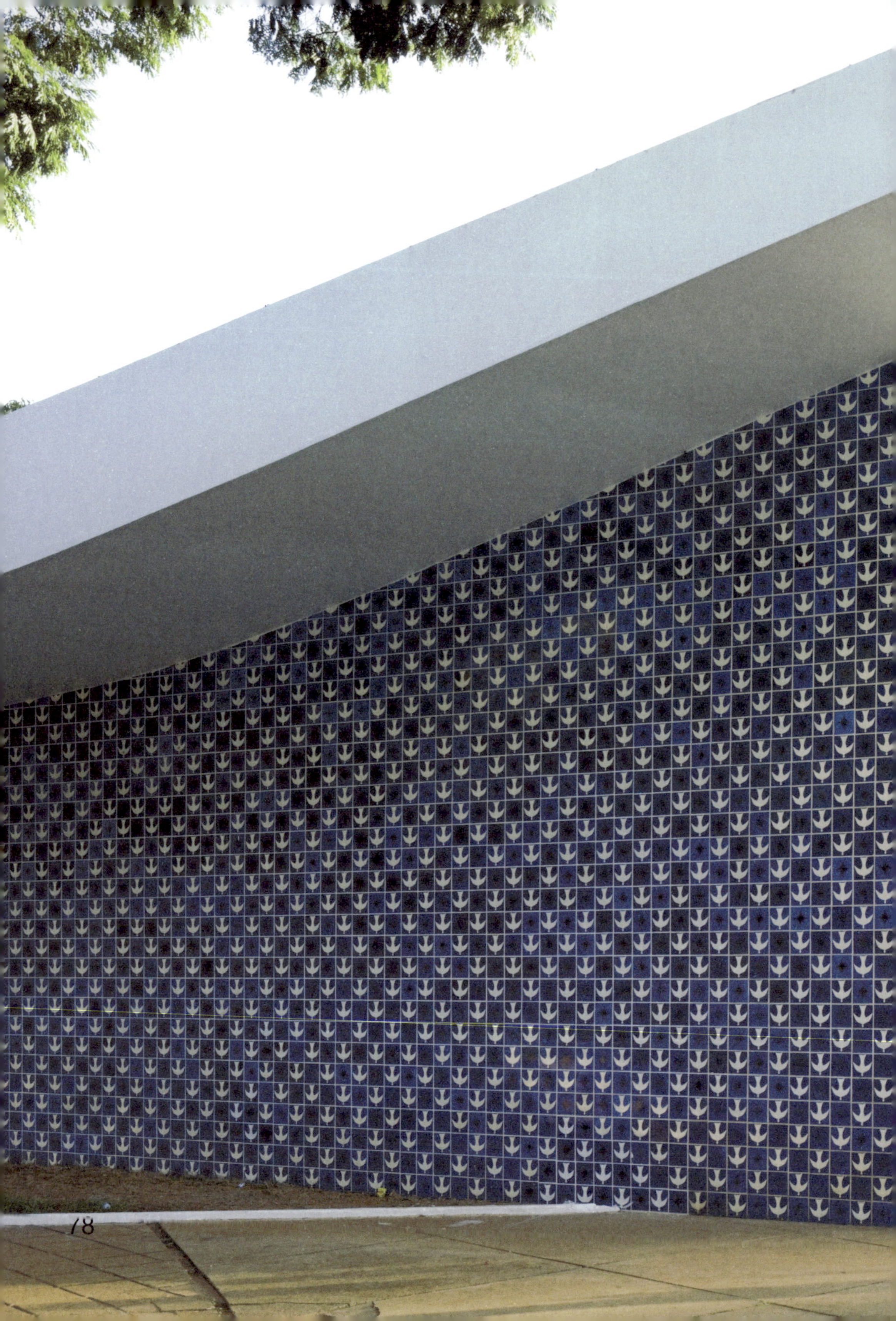

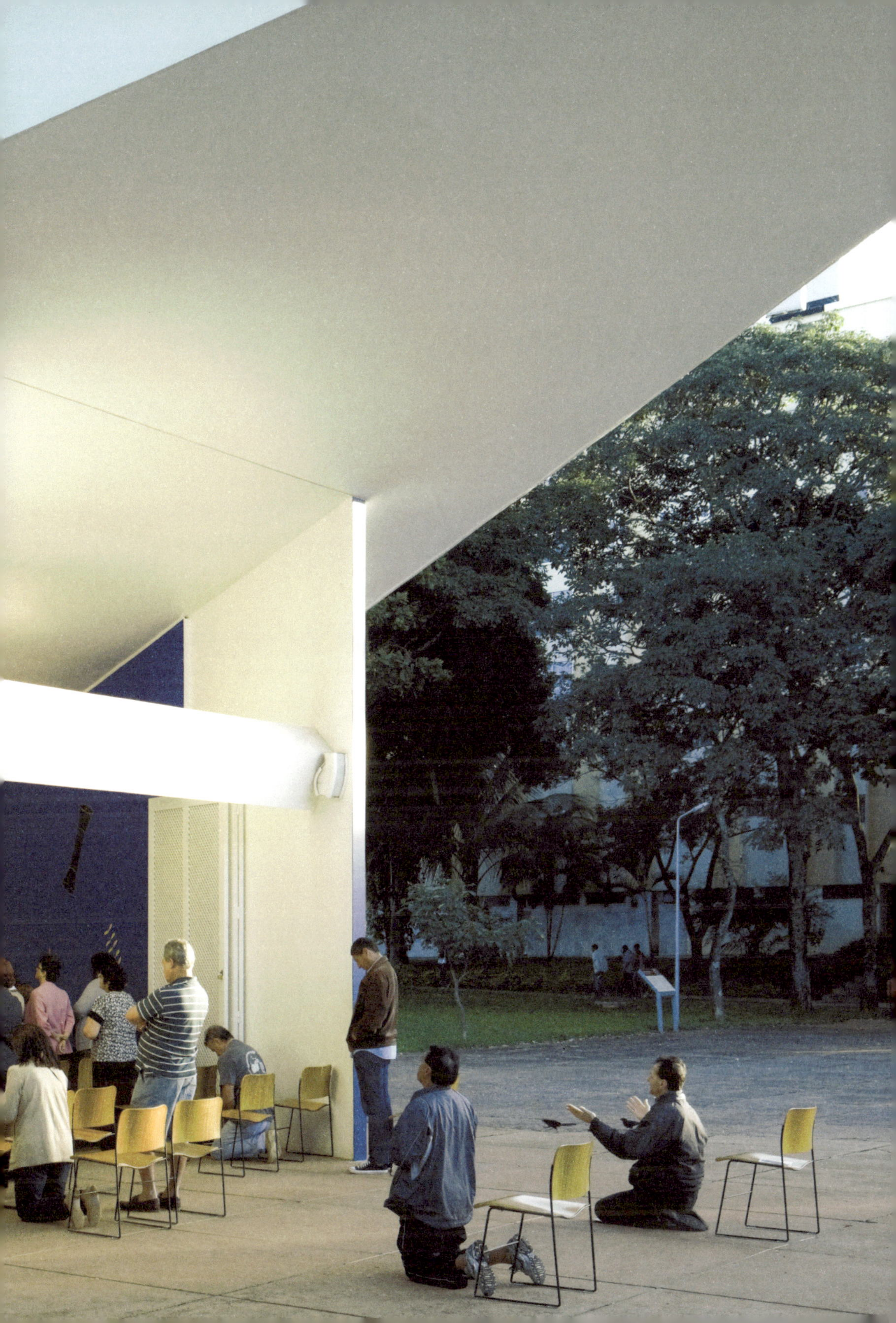

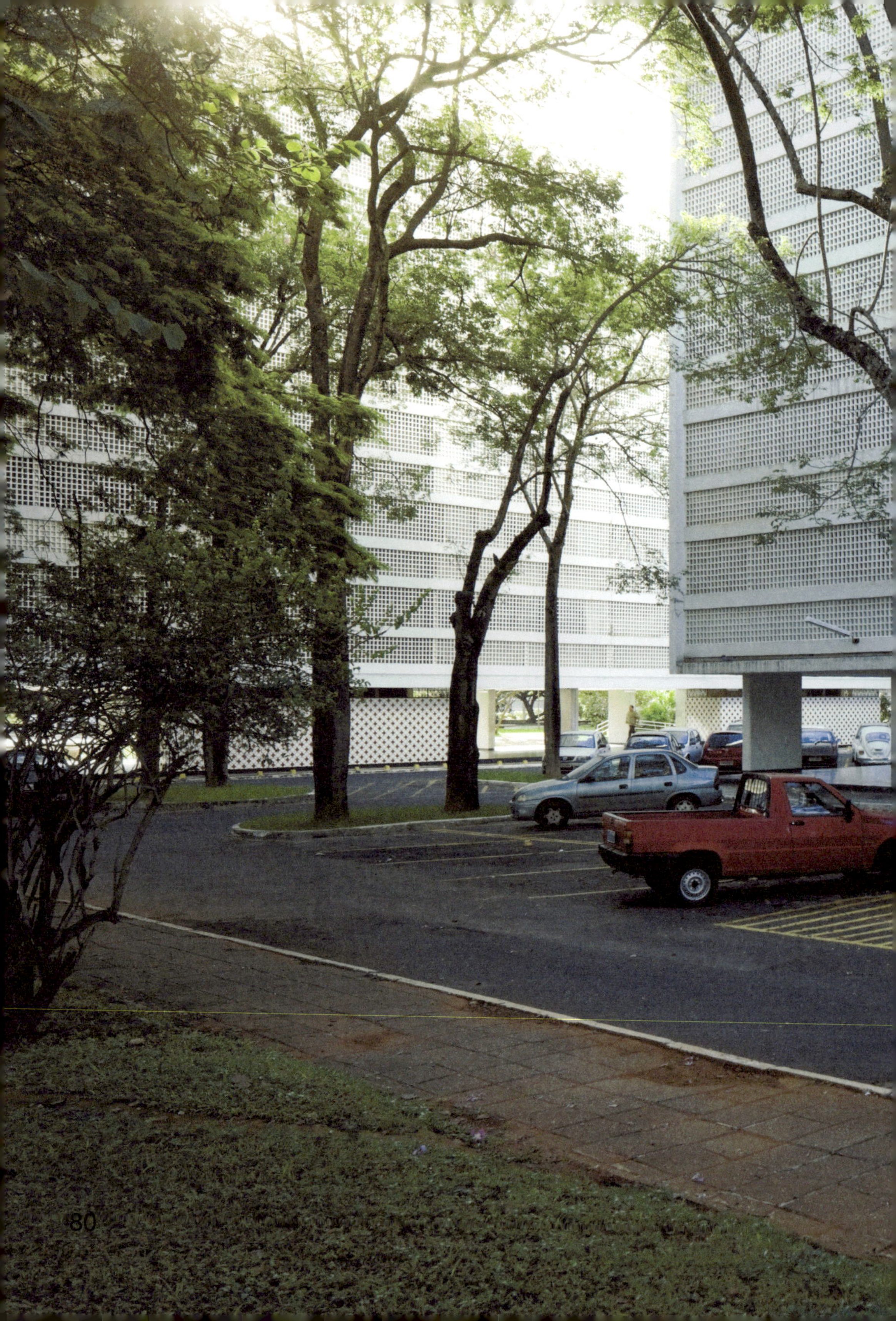

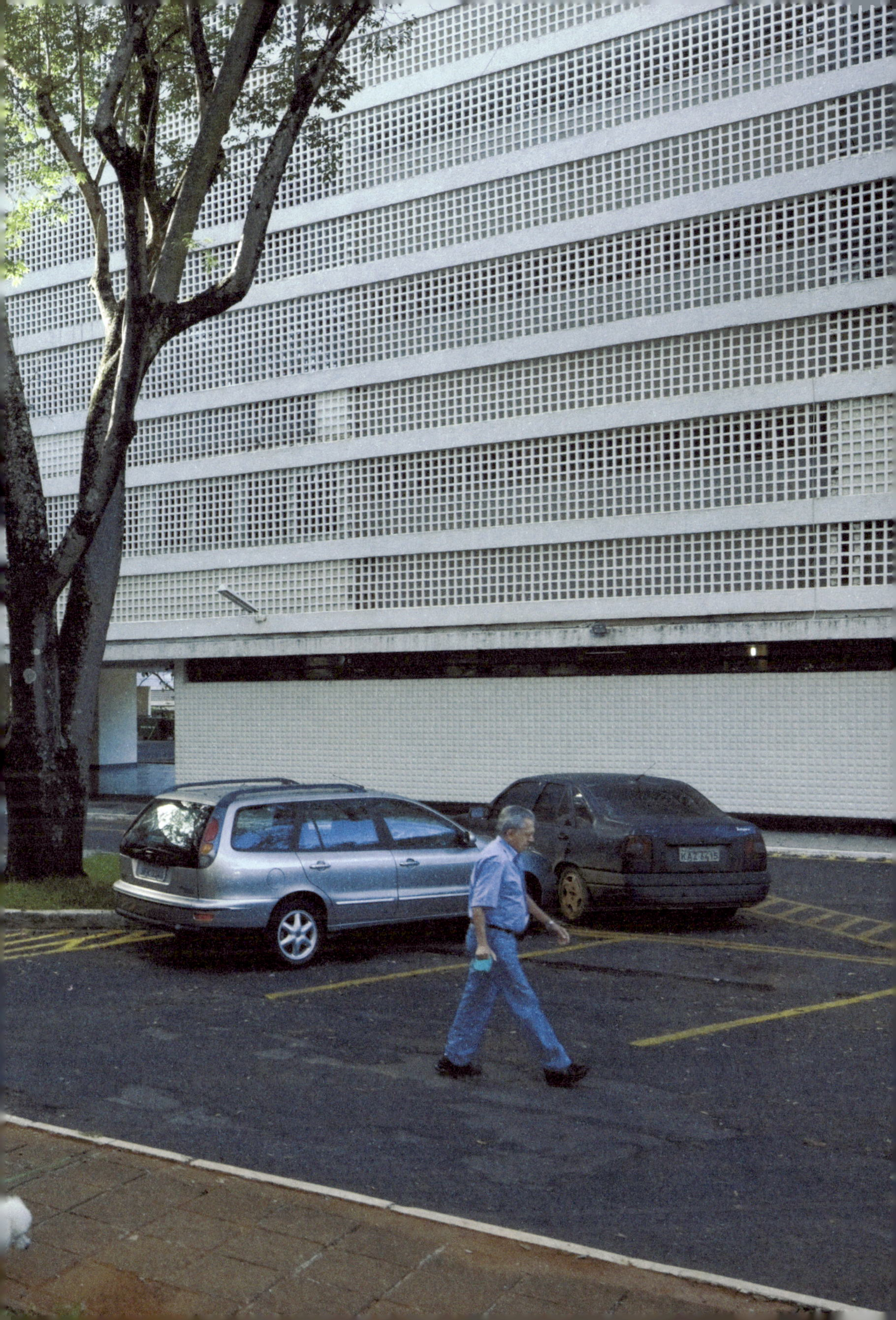

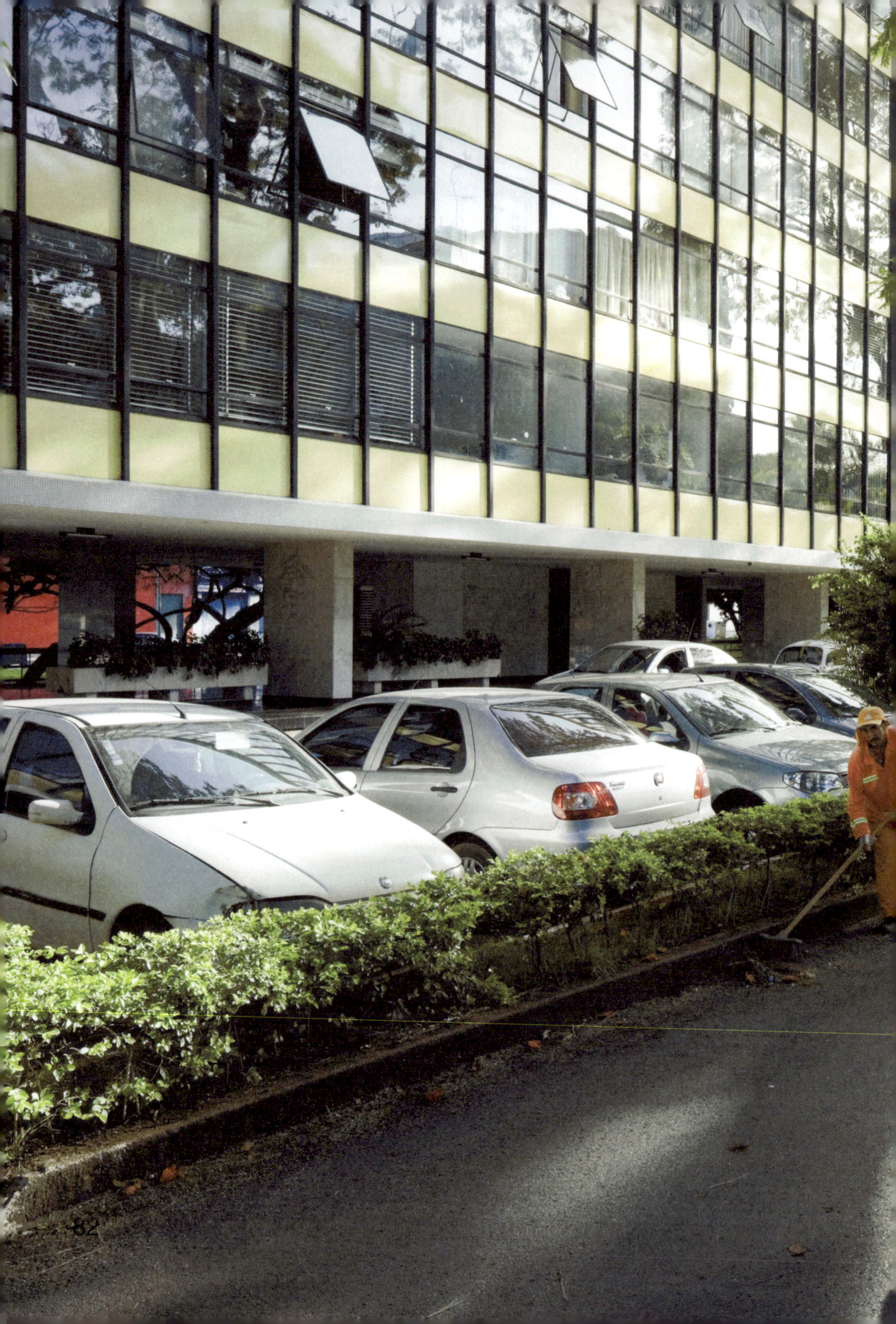

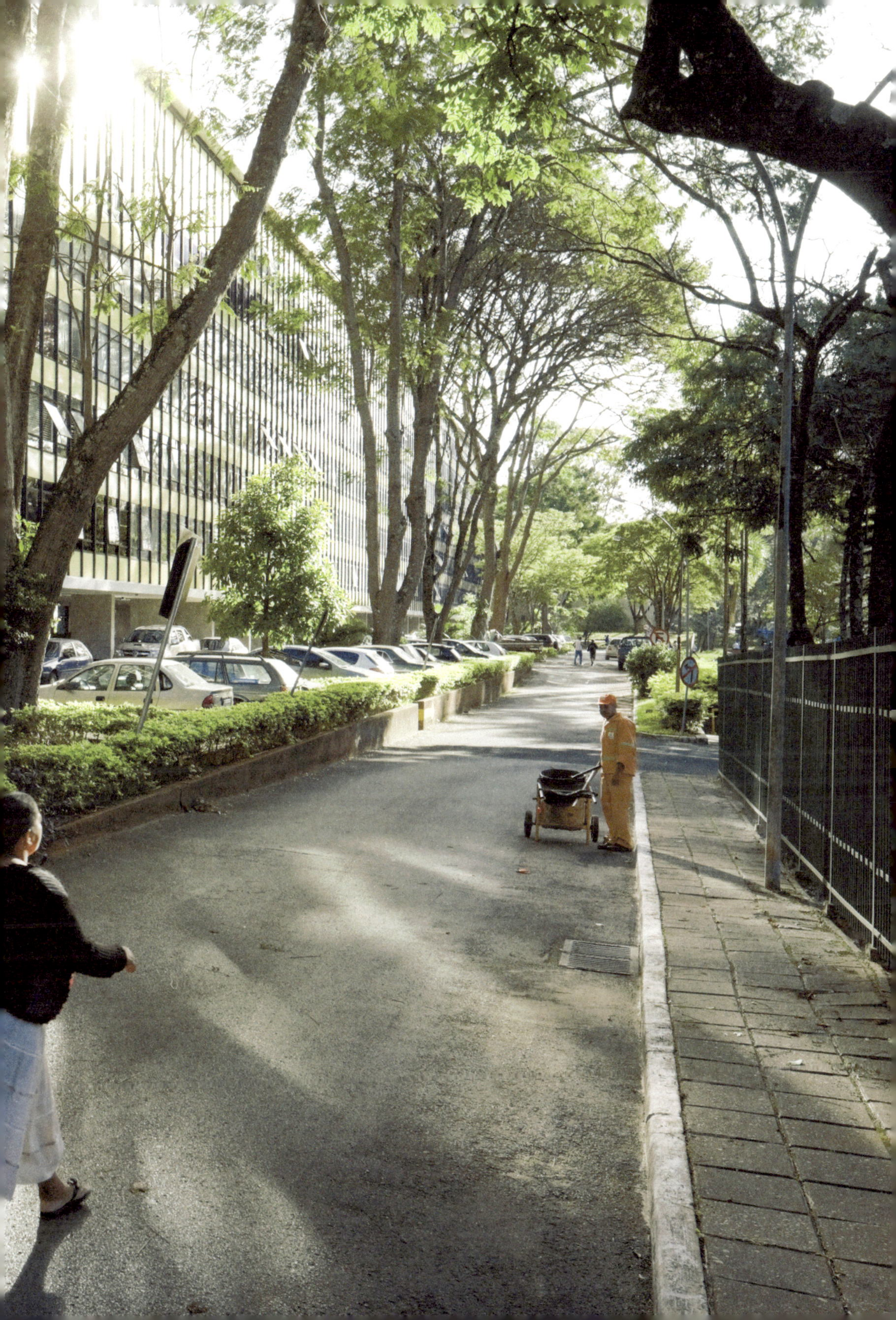

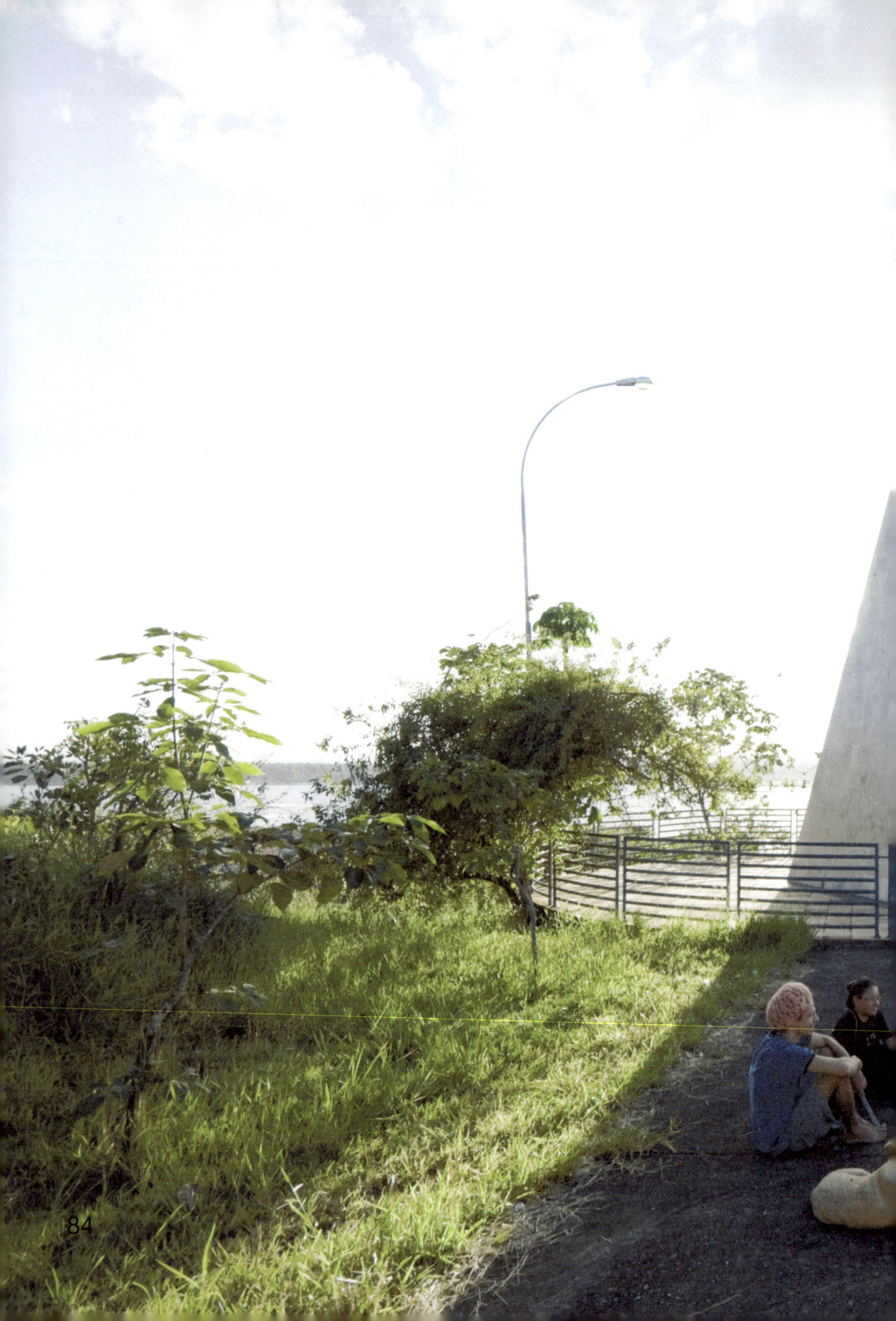

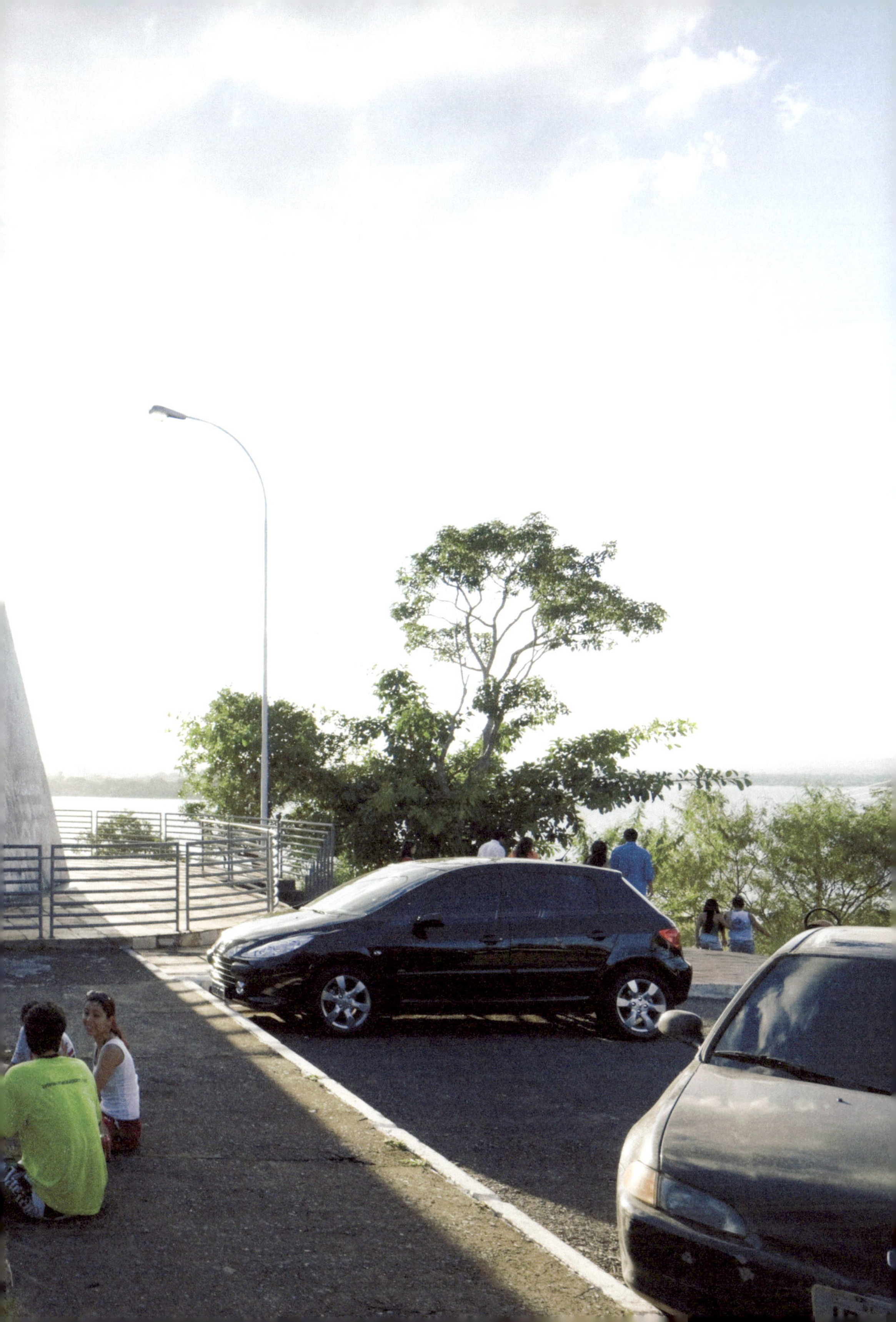

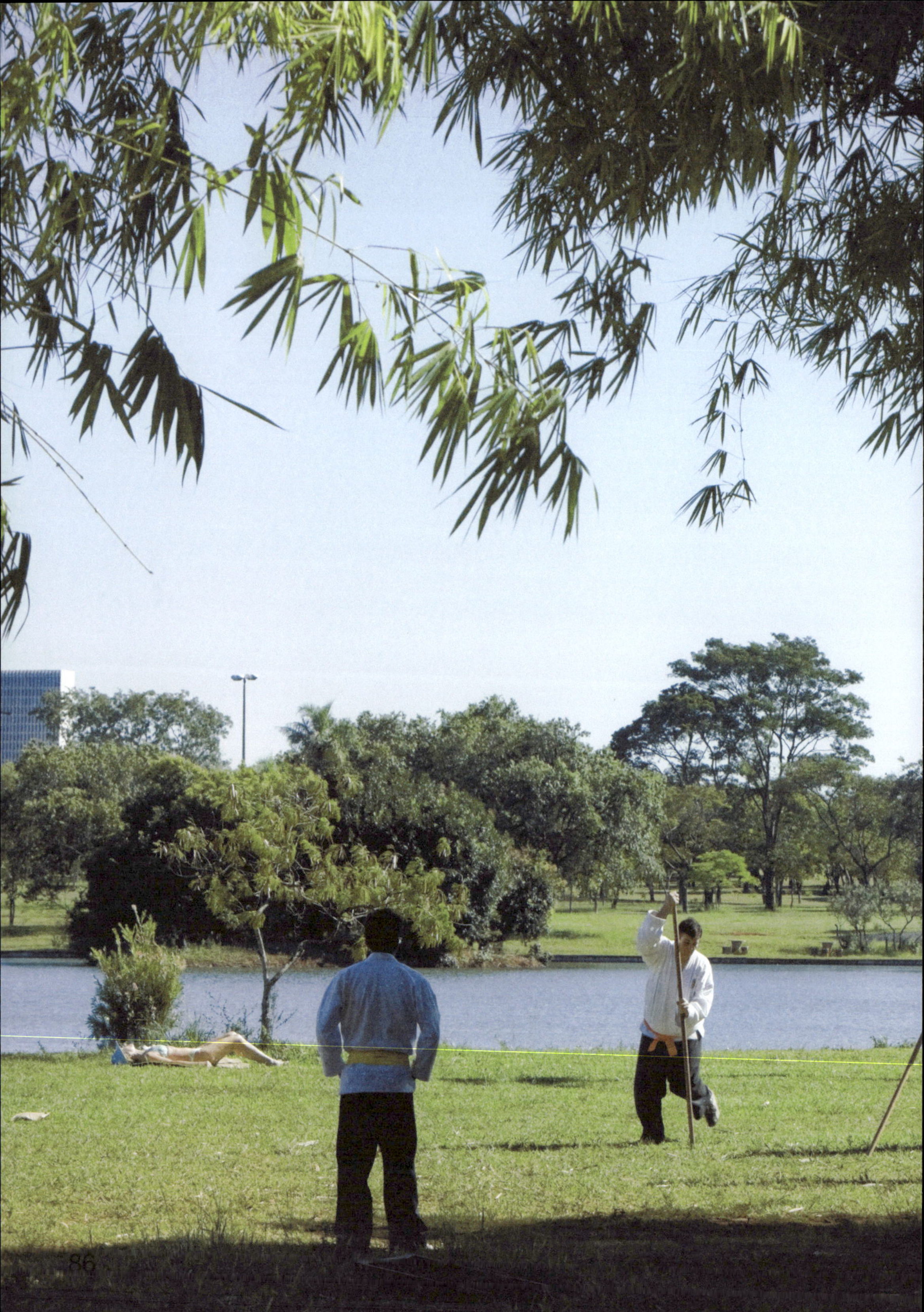

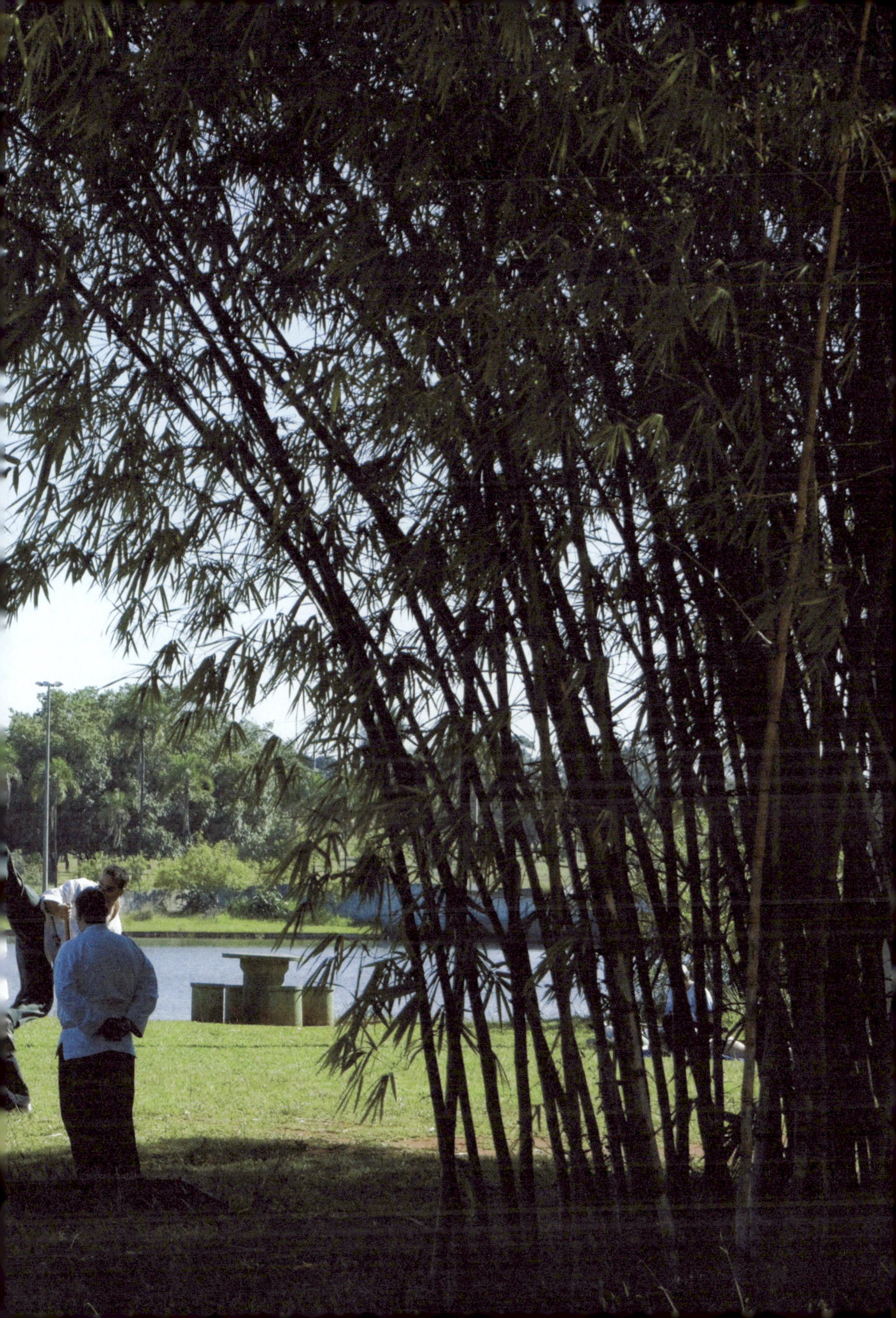

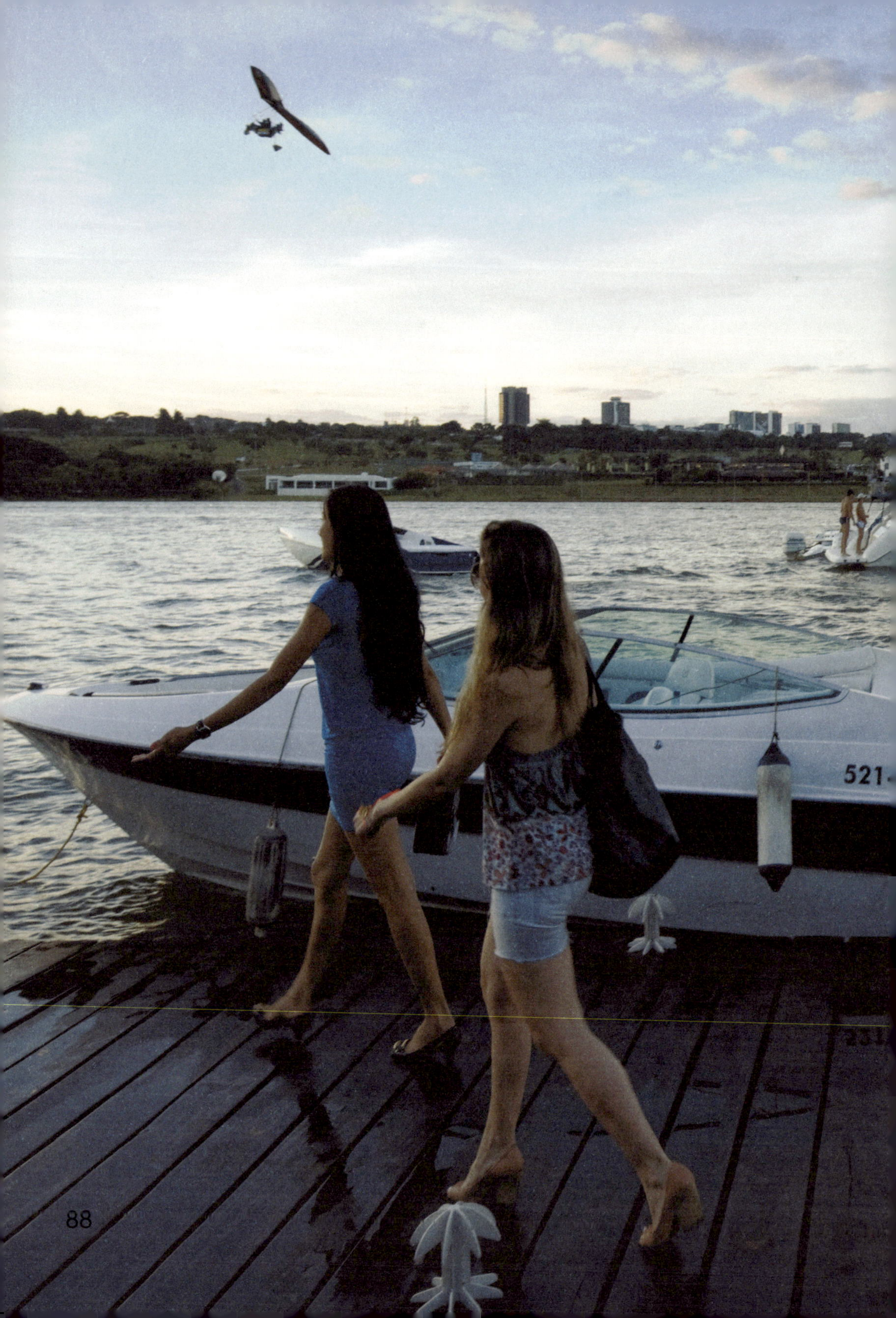
521

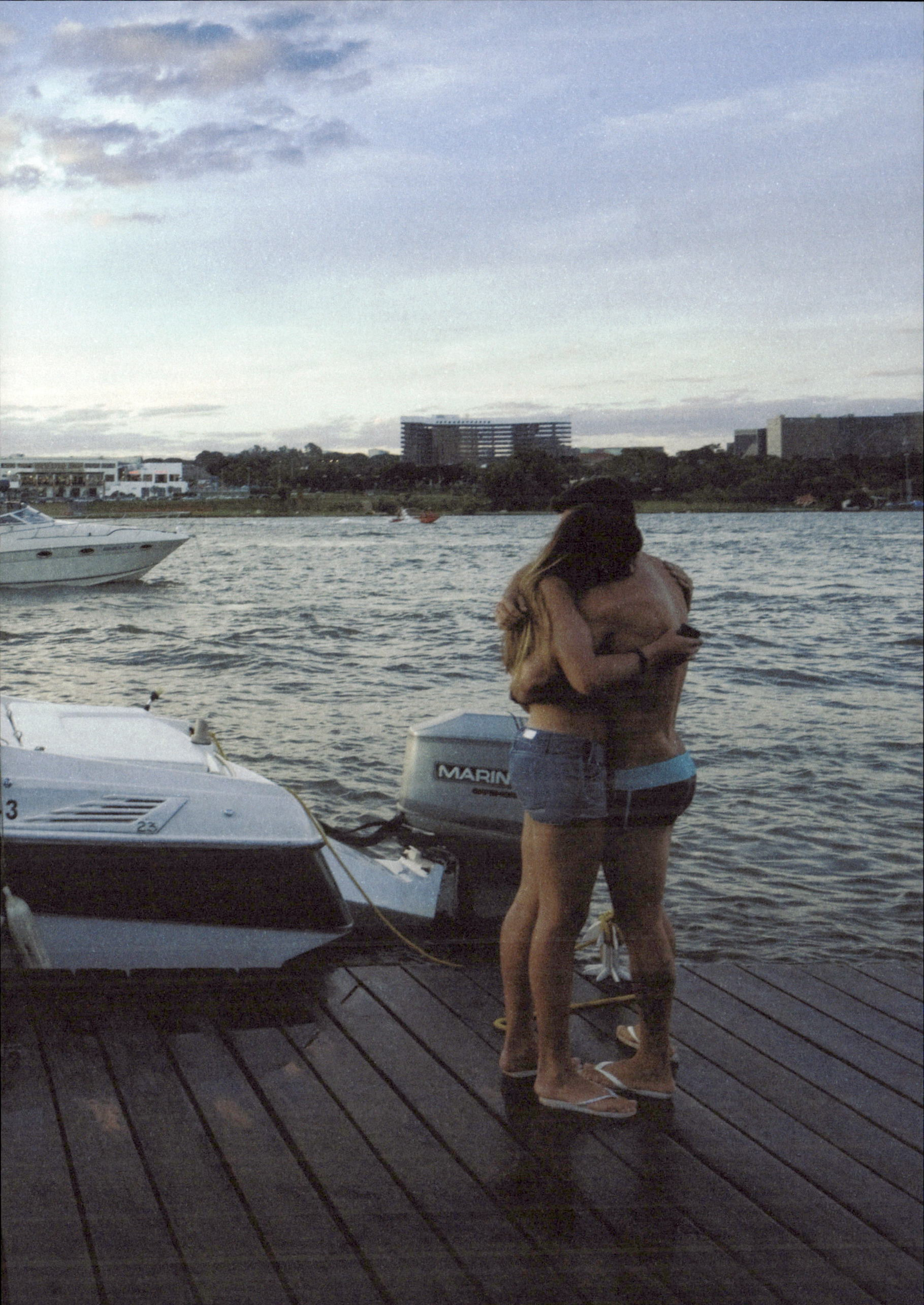
MARIN
23

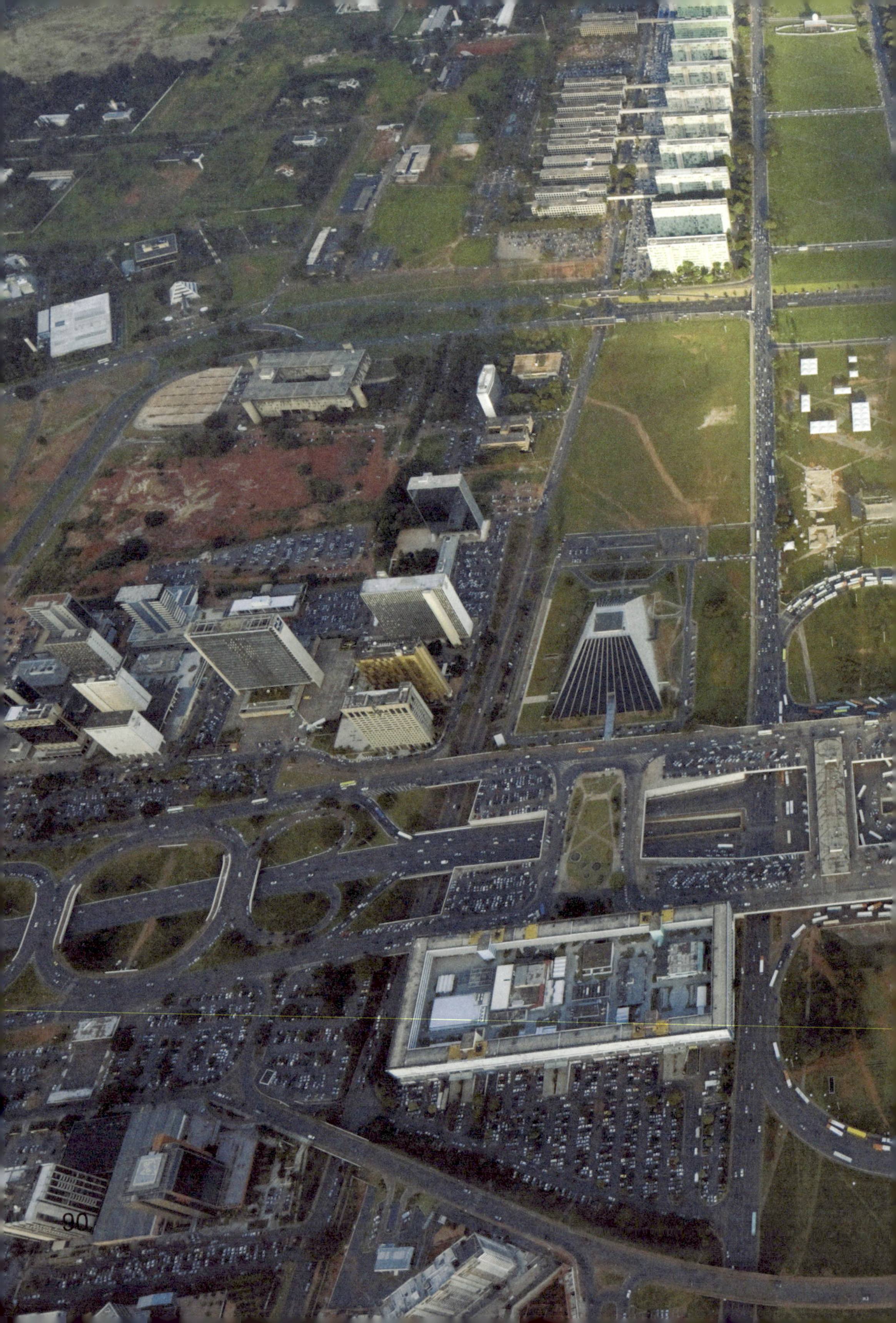

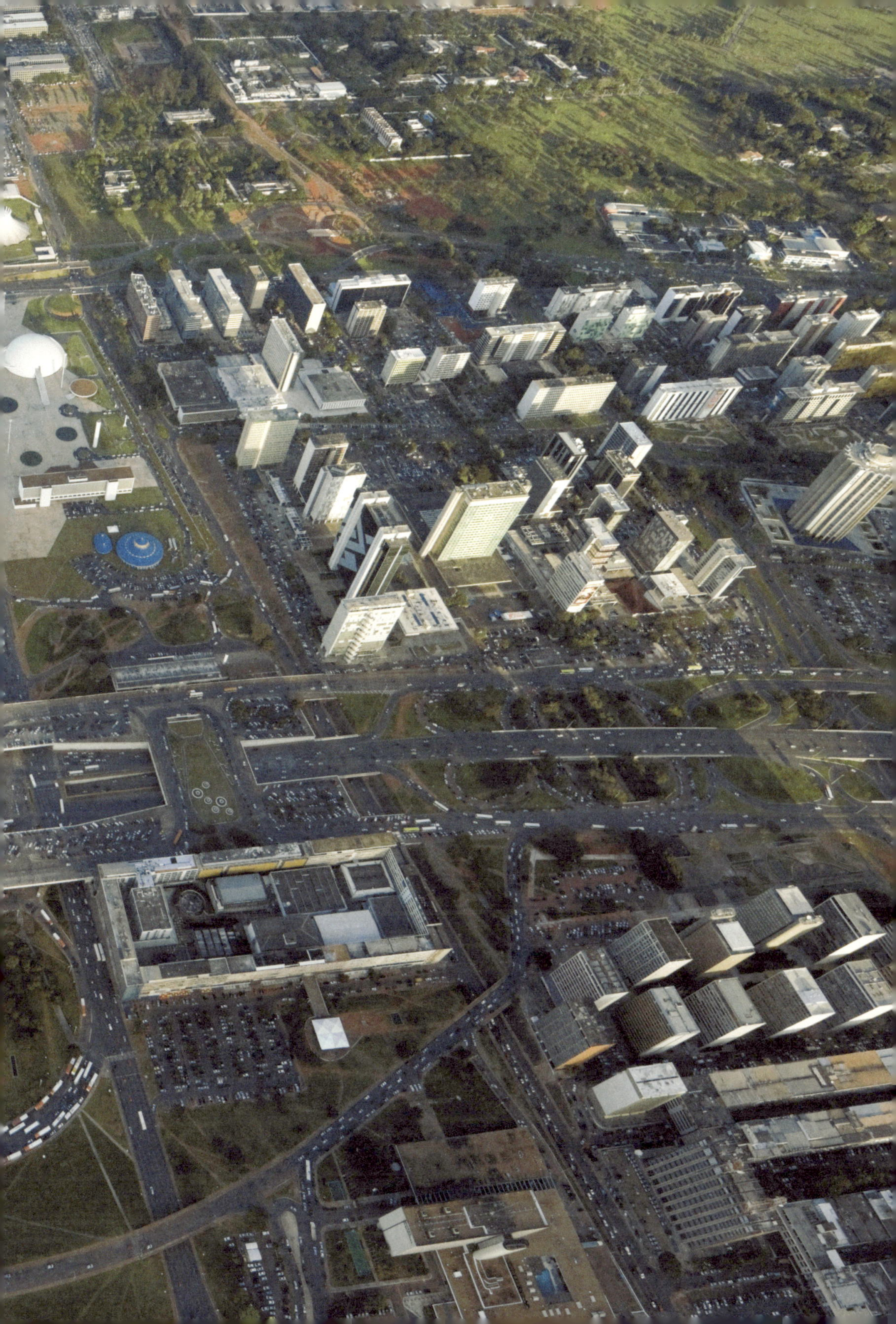

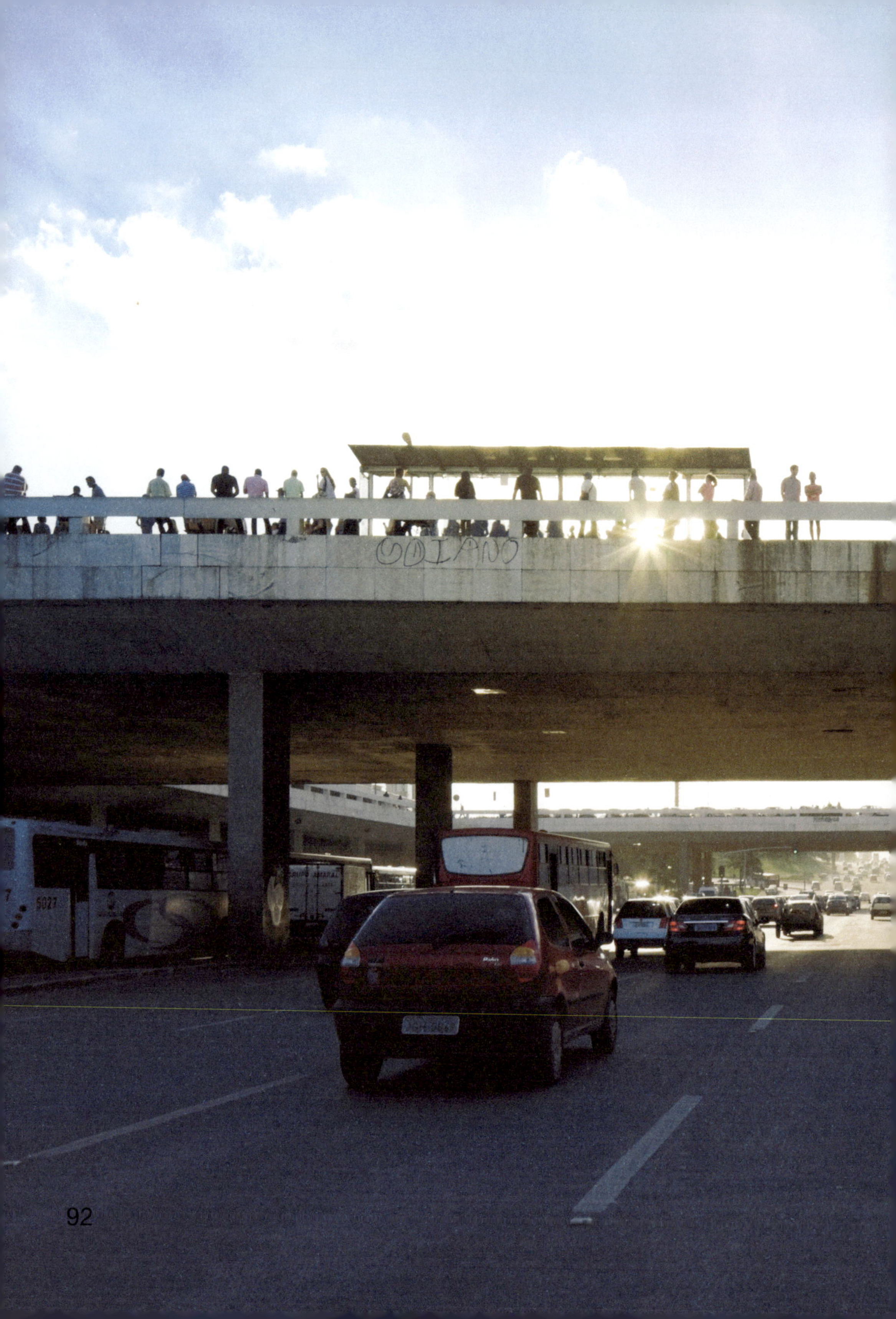
GOIANO

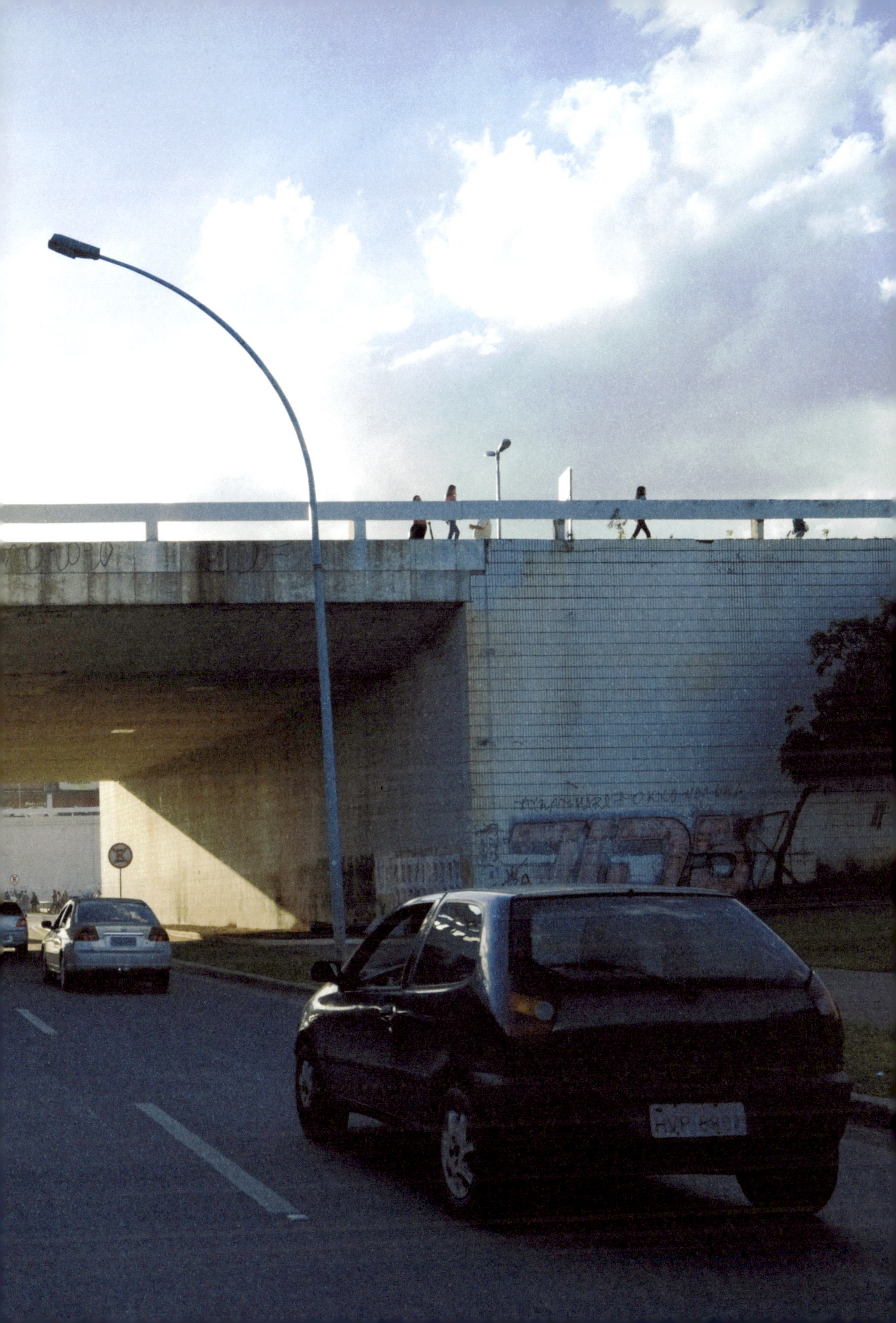

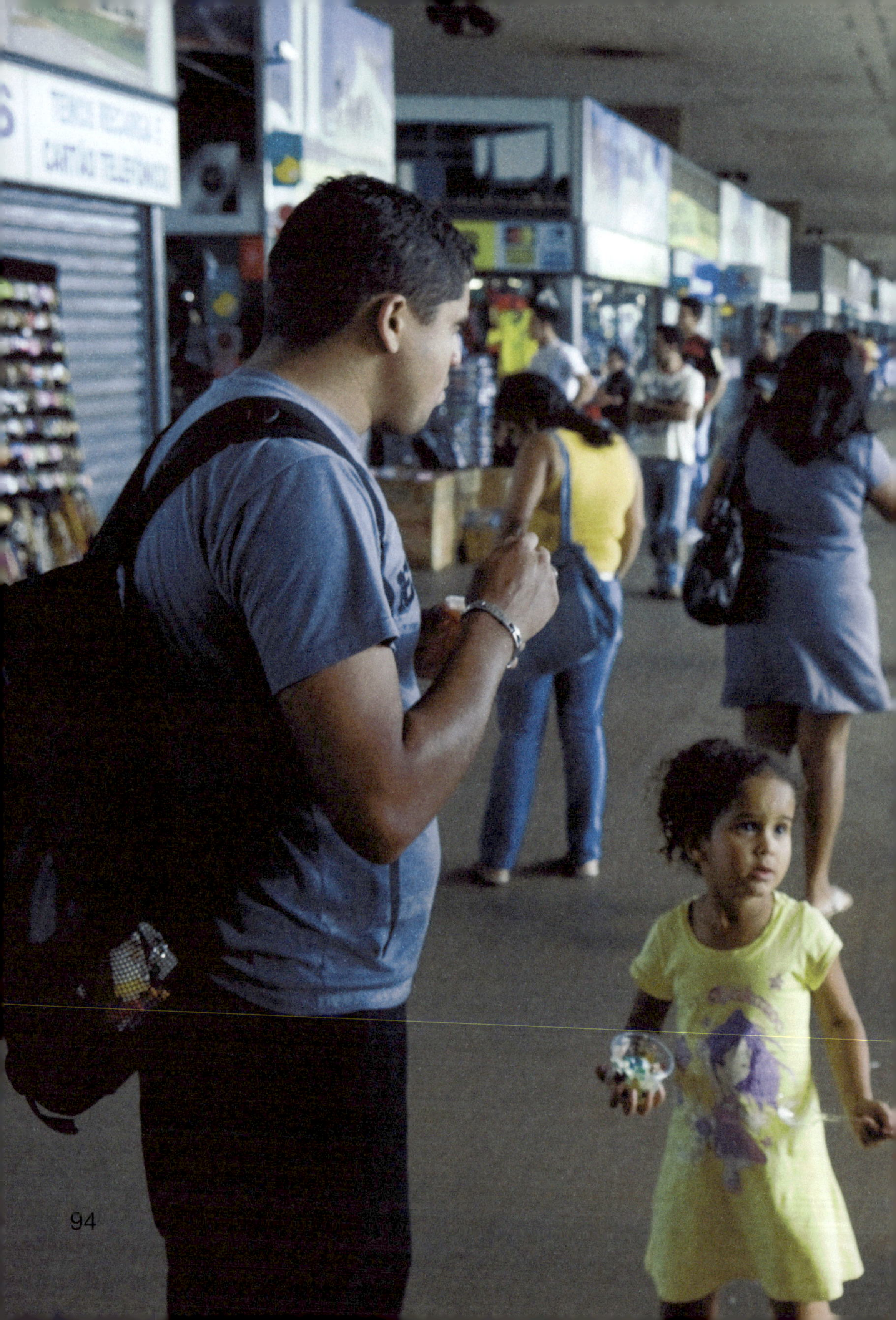

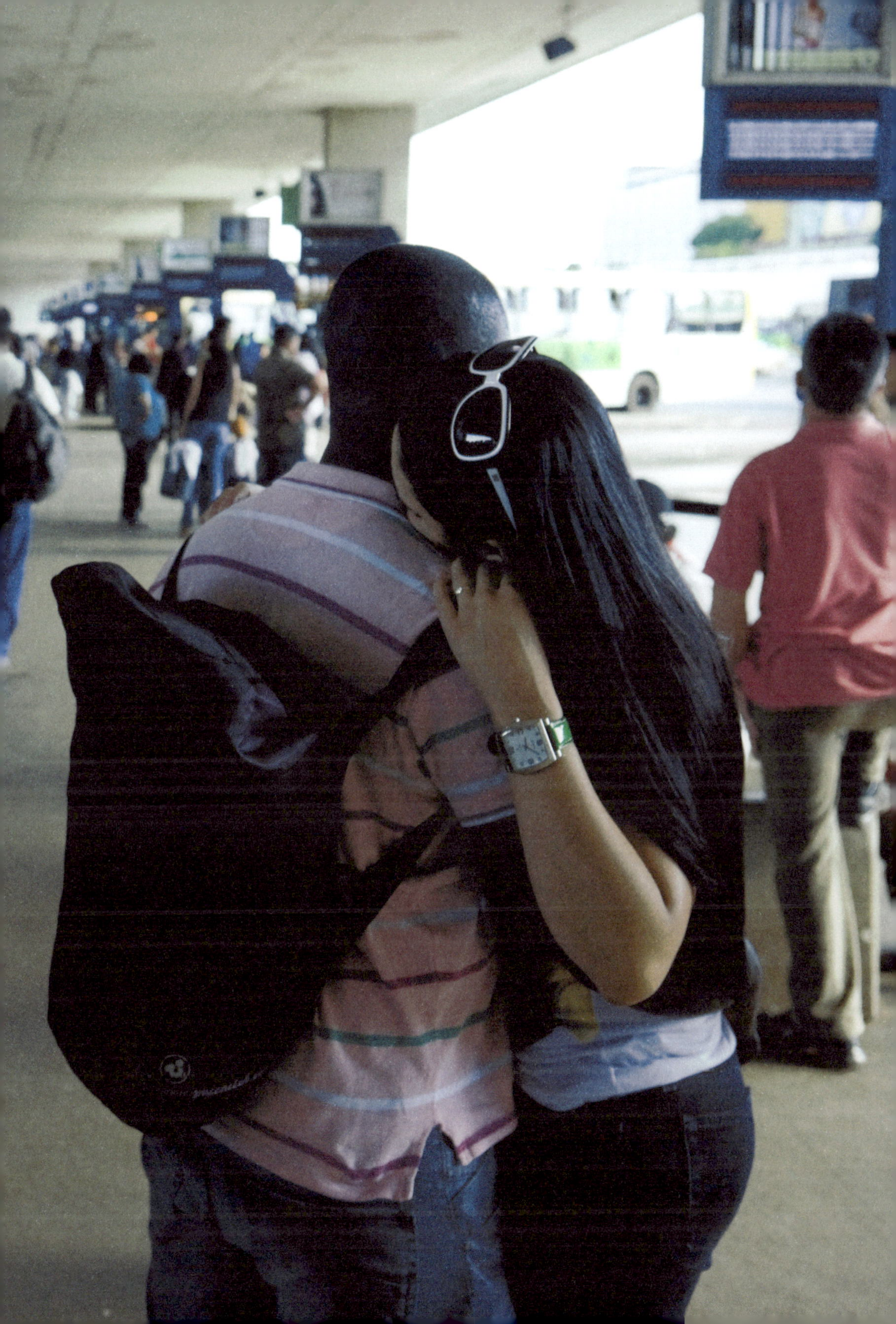

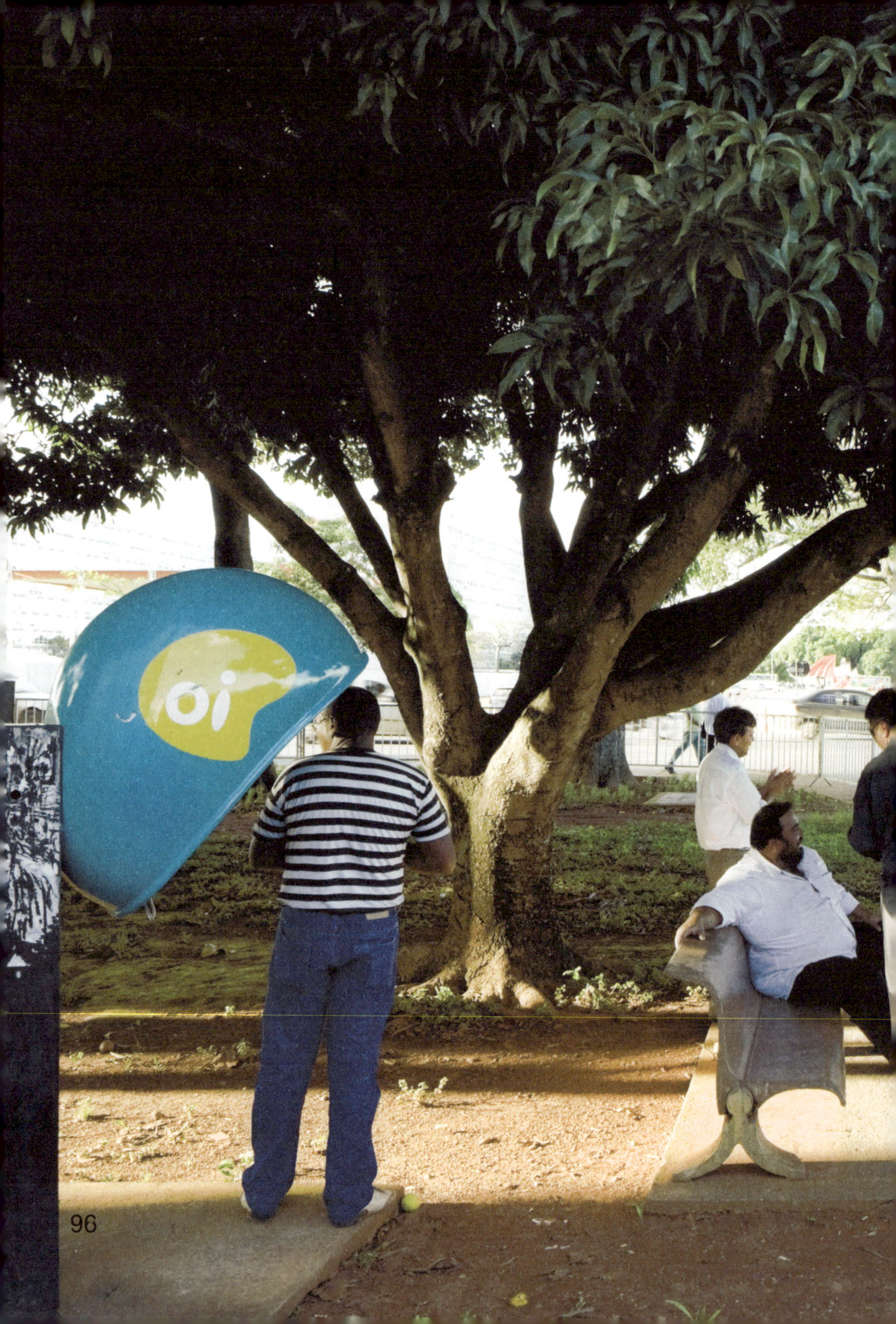
oi

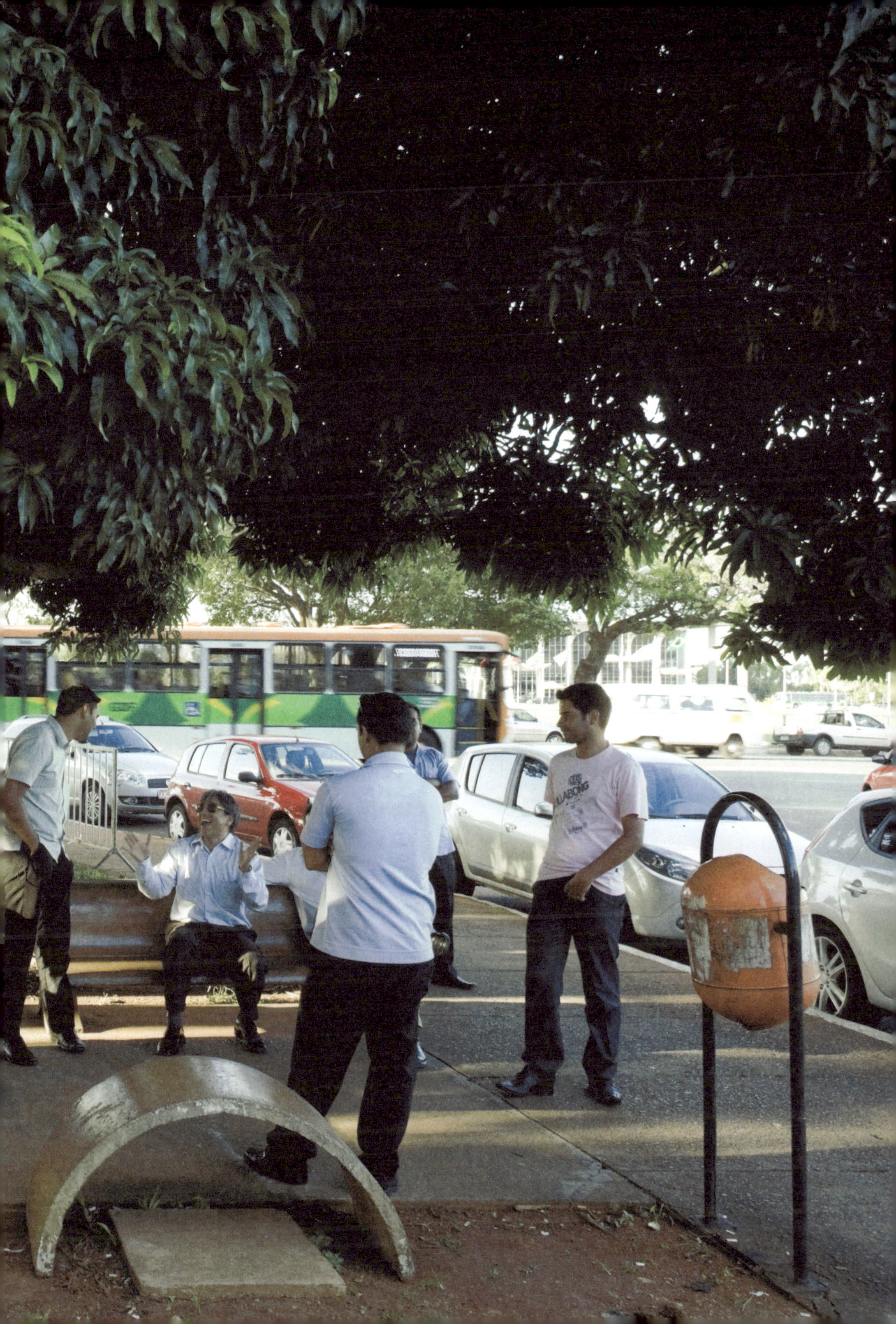

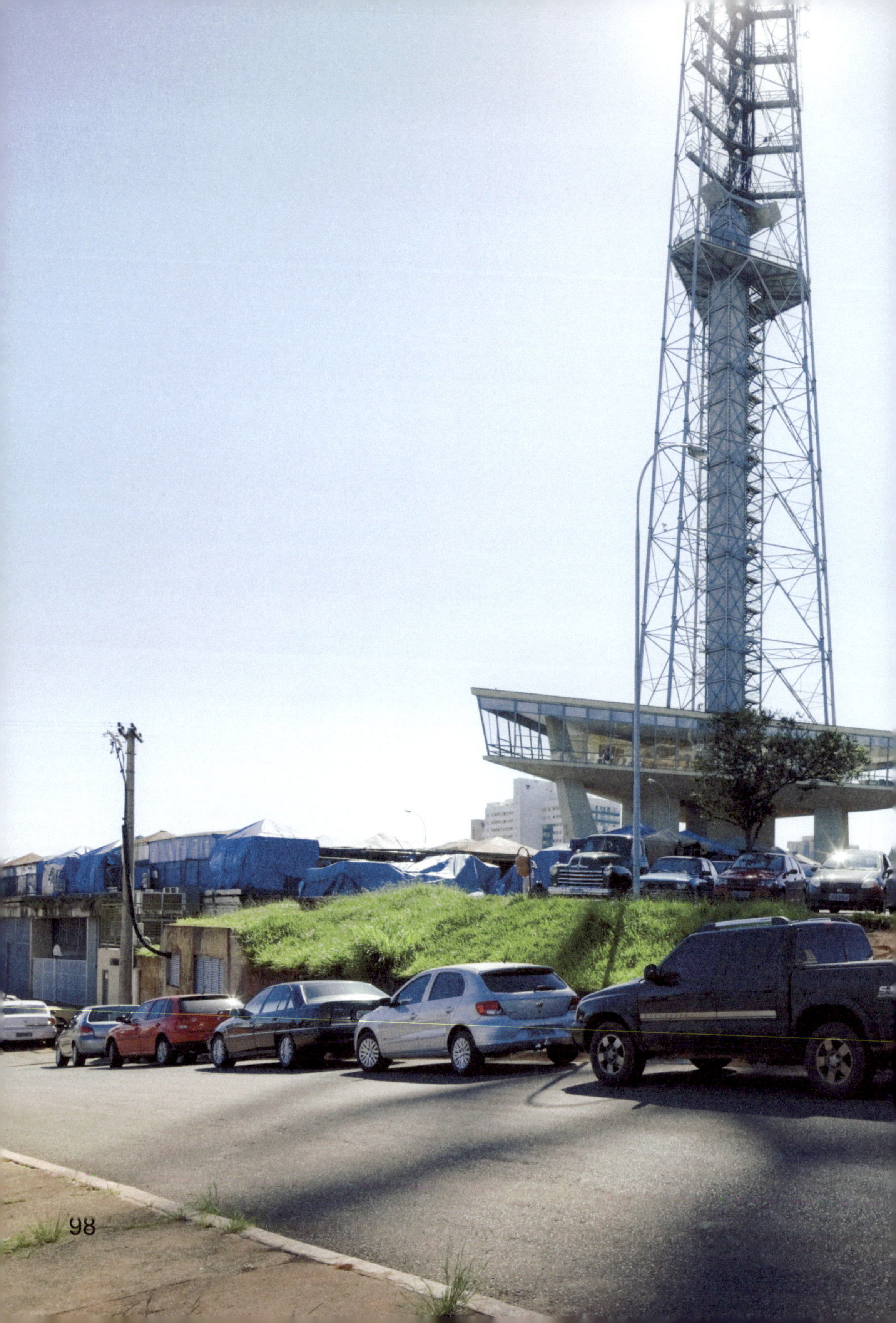

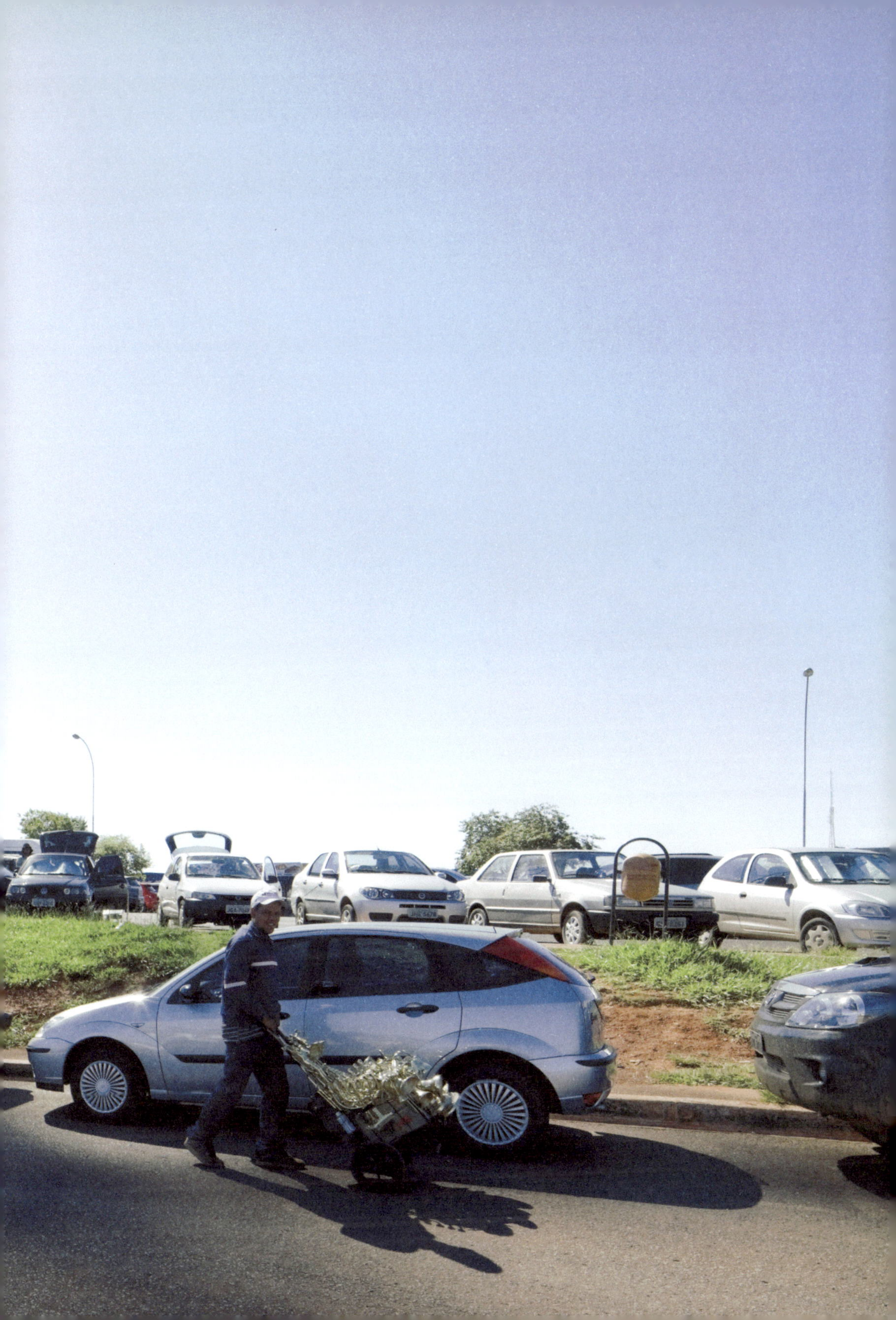

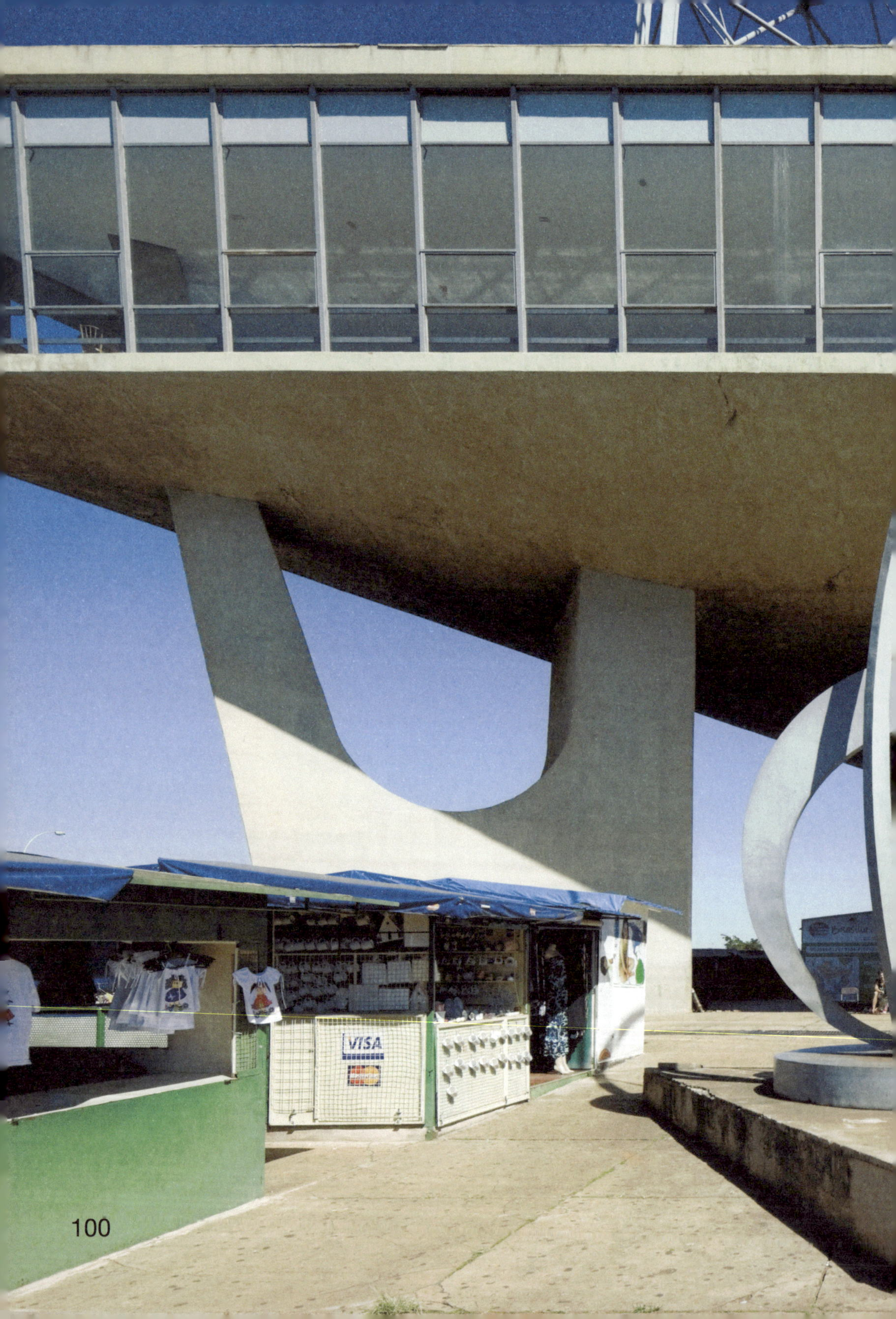
VISA

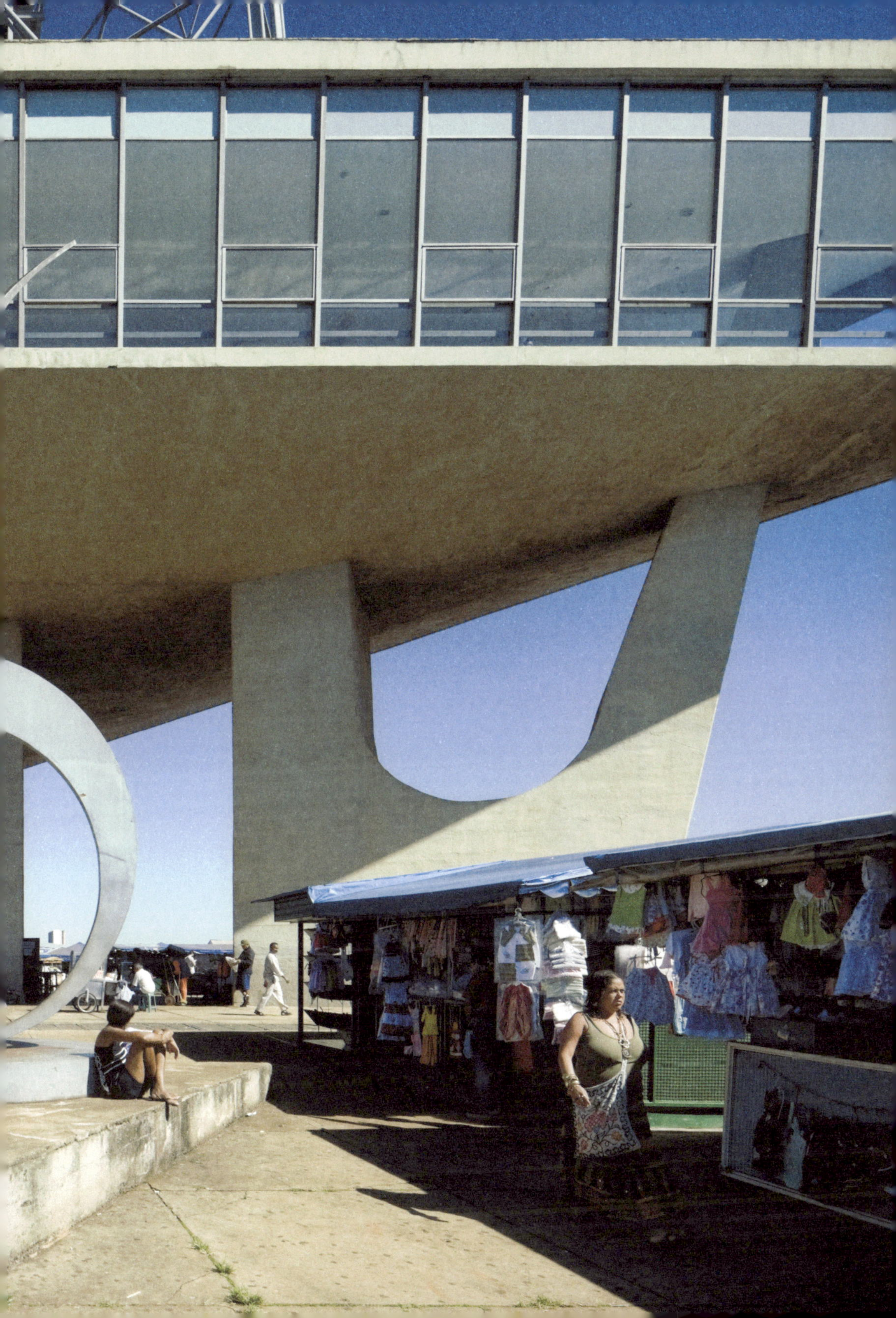

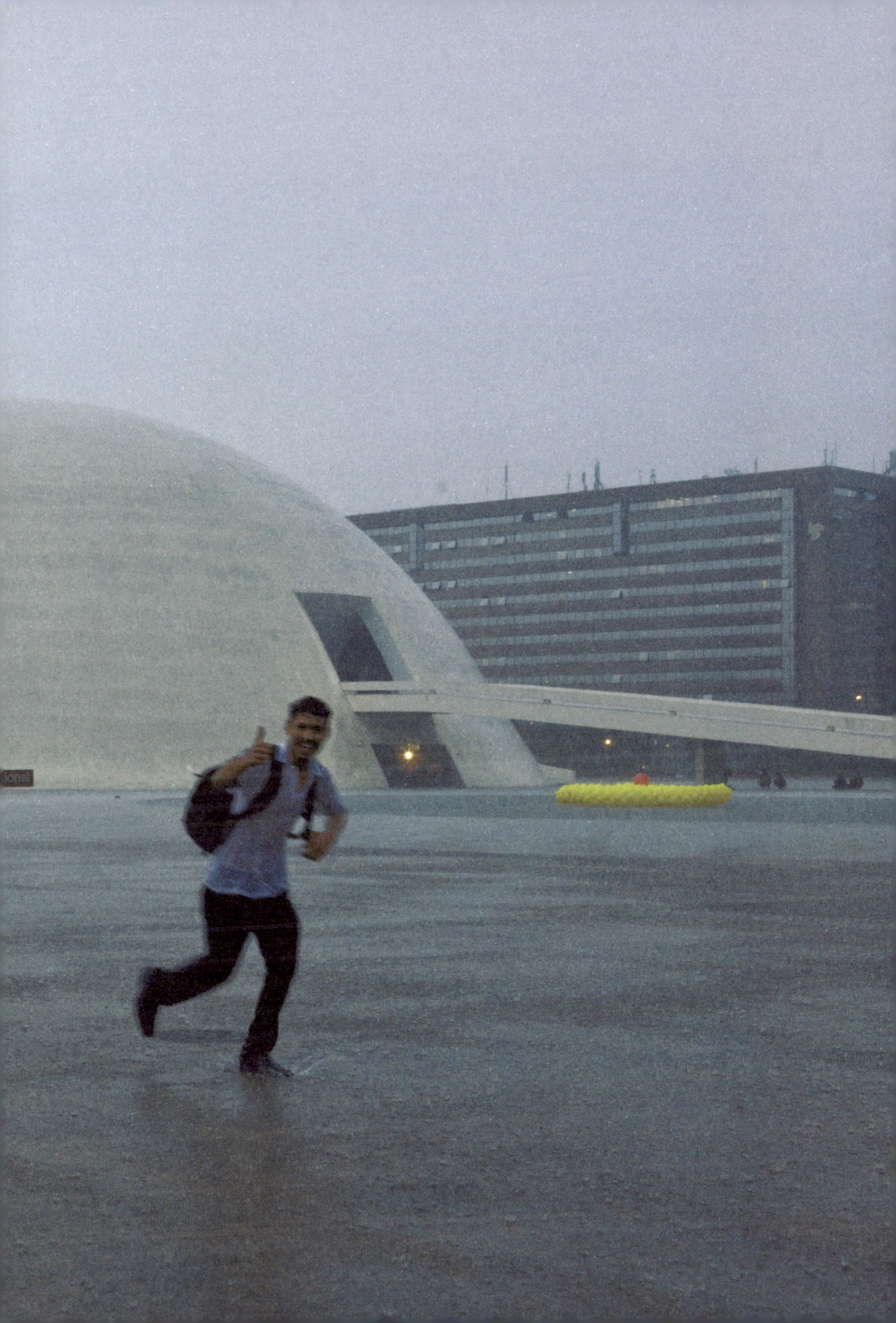

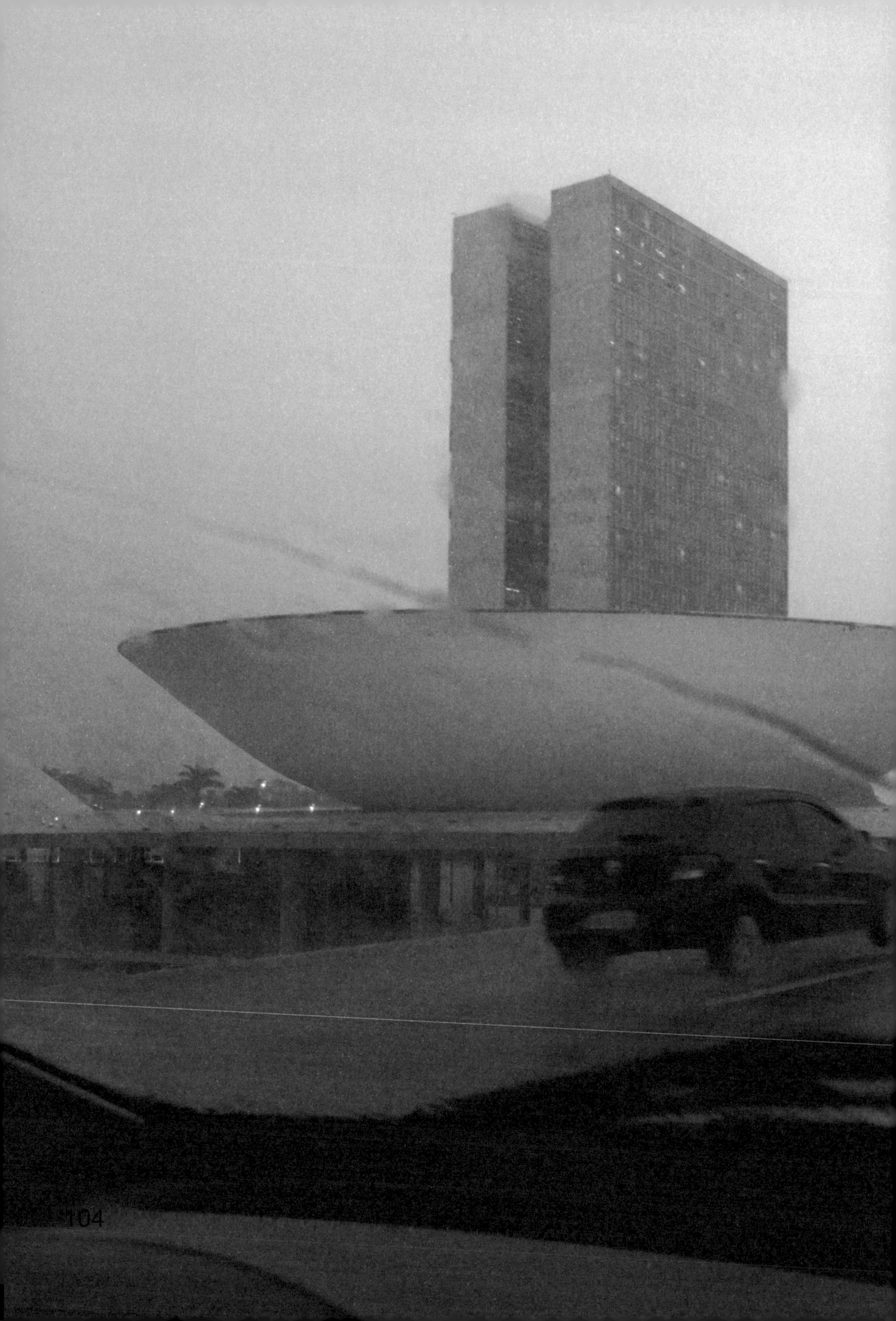

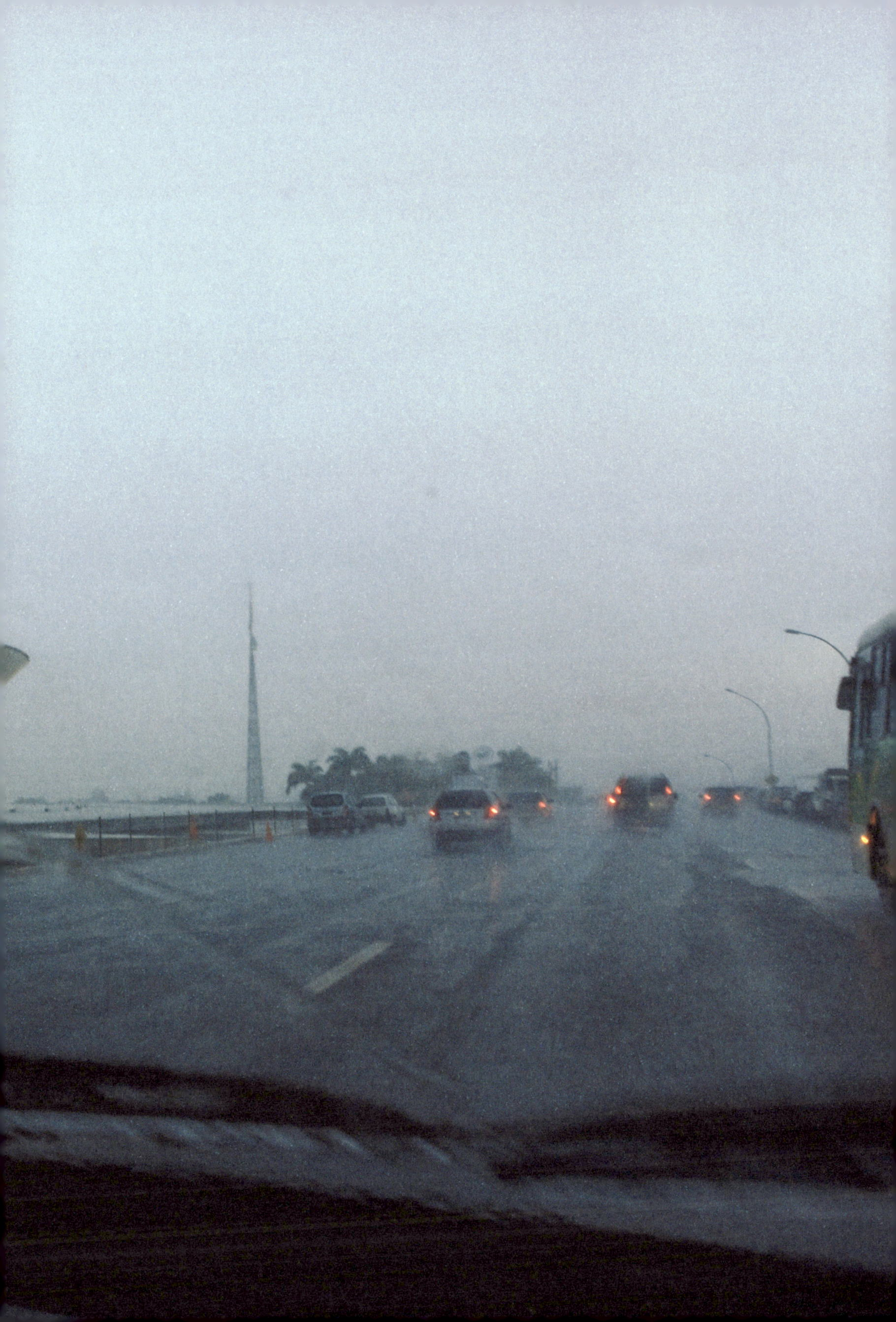

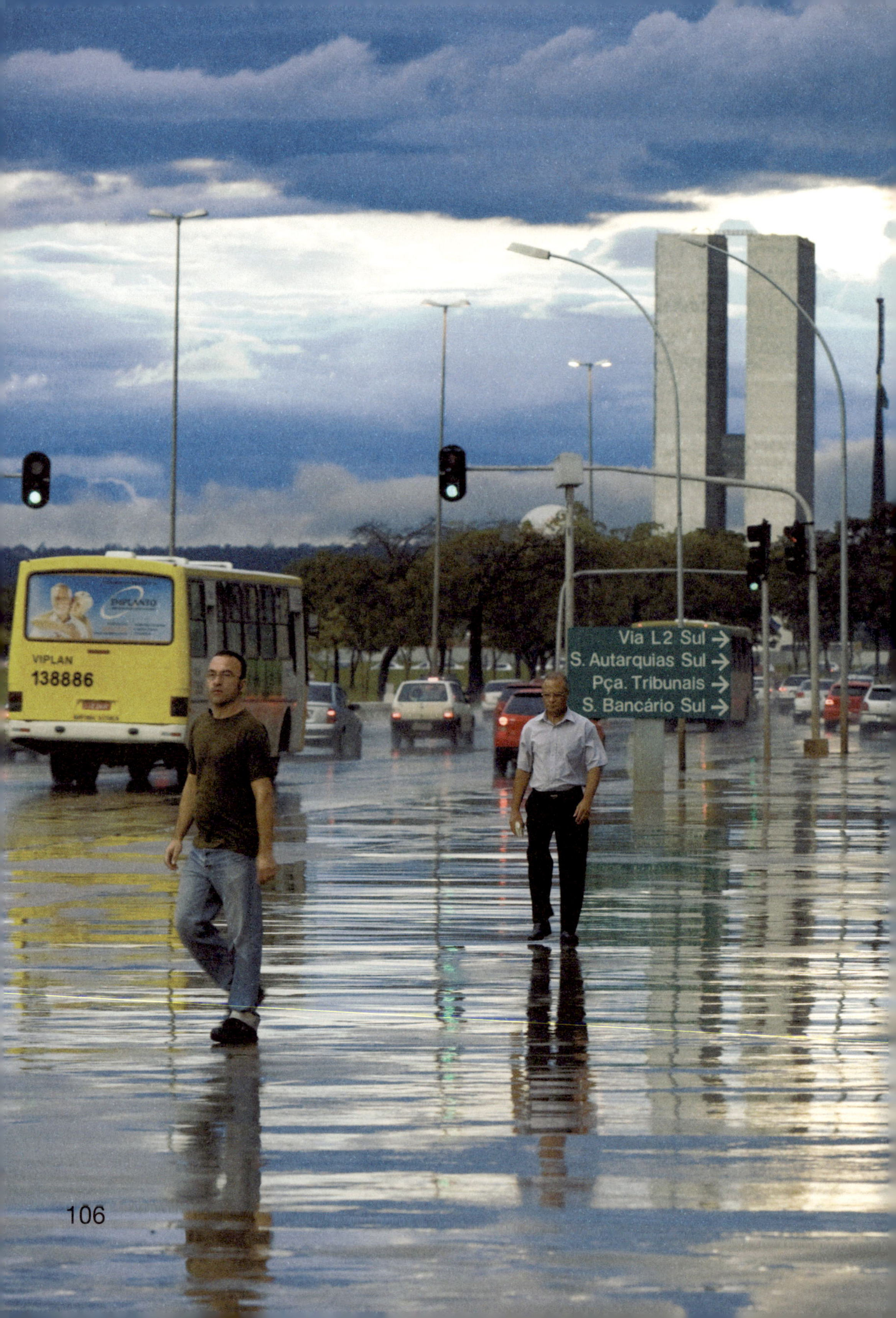
VIPLAN
138886
Via L2 Sul
S. Autarquias Sul
Pça. Tribunais
S. Bancário Sul

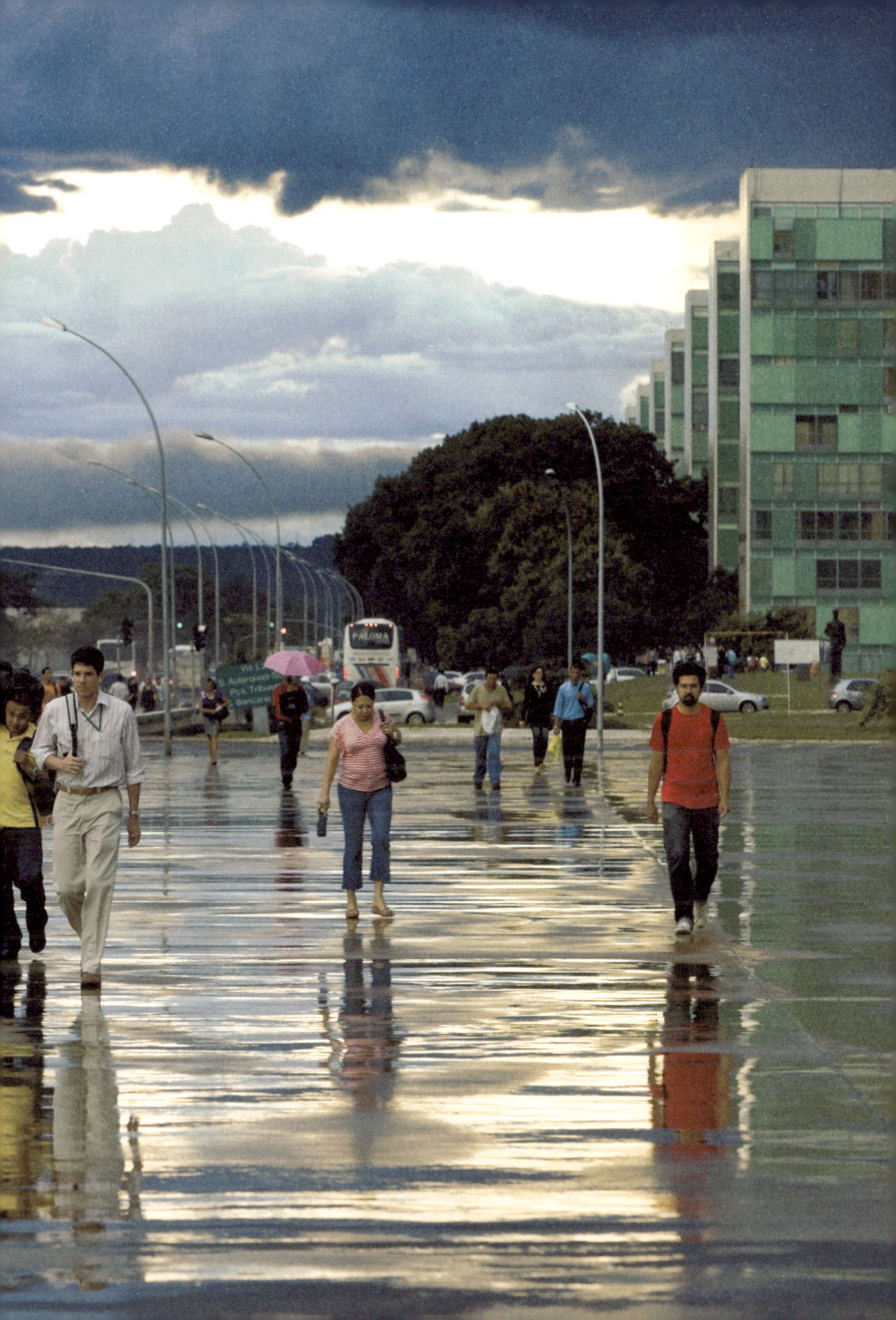
PALOMA

EX NIHILO: A Tale of Two Cities

Cees Nooteboom

In the week I am writing this piece, all kinds of newspapers have published a photograph of the place where I live: the Universe. The Dutch word for Universe is *Heelal,* Whole-All, as though my magnificent language wished to make it clear that absolutely nothing is lacking. It is oval in an elongated way, very old, mostly blue, with a strip of white running through it, and a touch of red on the underside. Some people are able to use these colors to read it like a calendar or a diary; others view it as a perfect architectural blueprint, a design, fresh from the drawing board.

You can't just create something like that. There has to be a plan, unless the design has somehow fabricated itself, which would make it a miracle.

The next miracle is the fact that I am sitting in my studio on a Spanish island with the newspaper page so attractively portraying the Universe here beside me. The whole Universe on my desk. Somewhere in that long white strip that appears to cut the Universe in two must be that distant star called Earth, which in this photograph, because that's what it is, is visible not as itself, but only as a distant nebula floating through the void.

So I am sitting on an invisible island in an invisible sea on an invisible star, contemplating how wonderful it must be to design something that has never existed before. The first time I reflected upon this kind of thing must have been a long time ago, when land had just been reclaimed from the sea to make the North-East Polder back home in the Netherlands. You may have heard the quip that God created the world and the Dutch created the Netherlands. We've been doing so for centuries. This has perhaps made us a little idiosyncratic, maybe even conceited, but then it's no small matter. Where once there was water, now there is earth. Let there be land. I remember the films that were made at the time, men in black and white on dredgers, soft, wet clay, the construction of dykes, land slowly surfacing through the water: another miracle. Documentaries gave viewers the opportunity to take a look at drawing boards where men were busy marking out straight lines, no curves allowed. Lines for roads, canals, ditches, and rectangular plots for agricultural purposes. The accompanying sense of omnipotence may exist only in my imagination, but still. The sky was already there; they didn't have to do anything to that. The sea was there too, as it had been for centuries, salt water that was to become fresh water behind a long dyke that separated the sea from the sea, a sea that was to become a lake. And then there was the land. Land on paper, not yet made of earth, land brought out from beneath the sea until one day it is simply lying there, flat, bare, undeveloped, the straight lines of the blueprints not yet visible in the new ground, the towns and villages that are to come still just the rational dreams of the planners.

A peculiar thought. Somewhere, all of it already exists: bricks, bluestone, wood, glass, lead, rubber, plastic, the essential materiality with which a town is constructed. These materials are not as yet physically present, but the town planner and architect is aware of that and knows where to obtain them. The building he sees is still virtual, a possibility. The air in the place where it is to be built still remains empty. Suddenly everything is possible. Possible feet that will walk down possible streets, possible trees around a possible farmhouse where a possible shed will shelter possible cows. The possible church, the possible school for the possible children – as yet unknown, but oh so possible – the possible churchyard for the possible deaths, the possible bell that will ring out from the church that does not yet exist, to accompany the dead to their graves – inconceivable, yet already designed – its bronze sound echoing over land where the wind already blows, but where nothing yet grows, no man's land that is set to become someone's land.

Sometimes, back then, I used to cycle along the straight lines of paths that had already become reality. Where I watched my front wheel turning upon the brick path, fish once swam, and within that amphibian vision

I saw not only those vanished fish, but also the tall wooden ships that, centuries ago, had returned home after journeys of many months, sailing over a sea that no longer existed. But how did it happen? The paths and roads were first to arrive. My point about the possible graveyard was not merely poetic license; I saw it with my own eyes. There was a fence around it, with a gate, and I looked out upon a bare, elongated rectangle; no one was buried there as yet. It was waiting, the graveyard, just as the land was waiting for villages and towns, and the villages and towns for residents, the farms for people and animals, the land for tractors and trees. And the trees, if they were to come, would have to wait for the wind to carry their scent so far that the birds would fly from the old land to build their nests and blend their own sounds with those of the people for whom all of this had been designed and built.

Now that is all history. We drive along large motorways from Amsterdam to cities that were not there back then, such as Almere and Lelystad. Generations have grown up with the feeling that these cities have been there forever. They treat their cities just as people have done for centuries. It makes no difference that their hometown was created from nothing, and did not accumulate from deposits of silt, like Amsterdam, or originate a thousand years ago as a settlement of monks, like Munich. They use their city in the firm conviction that this is the purpose of cities: they are implements, large objects and forms that you encounter when you are born, your rightful property, to be used as you see fit, constructed for you. The residents of Chandigarh and Brasília must feel the same way.

I remember my first visit to Brasília. That was in 1968, and even then it was no longer new. Of course I had seen the city in photographs, the strange, magical bell-glass form of Niemeyer's cathedral, curving first in, then out, the Ministry of Foreign Affairs and the Palácio da Alvorada, or Palace of the Dawn.

I had flown in from Rio de Janeiro and had heard from diplomats that no one wanted to leave the chaotic yet sensuous seaside city of Rio de

Janeiro and move to the hot interior of the country, where everything was to be built from scratch, as Washington and Canberra once were, and, before that, Palmanova and Sabbioneta, planned cities, unencumbered sites far from other centers, almost abstract places that would escape any rivalry from that which already existed, cities from which the country would be ruled. I had flown in from the sea, had seen tropical rainforests from the airplane and red earth the color of freshly dried blood, followed by the brown of the upland plains. Everything looked violent, dramatic, and the heat when I landed, with no cooling ocean breeze, only reinforced that impression.

I had seen a book of the town-planning designs for Brasília, as devised by Lúcio Costa, Niemeyer's friend, with the straight lines I mentioned above arranged inside the widespread outline of an airplane that was projected onto the landscape, and within this shape the buildings of Niemeyer himself, which now were a reality, female forms, curving, sensual lines, inspired by the voluptuous hills of his hometown of Rio, curves that appeared to act counter to the grid in which they were situated. A few hours later, I was walking inside that grid, but walking was not the simplest way to get around, as it is in some old cities. The scale was vast and the distances were a challenge in the heat. My own, human proportions cowered at the violence of these dimensions. Was I disappointed? That's not the right word. From afar, the cathedral, the National Congress building and the Planalto Palace looked like wondrous sculptures; they had something breathtaking about them. There was something else I hadn't expected: not only the human element, but also the effect of nature. In architectural blueprints, no grass grows between the stones. The concrete shows no sign of efflorescence and rust is not part of the design. People in architectural sketches are faceless outlines, predictable shadows with the task of indicating the scale of the sketch, moving from A to B in a straight line that is in keeping with the design, not suddenly falling down drunk or dead or unexpectedly retracing their steps. Now I was one of those people myself, the sketch had become reality, concrete looked like actual concrete. Even then, only around ten years after the construction, the tropics had done their work, and human beings had inserted themselves between the design and the practice. To be clear, perhaps you could put it this way: architectural sketches are always silent, whereas cities never are. It is not drawings that live in cities, but people, unpredictable individuals who might at any moment disturb the order that has been designed for them, who may break through the silence of the sketches by making use of that unique instrument that makes a city a city: the human voice.

I once came up with a new phrase to describe this aspect of cities: *de gestemde stad,* the voiced city. My thinking was that conversation never stops in cities, that in old cities like Rome, Amsterdam, Zürich, right from the very beginning, there has never been a single moment of complete silence, because even when nearly everyone is asleep there are always some people who are not.

A city is the accumulation of everything that has ever been said there, every word spoken, a proclamation, an outcry, a death sentence, a prayer, the whispering of lovers, the groans of the sick, a drunken argument, a parade with chants and songs: all of these sounds combine to form a ceaseless litany that has always accompanied the history of the city over the centuries, and continues to do so, a conversation that will never end as long as the city continues to exist.

By the end of World War II, Berlin was almost completely destroyed, but the city never fell entirely silent, echoing with words of fear and defeat, final orders, the foreign voices of the troops as their grip on the city became ever tighter. All of that added, layer by layer, to the previous, earlier conversation once started in a past that had become invisible.

And that is what is so mysterious about new cities, that initial lack of speech, just before the beginning, when the first word is still to be said. No matter what, there is always a first word. Antiquity has to be created; anyone who does not believe this fact is operating in a vacuum. It has to start somewhere, when the first words are spoken which will form the beginning of an endless series that, if all goes well, will echo down the centuries. Livy came up with a term for this, which surfaced from my memory as I was writing these thoughts, a phrase that made an impression on me during my schooldays when we had to translate sentences from his marmoreal Latin: *Ab Urbe Condita* (From the Foundation of the City), which was the title of his book. It dealt with the moment when the city was founded: *Romulum Remumque cupido cepit in iis locis, ubi expositi ubique educati erant, urbis condendae*… "Romulus and Remus were seized with the desire of building a city on the spot where they had been exposed and brought up." But where exactly should that be and who should be king? They decided to look to the skies for the answer. Seers were able to read the will of the gods in the flight of birds and so discover which of the twin brothers was to give his name to the city that was not yet there. Romulus chose the Palatine Hill; Remus the Aventine. Remus saw the first birds, six vultures, but Romulus later saw twice that number, which is why Rome is now called Rome; Remus was killed in the jealous fight between the two brothers following the judgment of the gods. It was only then that the conversation of the city could begin, one that continues into our own day and age, and in which elements of myth and history fuse alchemically to remind us of antiquity, an antiquity that has never released its hold on the city, even with all its modernity.

New cities have no antiquity other than that of the ground upon which they are built and the traditions from which the ideas of the designers flowed, because no matter how new, original, modern an architect might be, no one comes from nothing or from nowhere. Just as no writers could exist without a never-ending series of predecessors, Plato, Homer, Ovid, Cervantes, Shakespeare, Tolstoy, Kafka, no architect could exist without Vitruvius, Boullée, Palladio, Herrera, Loos, Berlage, Rossi. The names I have listed here are random; any reader or student of architecture could add hundreds more. Every great architect stands at the top of a pyramid, nourished by everything that he has seen, read, studied, and by the accumulated philosophy and practice of centuries. This is what he uses to build his house, his church, his library, his housing project, and what he creates is a philosophy in practice, a train of thought based on a philosophy about the world, about how society should be, and of course this applies especially to the architect who is allowed to build a city. What he makes will influence the lives of the people for whom he is making it, positively or negatively. The influence is negative if he is not permitted to follow his ideas in their entirety: what he is not allowed to build will remain invisible. No one can fall in love in the shadow of a building that does not exist, by which I mean that the *not*-built also has an influence on our lives, simply by not being there. The influence becomes positive if he succeeds in improving the lives of the people who will use his building or his city to work and live in, if he creates a better place to be. But how will people use the city? Does he know that beforehand? When the fleeting abstractions and the sketchy outlines of his designs have become people of flesh and blood, is he still master of their behavior? Of how they *feel* inside his buildings?

The photographs in this book are pictures of everyday life in two invented cities, Chandigarh and Brasília. They do not show how Le Corbusier and Niemeyer thought their cities would look; they show what the cities look like now, fifty to sixty years later. On the one hand, there is Chandigarh, which, in the visionary plan created by Nehru after the 1947 partition of India and Pakistan, was to become the administrative capital of the orphaned Indian Punjab. Brasília also dates from this period. The Belgian astronomer Louis Cruls had already identified the location for Brasília back in 1892, in the Cerrado, Brazil's highland savannah region. Le Corbusier's urban plan for Chandigarh could be described roughly as a grid, while Brasília's resembles an imaginary airplane, but, that aside, this city was also built with a central axis, the Eixo Monumental, with other streets leading into it. In 1968, I was able to experience for myself just how monumental Brasília's distances are, by measuring them out with my own footsteps. Another factor in the growth of these metropolises is the force of attraction naturally exerted by large cities, which cannot always be kept under control, particularly in the Third World. In both cities, the original plan has been tampered with for all kinds of reasons, politics, economy, demographic and industrial developments, changes of government; in short, the passing of time and all that it entails. Indeed, many people believe that India missed out on a huge opportunity by not adhering to Le Corbusier's revolutionary ideas. They think that Chandigarh should have served as an example for other potential cities in this developing superpower, which is growing at such a rapid pace. The icons of both cities, the world-famous buildings that we know from so many photographs, stand at the center of a living reality of satellite towns, but Chandigarh is also located in the midst of an uncontrollable sprawl of slums that most certainly weren't part of the plans. When I look at Iwan Baan's photographs, I wonder how Le Corbusier, who once said that a house should be a "machine for living," would have reacted, for example, to the sight of the incredible chaos in the office on pages 158–159. Machines are pure devices, or are at least intended as such. When Le Corbusier was growing up in the early years of the last century, which is already so distant, futuristic circles shared a veneration of machines, but the photograph of this room blatantly disregards the originally futuristic element of the city. There are no computers to be seen, but there is an elderly gentleman in a turban holding a mobile phone to his ear, and a book lying on the table looks modern enough to belie the date of 1932 on one of the pillars. The photograph was taken recently, but the man working away with his ballpoint, with the slogan "Work Is Worship" attached to a poster-covered column behind him, must be a genius if he knows his way around the staggering volume of pieces of paper, both loose and tied up with string. Is this a modern city? Did the architect imagine that his functional buildings would be used in this way? There is less chaos in the spacious room occupied by a number of serious gentlemen who look like legal experts in a law library (pp. 154–155), but, with the exception of the white plastic chair, this could just as easily be a nineteenth-century room. Another picture (pp. 166–167) shows a sort of storage space in which piles of books have been thrown together in no particular order. The glass in front is broken, the wall is damaged and the wood of the door is unpainted; no one has gone to the trouble of putting the books into proper piles.

"Urdu Novel" says a sign in one of the photographs (pp. 164–165). Urdu is one of the many languages of the Indian subcontinent, so this must be a library. On the right, light enters the room through the modern, rectilinear design of the large windows; on the left, the novels written in Urdu lean sluggishly against one another, longing for readers. The young woman in the picture is probably the librarian, and it is likely that she knows her way around what looks like chaos to me, but the architect would probably have been happier at the sight of the packed reading room (pp. 162–163), with its gleaming floors and bright white pillars, filled with young people reading and writing, none of whom had been born when he designed the city.

Baan is not trying to argue any particular point in these photographs; he is merely showing what happens when the chilly, impersonal drawing from the past is populated by real, live human beings. There they sit (pp. 146–147): Jatinder Joshi, "Advocate" and "Notary Public (Govt. of India)," two gentlemen at a small desk with official stamps and a chair standing at an angle, waiting for a client. Beside them, R.S. Rattan, "Oath Commissioner," sits at a rickety yellow desk with a fan of blue ink from his inkpad spreading out over its surface. The same job description appears again on the rusty green drawer beneath his desk. The only essentially modern element is the strange elliptical opening in the concrete wall behind them, which provides a view of the electric wiring on the white wall of the room behind. What you recognize, if you have ever traveled around this vast country, is India, the land of packed trains and endless multitudes of people, of what appears to the foreigner to be chaos, but which actually has its own secret order. This is visible in each of these photographs, almost like a jungle overrunning a city. The country and the people have taken possession of the design, and what else would we expect?

The students beneath the wondrously suspended reinforced-concrete ceiling (pp. 182–183) have no need to be constantly aware that it is actually part of a work of art that was designed for them by a revolutionary twentieth-century European architect. These are their normal surroundings, like the trees in the park that they walk past every day on their way home, which they either notice or do not. They probably have other concerns, like the young couple (pp. 176–177) strolling along without looking at a section of wall that resembles a painting, in shades of ochre, red and black. They are not in a museum; they live here and they pay as little attention to the work of art as they do to the weeds in the sandy soil in front of it.

The large sandals of a young boy (pp. 186–187) have combined with thousands of other feet walking past this same building to wear out a path that never featured in any of the plans. These anonymous feet have designed the path, as an addition, a correction, something that people just happen to do when they want to take a short cut, to get somewhere more quickly. This does not mean, however, that there is nothing more to the photograph. Something of the harmony, the curve of the protruding wall, the curious kink in the roof, the bright, pale gray color of the material, and its reflection in the small pond in front, whether consciously seen or not, will forever be intertwined with the lives of the passers-by, as part of a system of forms, like the unexpected and playful view through the hole on pages 148–149, which suddenly places the outside world and its uniform white cars down below in a different perspective. The point here, which Baan demonstrates so successfully in his photographs, is the interplay between what is designed and what is experienced, between the Platonic idea and the current reality of a practice that has taken possession of that idea. Nowhere can this be seen more clearly and yet more enigmatically than in the picture of two boys in school uniforms cycling past a red wall featuring a mysterious formula in brick letters (pp. 168–169). Three squares of different sizes contain letters, an E, an F and an H, which also appear above a bicycle rack on the same wall as part of a formula that I cannot solve: E + F = H. The paint has worn away from the frames of the squares and the red wall also looks a little like a shabby piece of clothing. Perhaps it is this photograph that most clearly illustrates the distance between origin, idea and thought, and what actually happens to them in everyday practice. Practice, or let us simply call it life: life as an extension of the architect, an unexpected and unpredictable henchman.

Brazil is not India, and so Brasília is not Chandigarh, but something similar is happening there. The people have taken possession of the city. They drape their graceful bodies over the polished marble (pp. 52–53); they walk within a work of art upon gently rising and descending concrete paths, which are not flights of stairs (pp. 48–49). They allow the light to wash over them; everything functions as it was intended to function. Like the girl studying on pages 46–47, they have made their surroundings their own. The graffiti and slogans on the wooden panels behind her are not by Niemeyer, but the bright light in the airy room with its simple school furniture certainly is. She sits there, writing intently, alone in the space that has become her own. The distance she has to travel to get home in the evening cannot be read on her face.

I heard that when the weekend comes many civil servants flee the compartmentalized city, which is divided according to function, because that was how the architect envisaged it. This is perhaps the price they have to pay to be surrounded by art on every side, or, if that doesn't mean anything, to be surrounded by harmonious forms designed by a benevolent person. I remember walking and walking with my oh-so-small footsteps, and always seeing one of those icons in the distance: the upturned bowl of the National Congress building, the hemisphere of the museum rising up out of the ground, the hyperboloid tropical plant of the cathedral against the evening sky, serving as a reminder of the endlessness of the land around us, the straight twin towers of Planalto Palace, the administrative seat of the government, symbol of power and organization, soaring up above the world of humans, who must look like the people in these photographs, reading in the coolness of a library or waiting for a bus to take them to some other destination in this same city. Maybe the praying man is among them, kneeling with outstretched arms on the pavement in front of the church (pp. 78–79), or perhaps they later disappear into the crowd, heading to one of the many places that did not appear in the design, such as the spot on pages 60–61.

As I remember it, everything was wide. You could spend days there, fanning out in every direction on one of those yellow buses: a wideness that I recognize in these photographs.

There is perhaps no better place to see this scale than in the photograph on pages 30–31. On the left is the futuristic flourish of the architect, who was in love with the seduction of rounded forms. It has been raining and the other buildings, tall and straight, are reflected in the wet surface, along with the solitary man and his backpack. He resembles one of those drawings, but with one difference: he is alive. We do not know where he is going, or how far he will have to travel to get there. It is his city; he has appropriated it. In the same way, the relative vulnerability of the girls, lying sunbathing on a stone bench in front of that expanse of fine latticework (pp. 32–33), illustrates something that is true of all cities, whether they are already old or have yet to become old: that they may indeed have been built for us, that we can use them as long as we are around, but that we and our fleeting figures will disappear from these powerful, wide and tall structures, because they were not built for us alone, but for those who will come after us. After all, cities must live longer than people. The buildings will remain, but we will leave behind our marks and our history upon them, because that is what a city is: a place that is written, right from the beginning, by all of its inhabitants, a stone book containing all that we have said and done, with the inhabitant as an invisible and anonymous architect who will also play a part in centuries to come in shaping the design, in writing the history. Iwan Baan's photographs bear witness to this process.

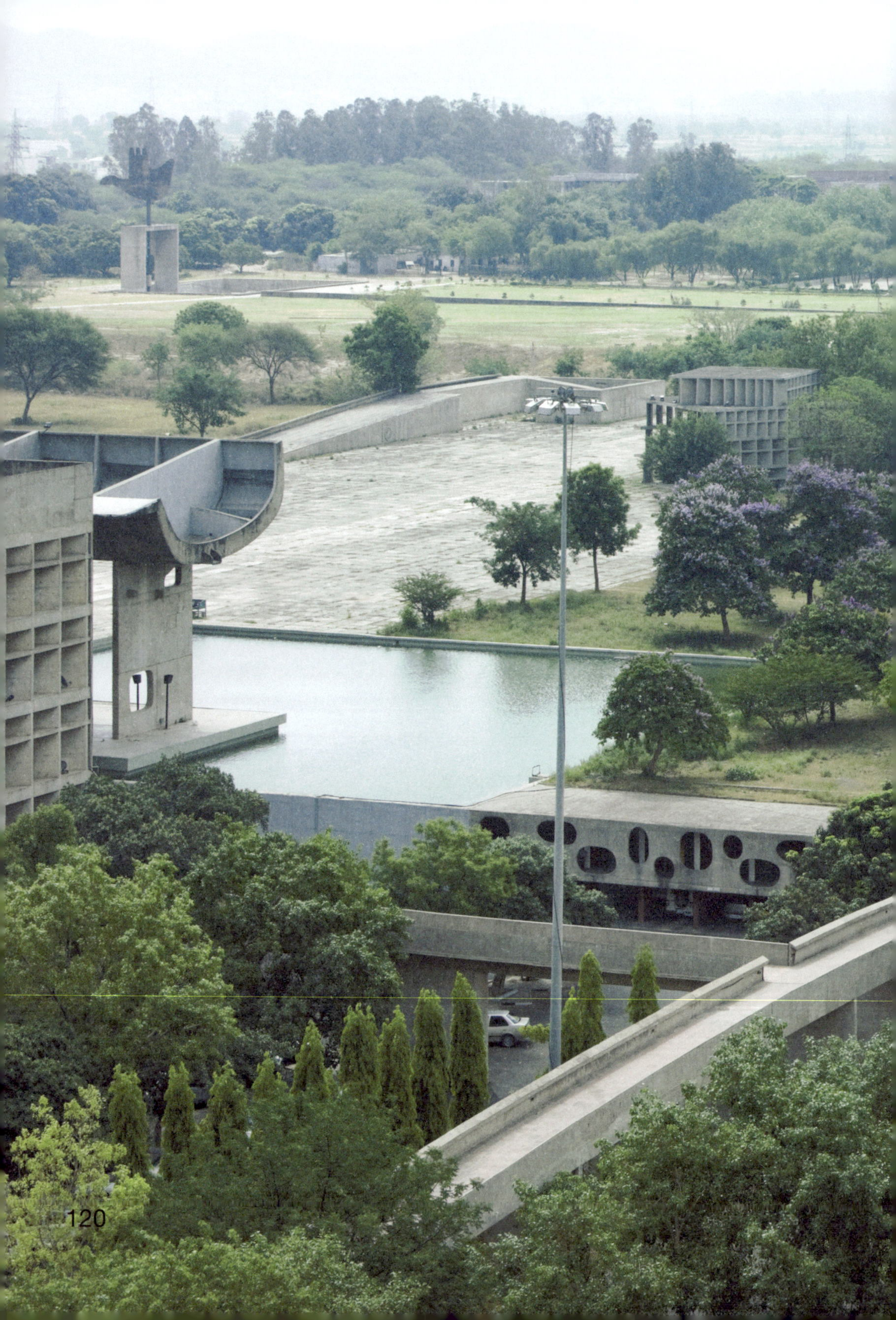

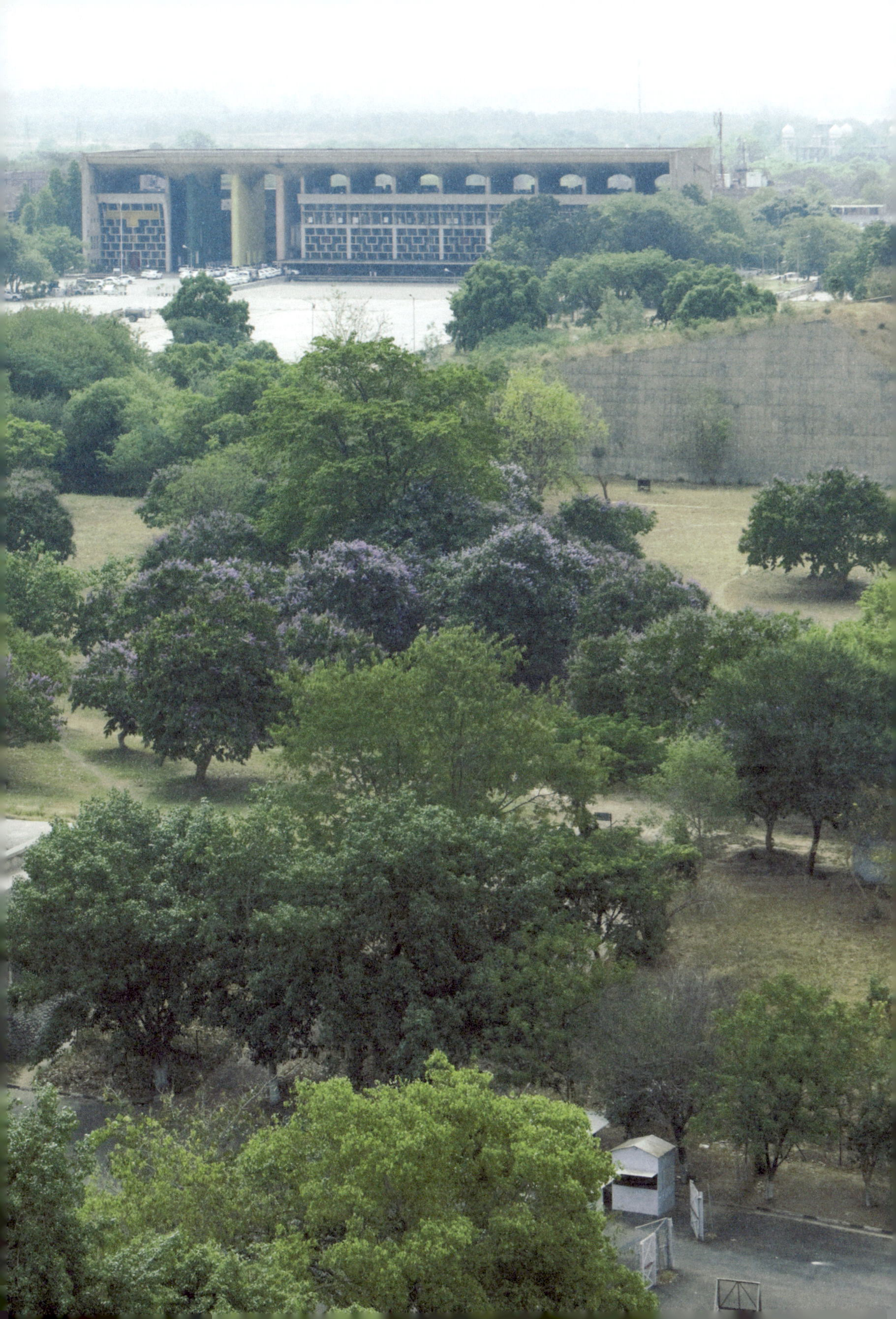

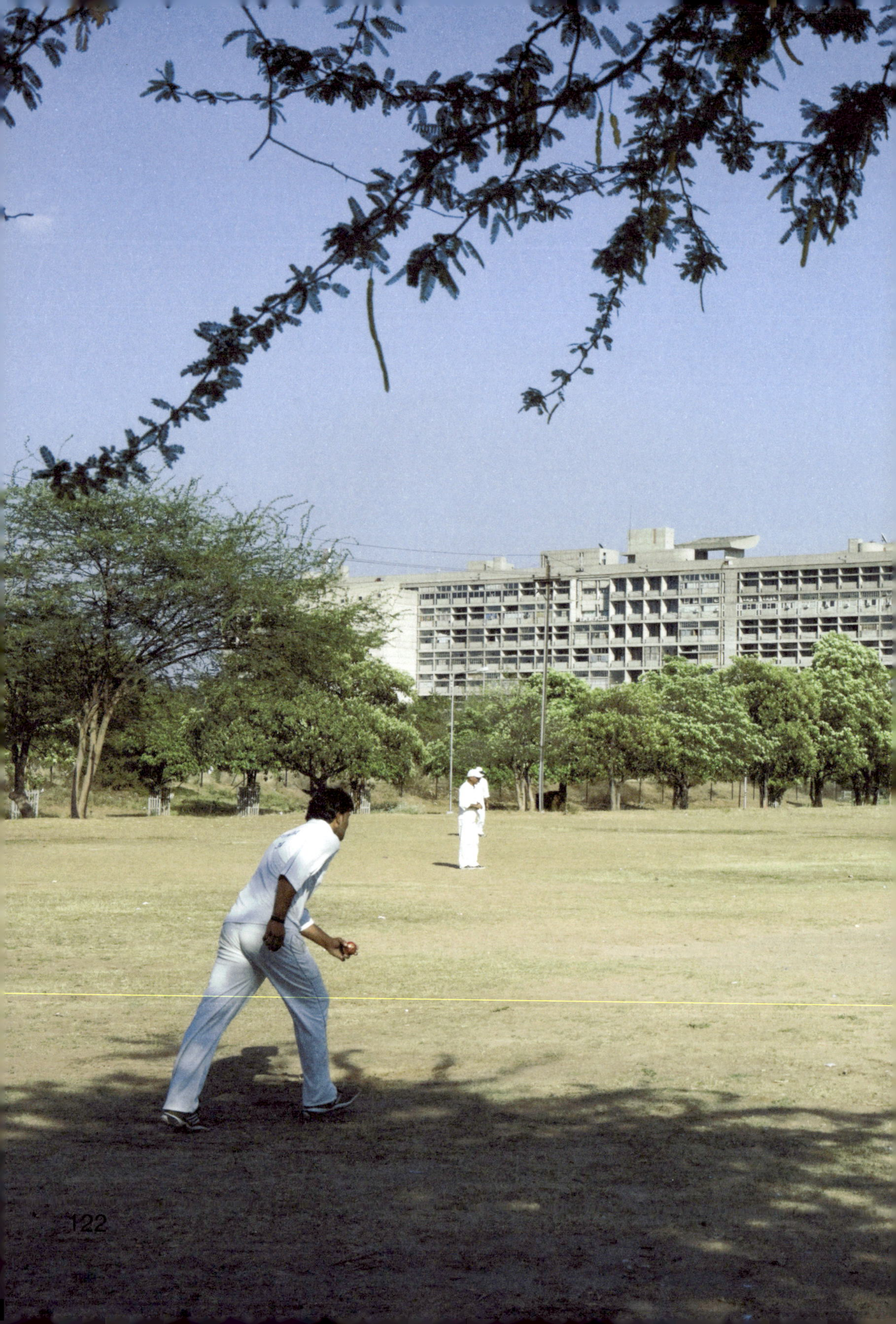

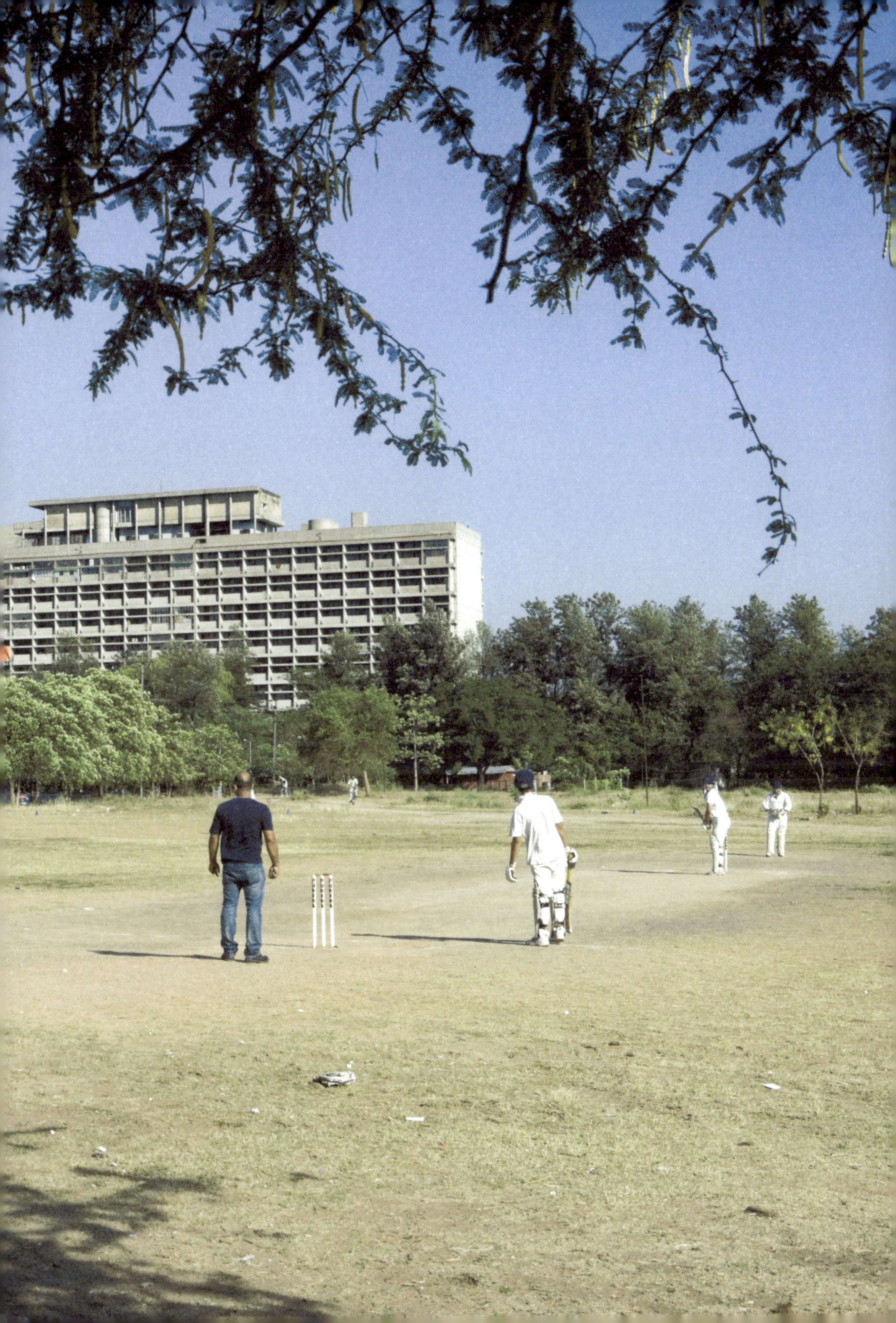

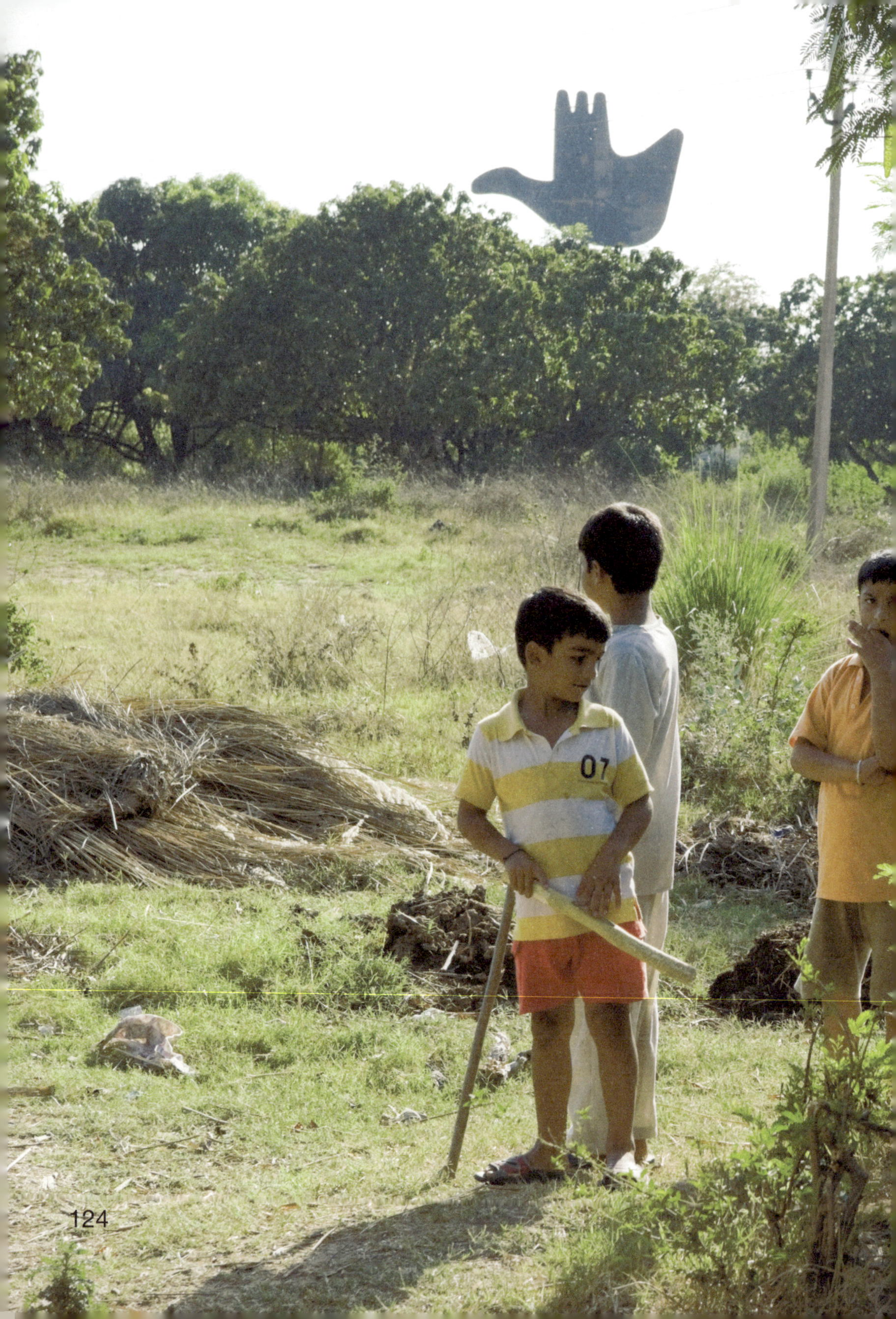
07

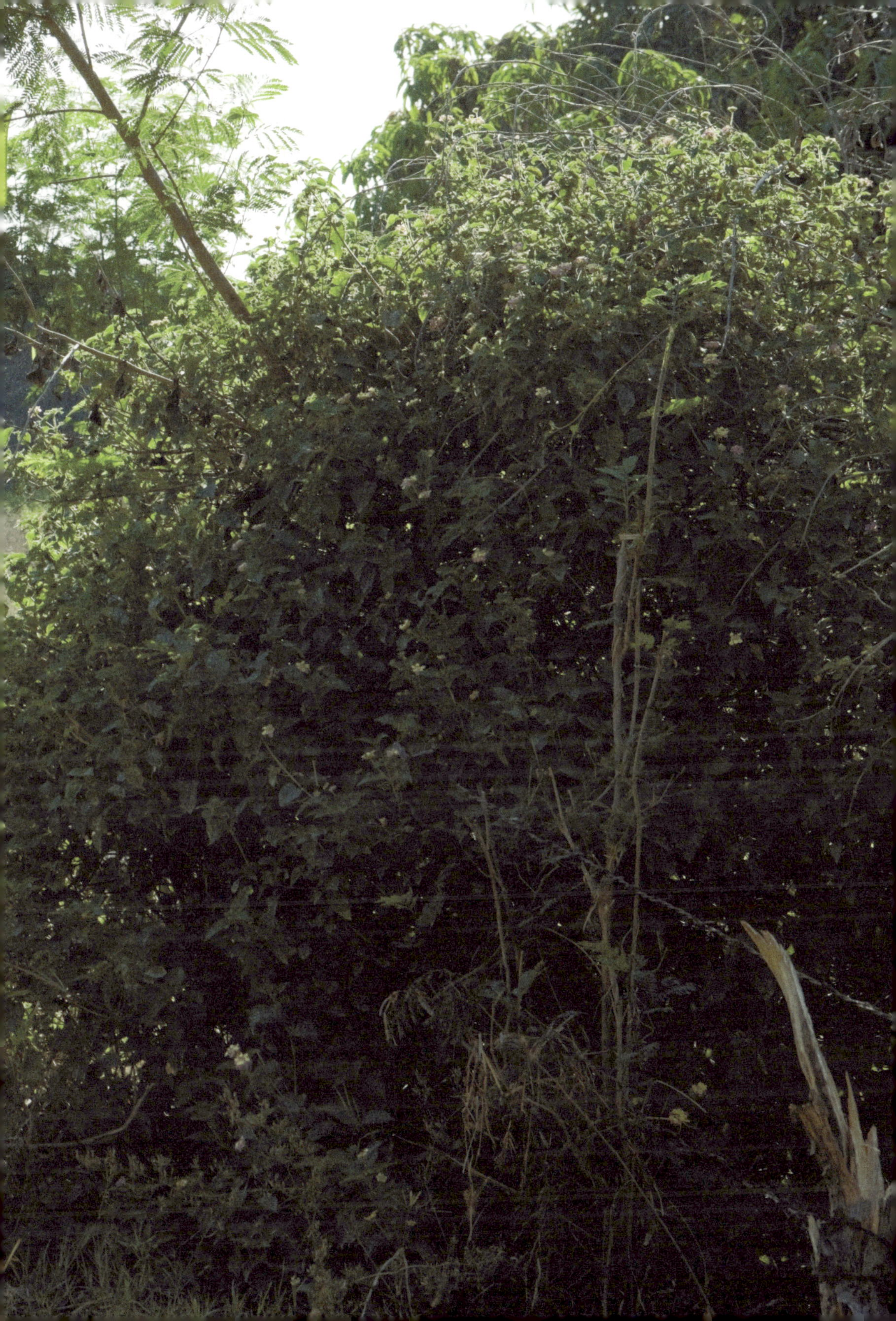

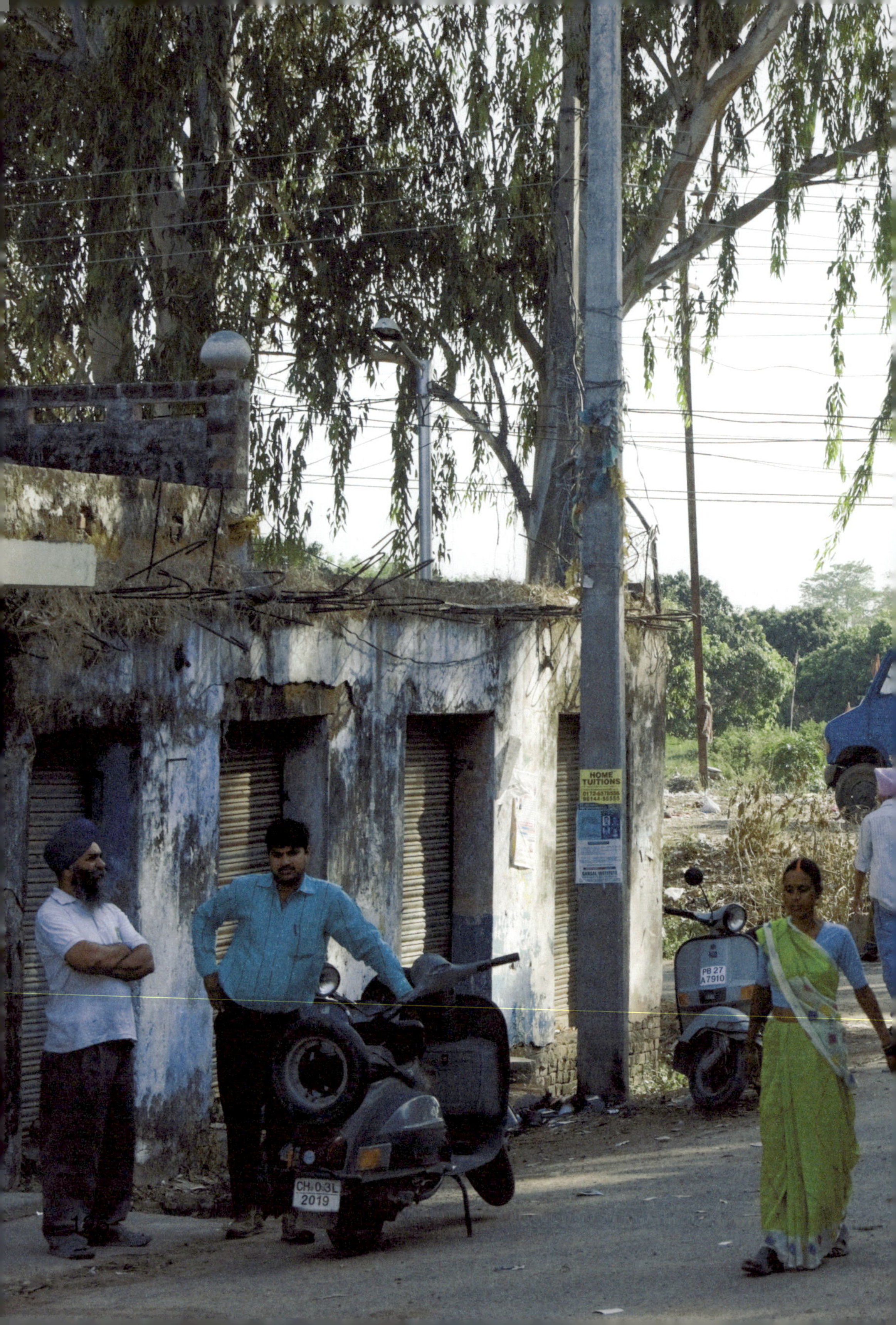
HOME
TUITIONS
PB 27
A7910
CH 03L
2019

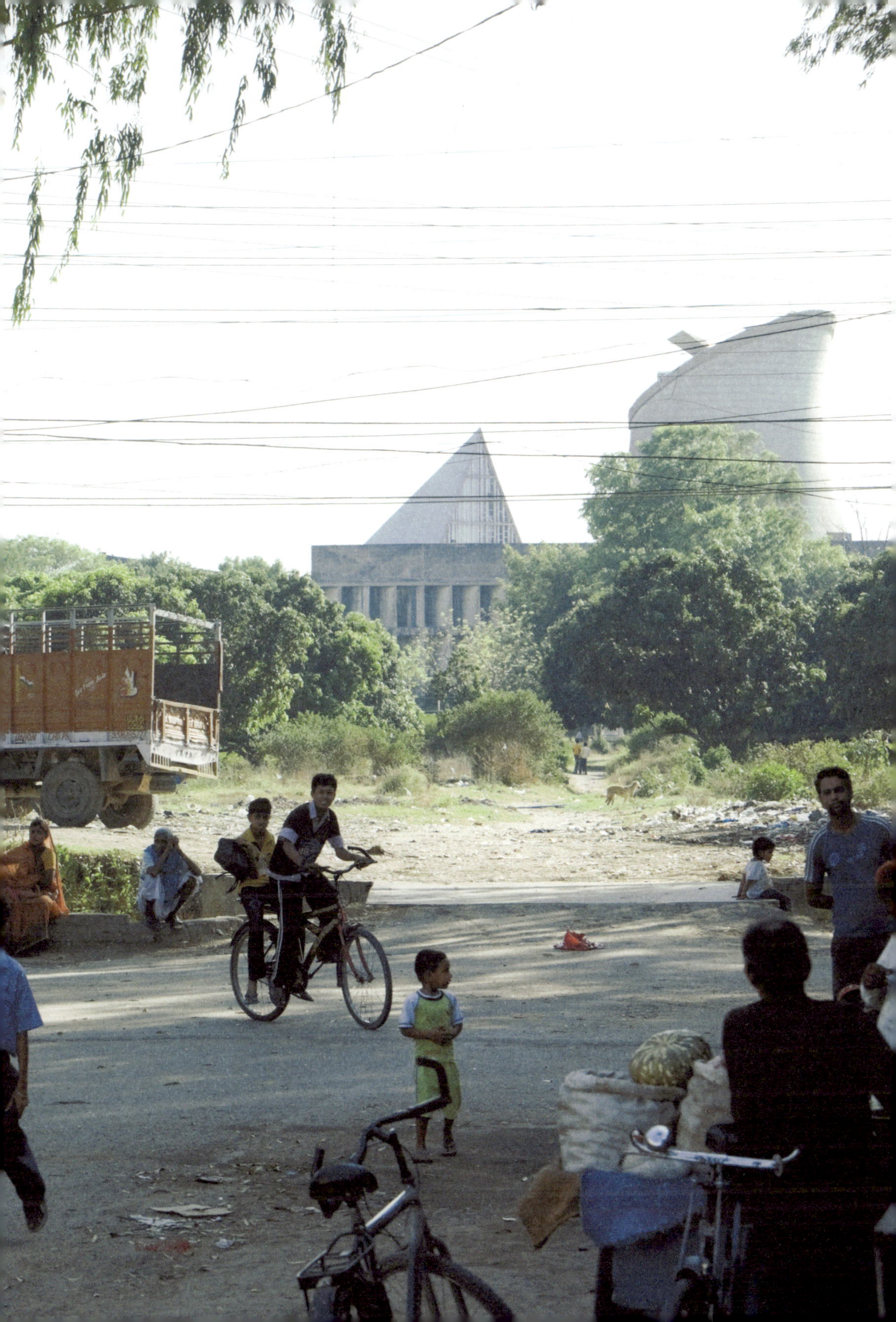

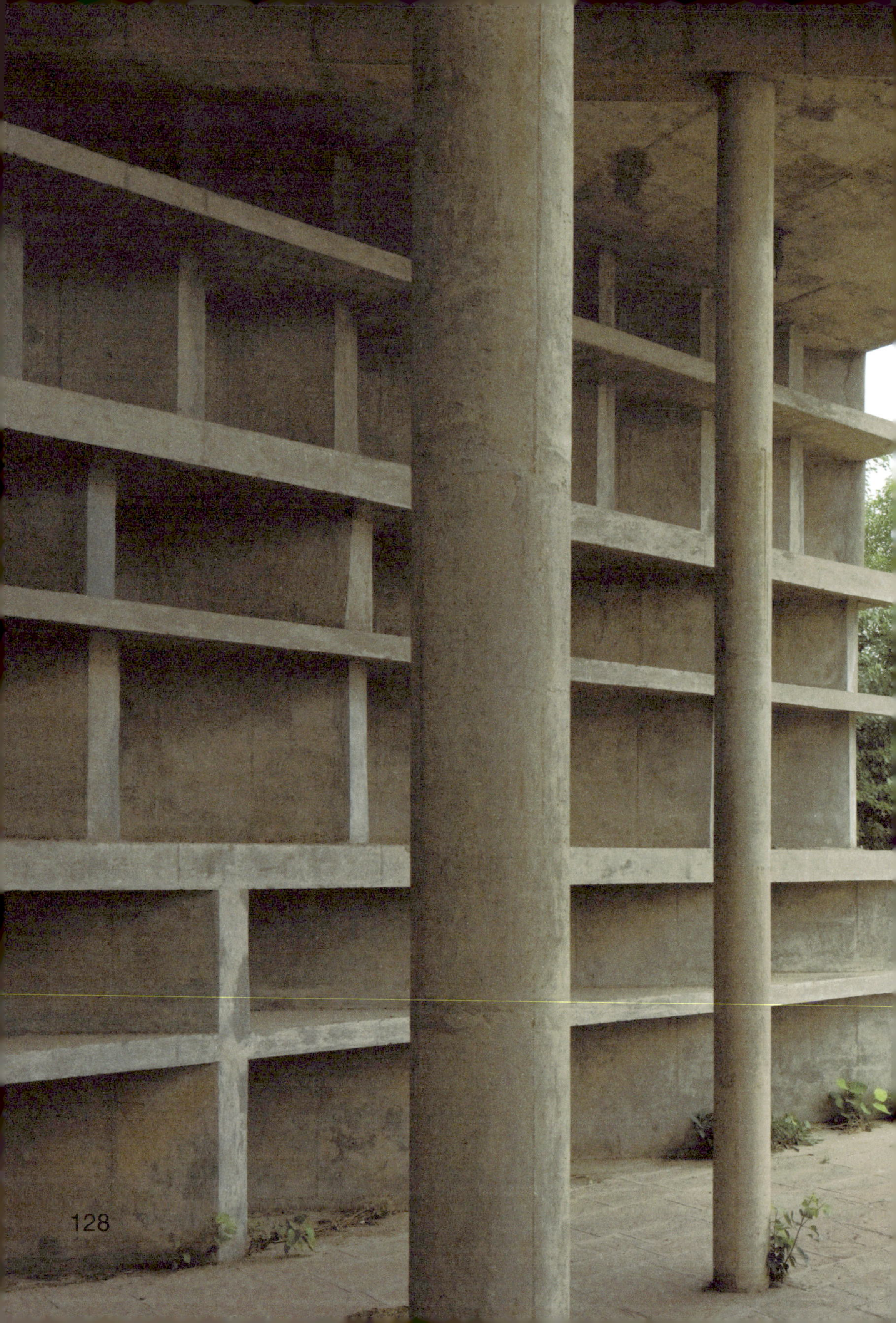

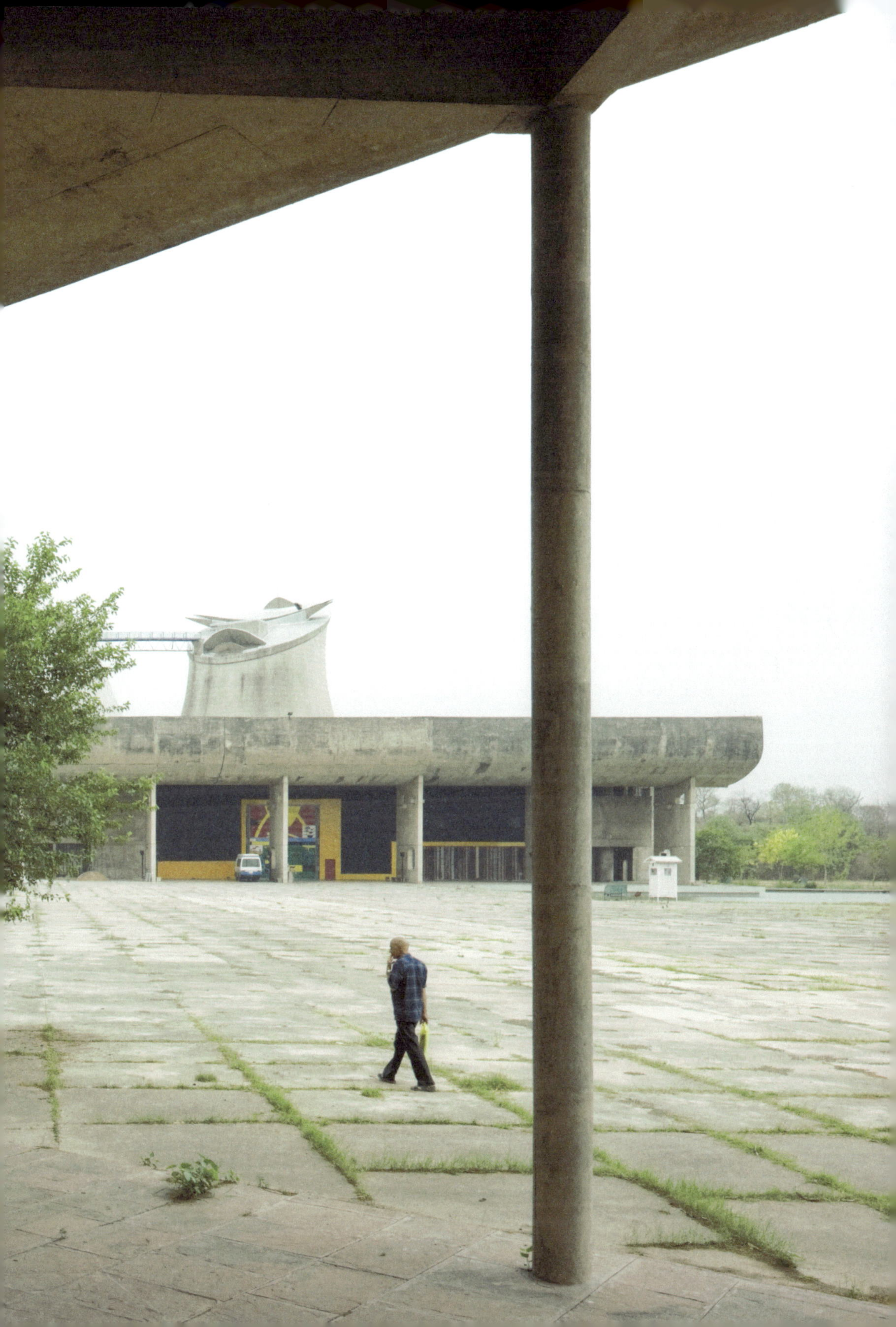

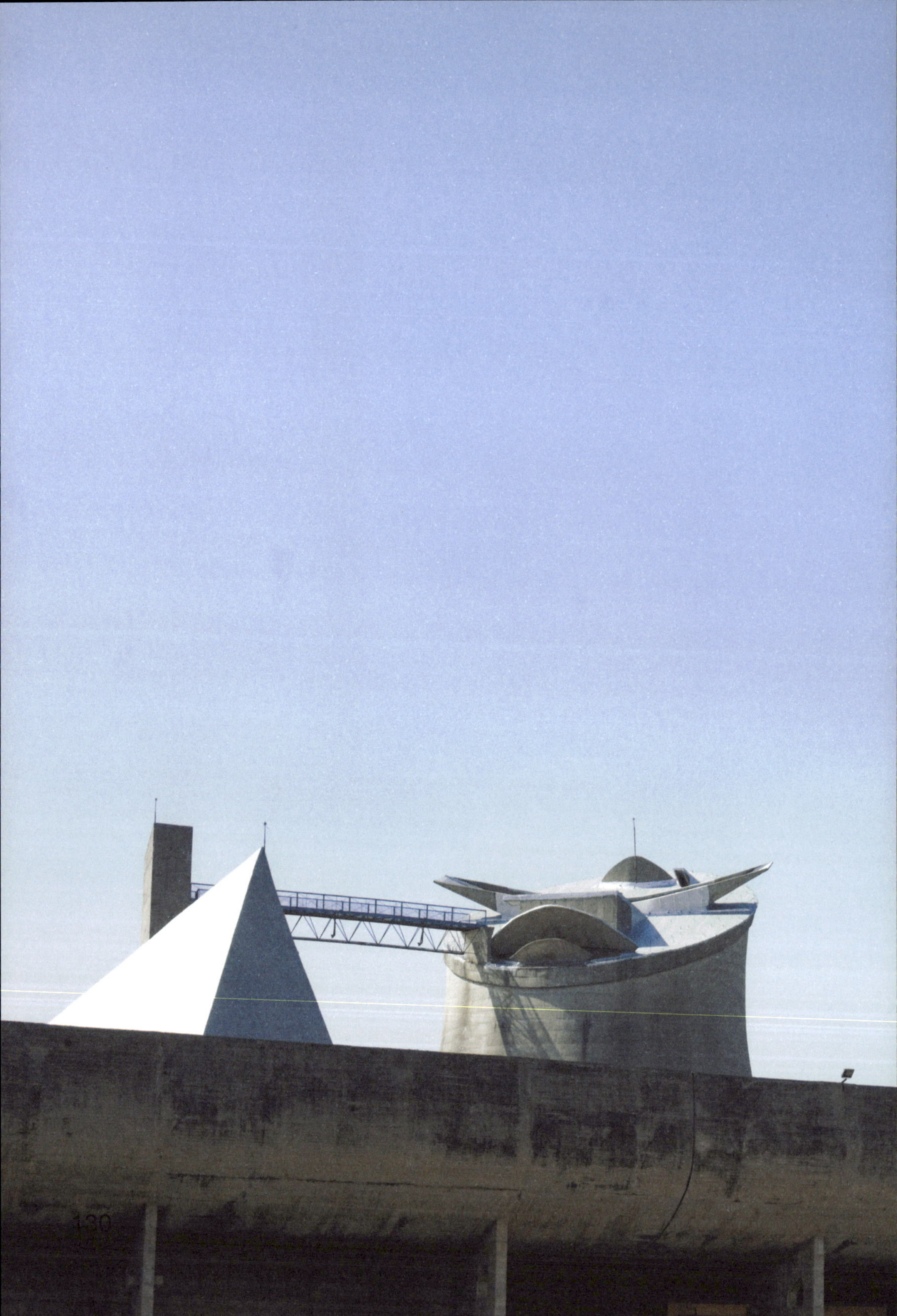

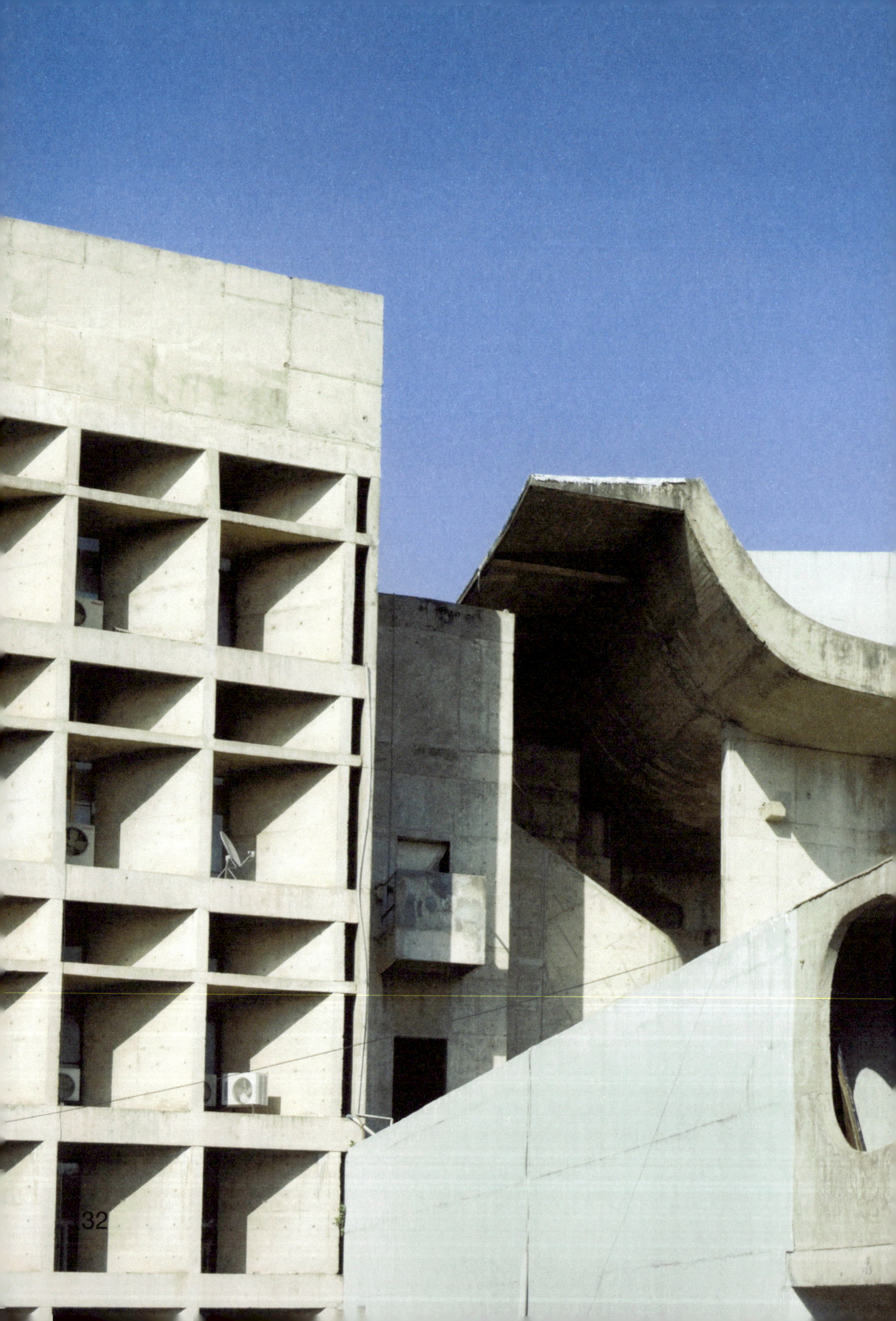

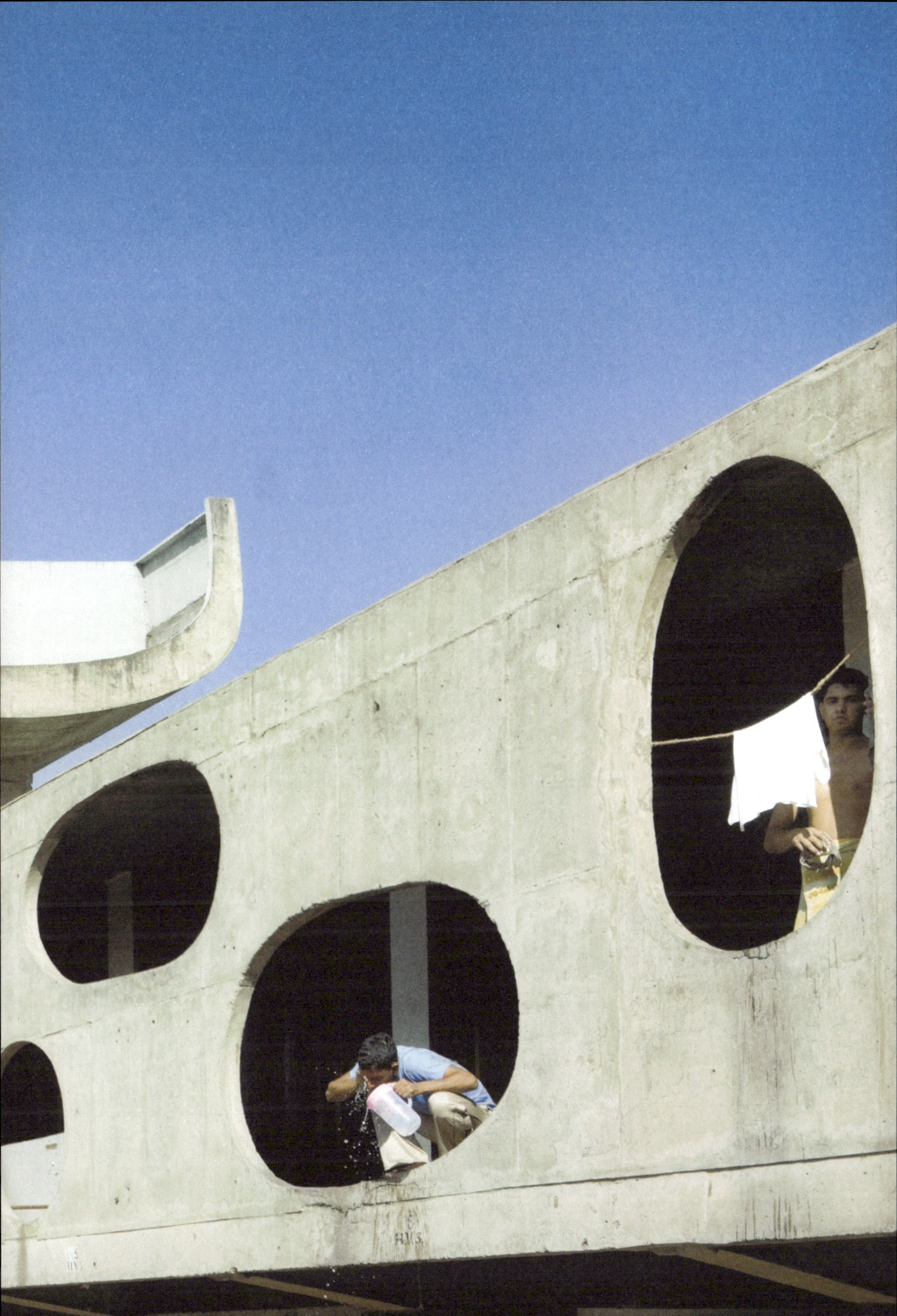

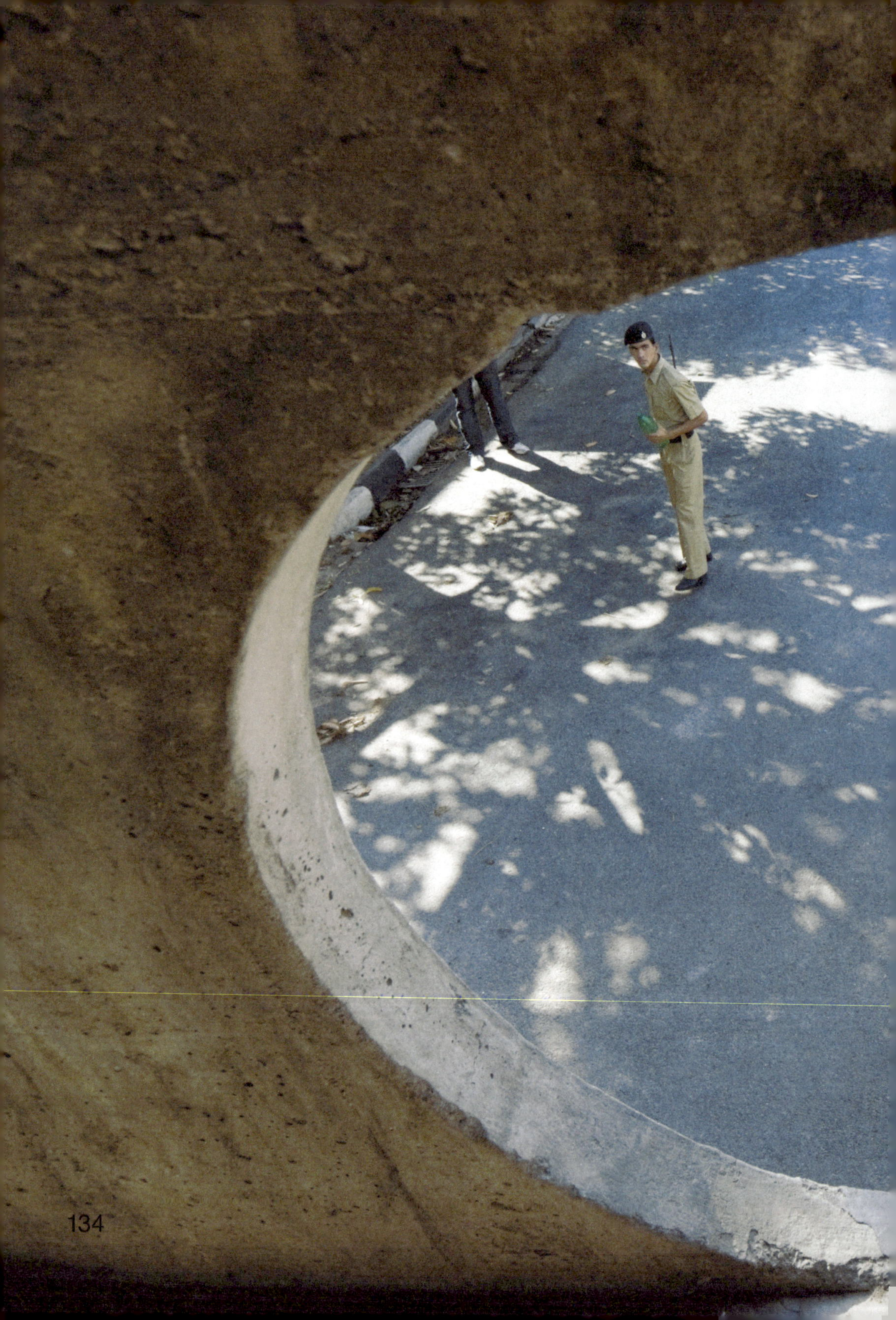

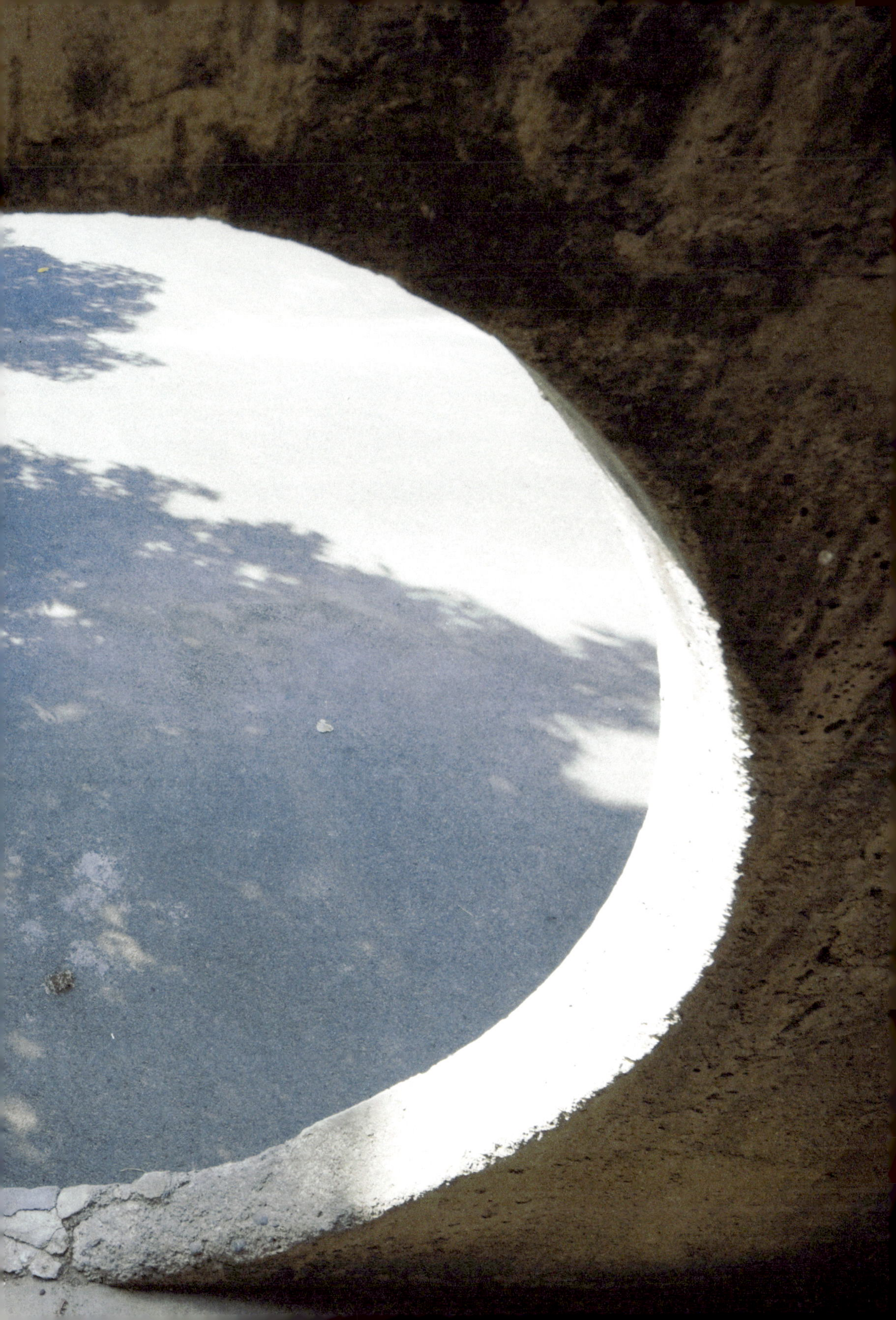

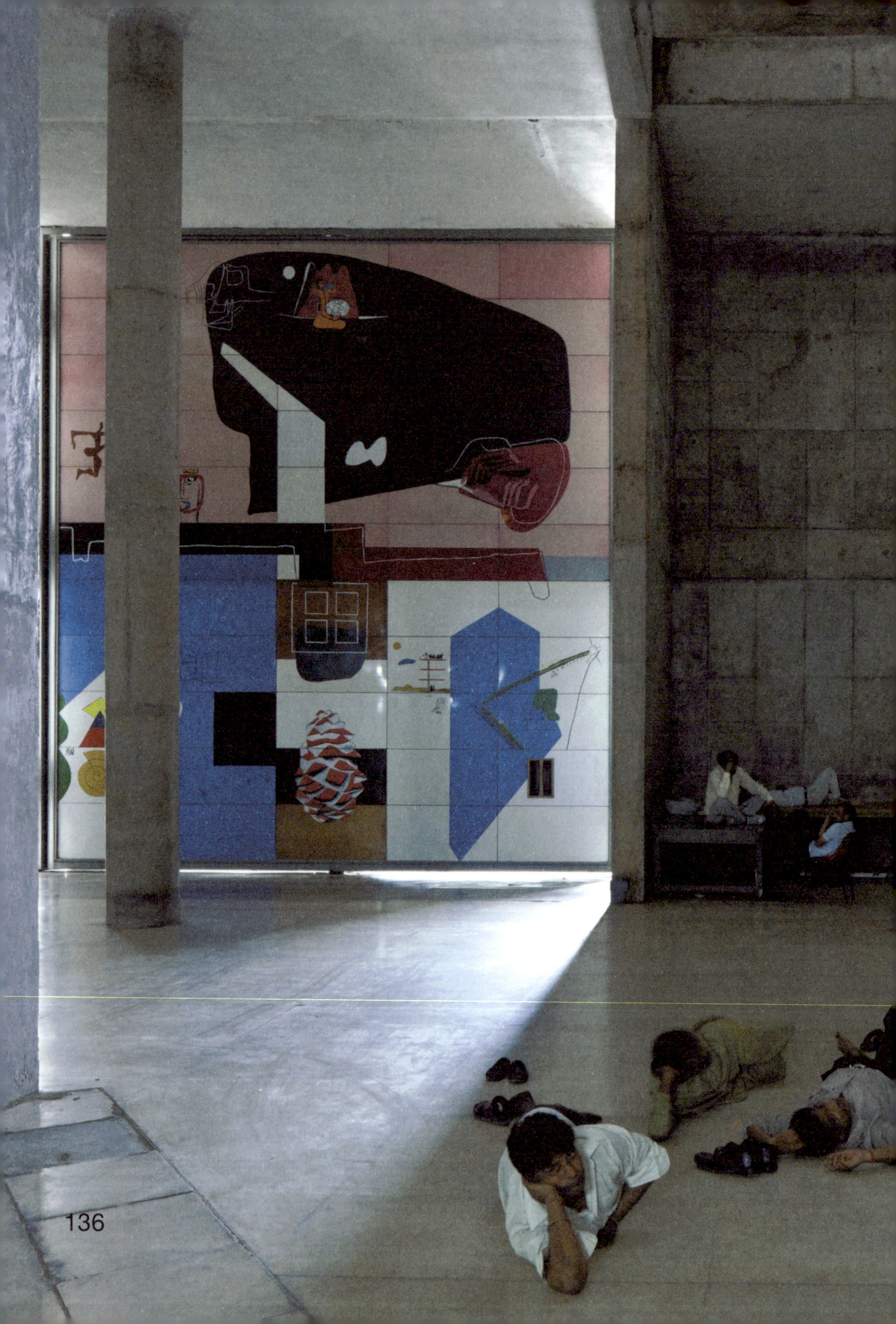

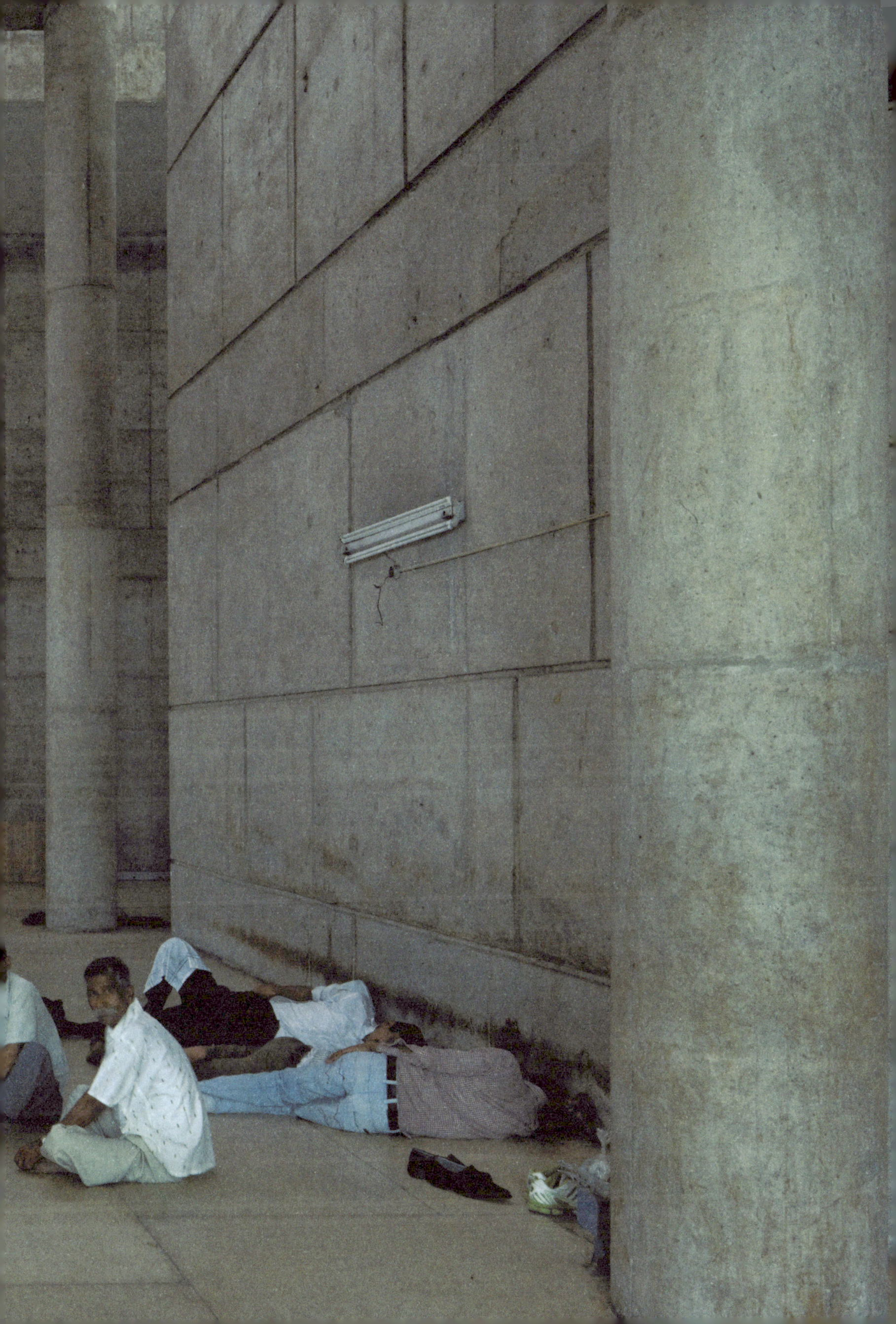

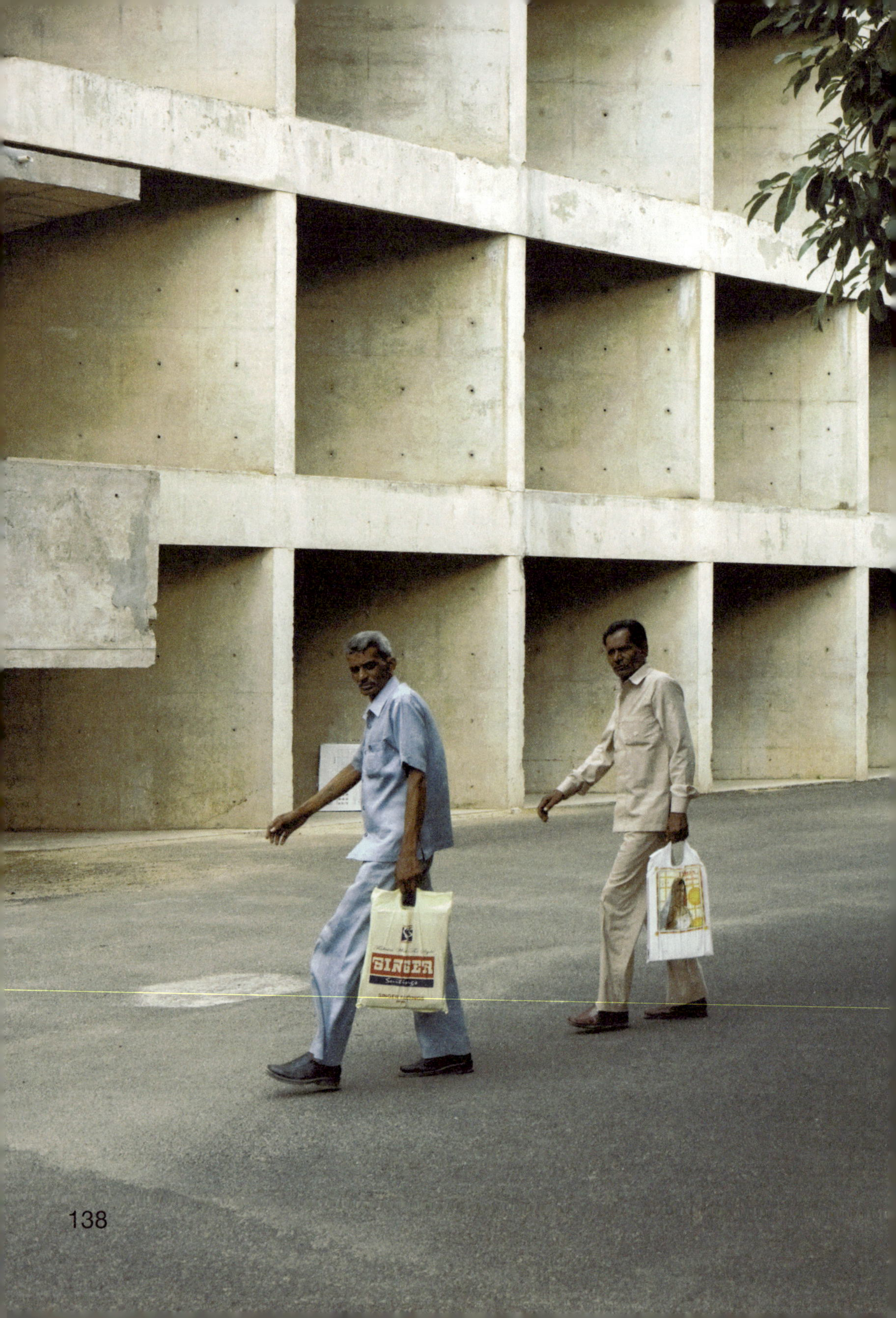

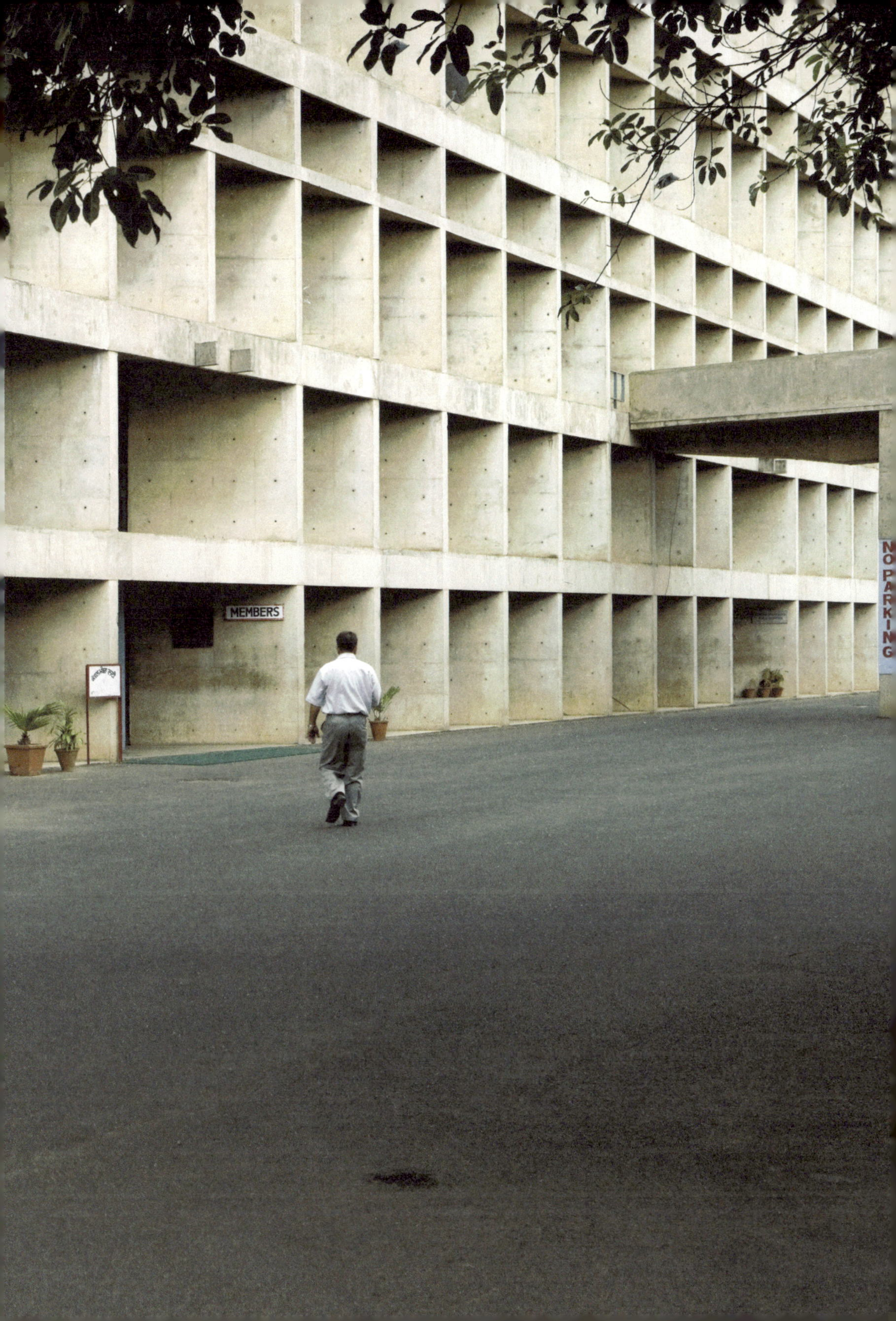
MEMBERS
NO PARKING

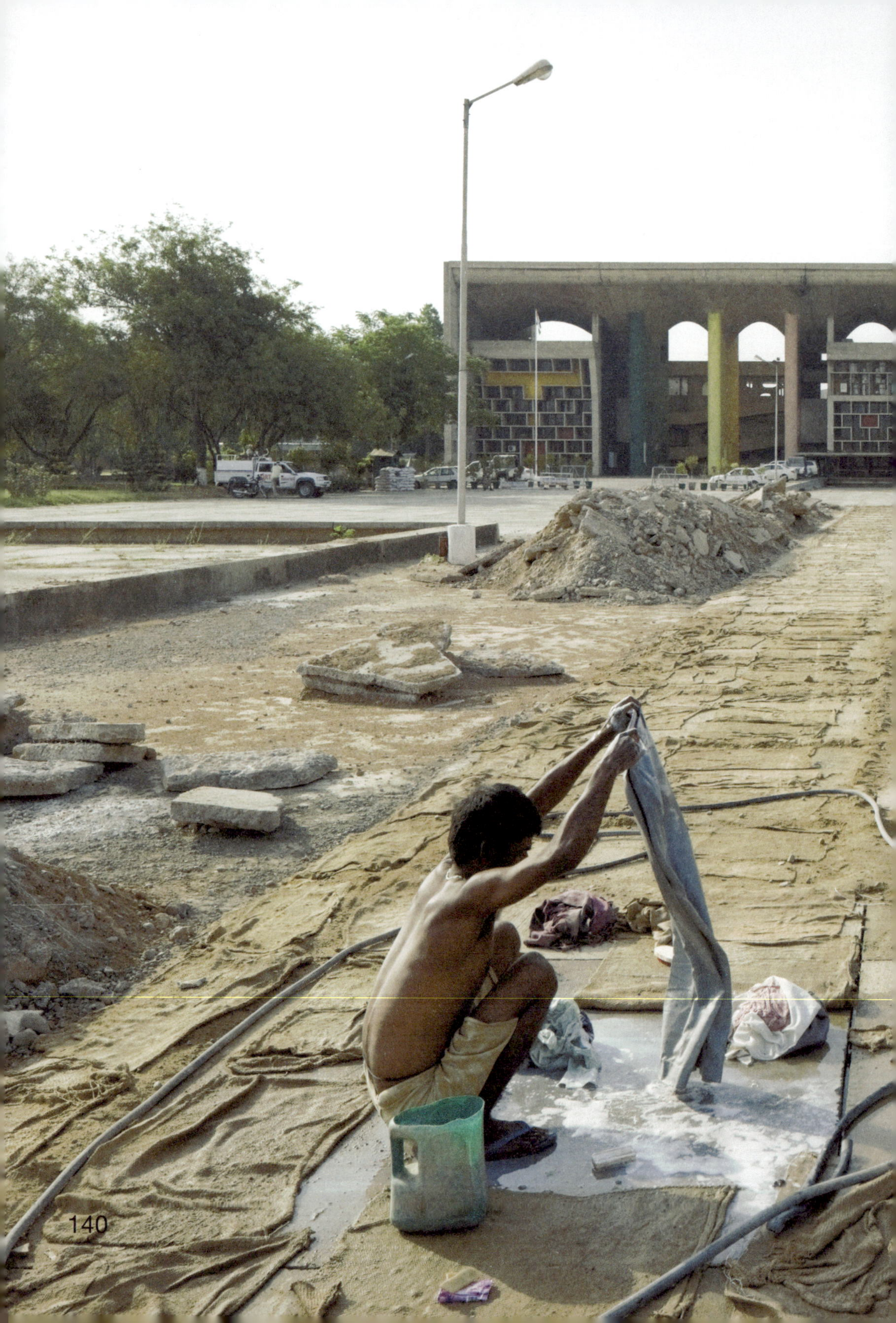

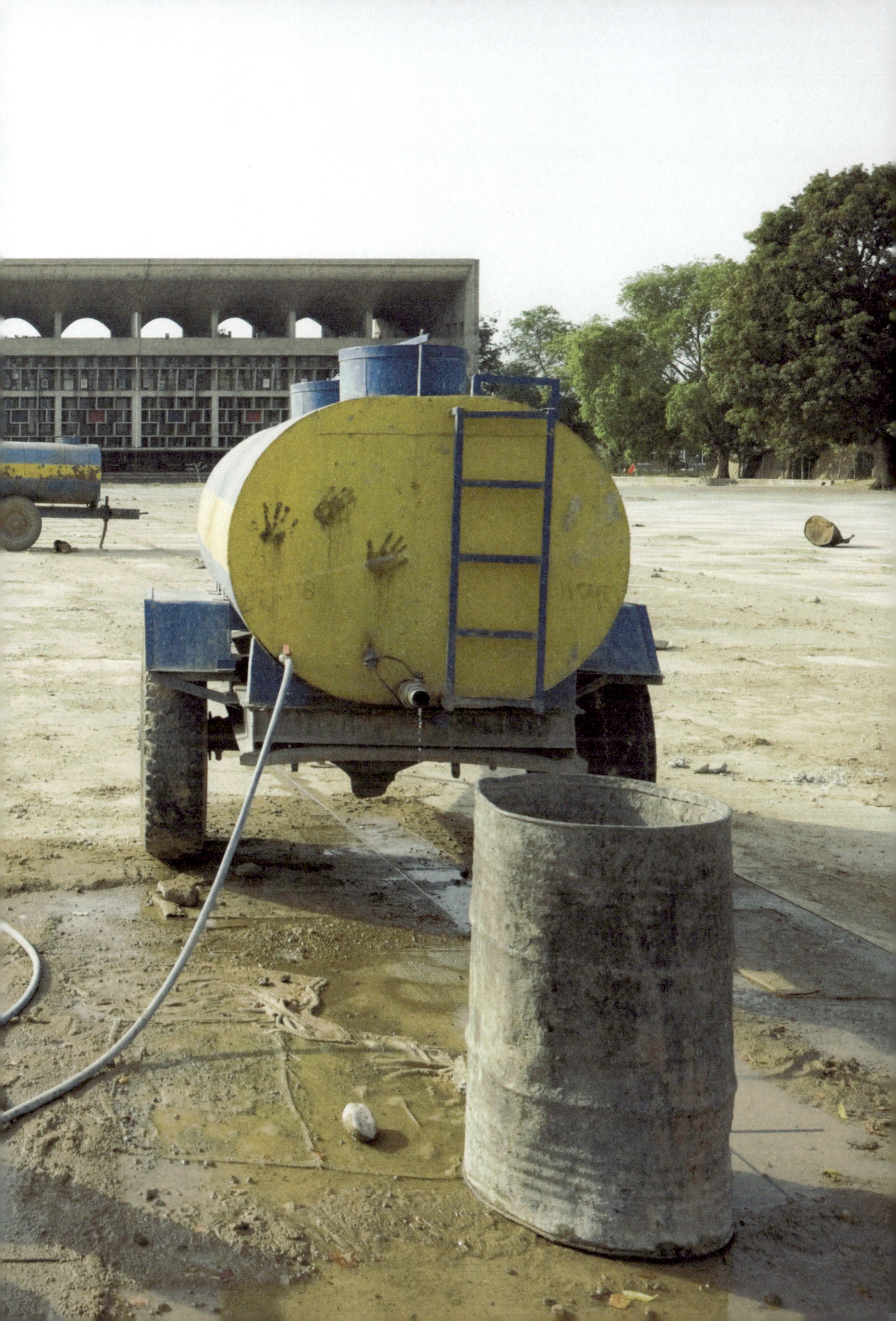

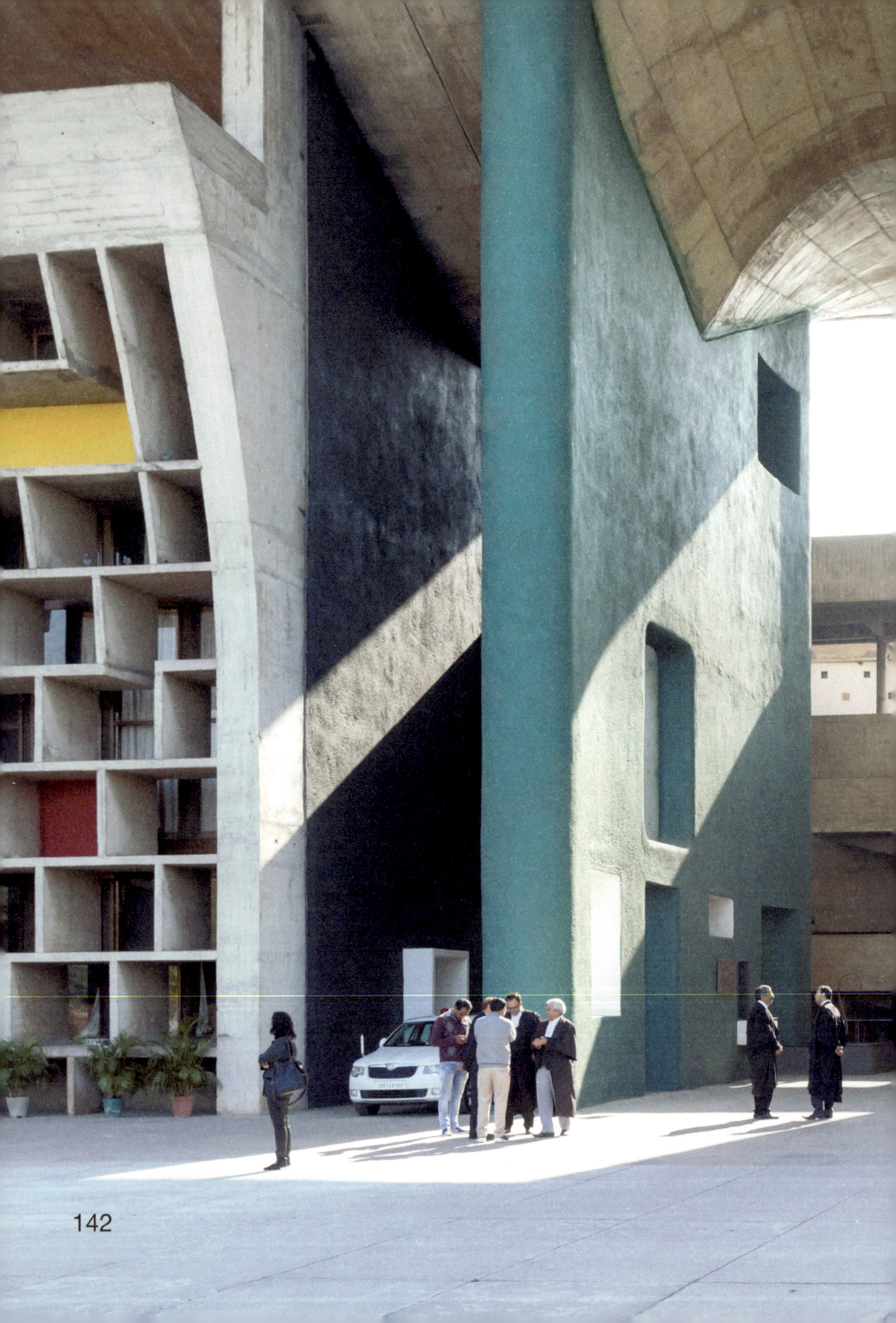

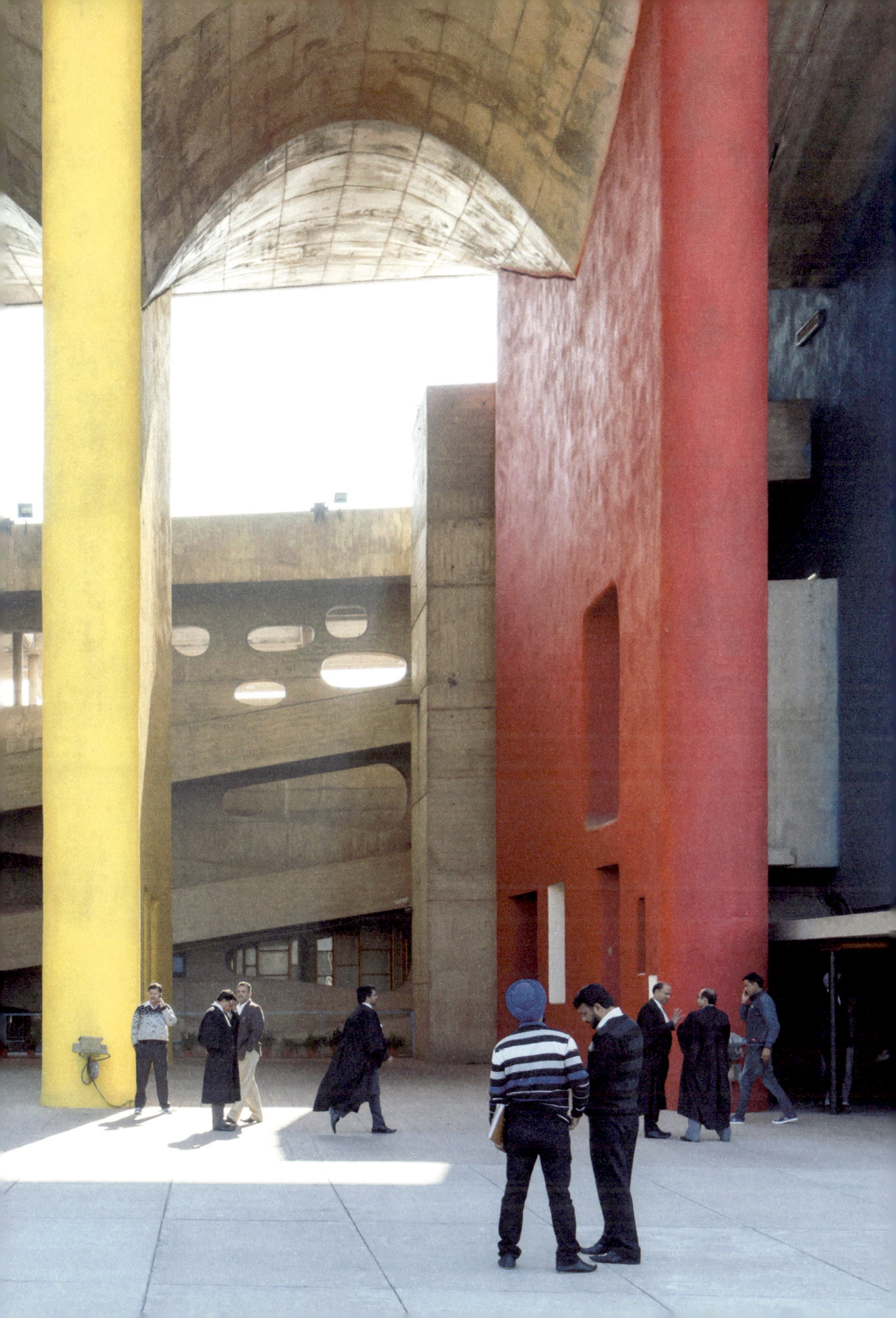

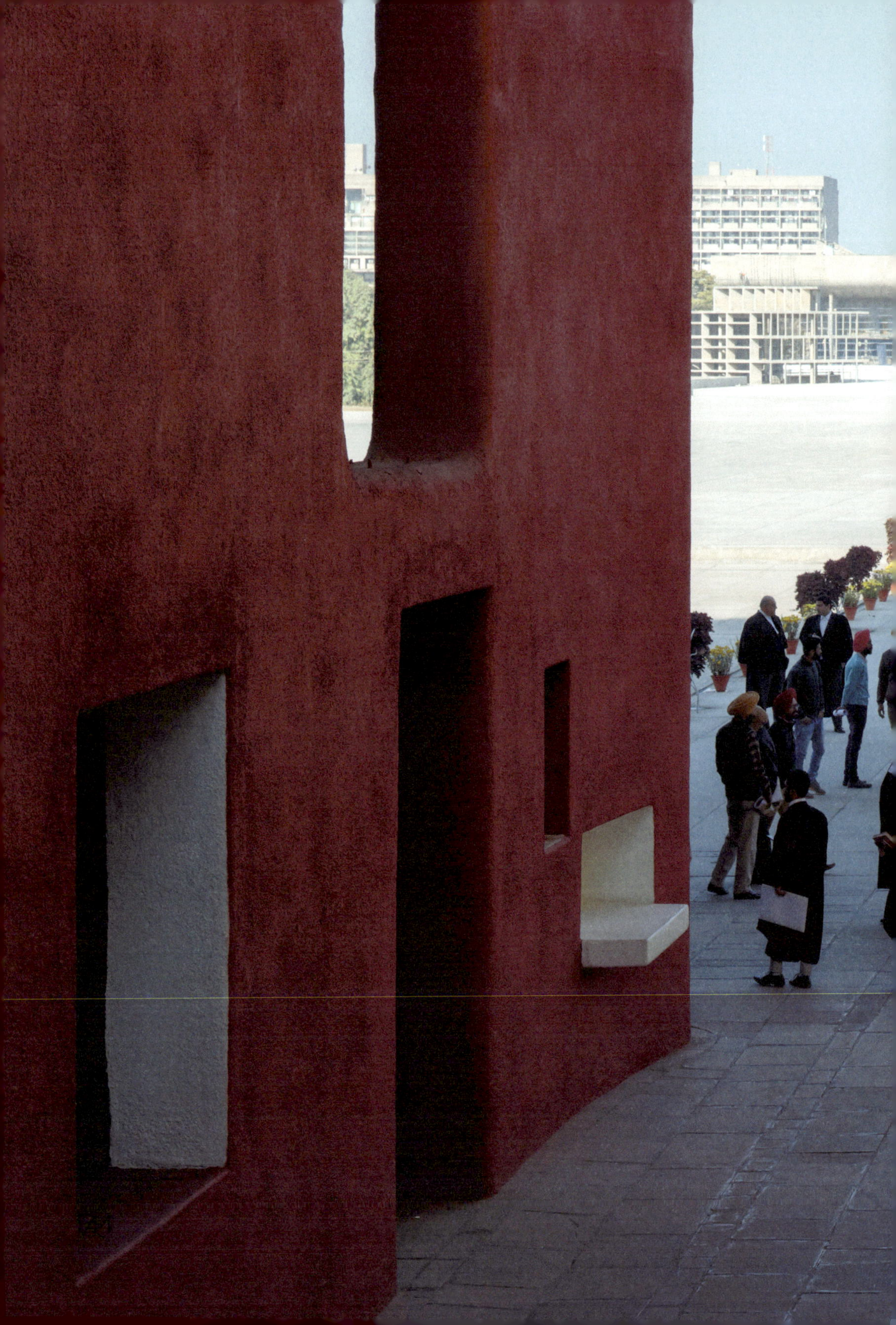

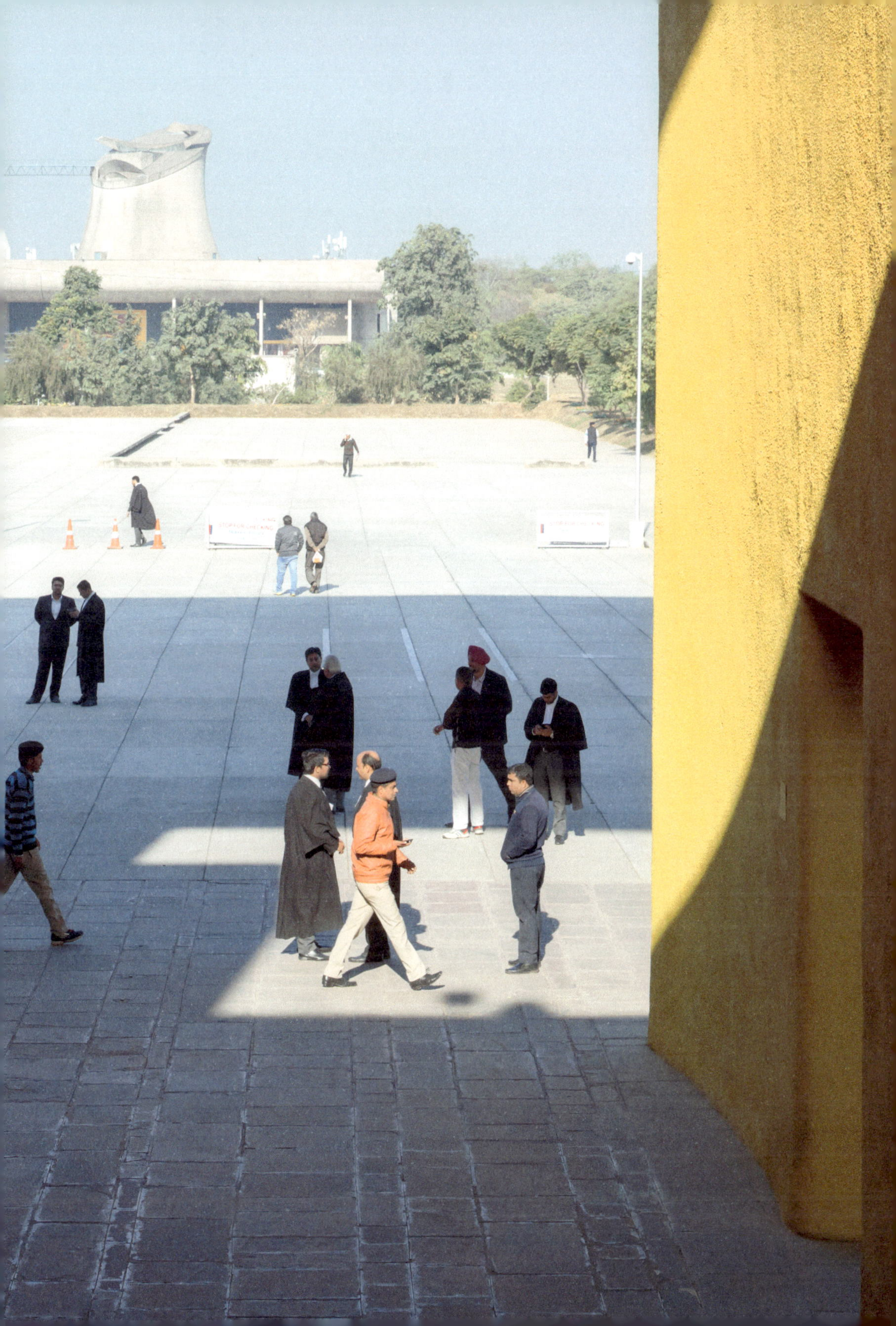

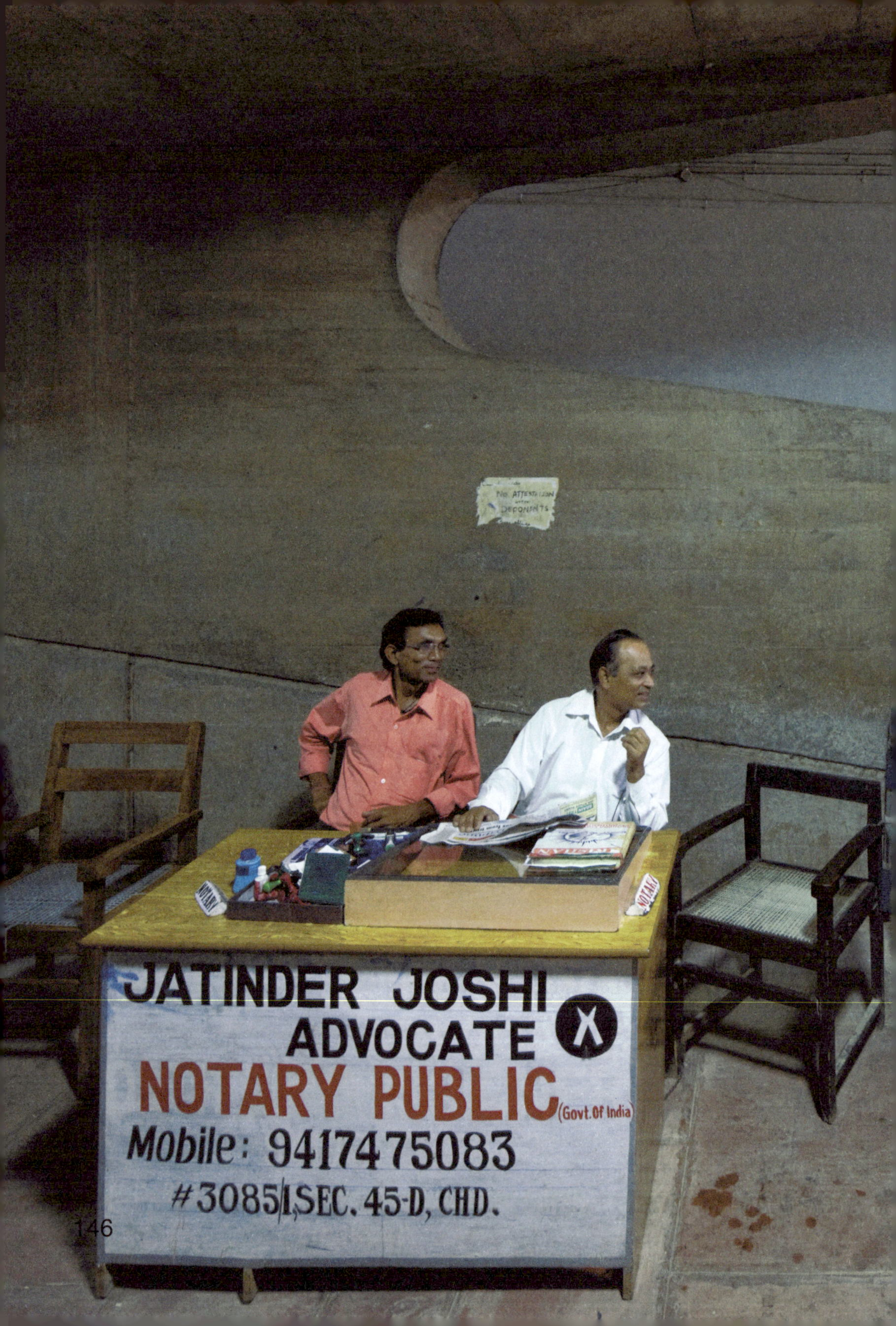
JATINDER JOSHI
ADVOCATE
NOTARY PUBLIC
(Govt. Of India)
Mobile: 9417475083
#3085/1, SEC. 45-D, CHD.

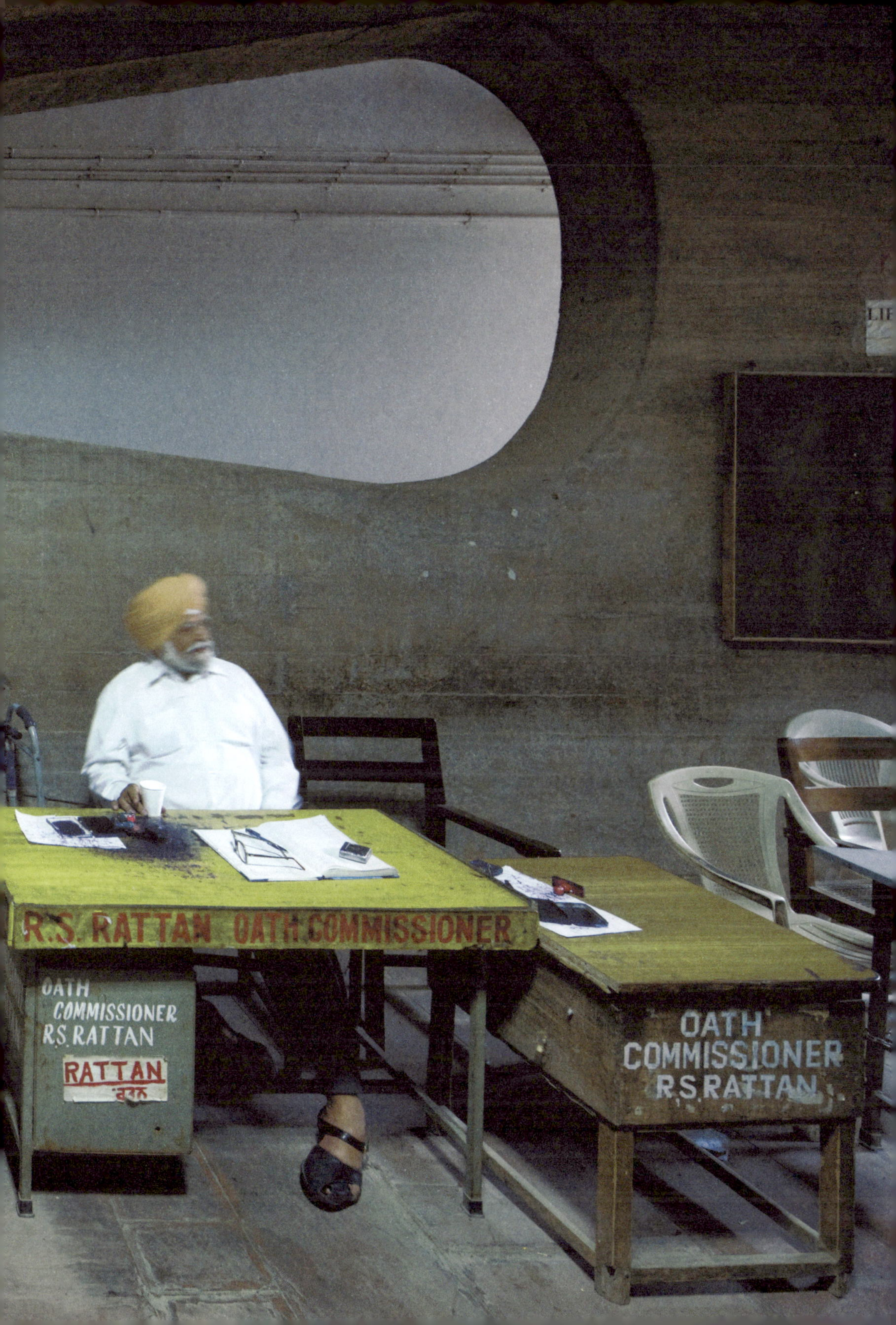
R.S. RATTAN OATH COMMISSIONER
OATH
COMMISSIONER
R.S.RATTAN
RATTAN
OATH
COMMISSIONER
R.S.RATTAN

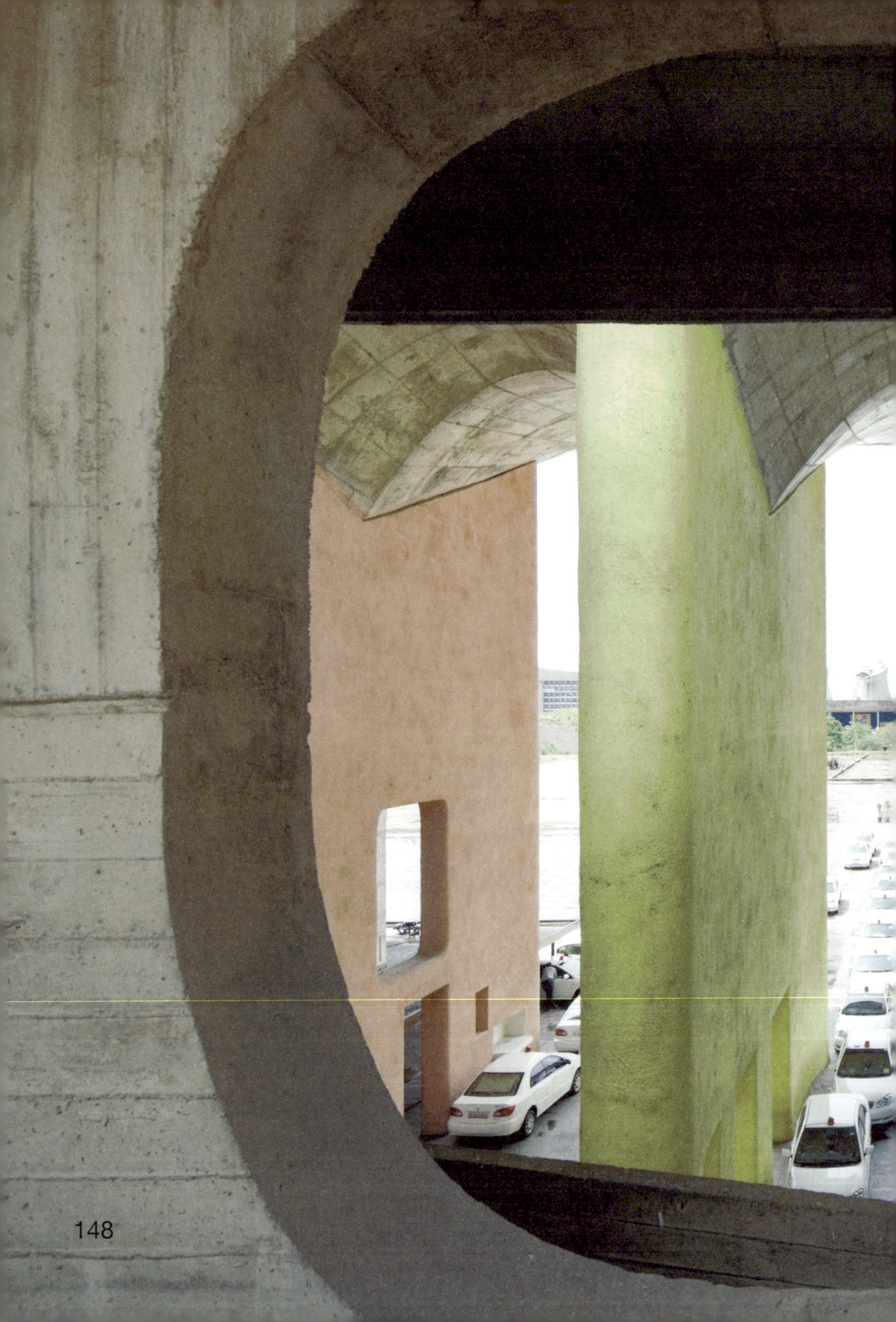

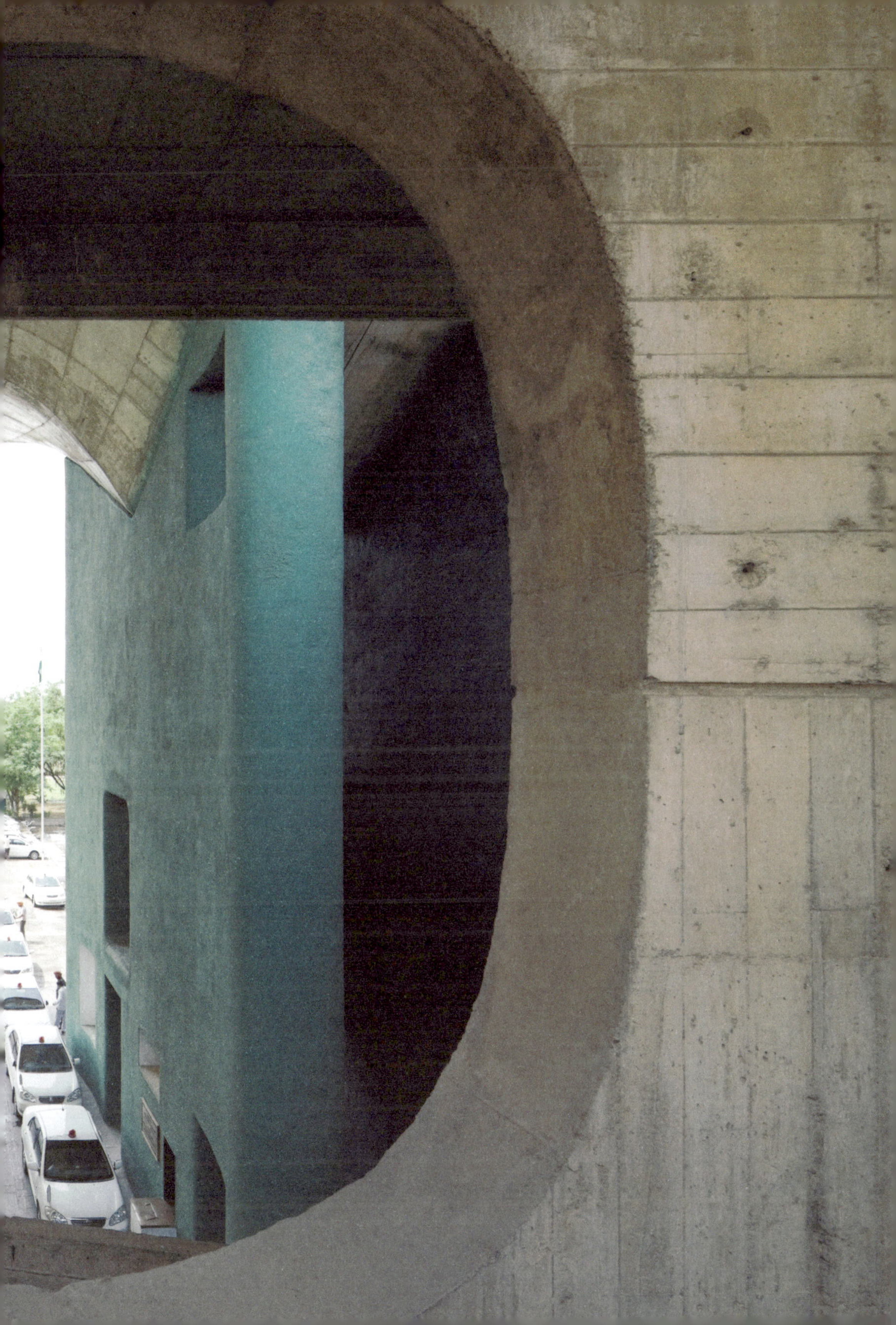

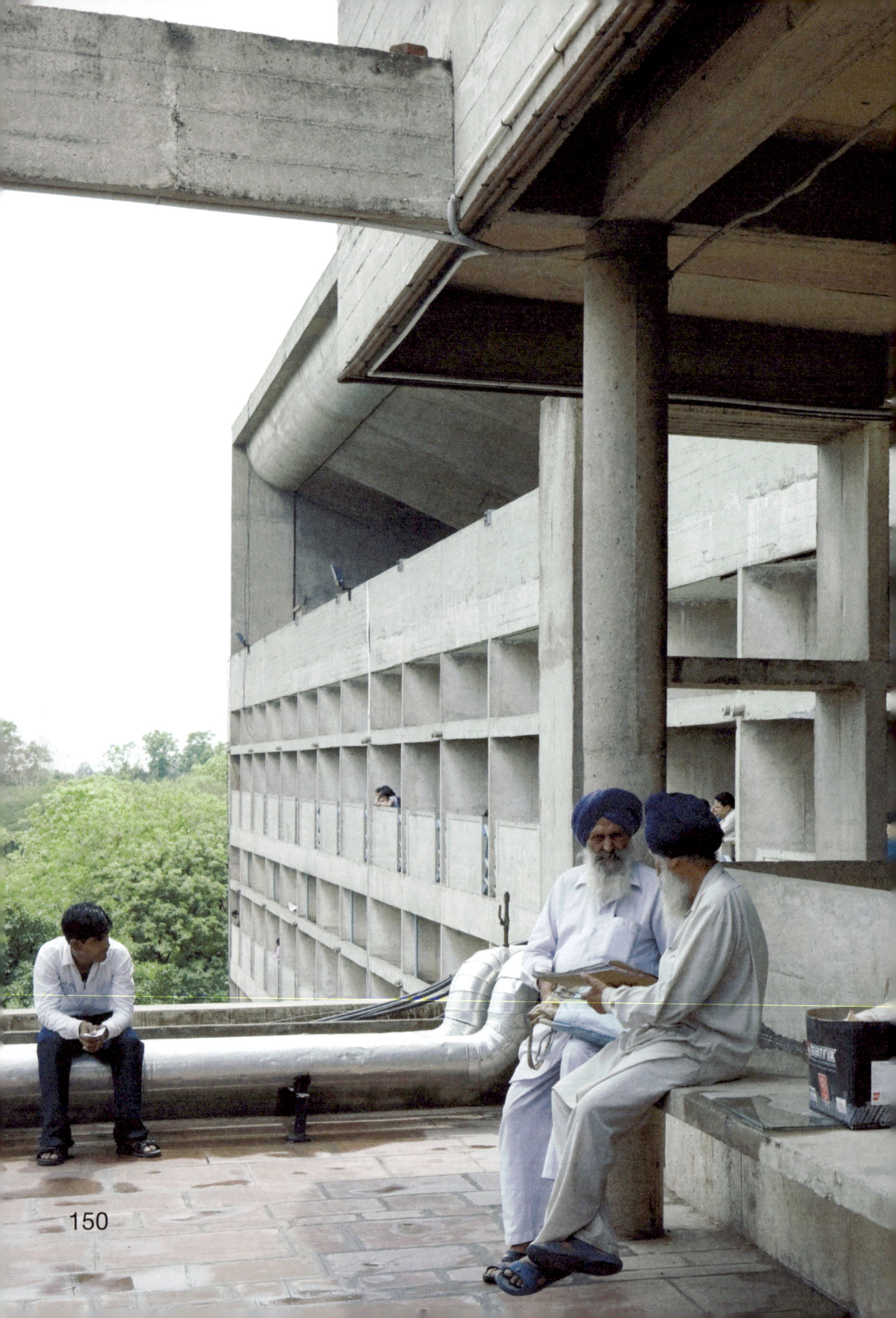

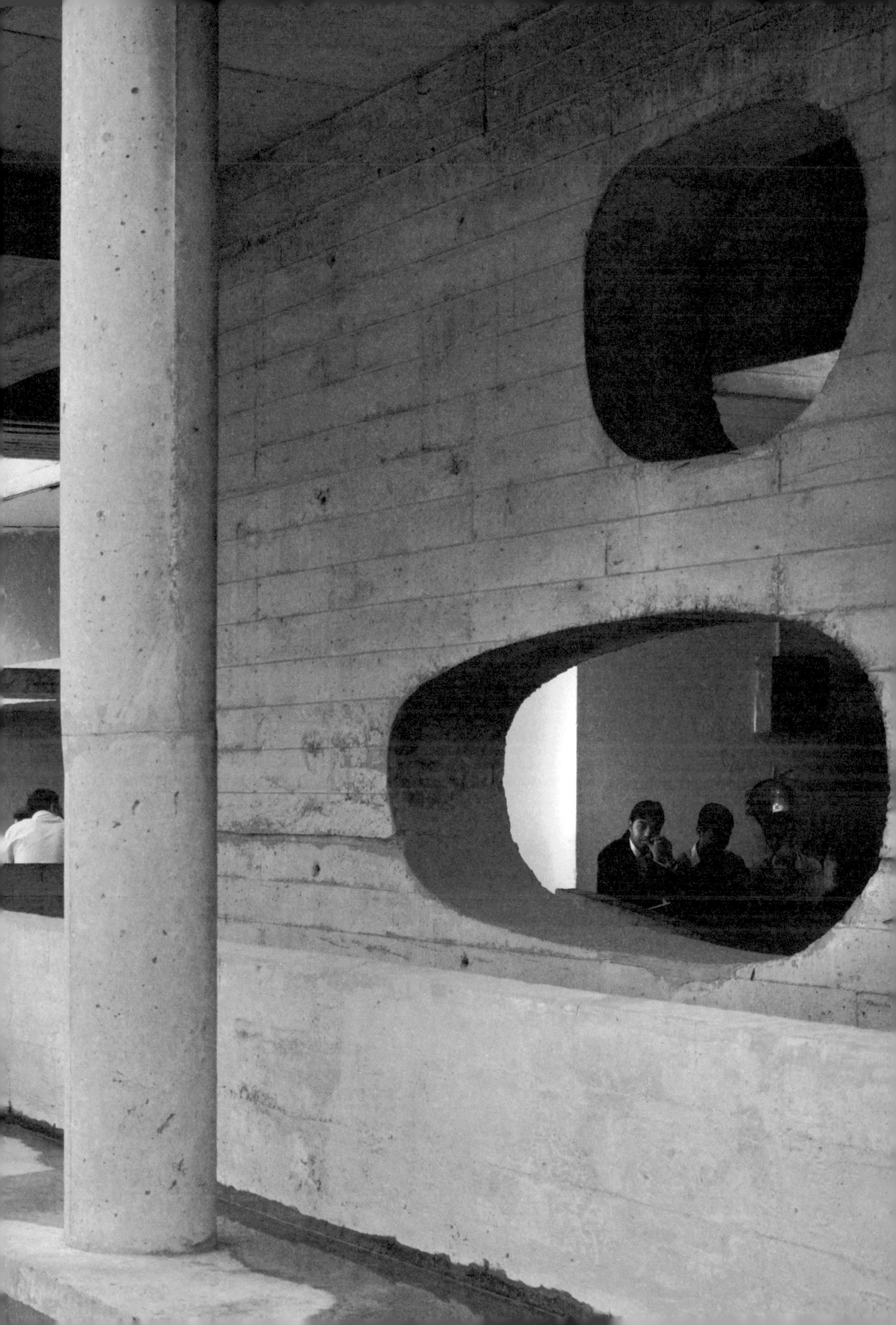

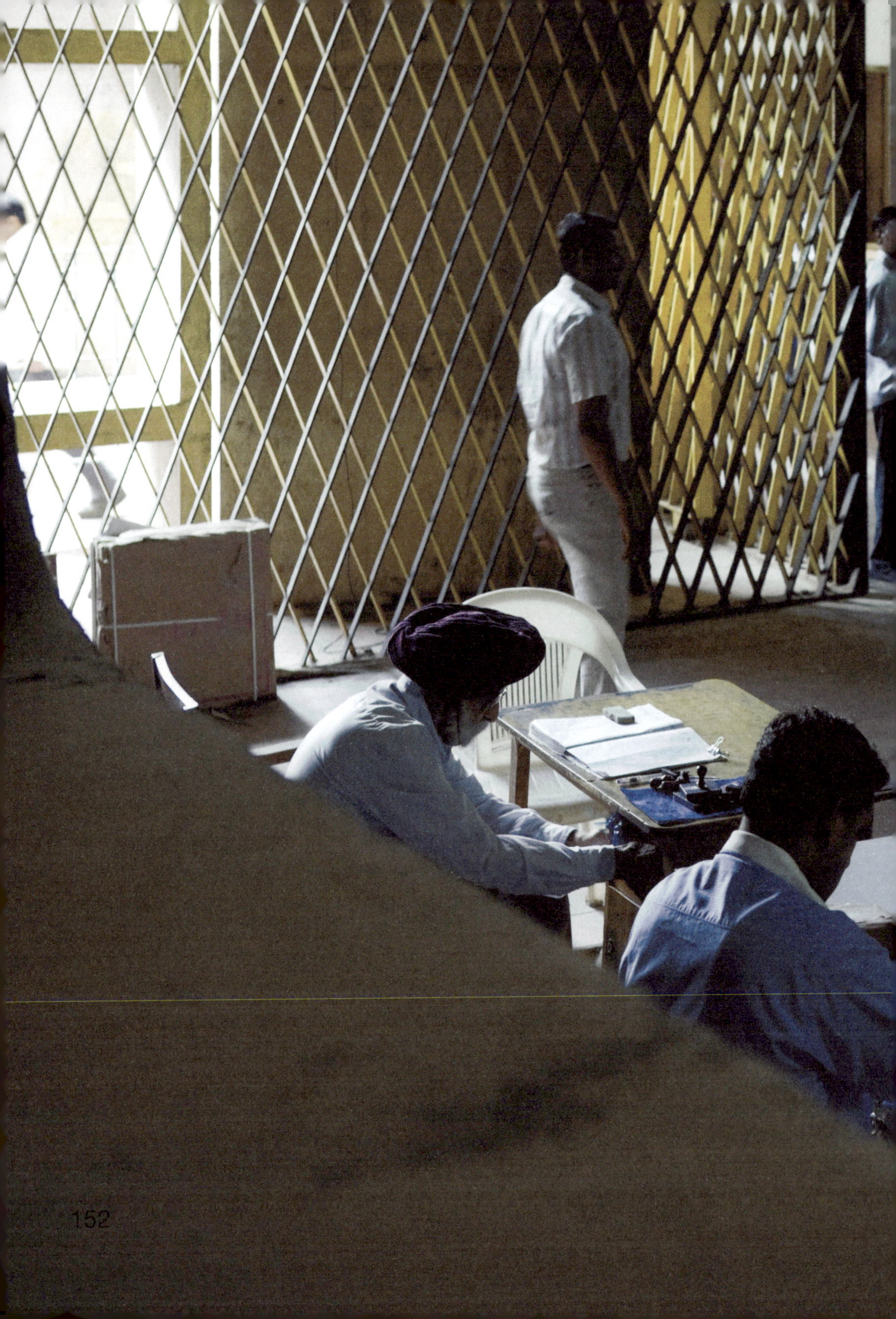

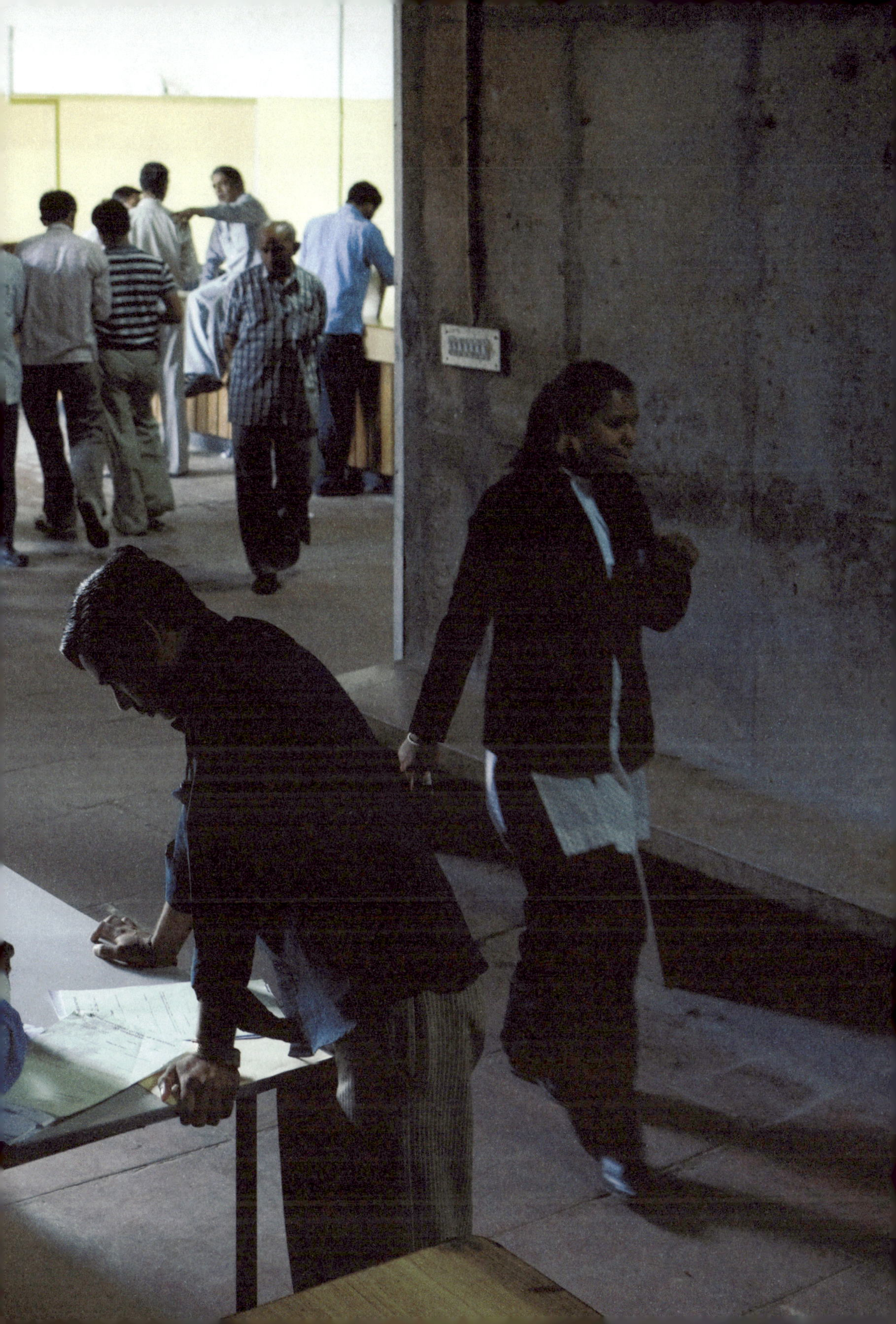

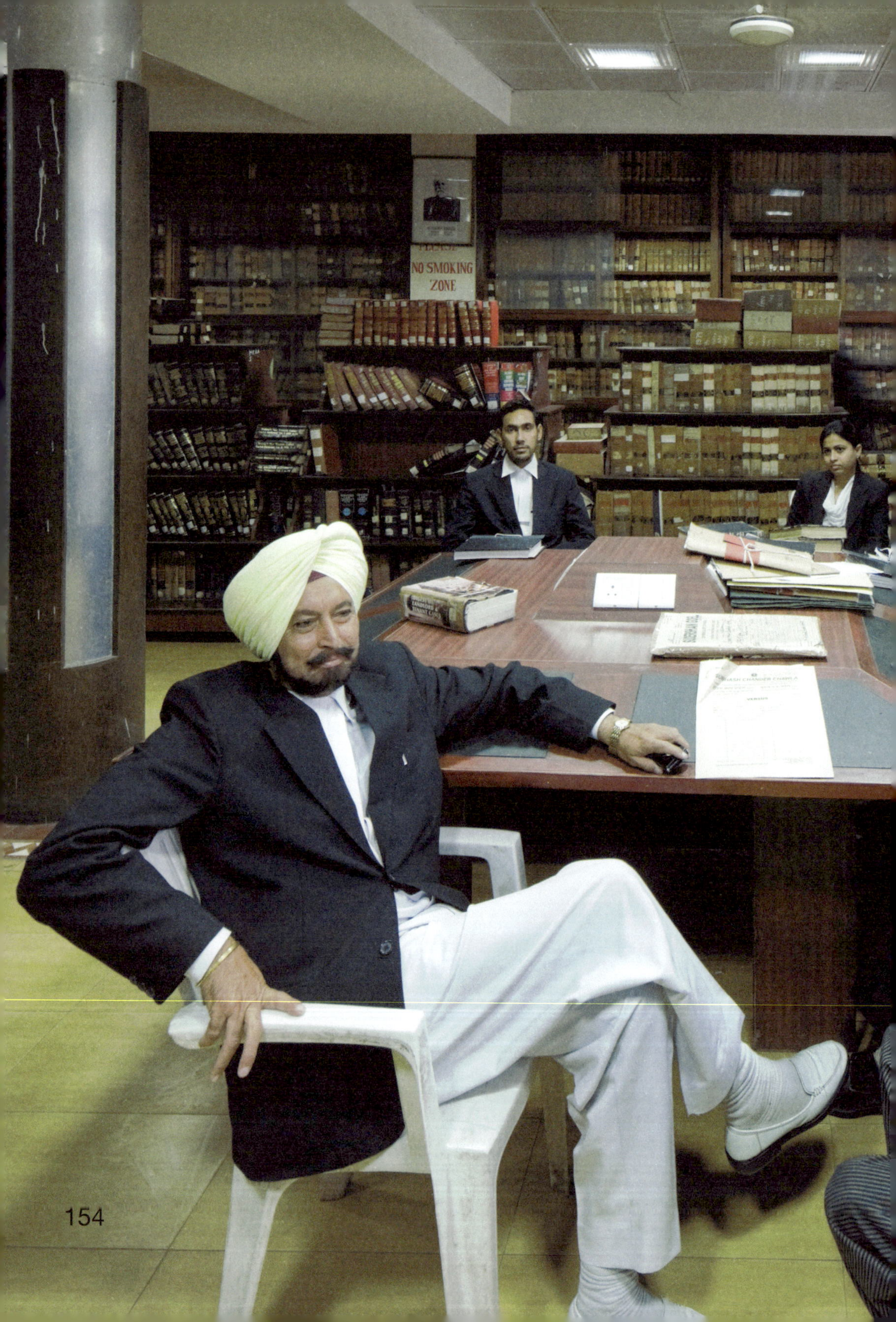
NO SMOKING
ZONE

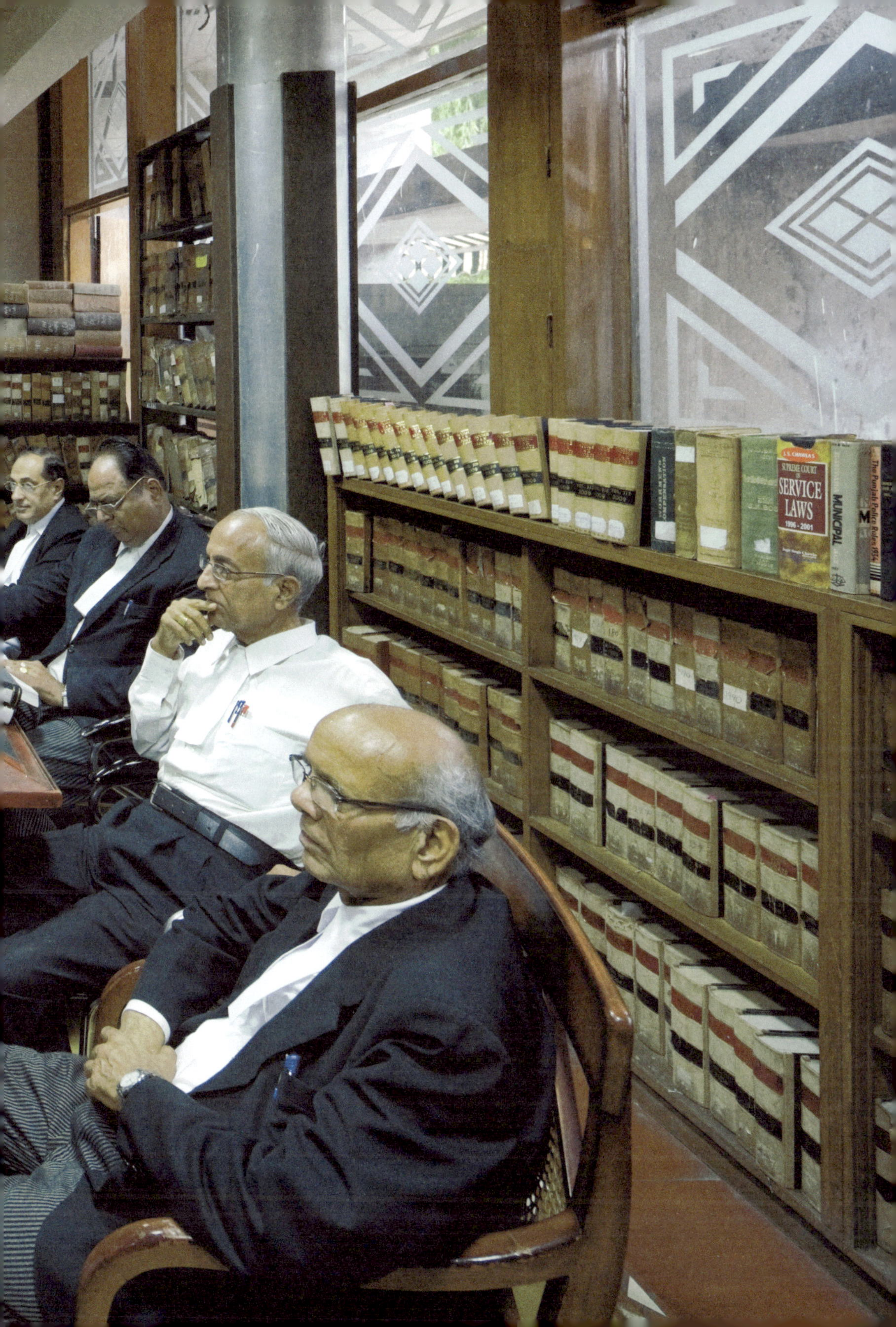
J. S. CHAWLA'S
SUPREME COURT ON SERVICE LAWS
1996 - 2001
MUNICIPAL
The Punjab Police Rules 1934

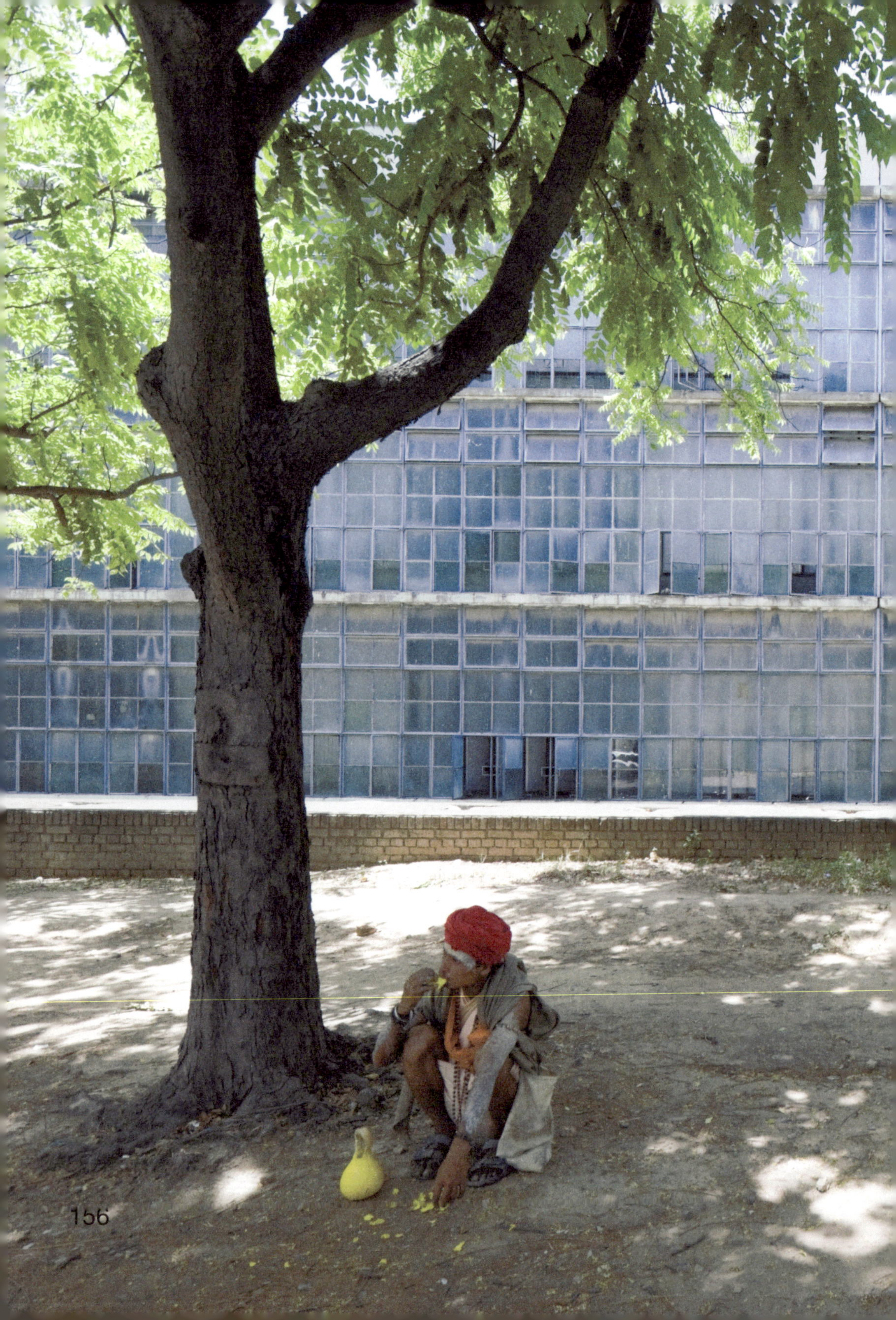

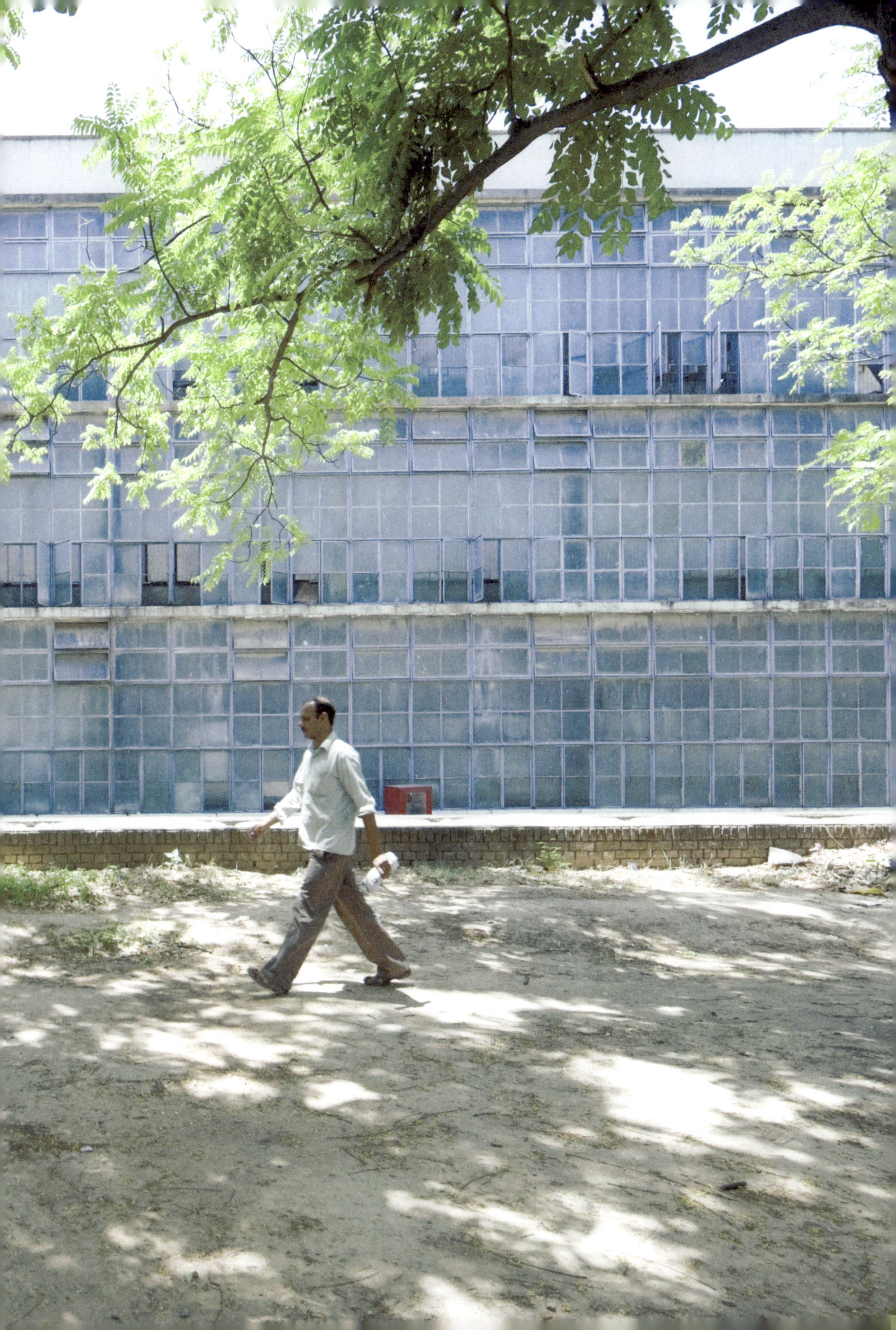

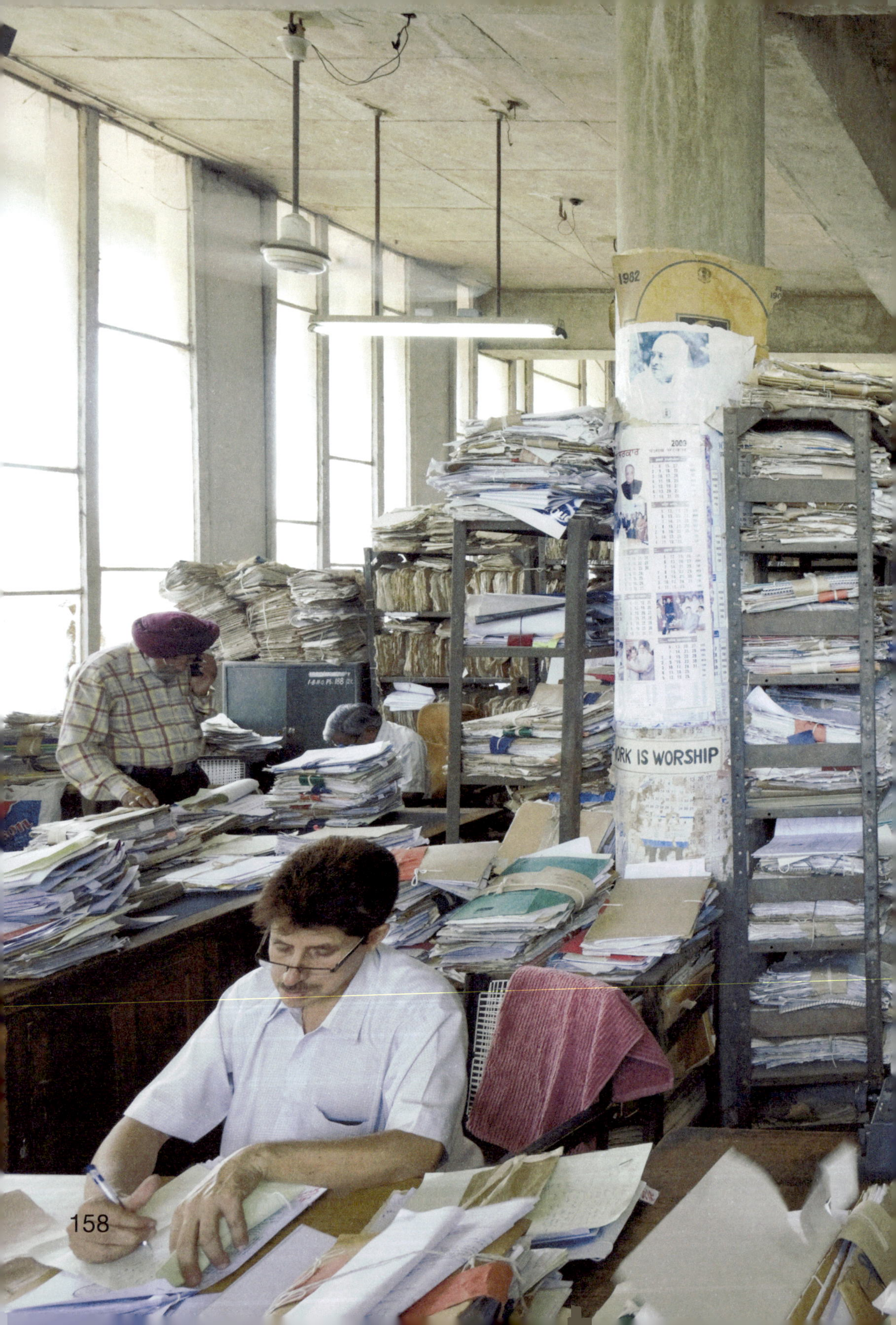
ORK IS WORSHIP

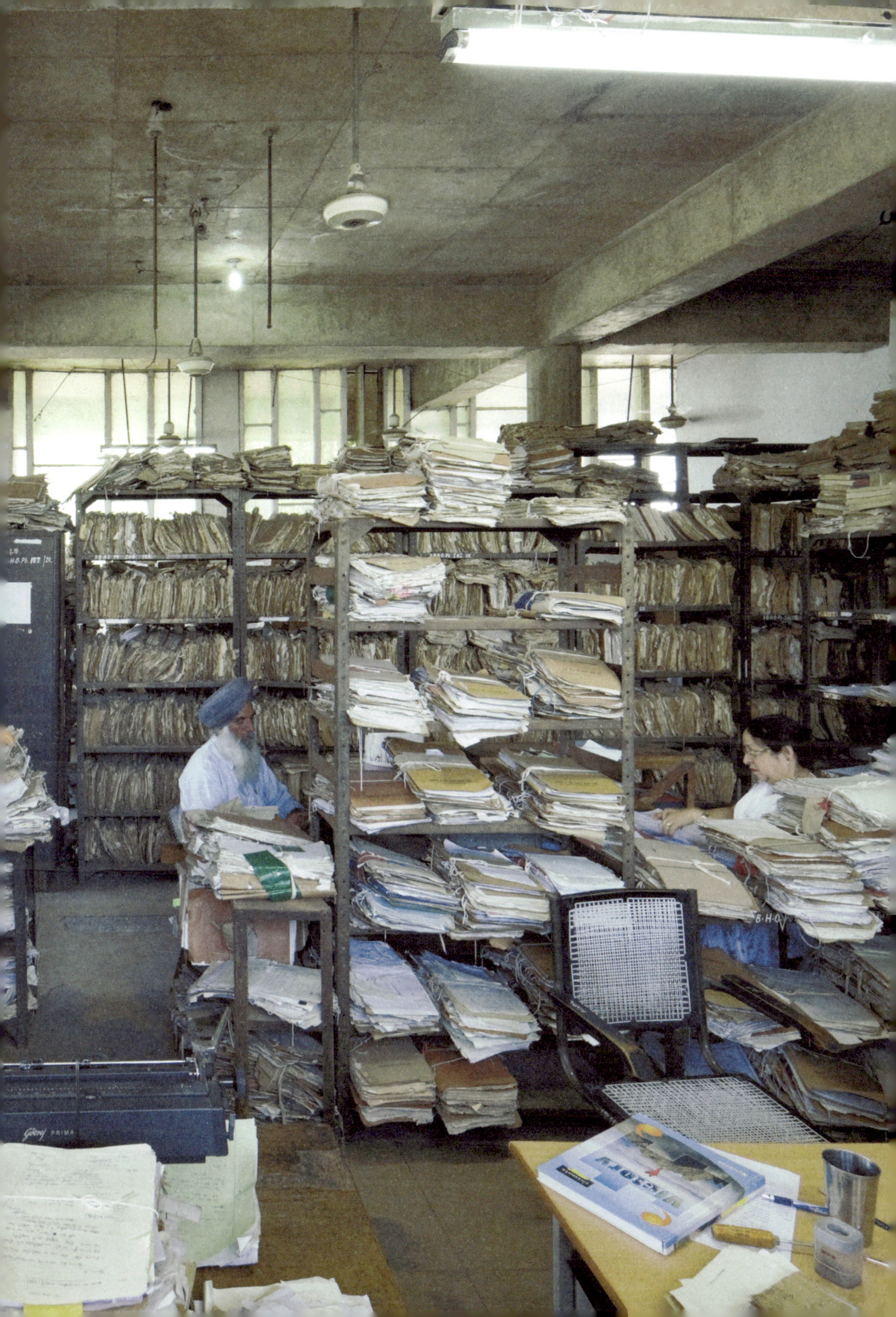
PRIMA

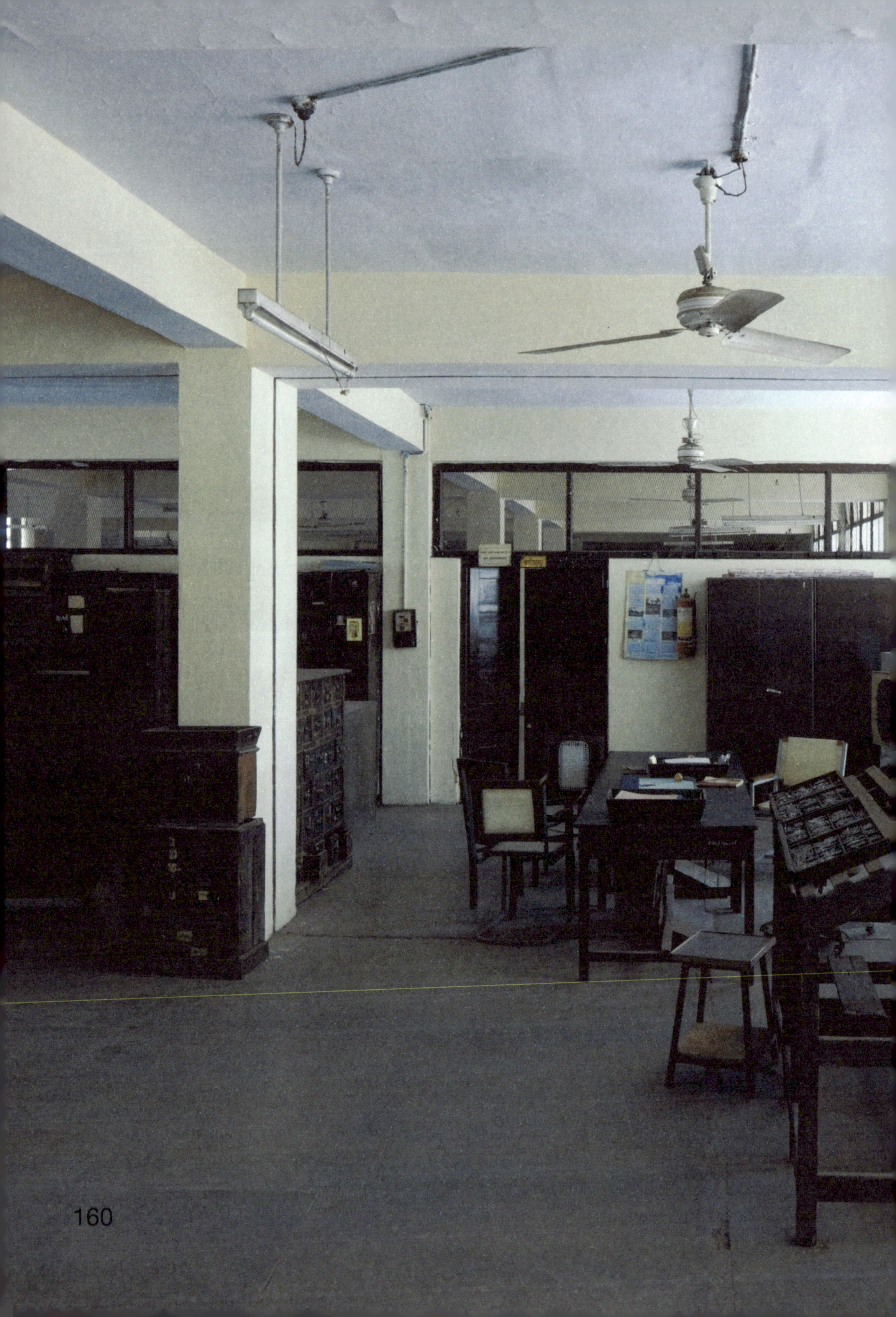

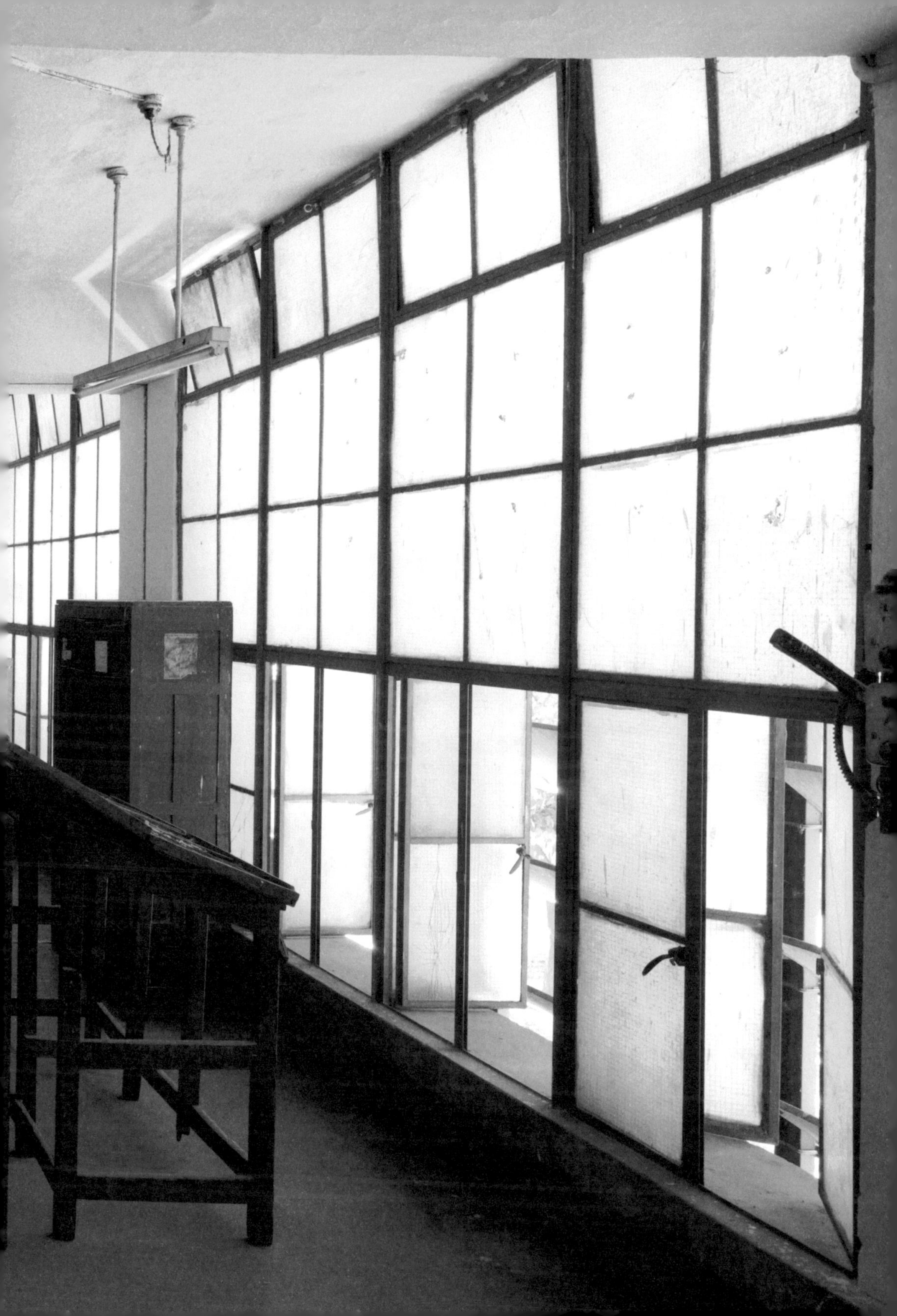

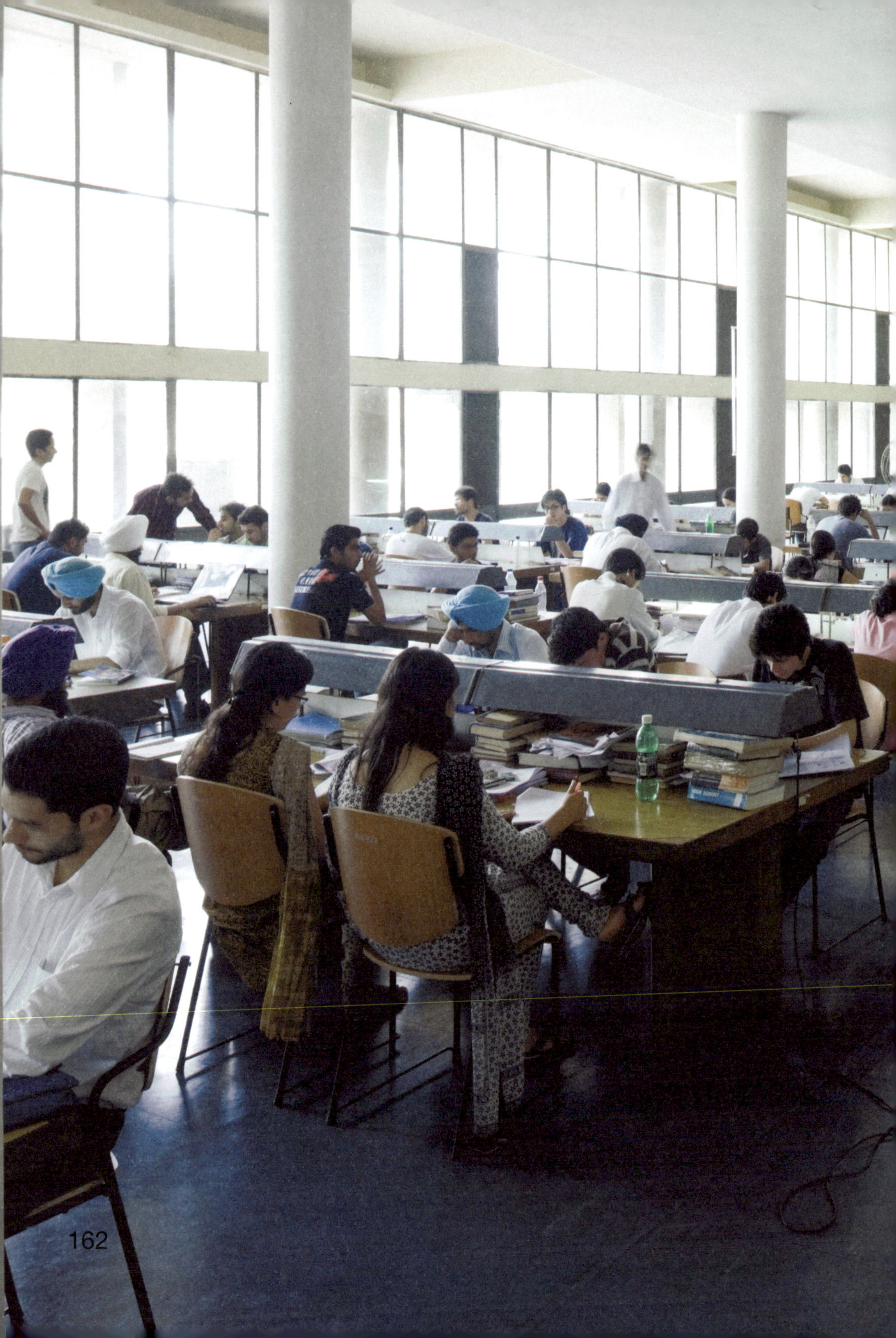

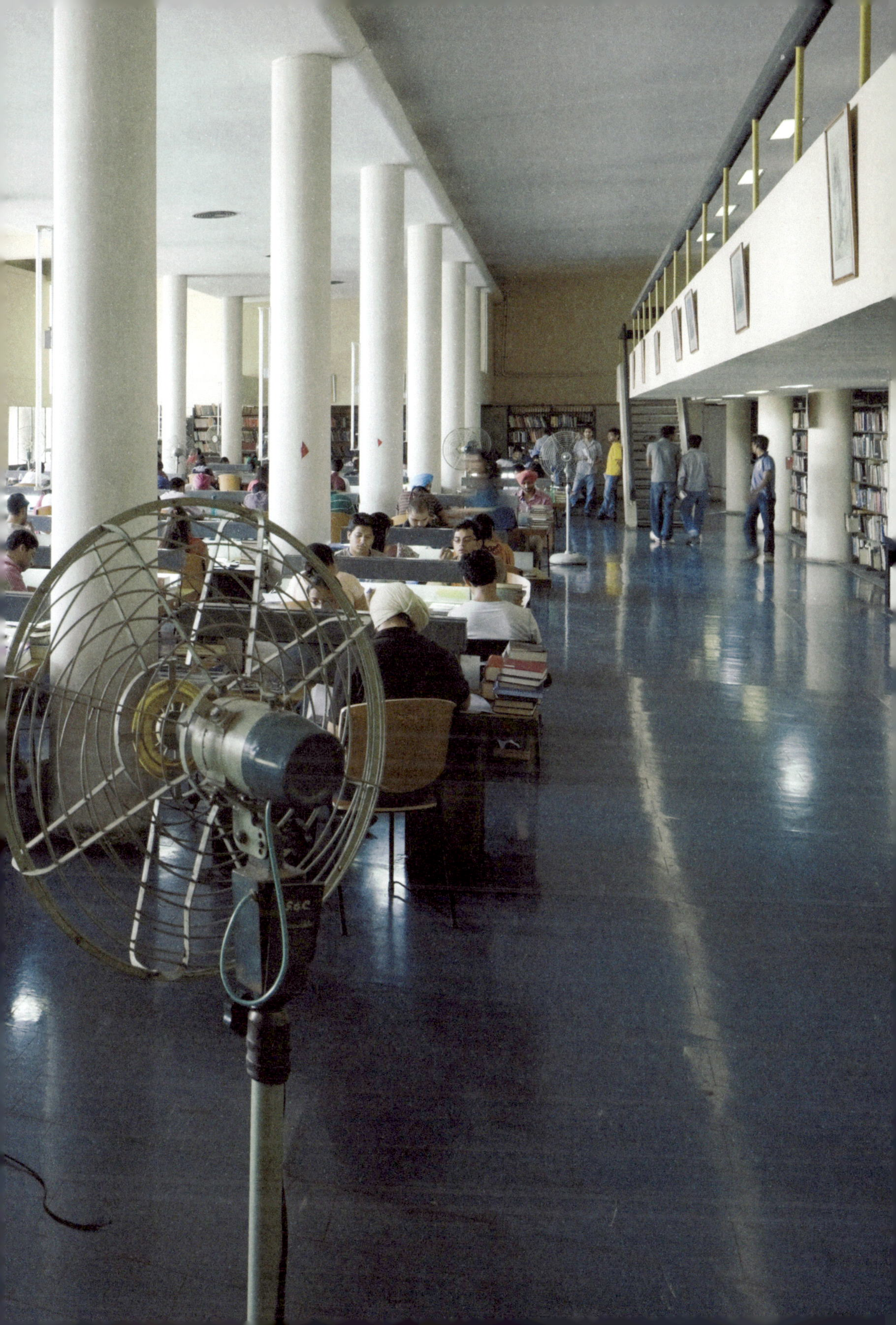

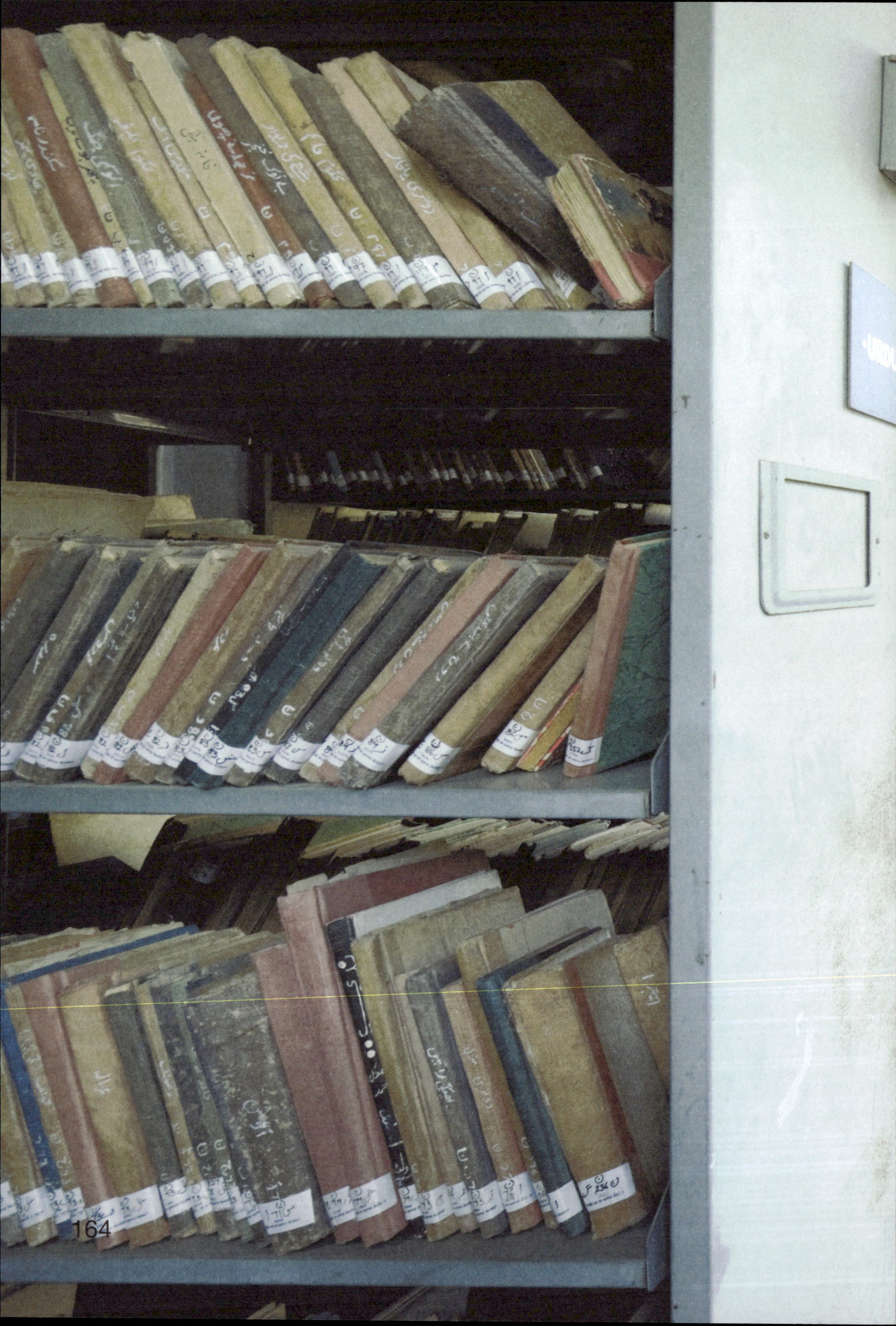
URDU

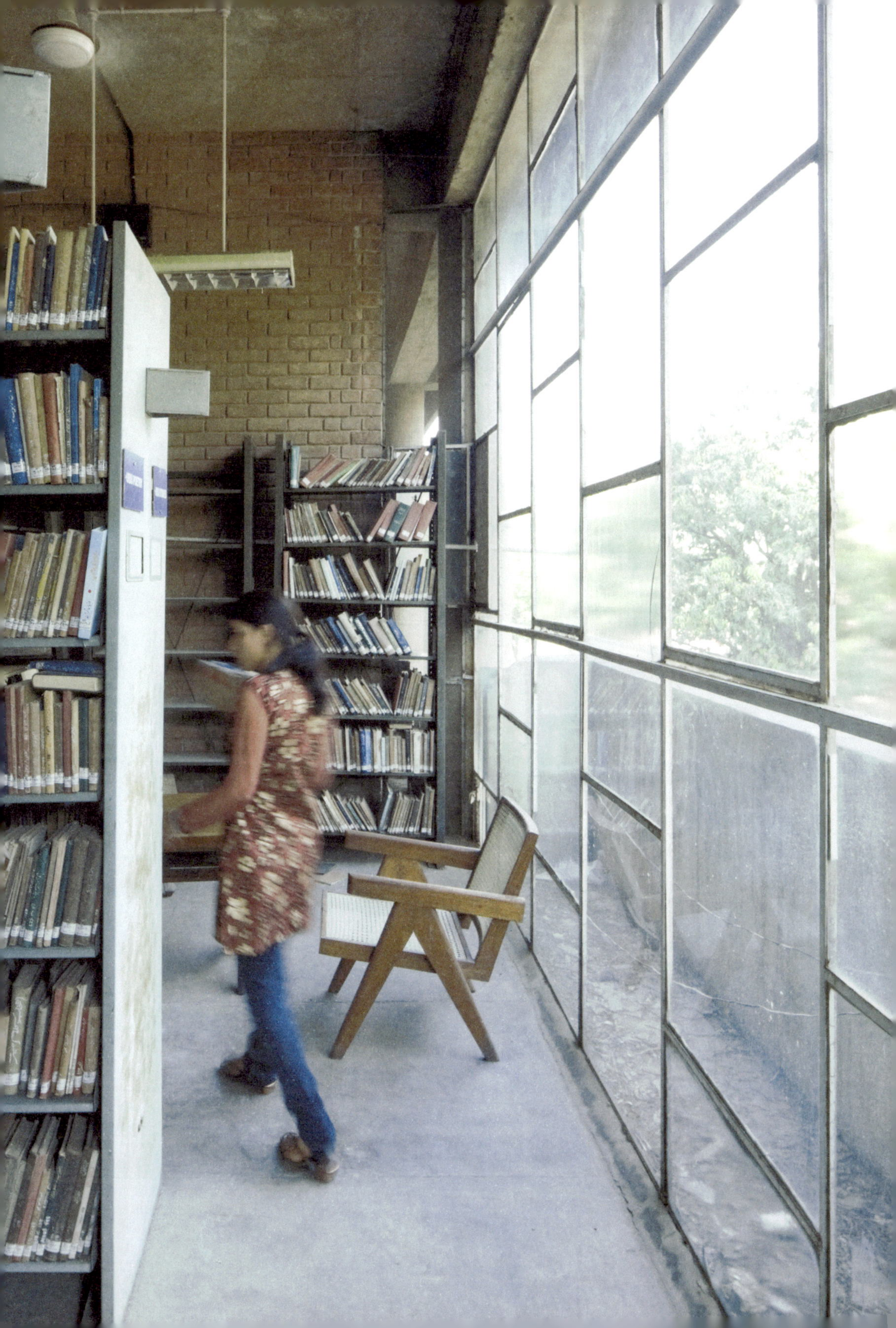

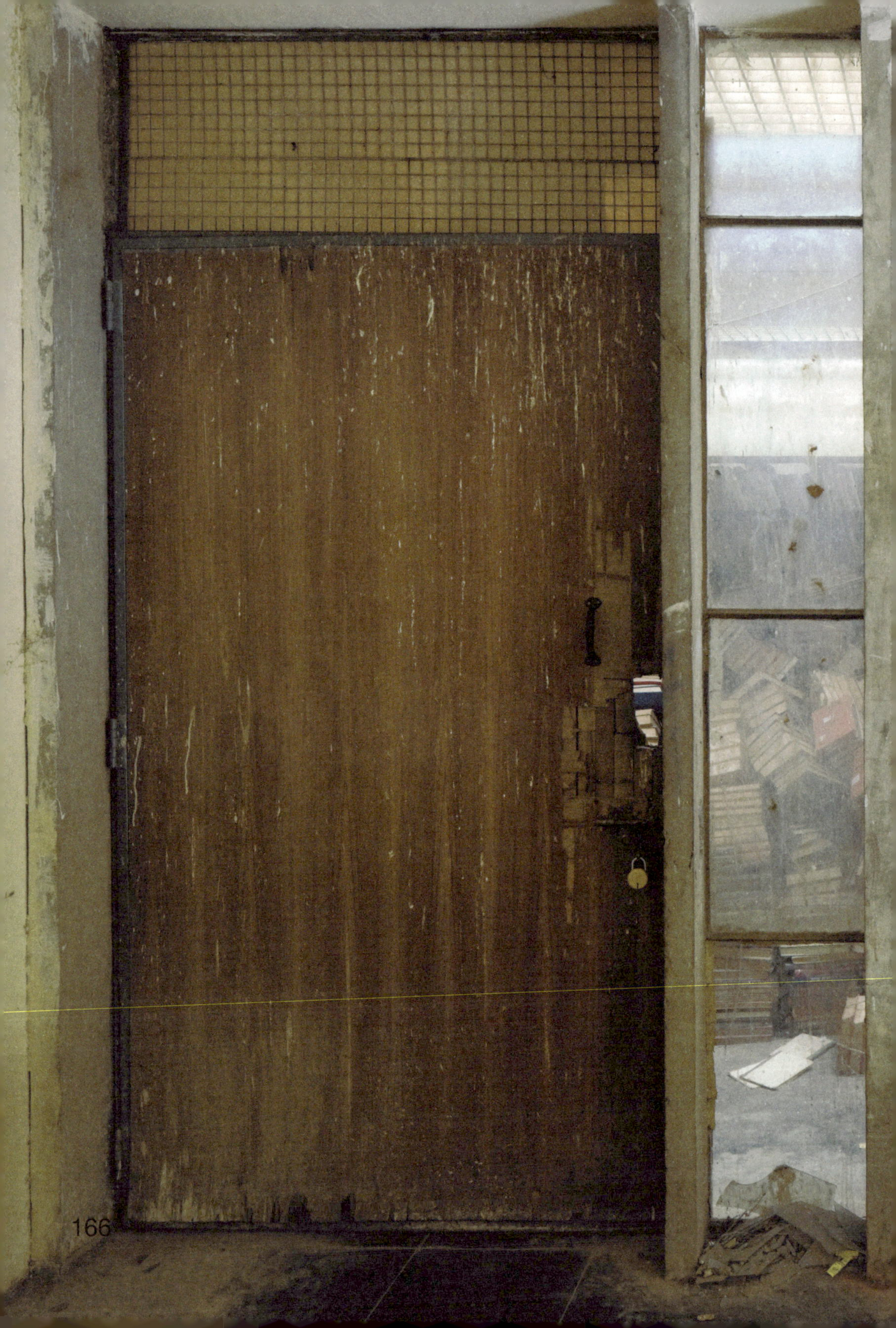

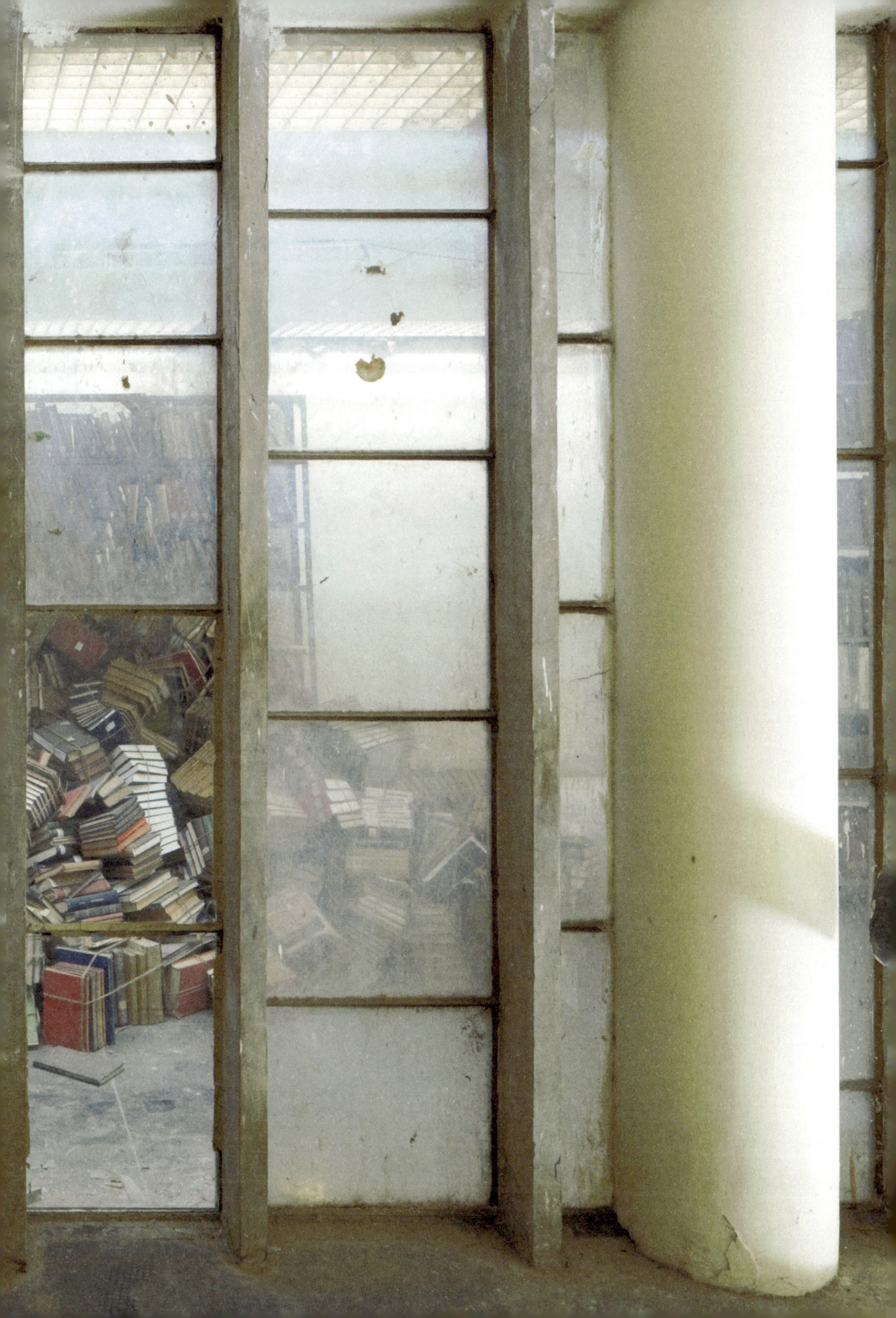

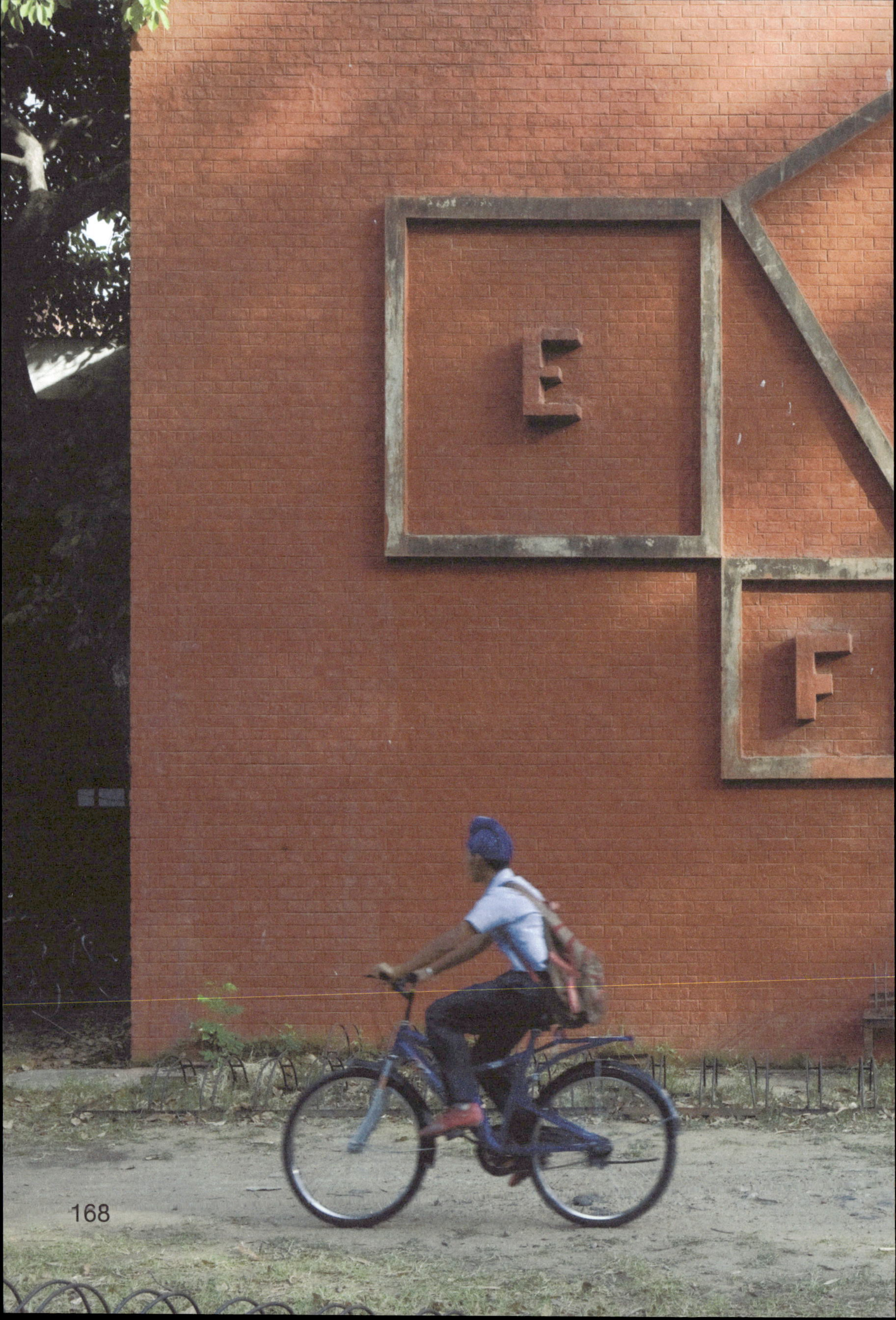
E
F

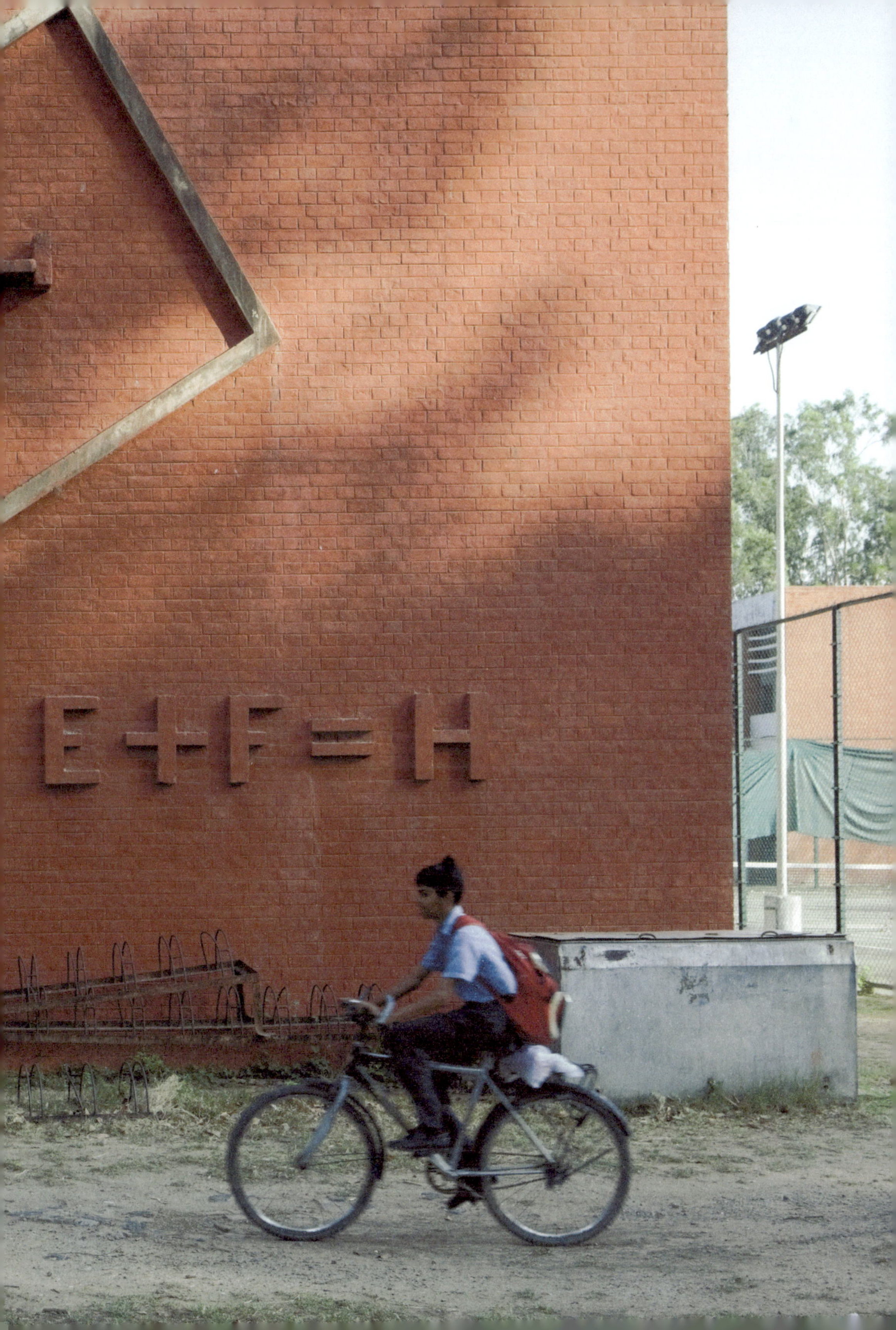
E+F=H

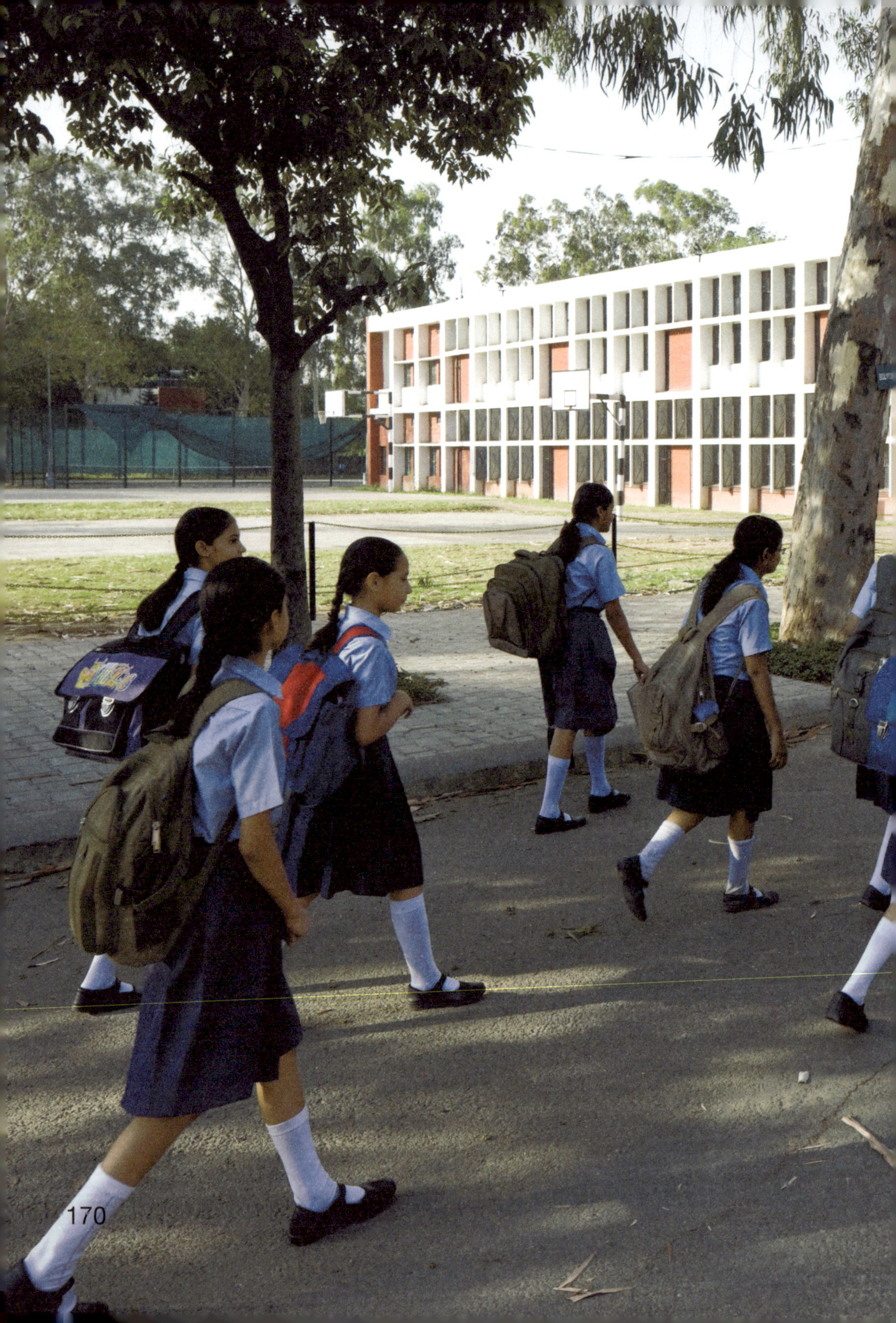

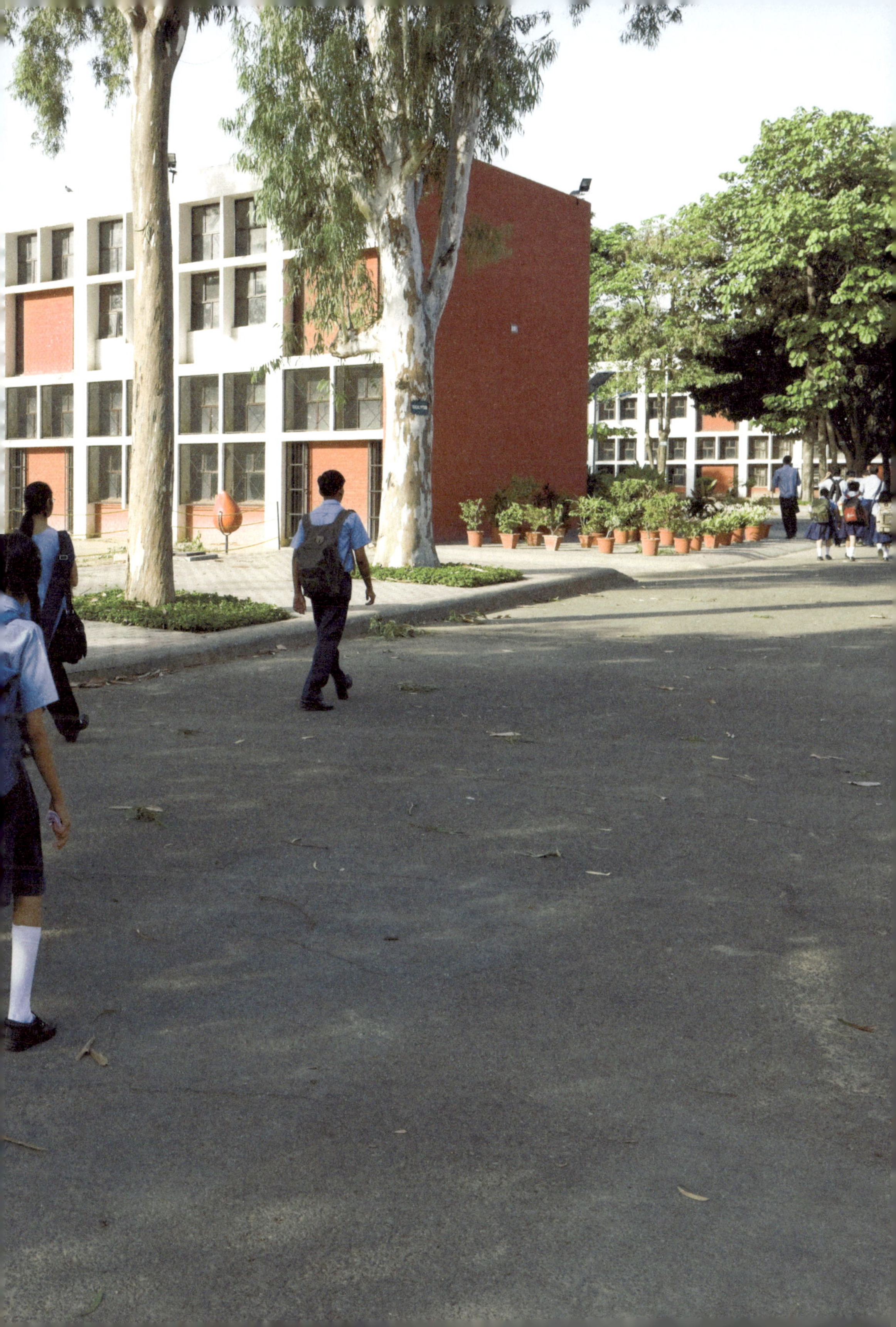

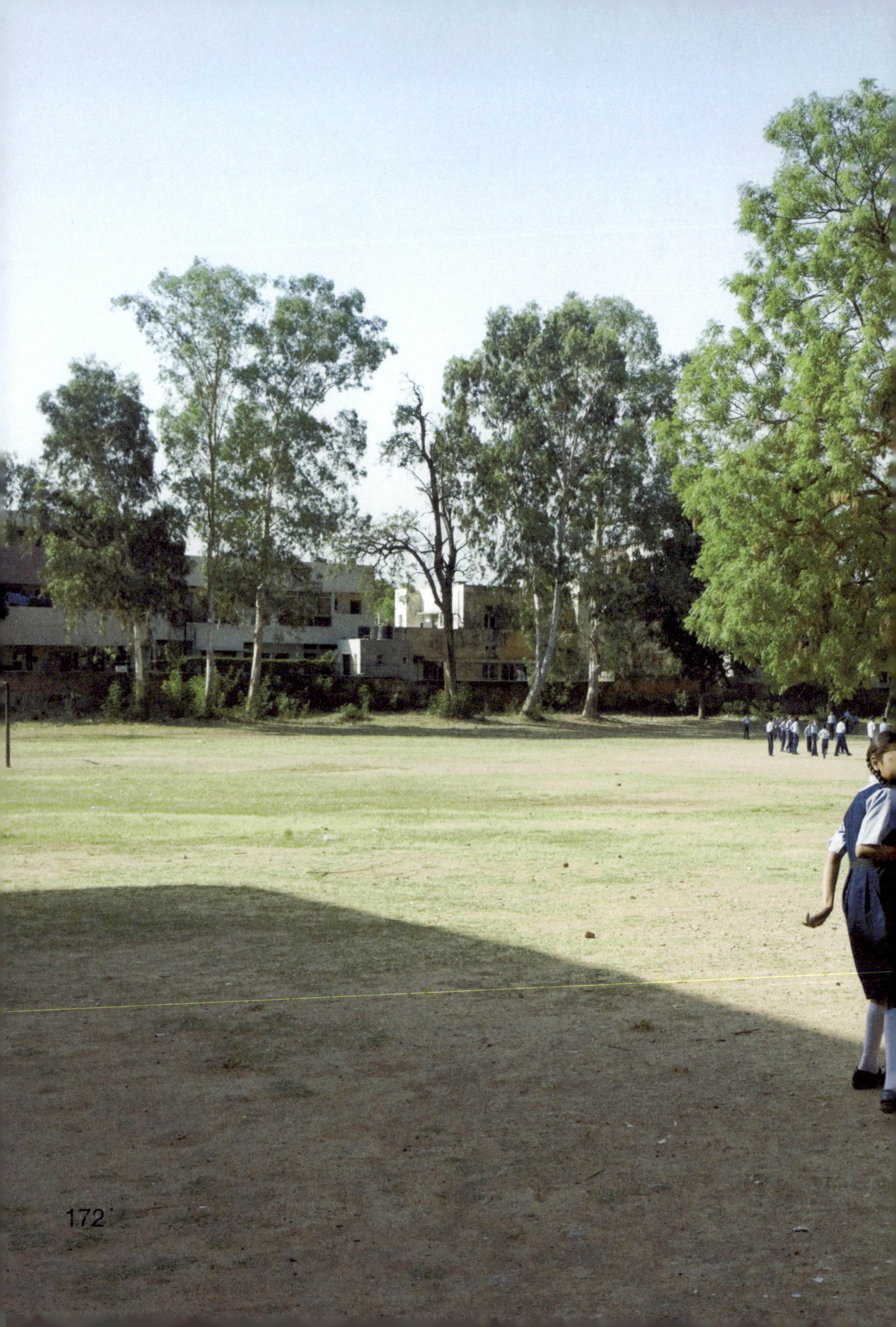

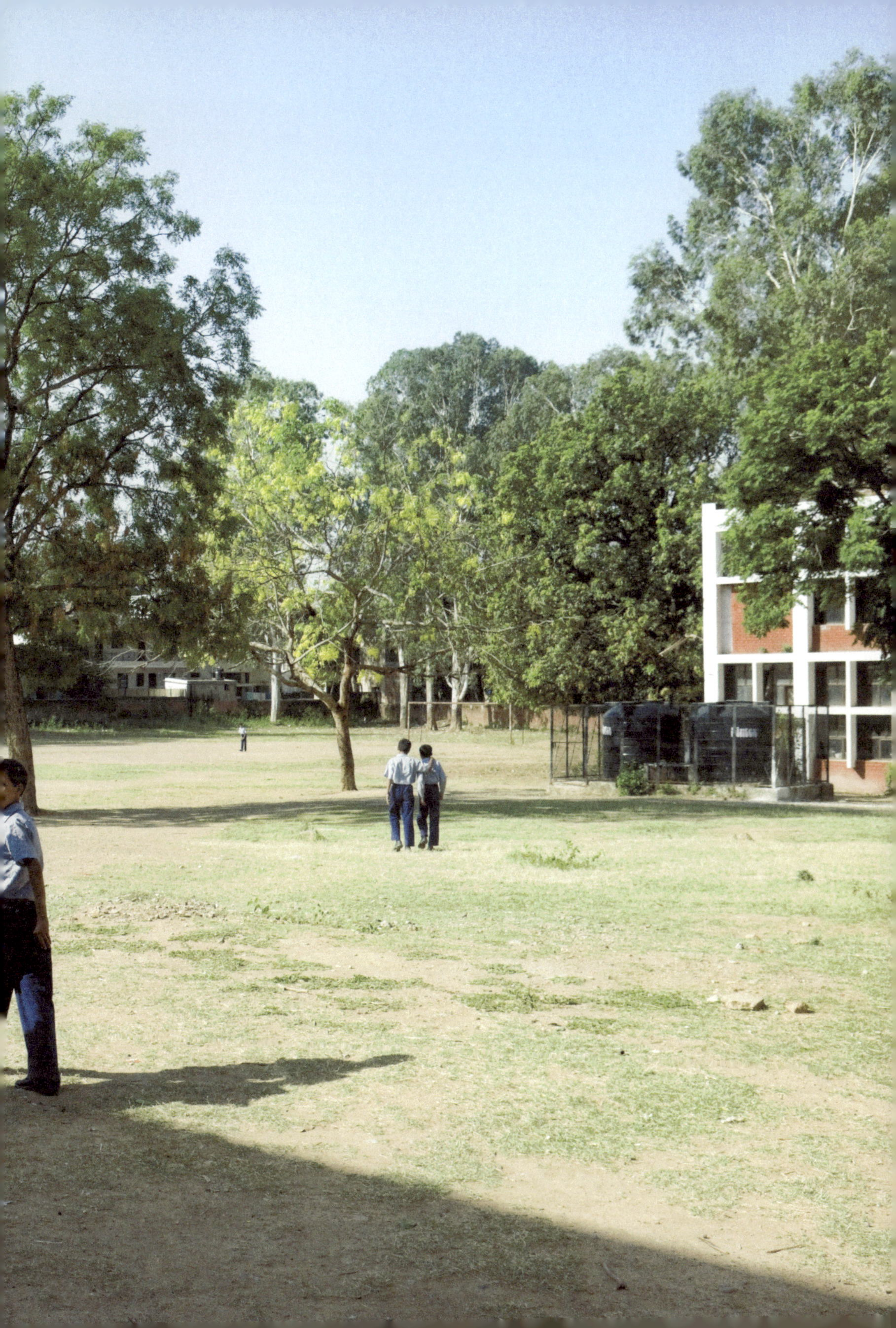

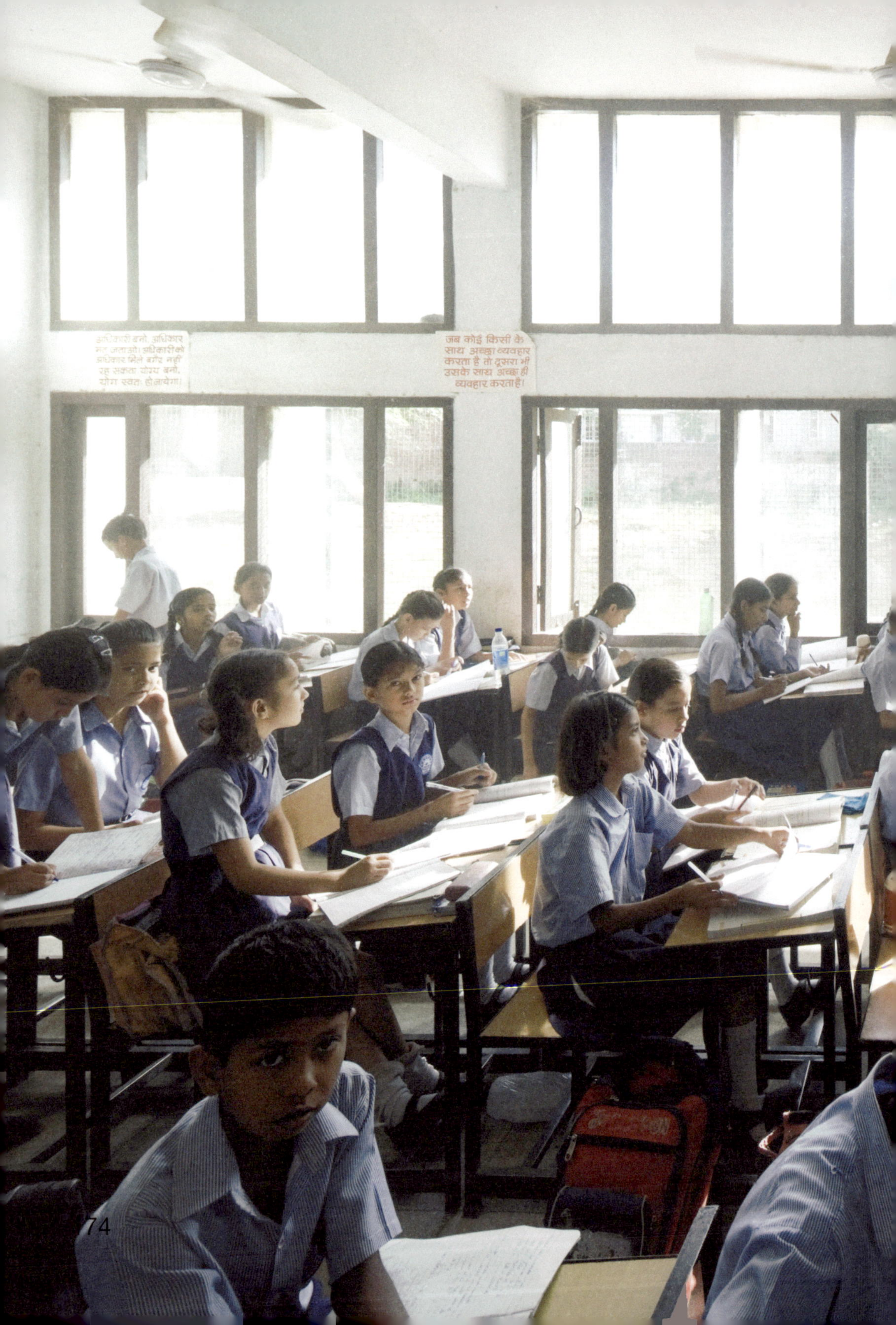
जब कोई किसी के
साथ अच्छा व्यवहार
करता है तो दूसरा भी
उसके साथ अच्छा ही
व्यवहार करता है।

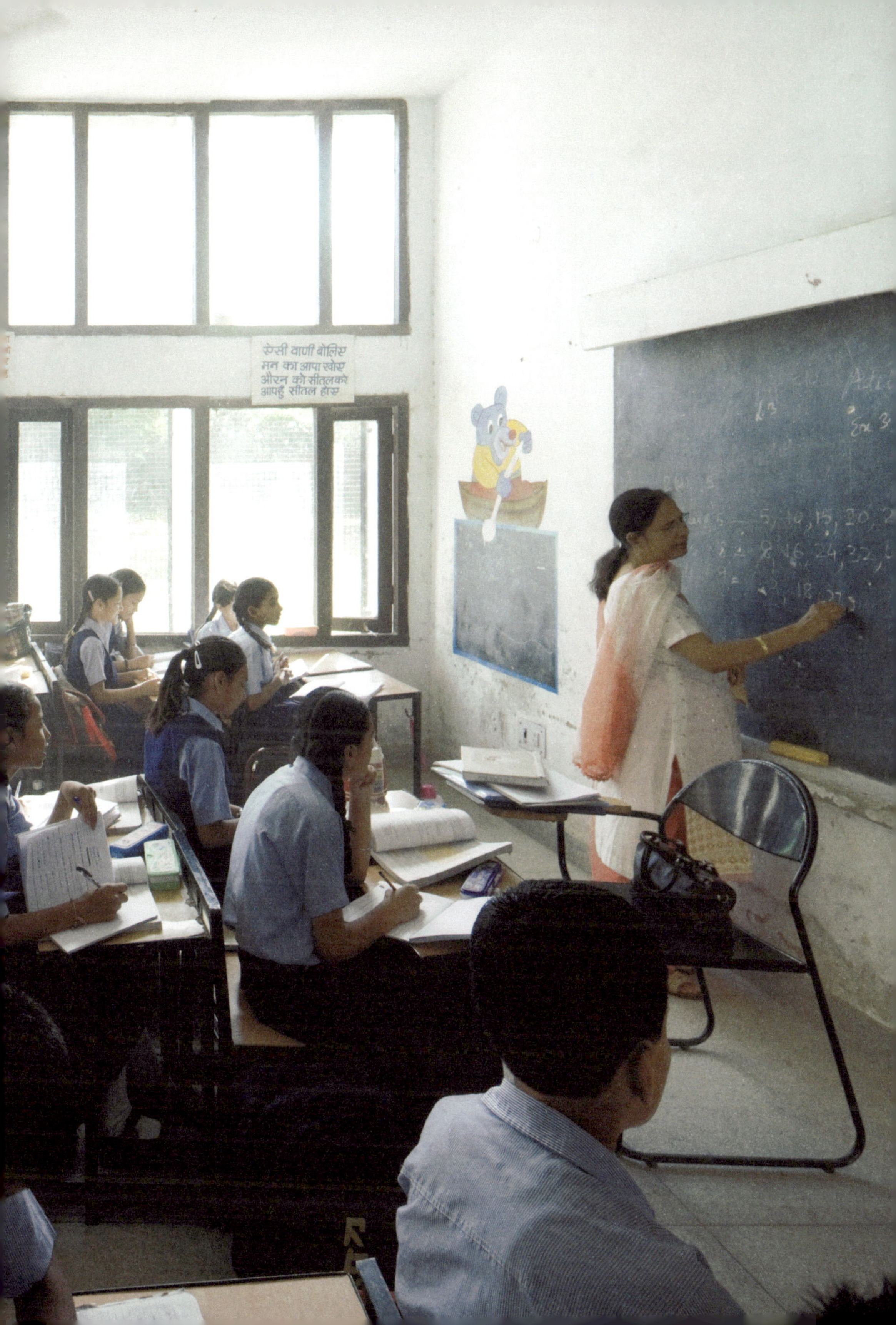
ऐसी वाणी बोलिए
मन का आपा खोए
औरन को सीतल करे
आपहुँ सीतल होए

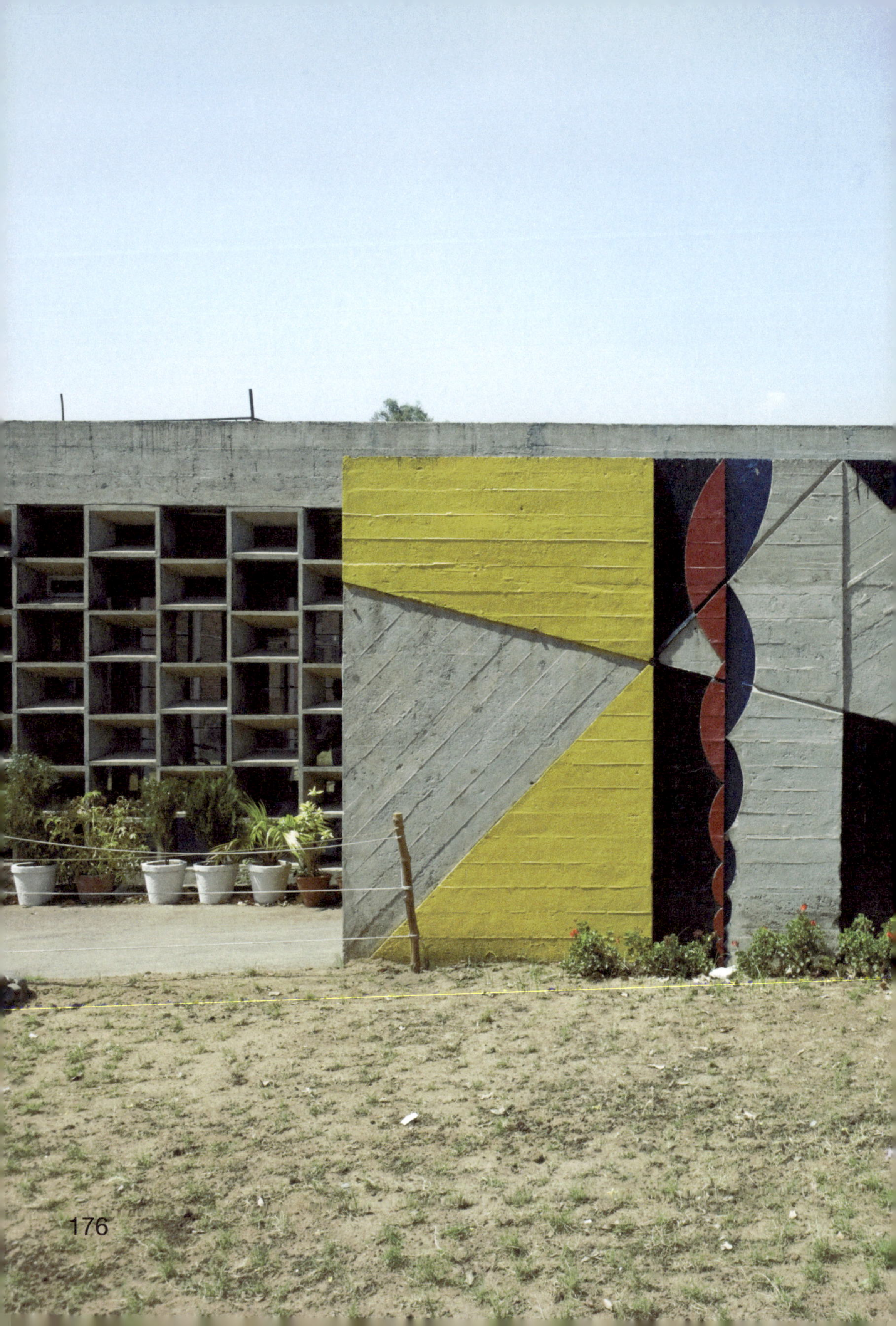

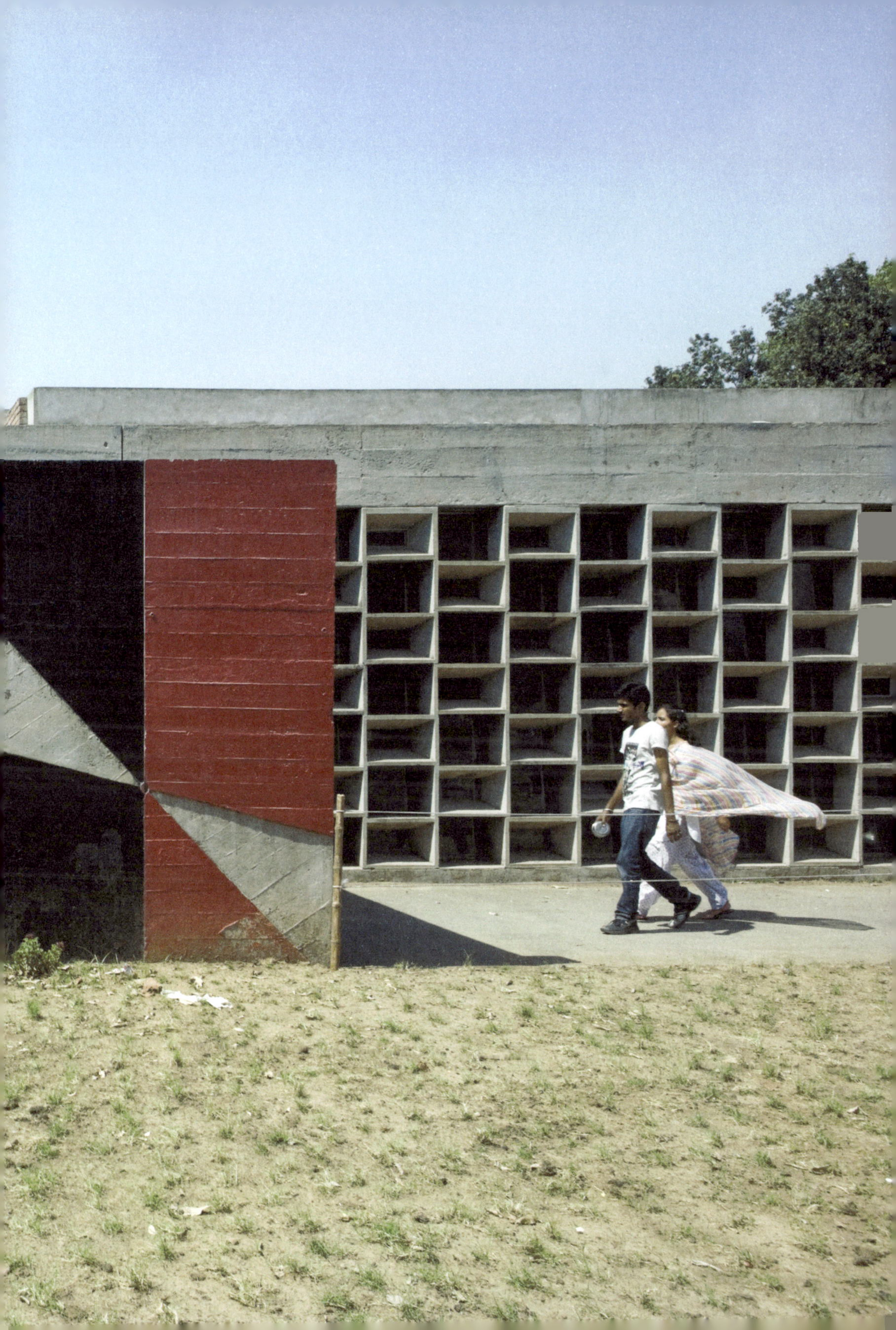

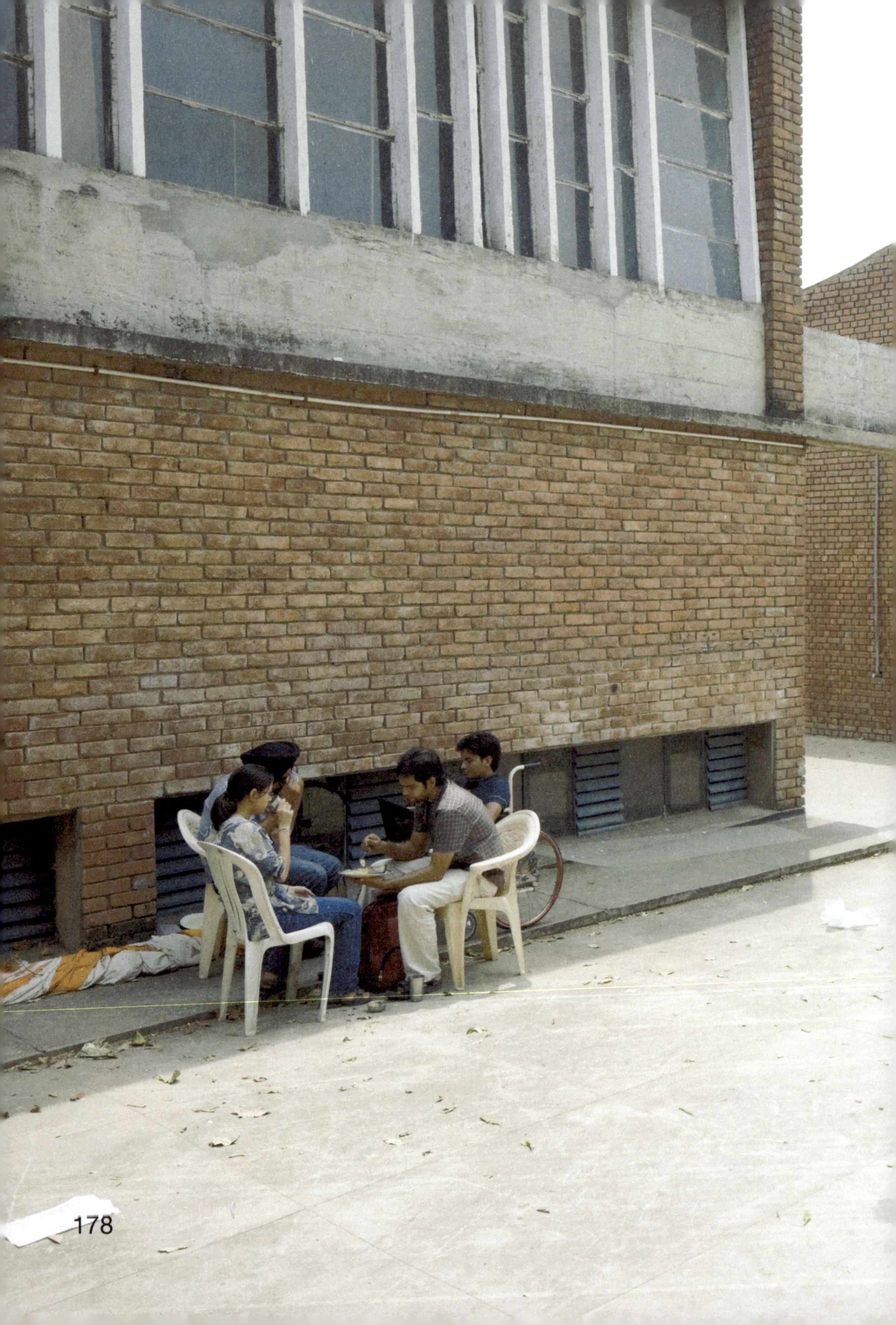

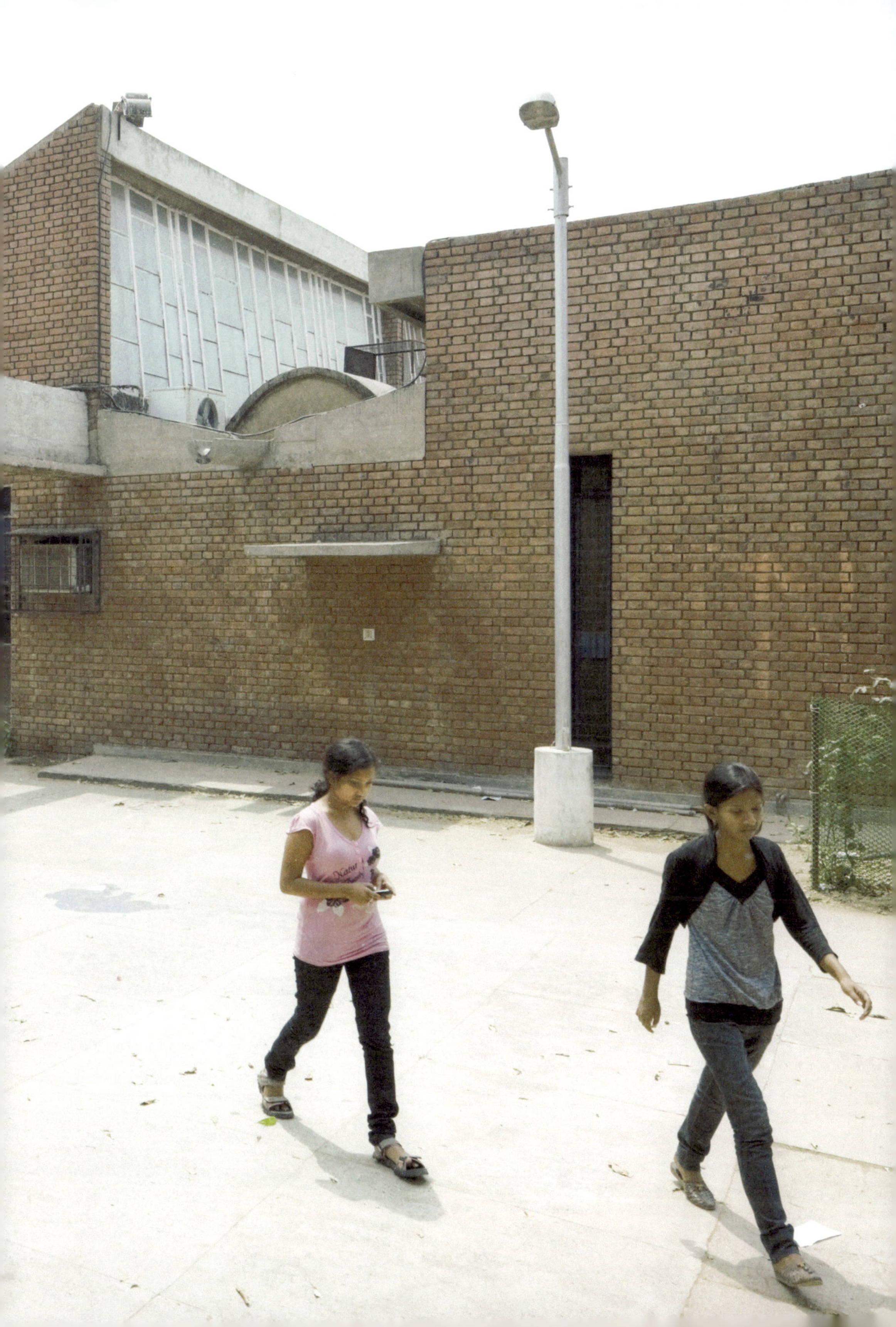

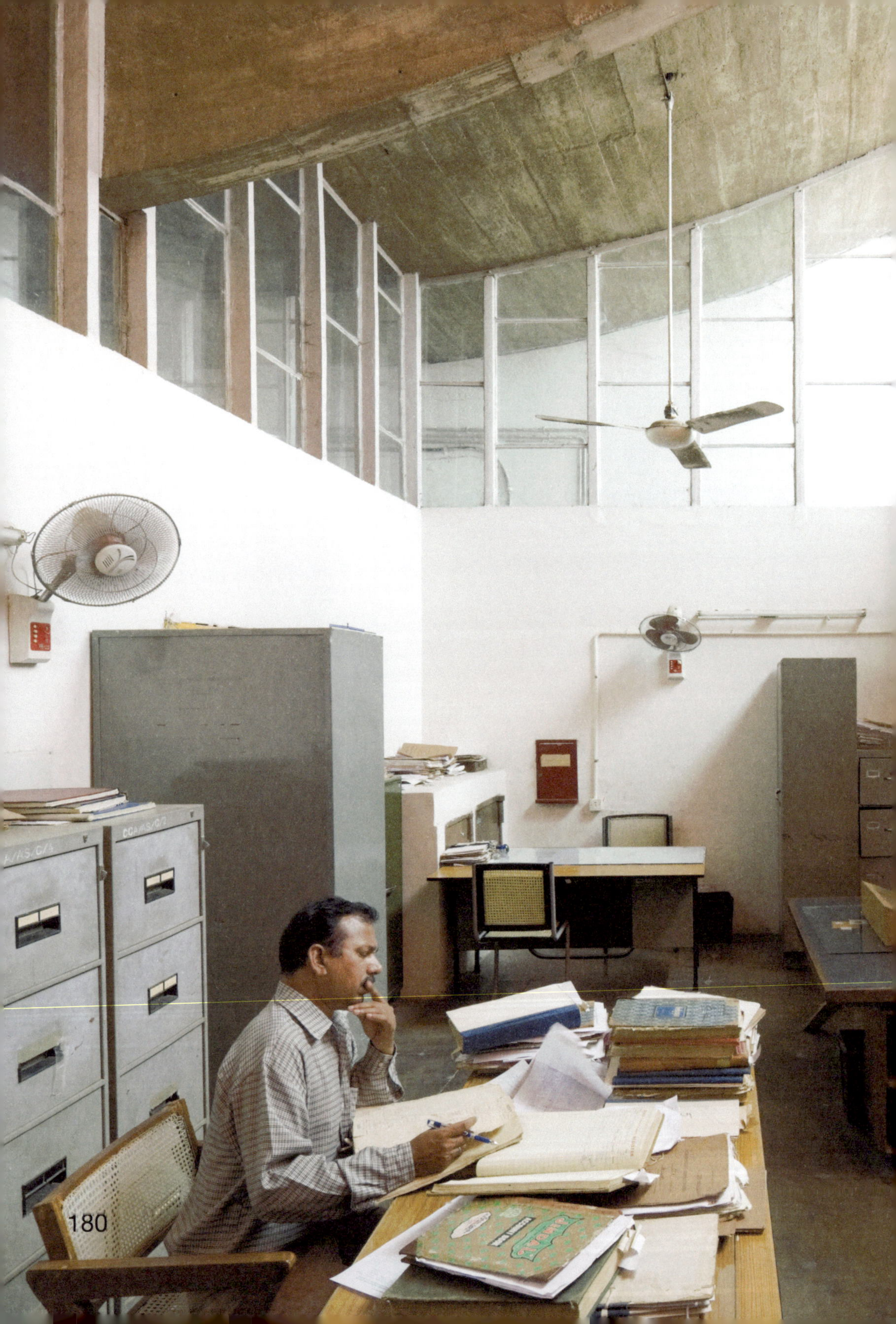

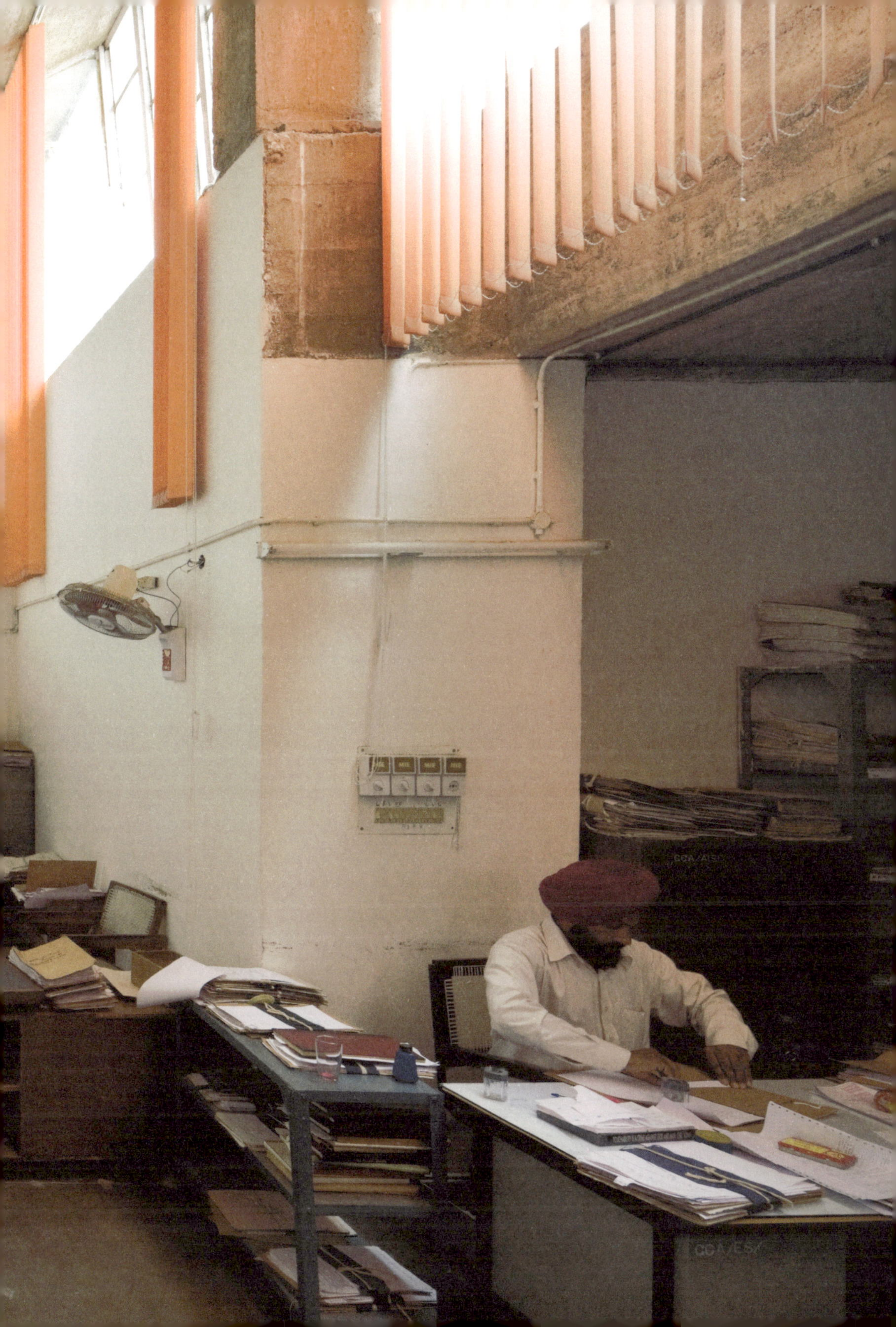

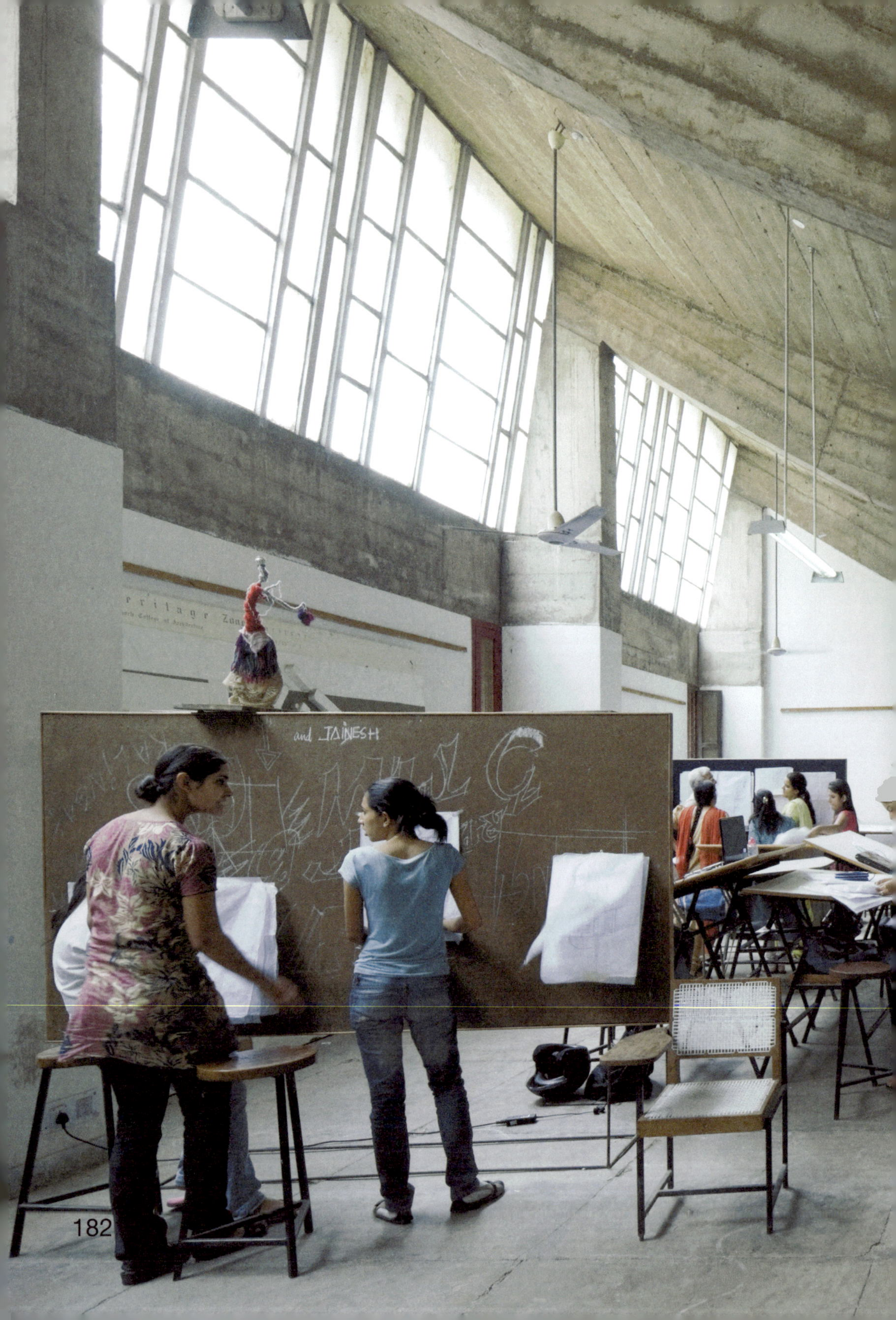

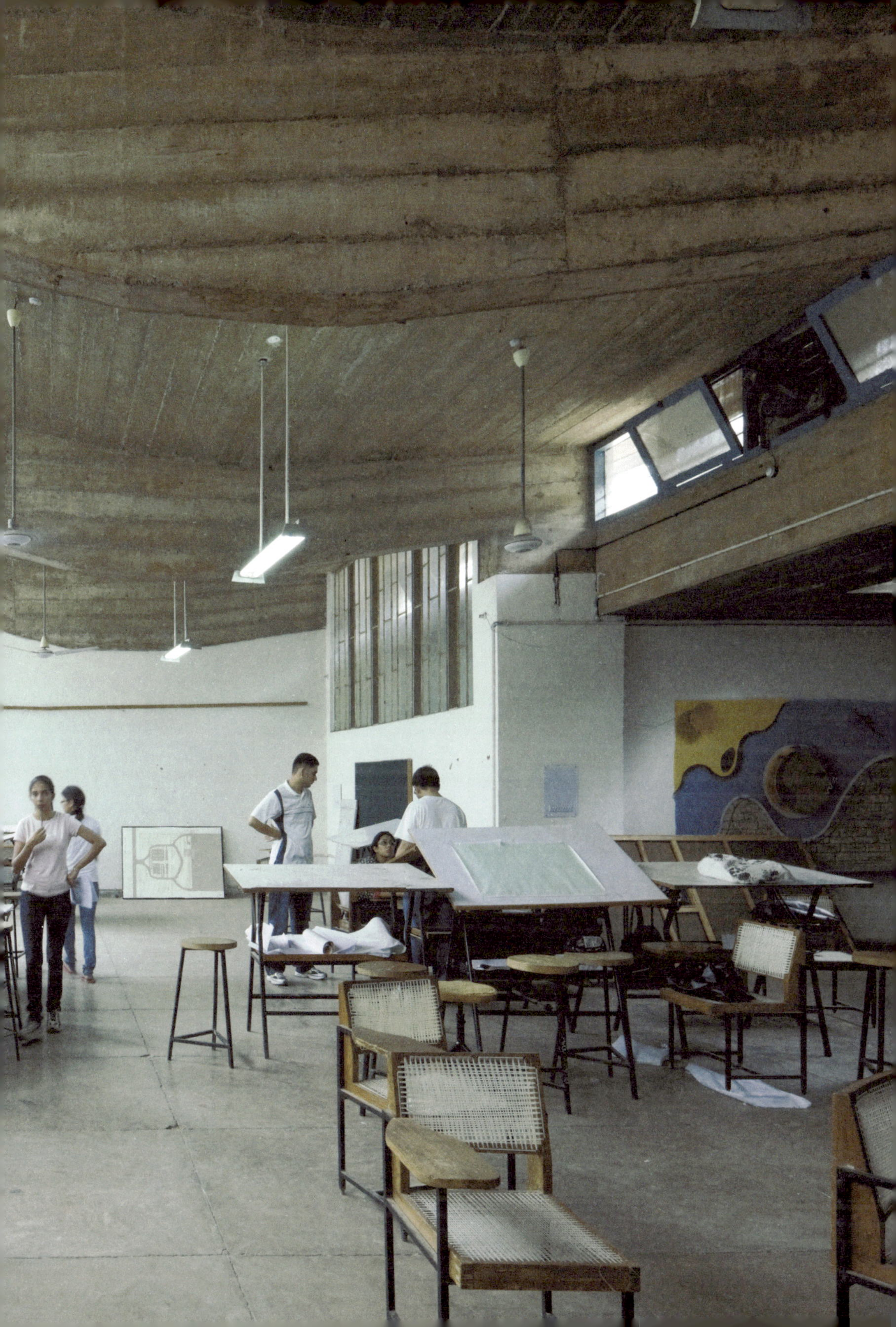

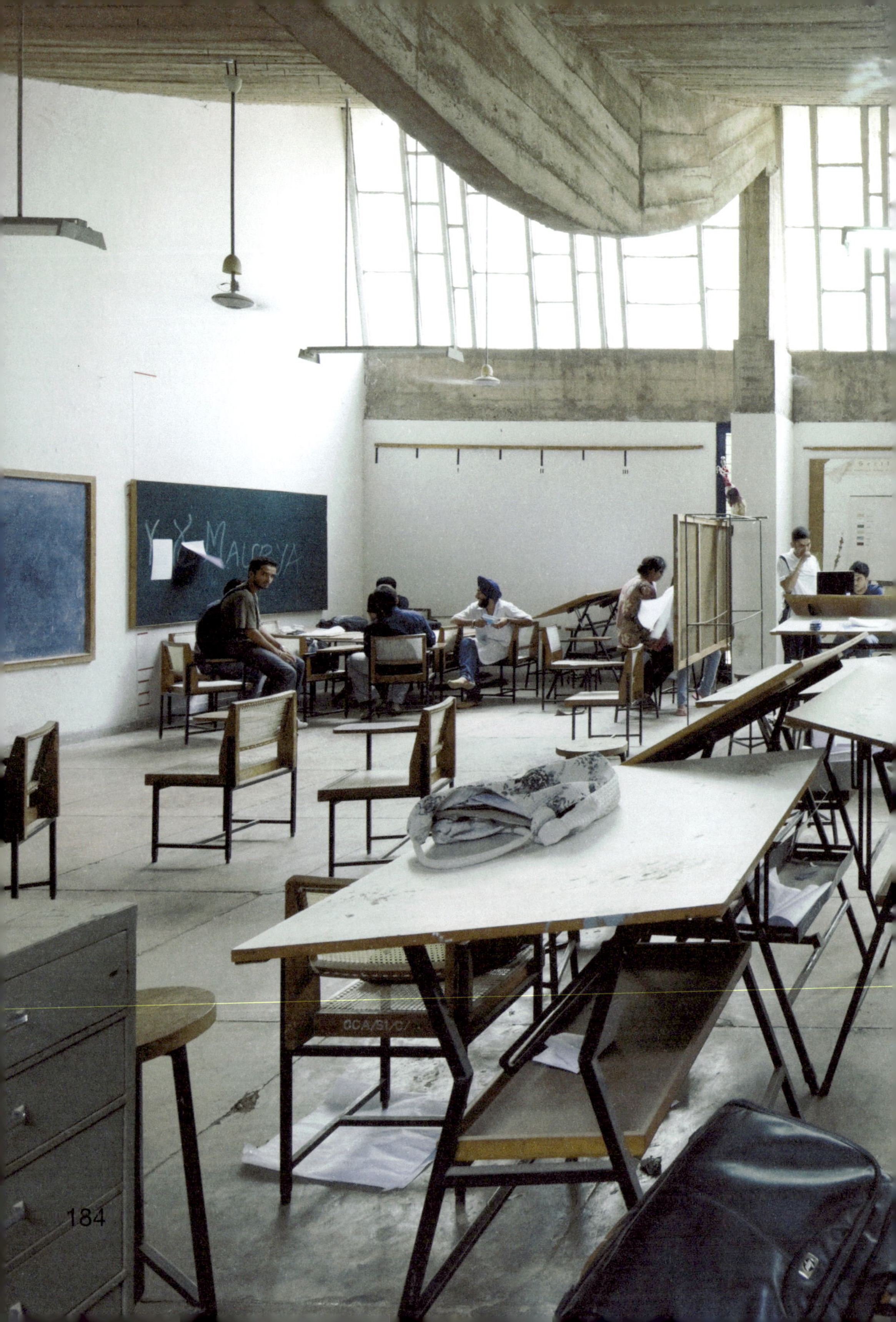

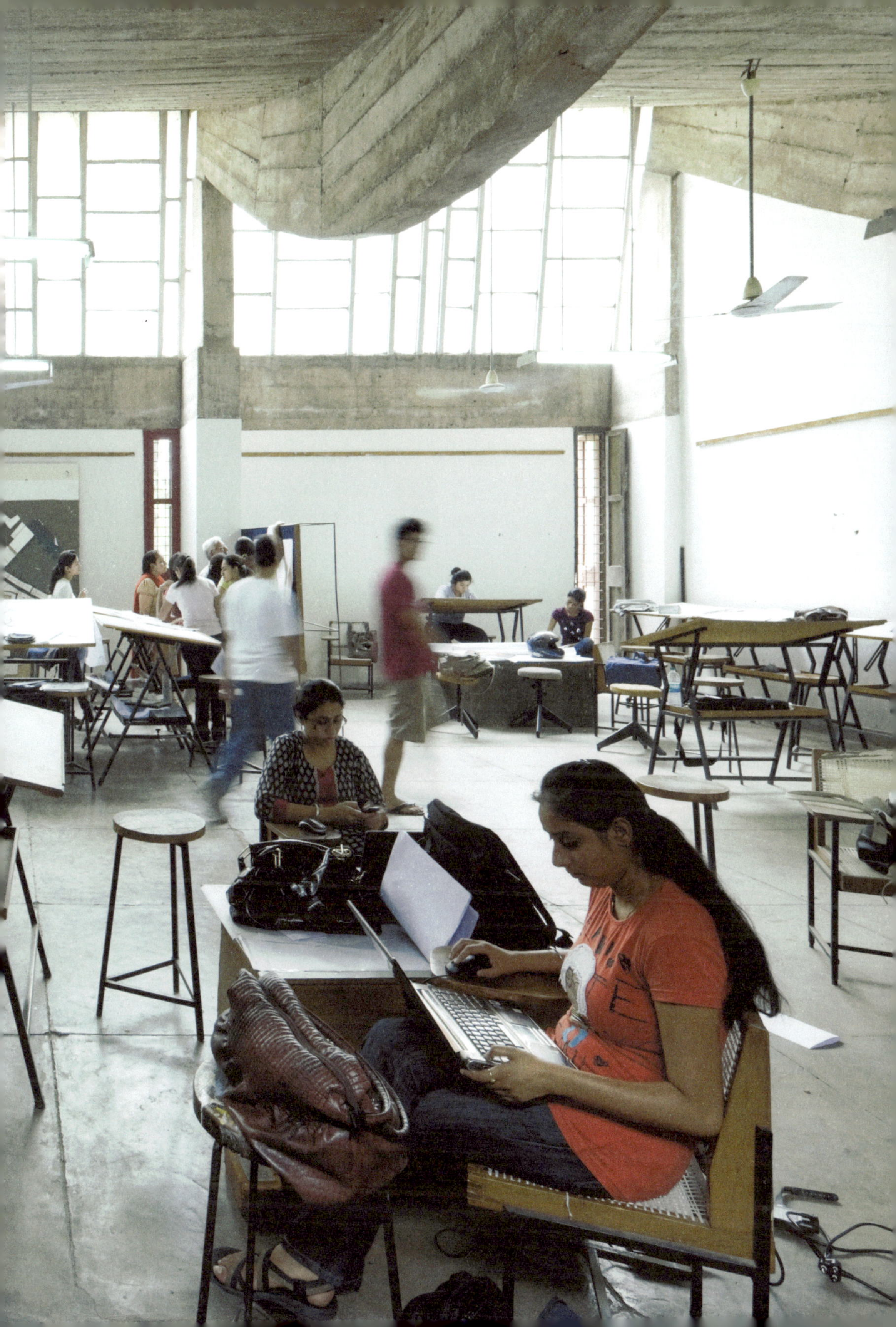

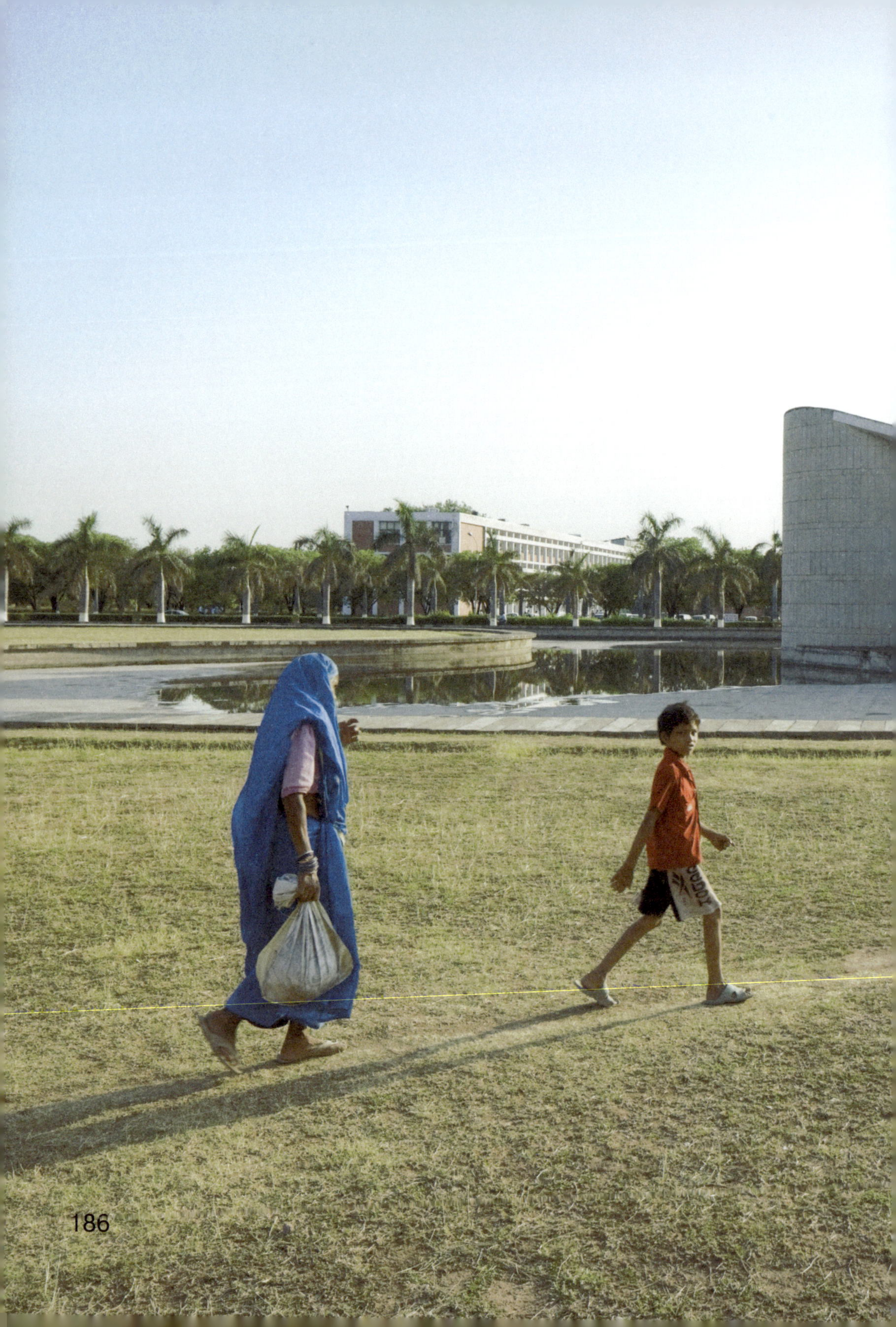

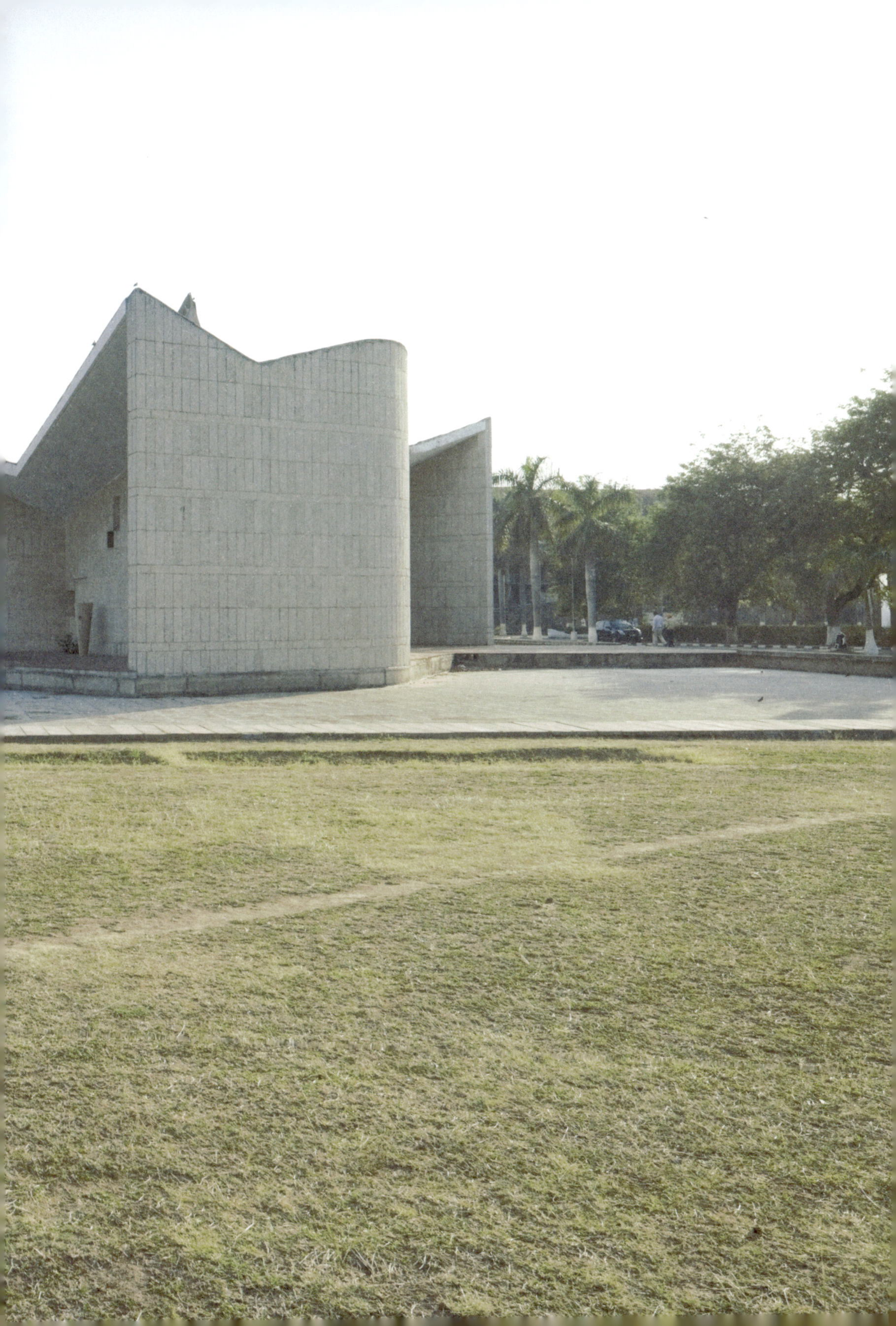

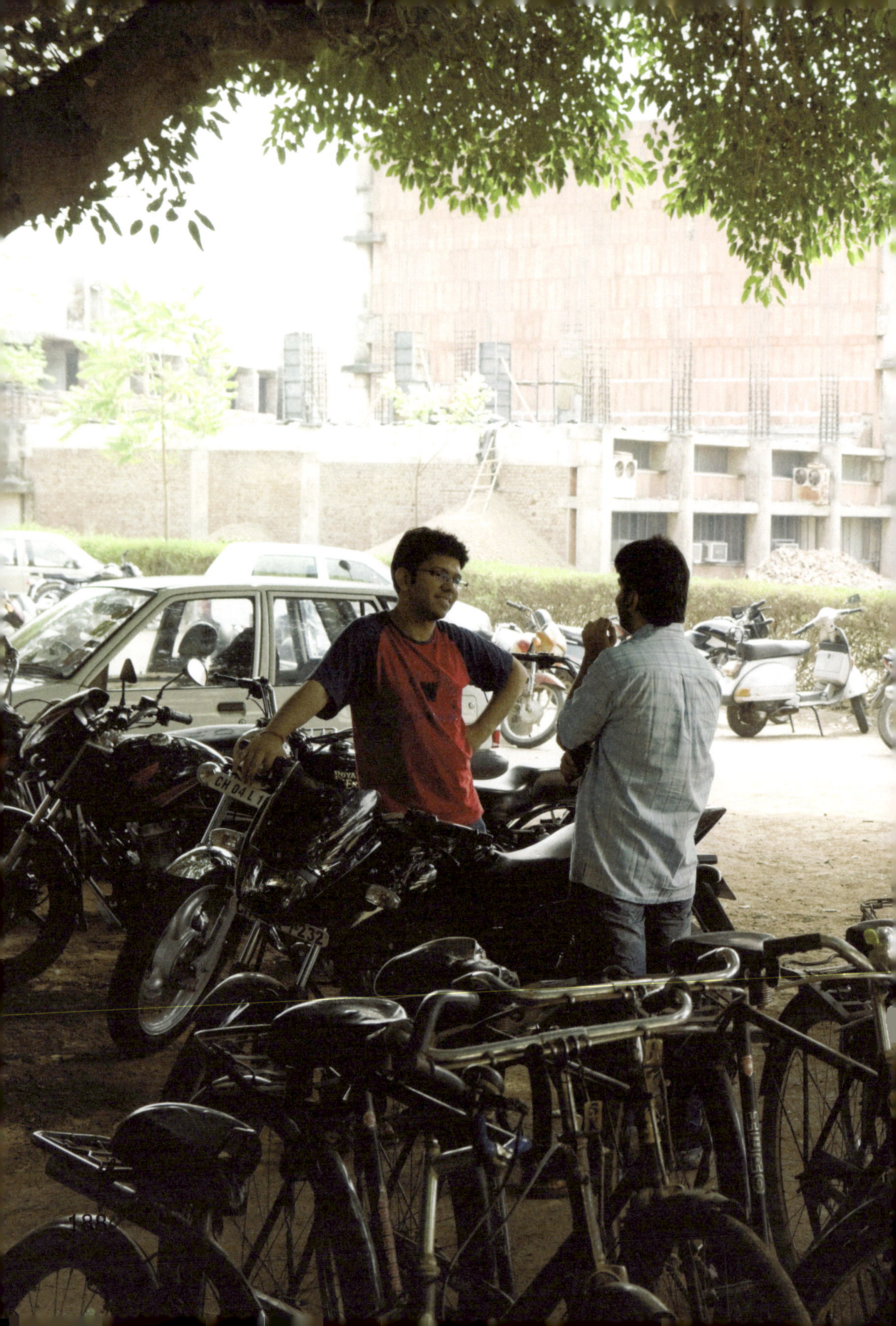
CH 04 L 1
232

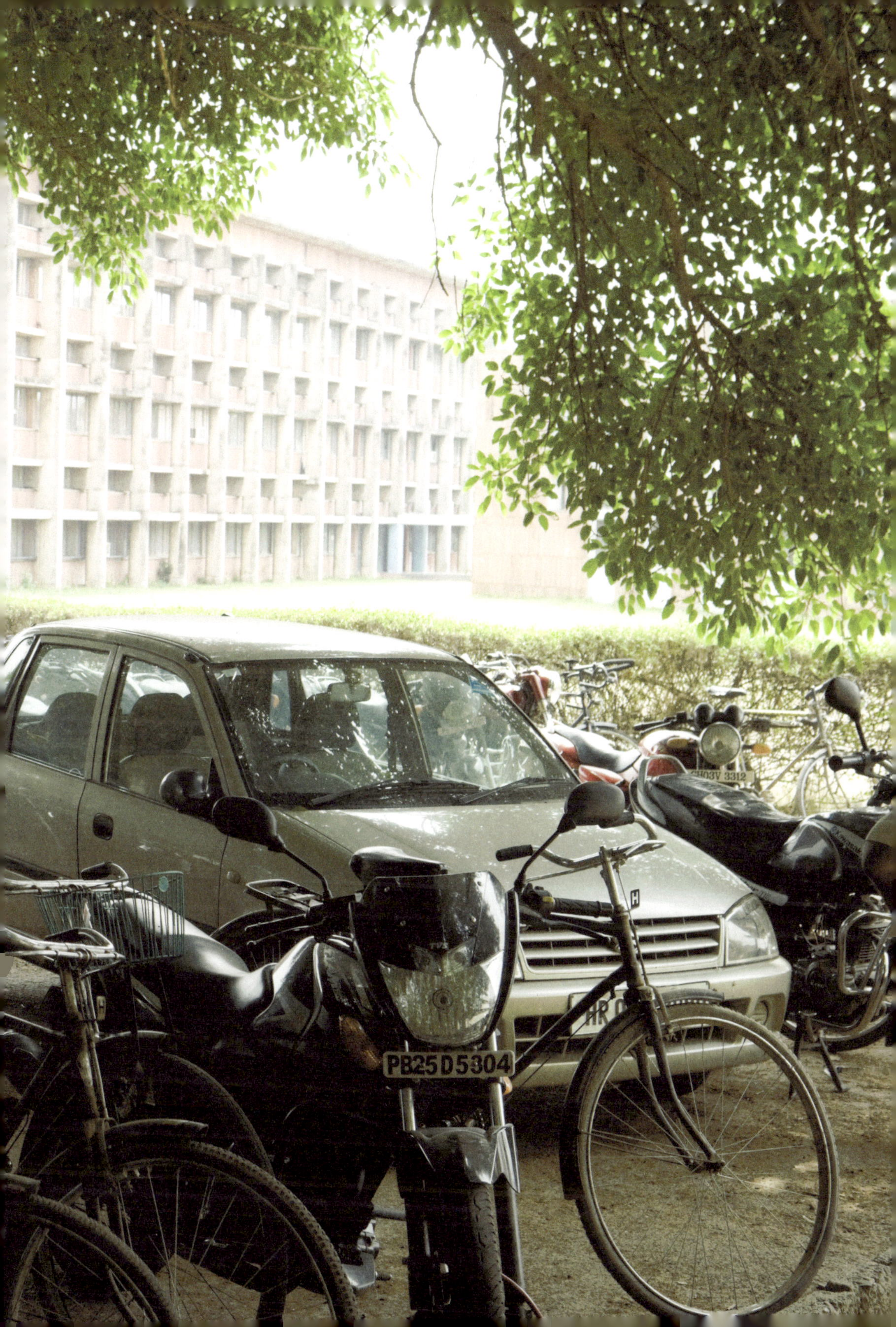
PB25D5304

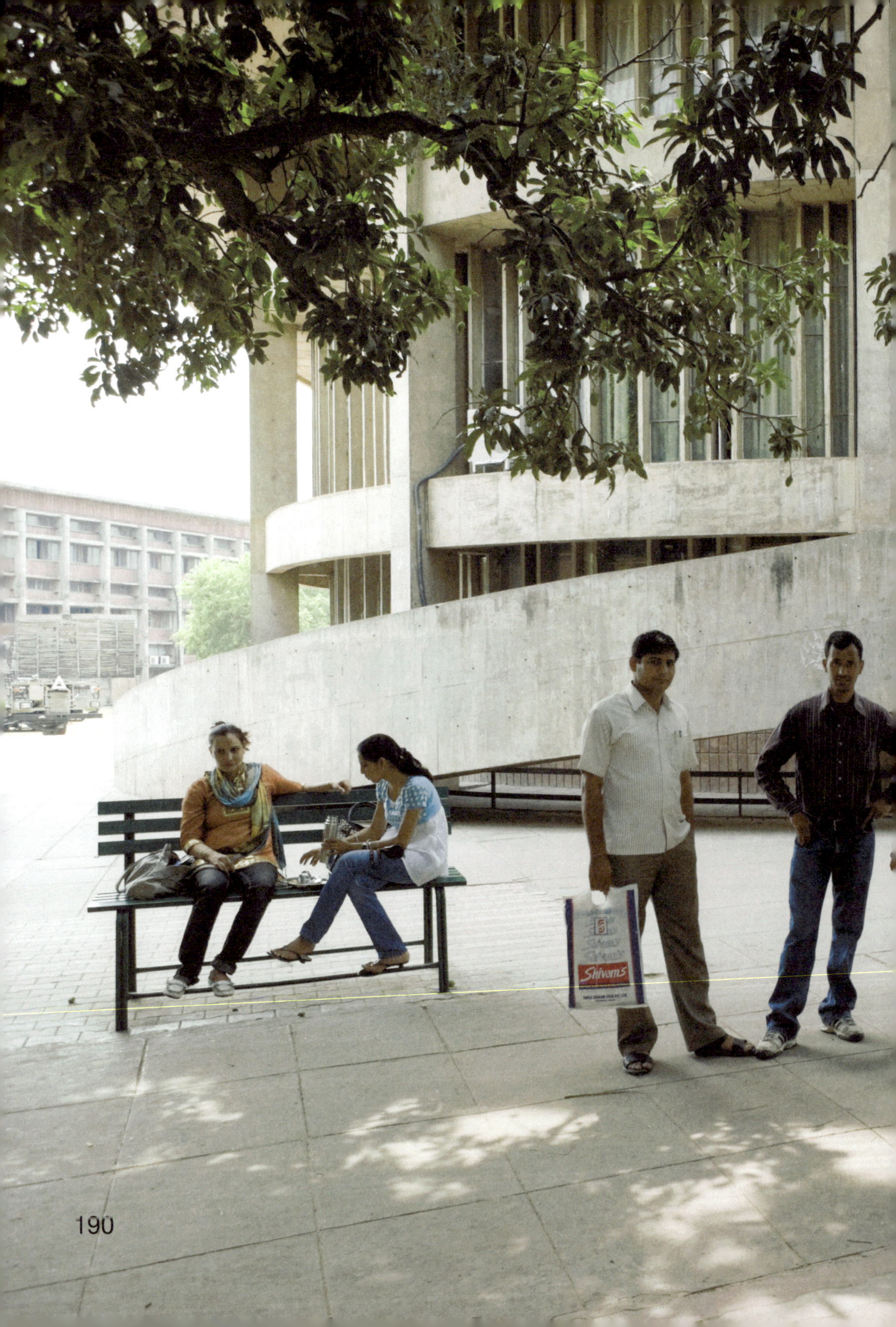
Shivam's

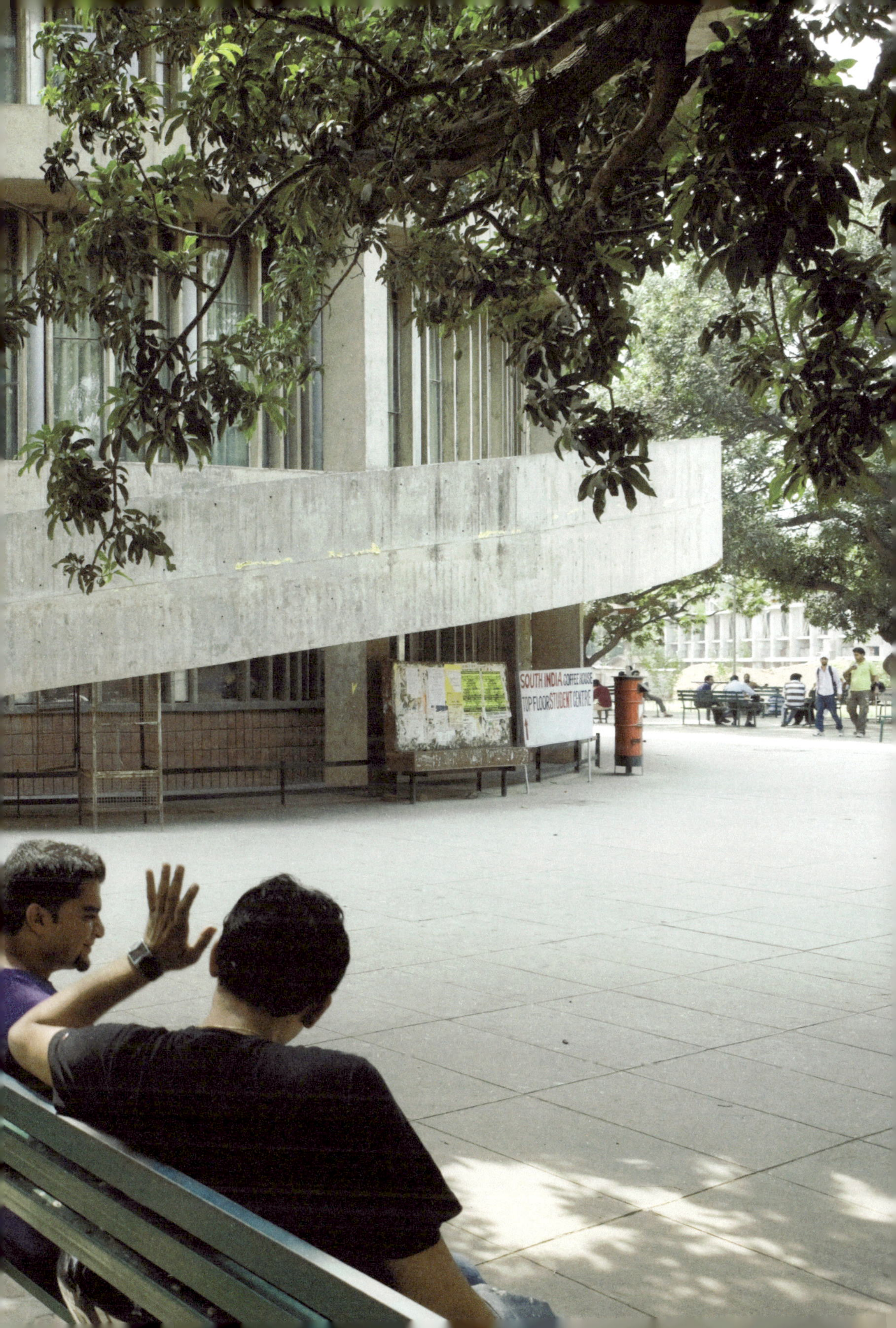
SOUTH INDIA COFFEE HOUSE
TOP FLOOR STUDENT CENTRE

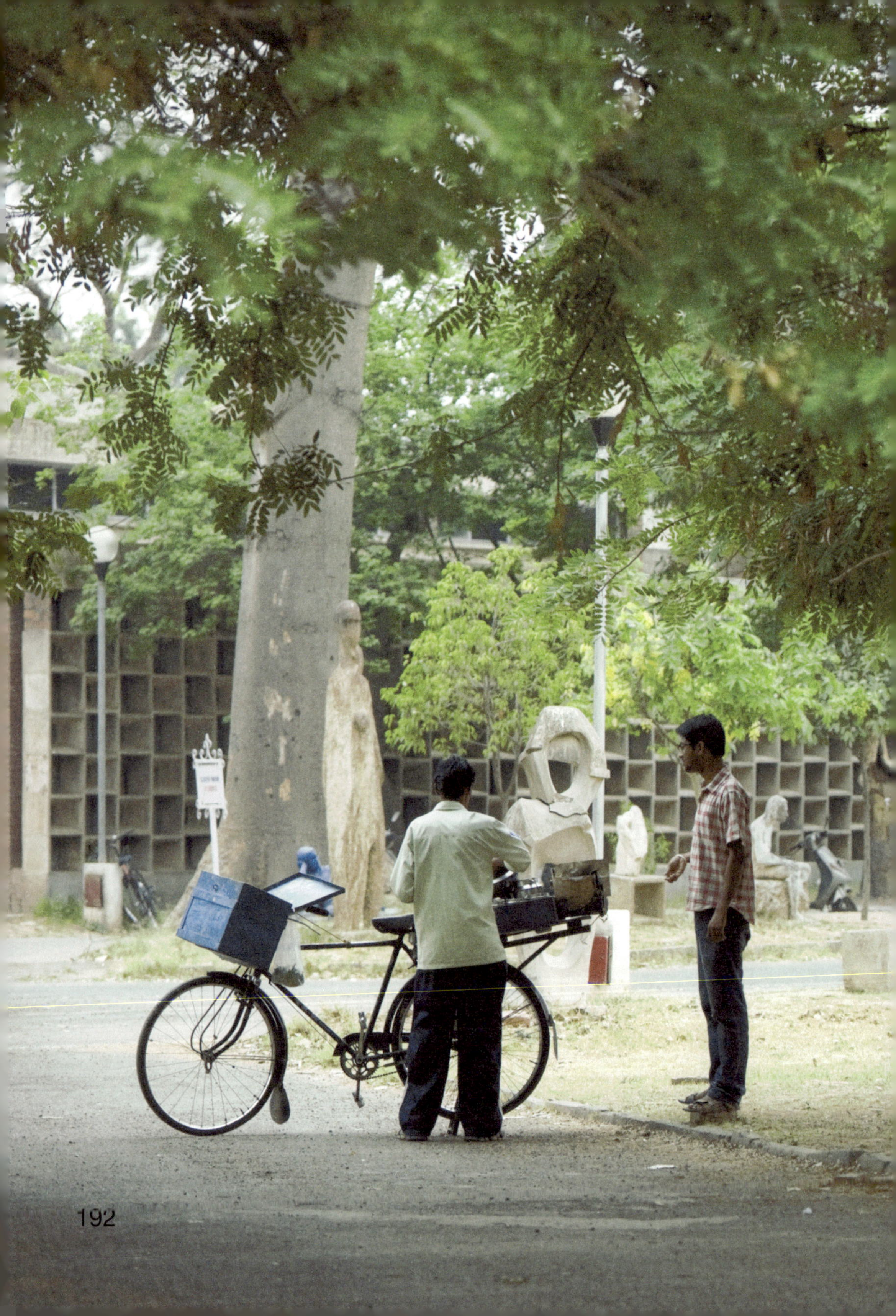

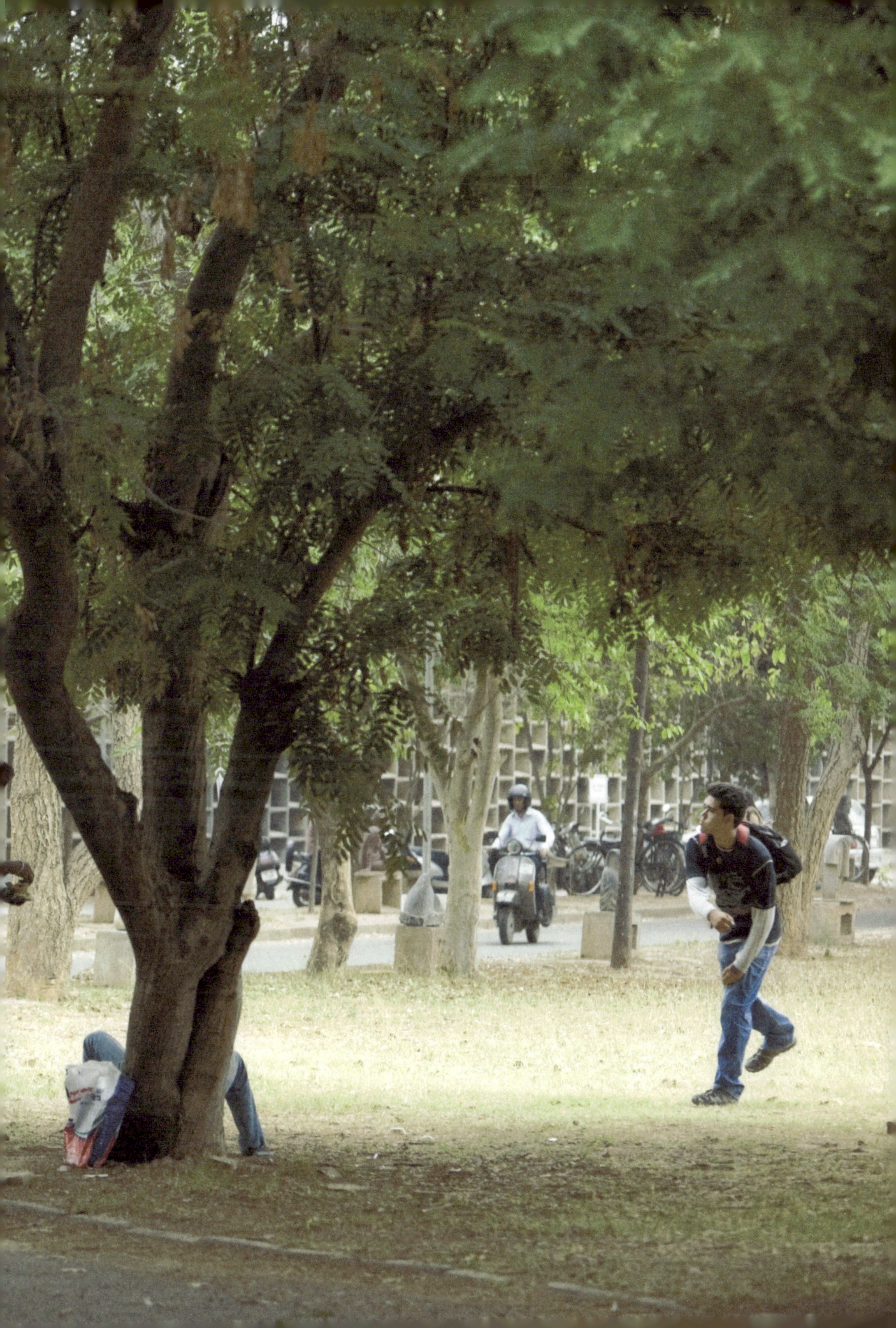

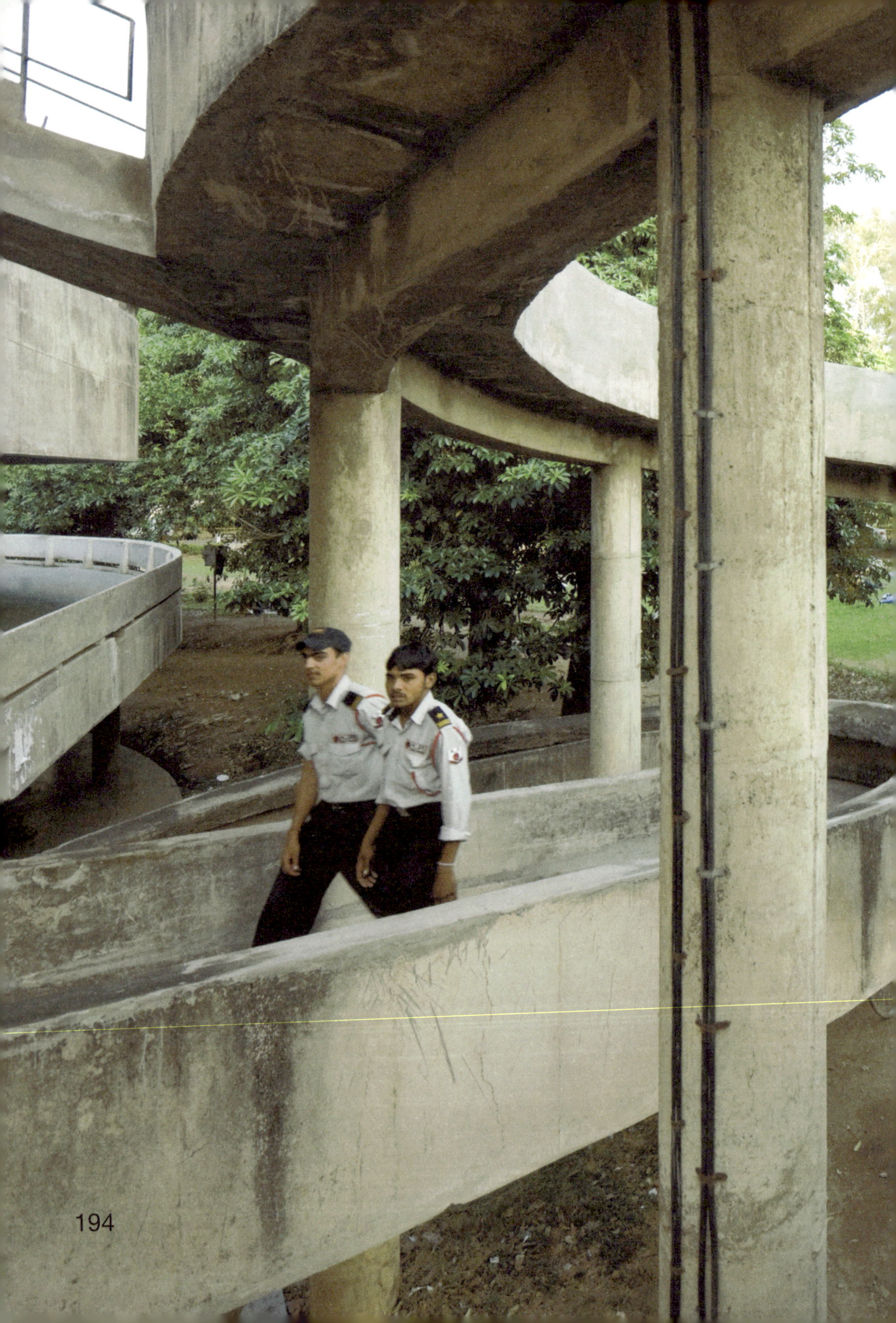

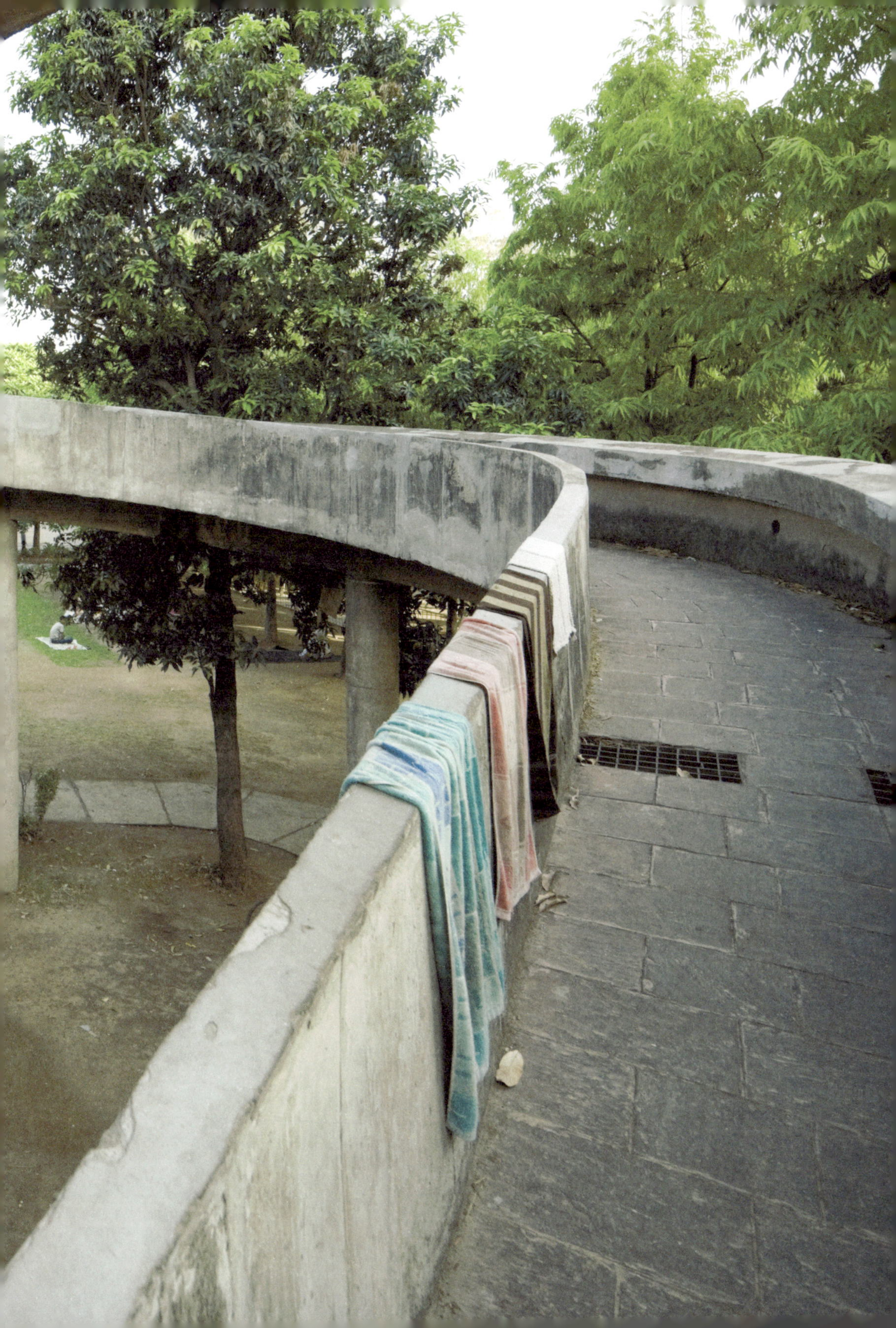

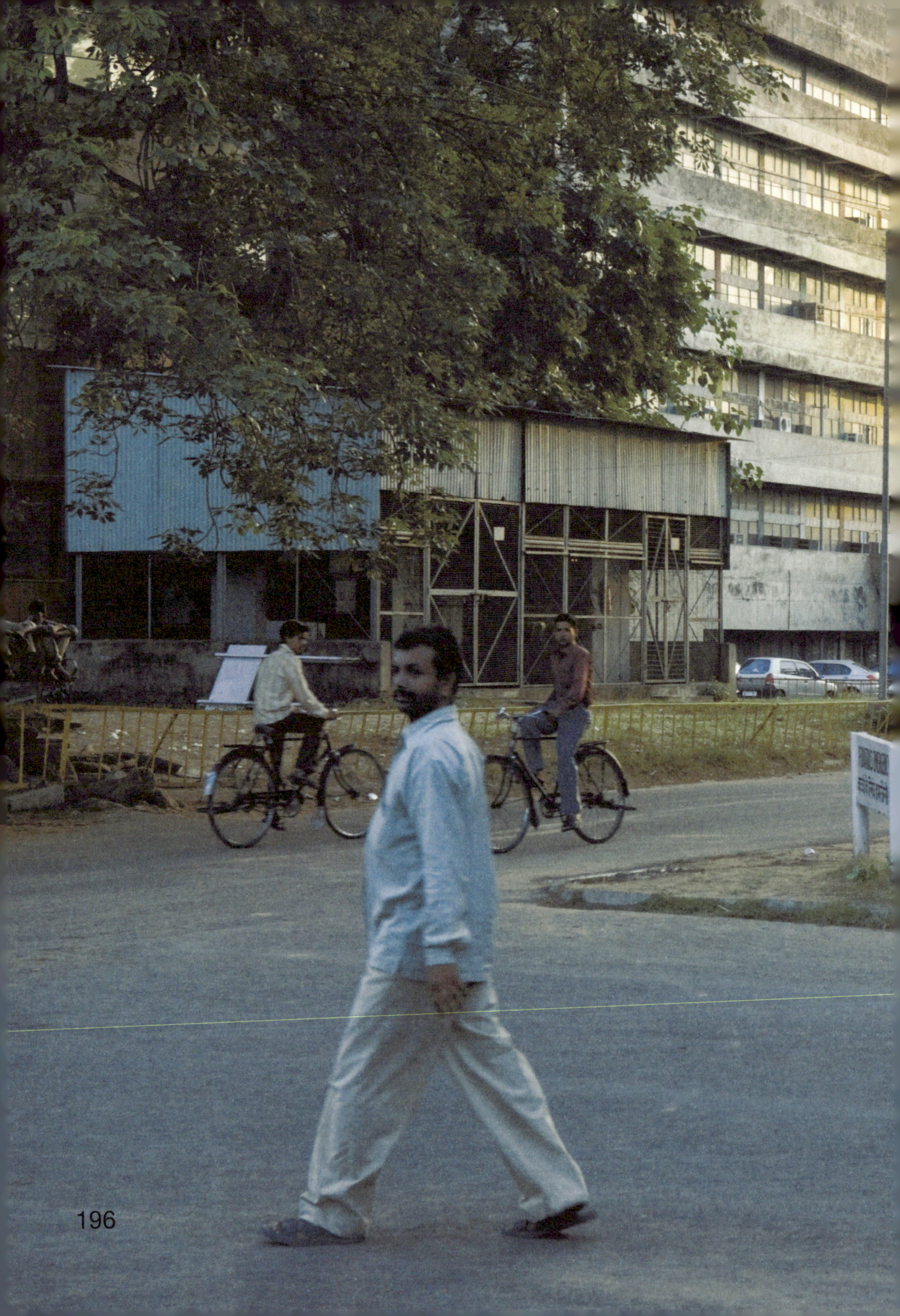

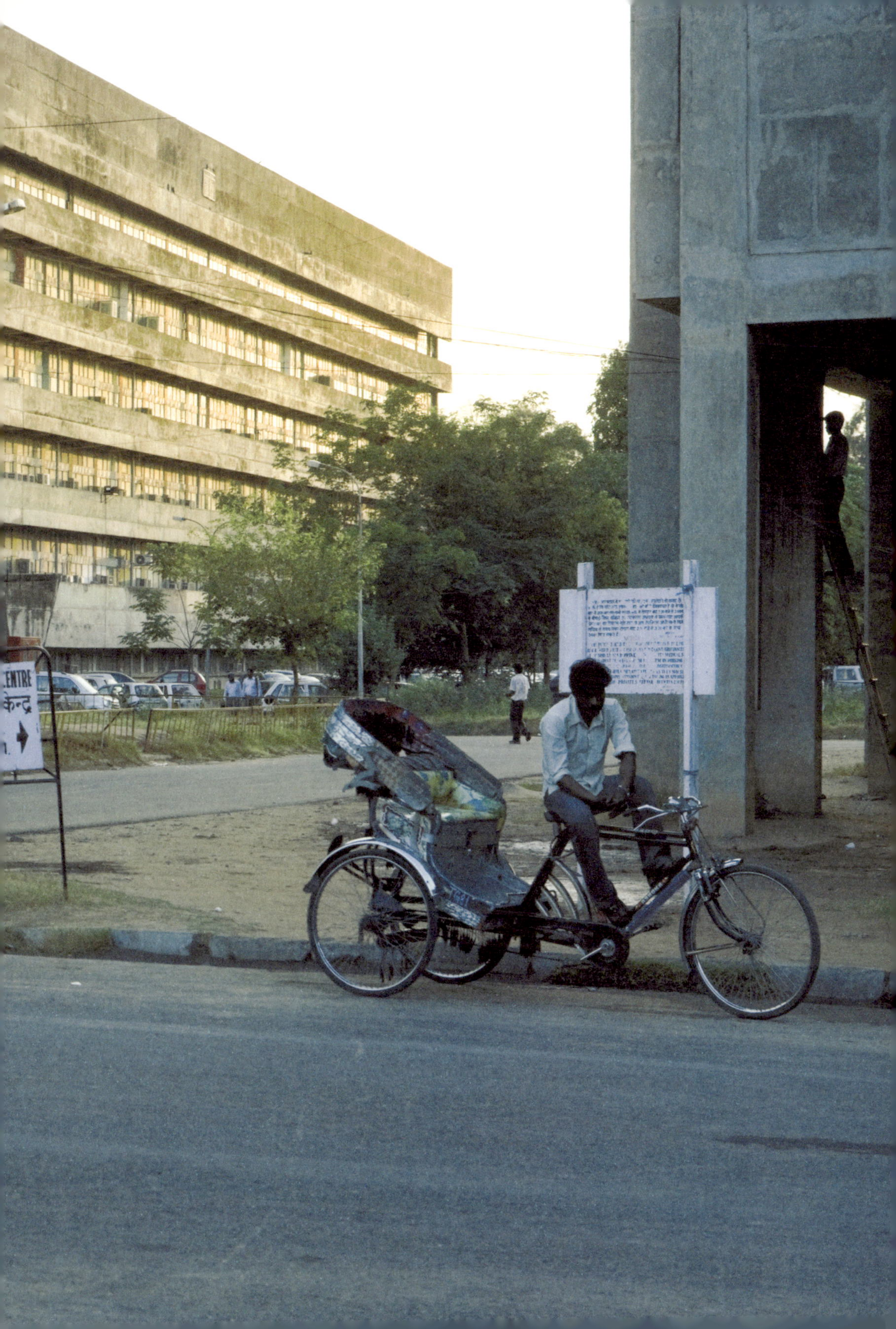
CENTRE
केन्द्र

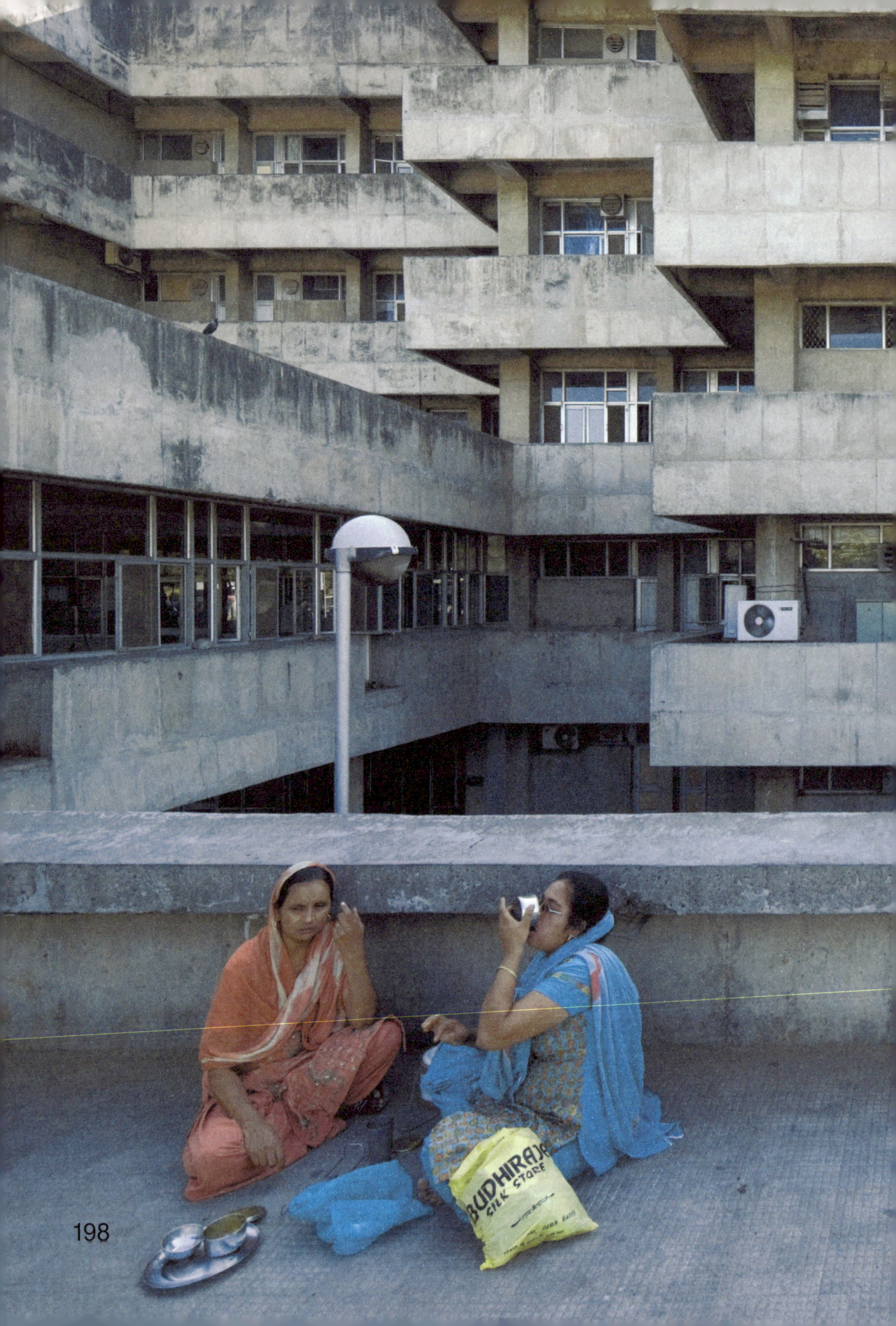
SILK STORE

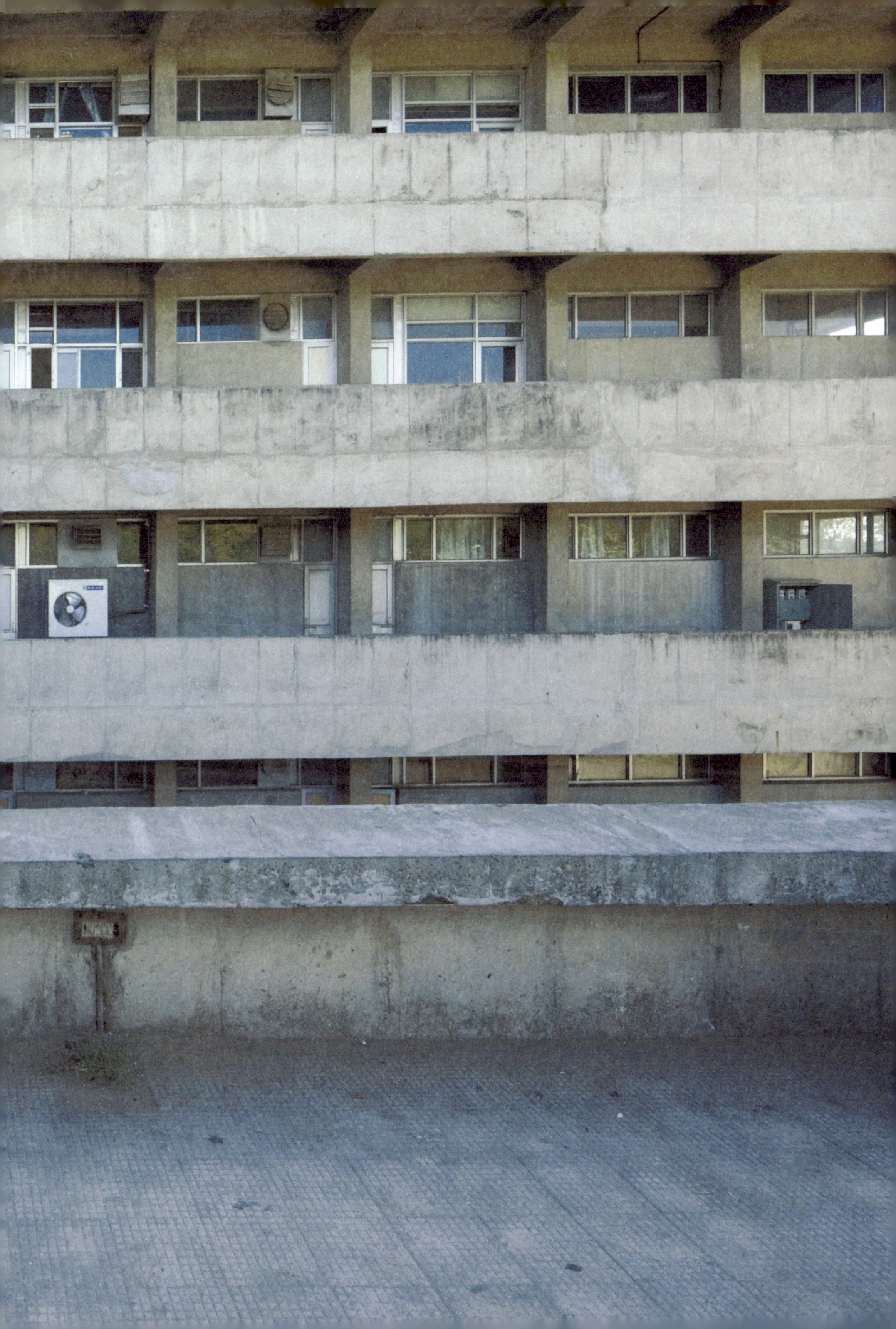

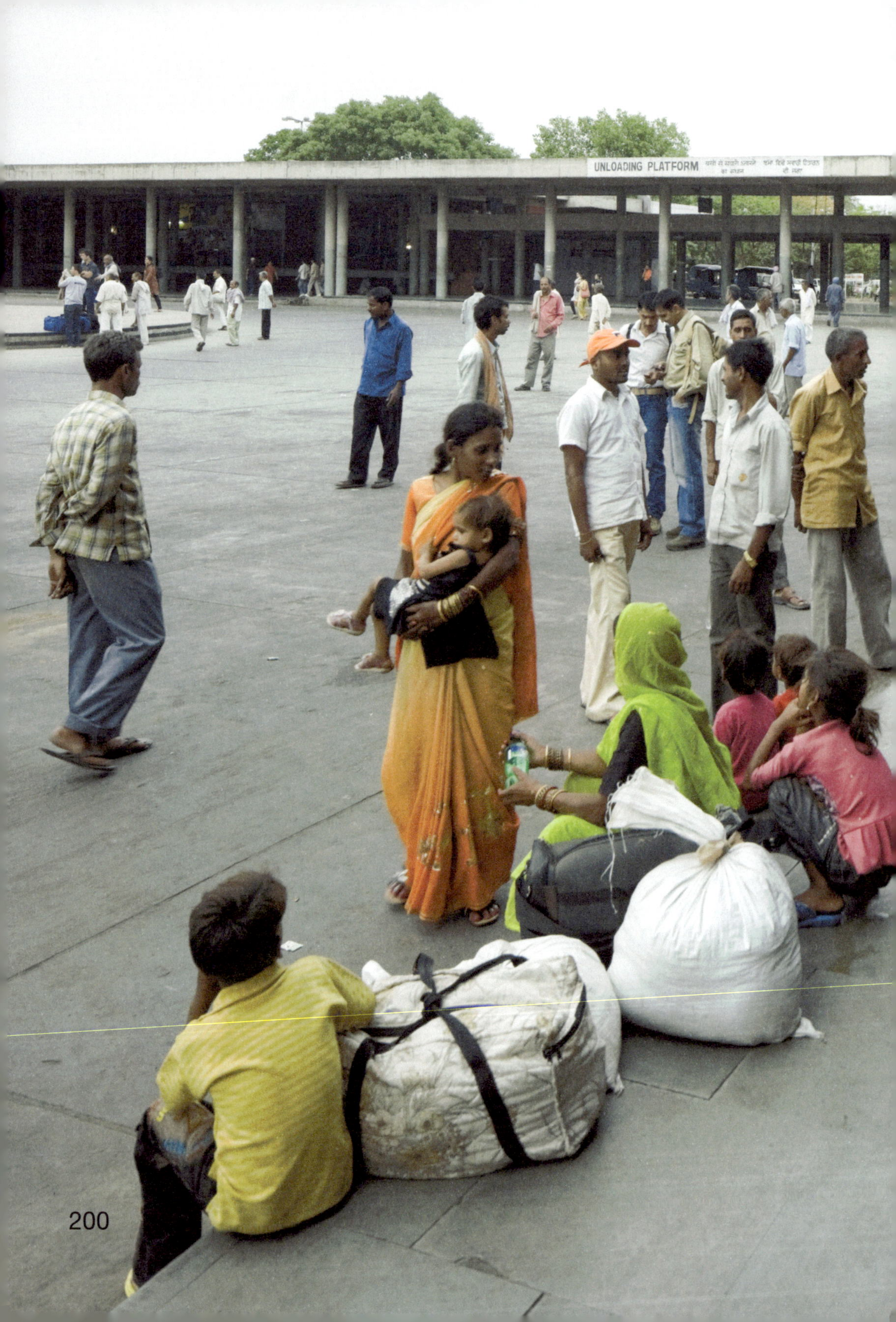
UNLOADING PLATFORM

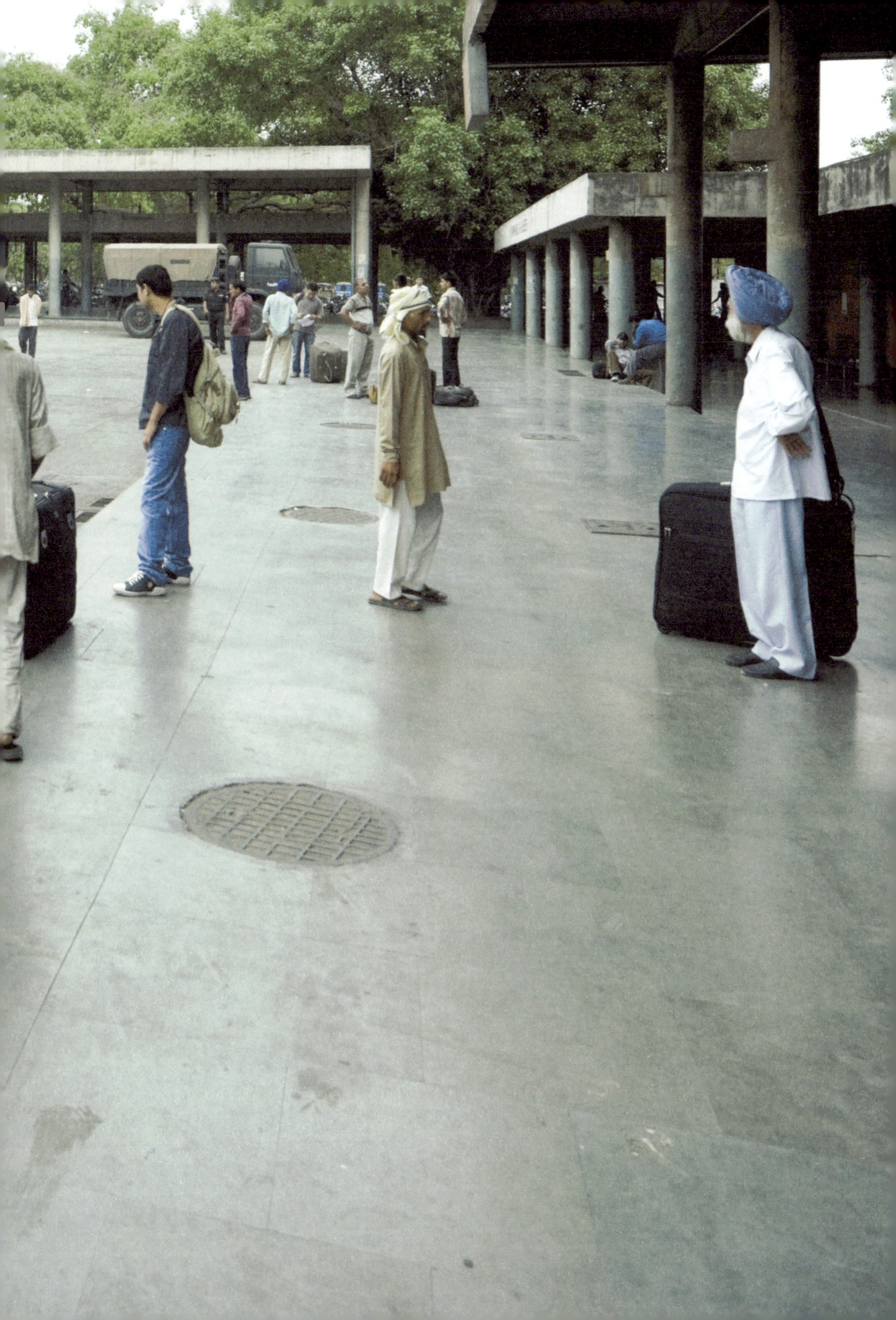

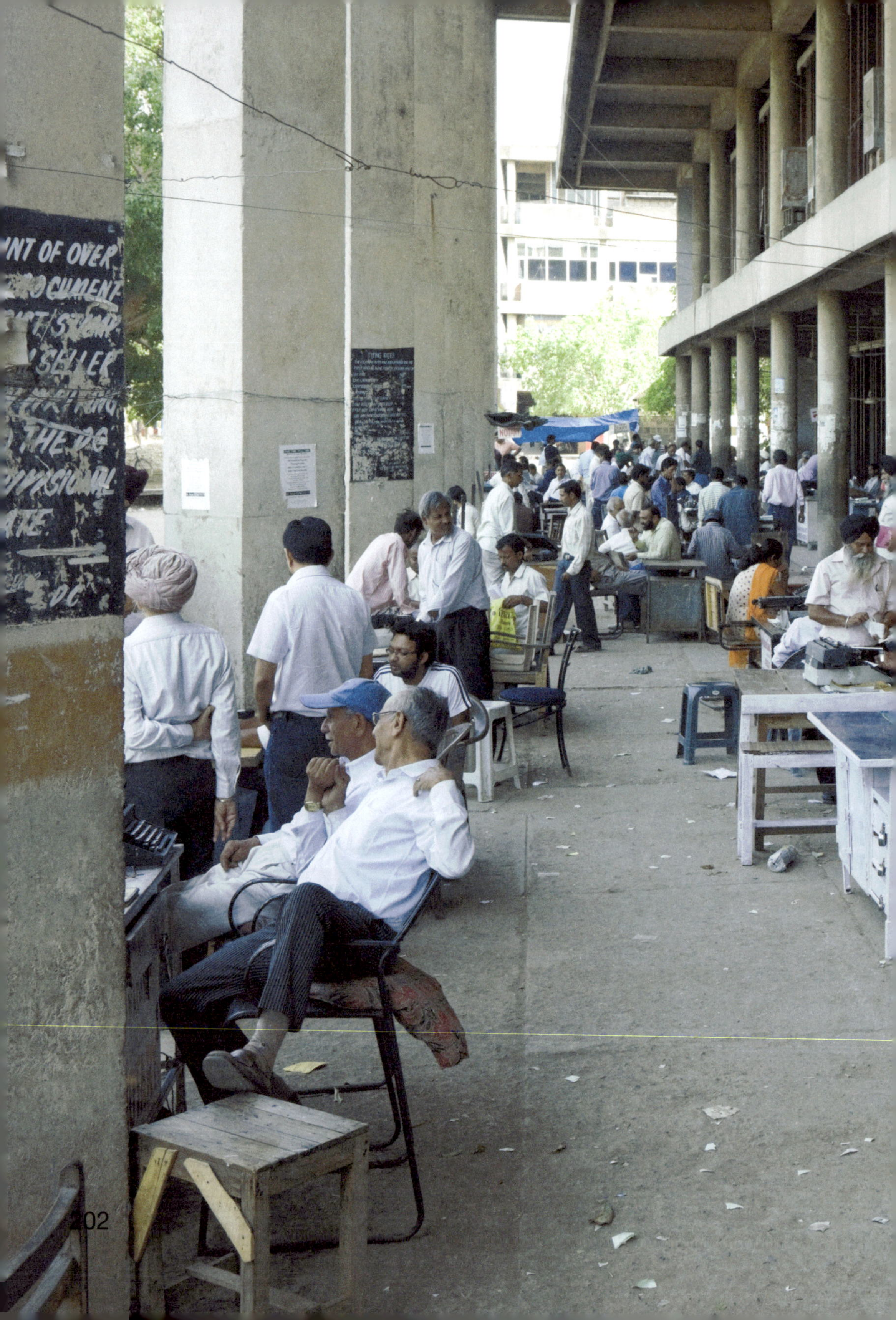
NT OF OVER
SELLER

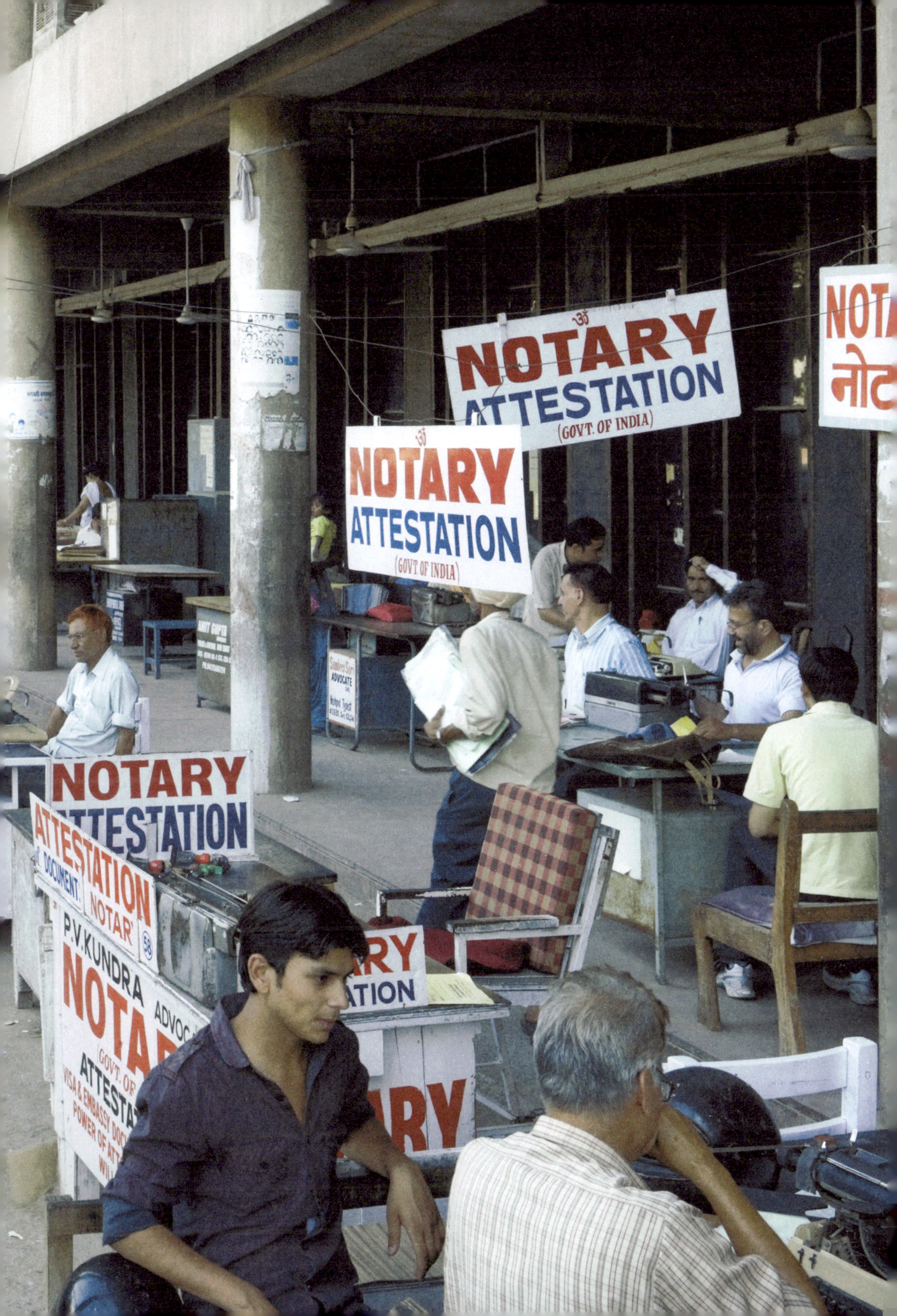
NOTARY
ATTESTATION
(GOVT. OF INDIA)
NOTARY
ATTESTATION
(GOVT OF INDIA)
NOTARY
ATTESTATION
ATTESTATION
DOCUMENT
P.V. KUNDRA

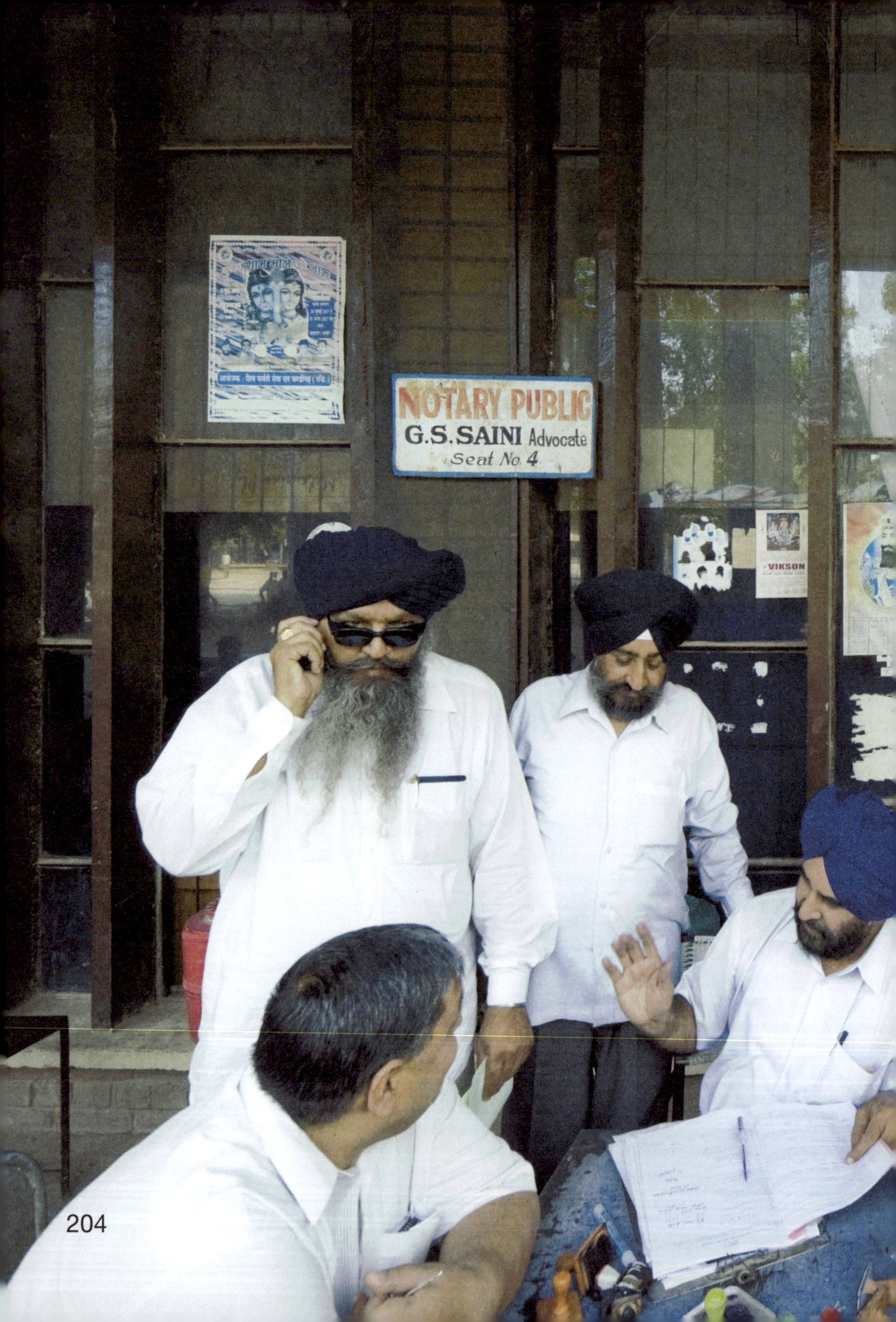
NOTARY PUBLIC
G.S.SAINI Advocate
Seat No. 4
VIKSON

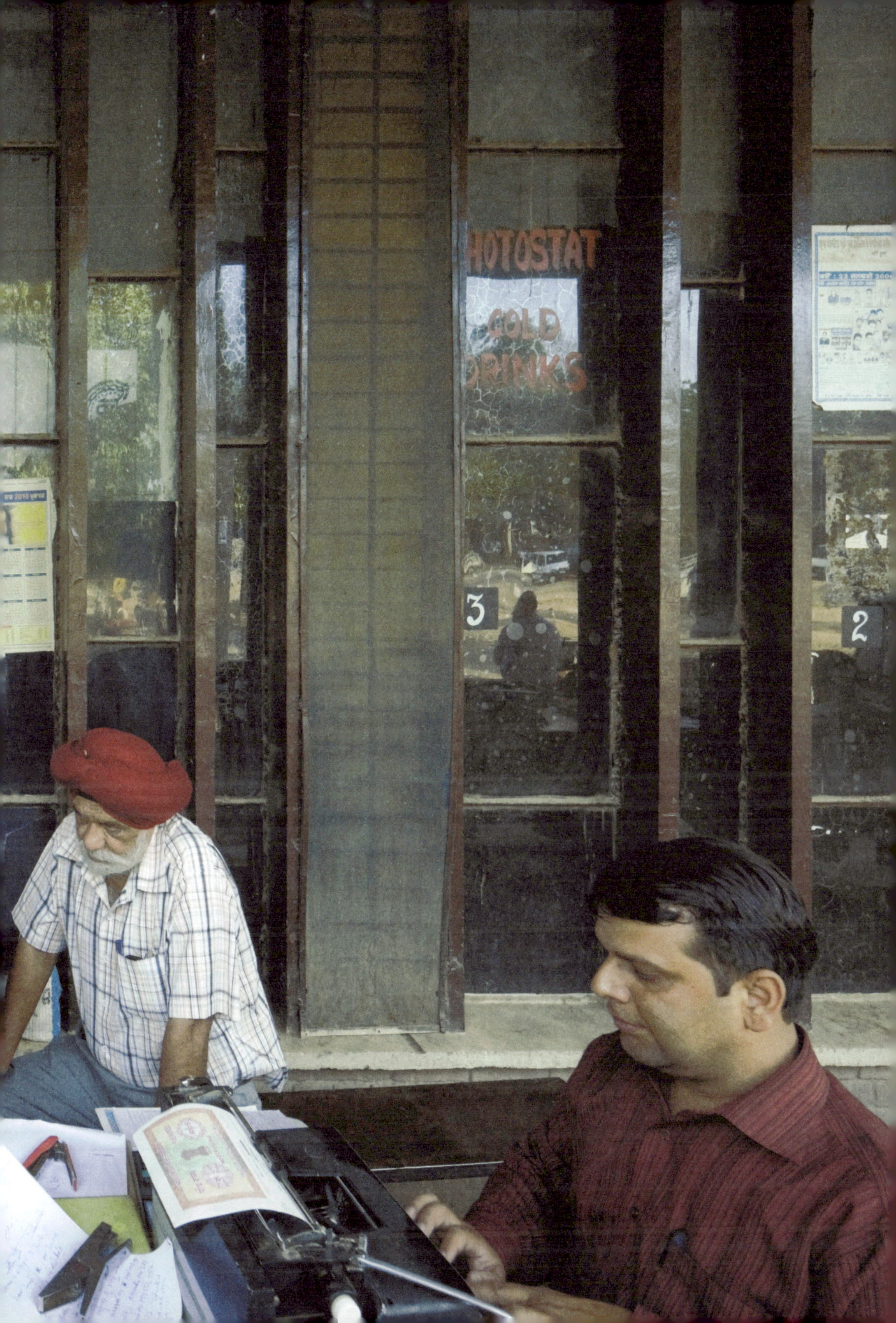
HOTOSTAT
COLD
3
2

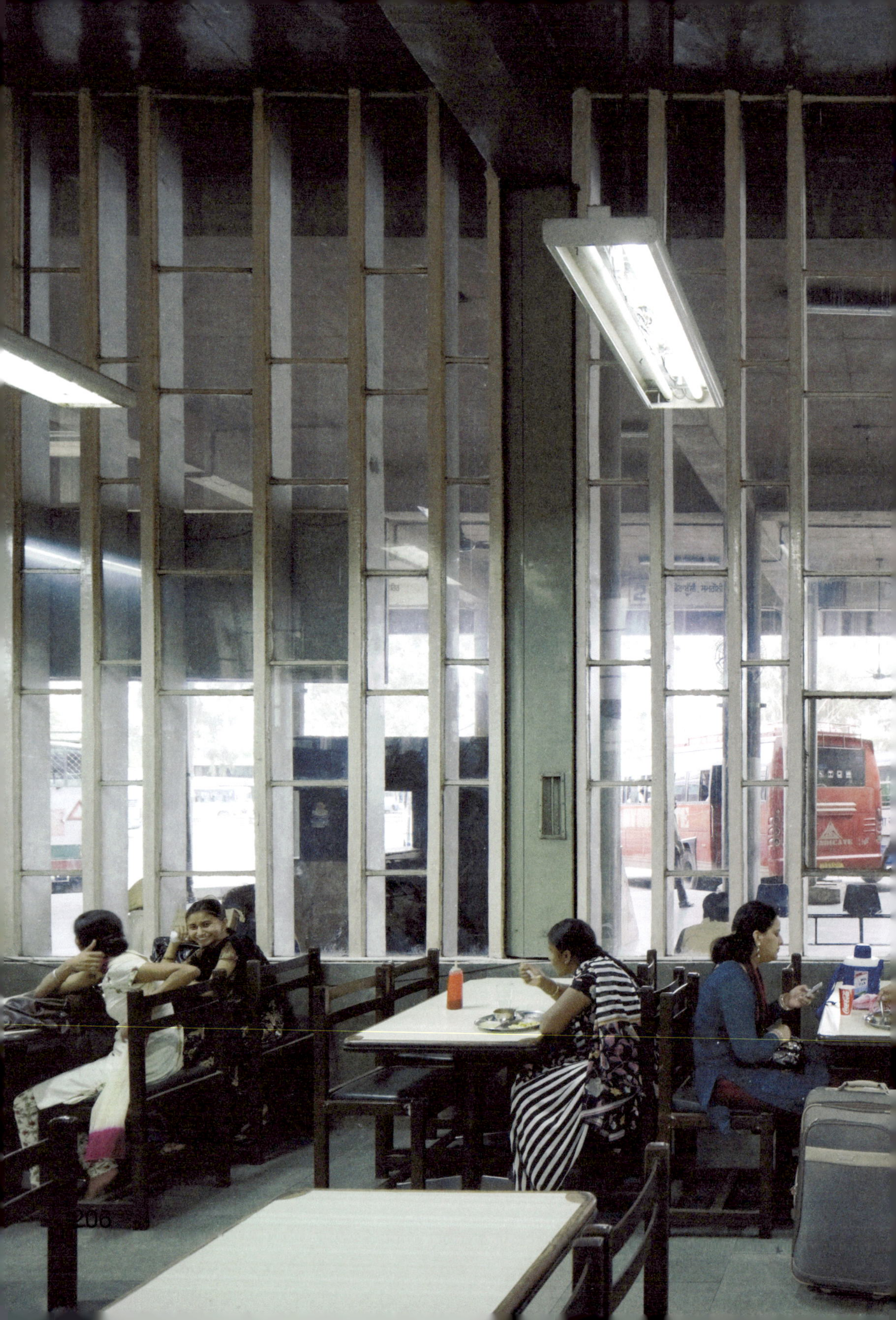

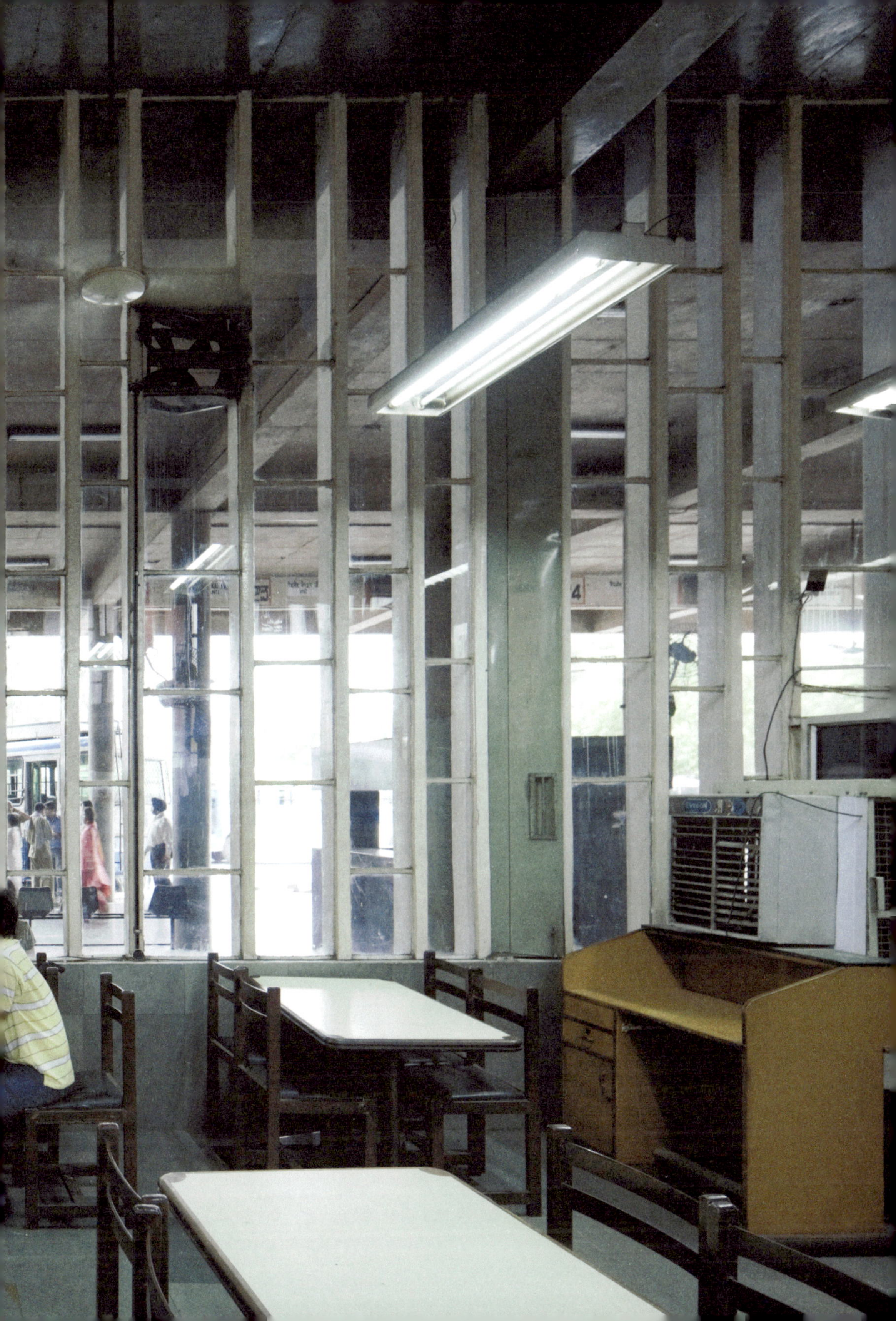

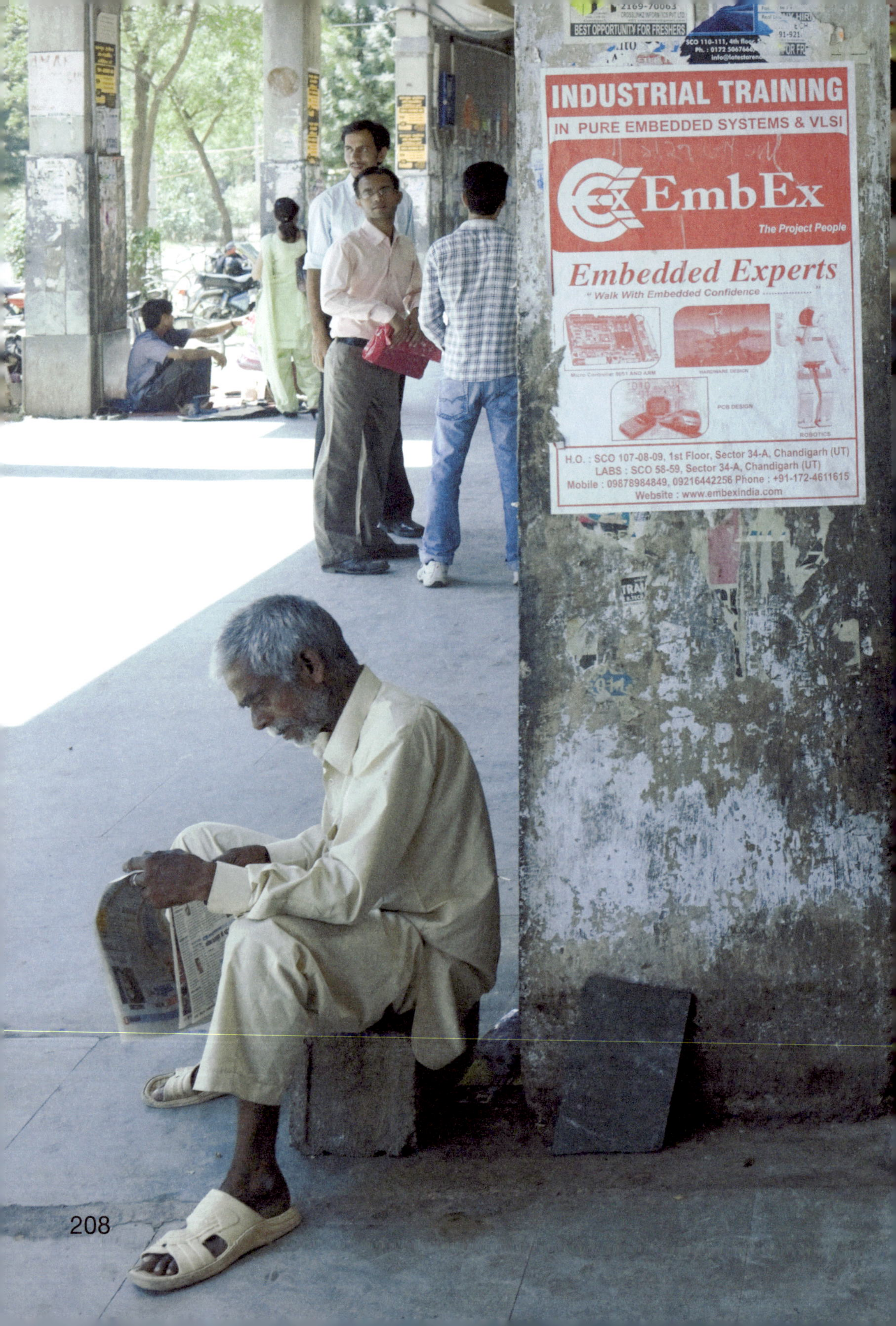
BEST OPPORTUNITY FOR FRESHERS
INDUSTRIAL TRAINING
IN PURE EMBEDDED SYSTEMS & VLSI
EmbEx
The Project People
Embedded Experts
" Walk With Embedded Confidence .... "
H.O. : SCO 107-08-09, 1st Floor, Sector 34-A, Chandigarh (UT)
LABS : SCO 58-59, Sector 34-A, Chandigarh (UT)
Mobile : 09878984849, 09216442256 Phone : +91-172-4611615
Website : www.embexindia.com

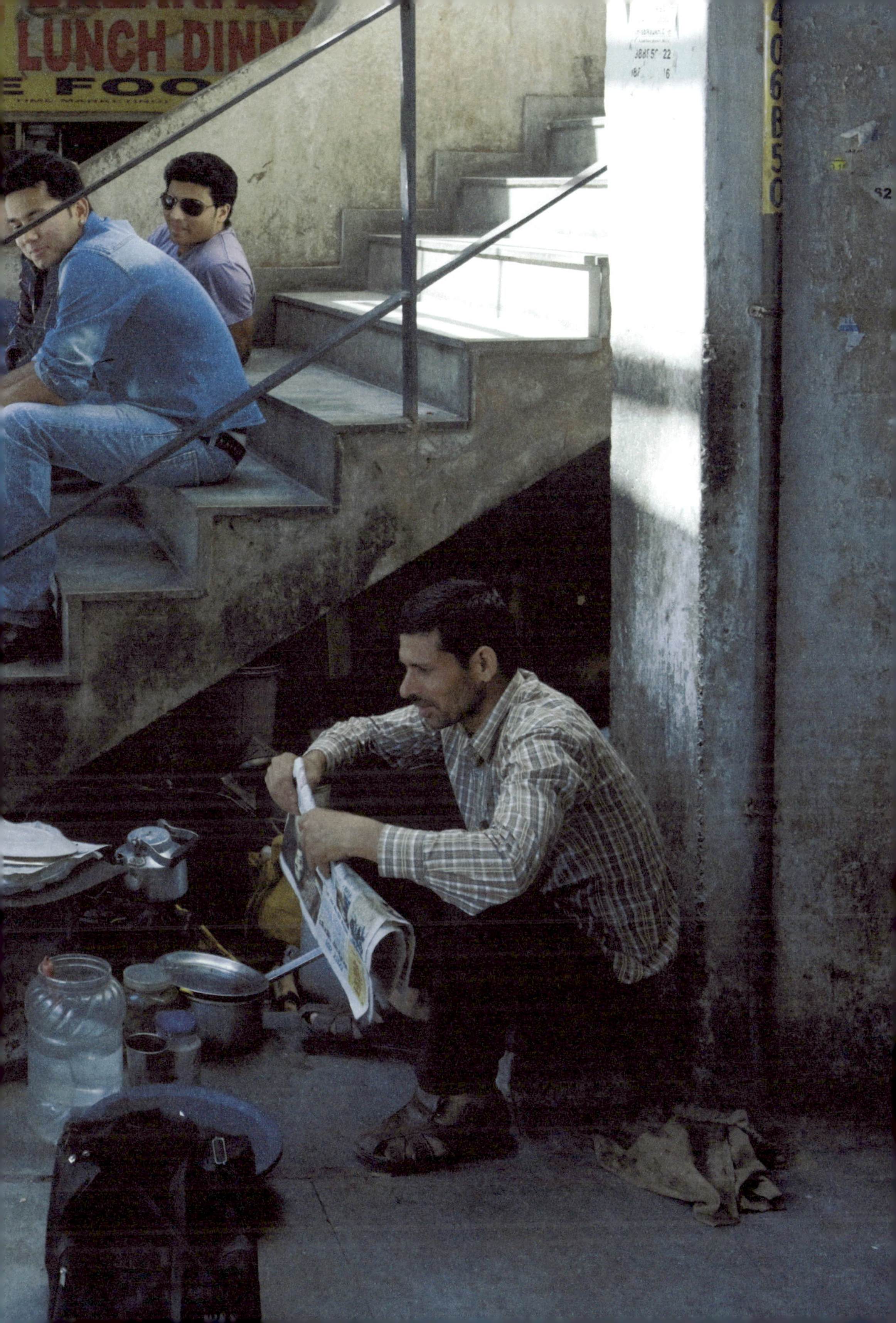
LUNCH DINN

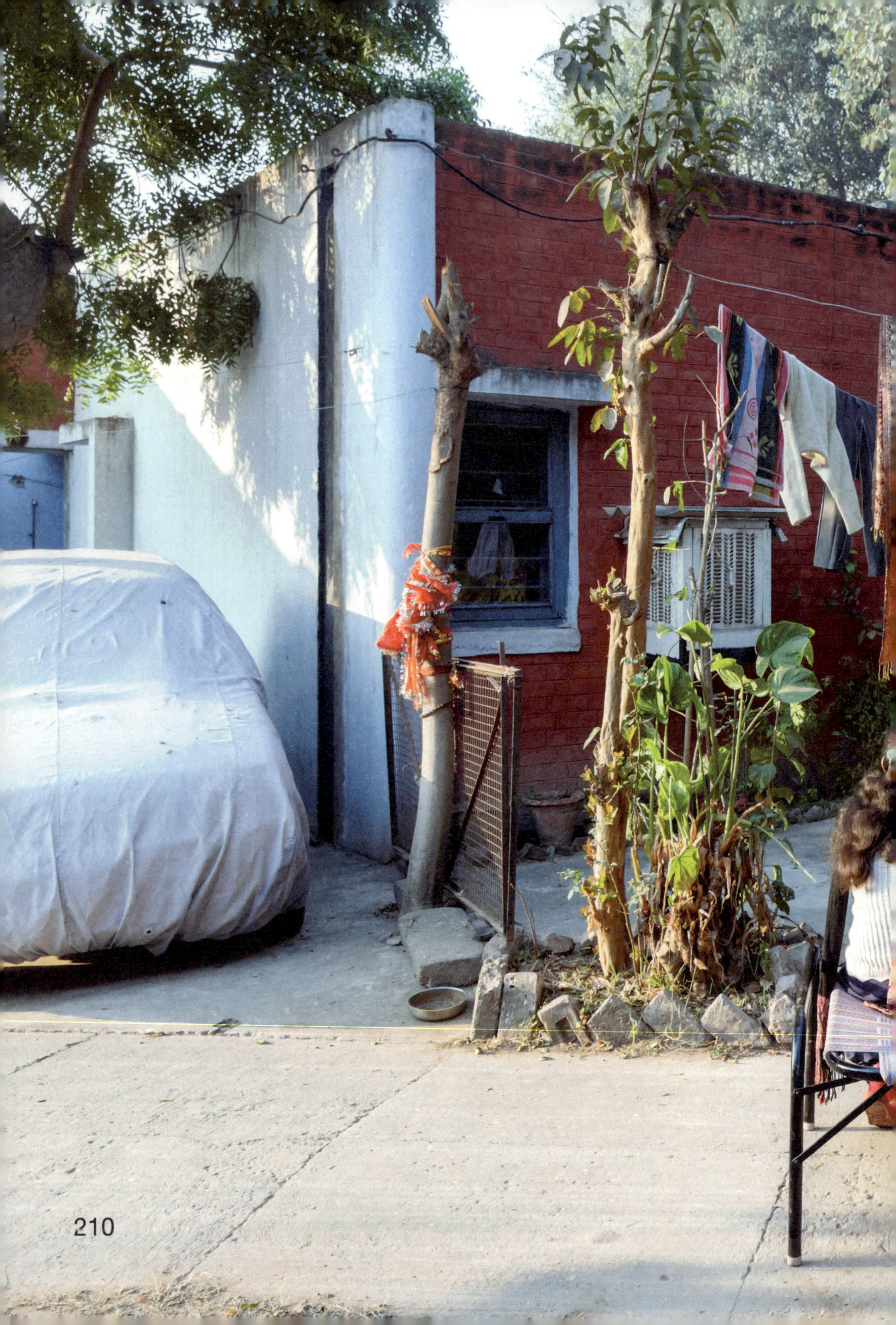

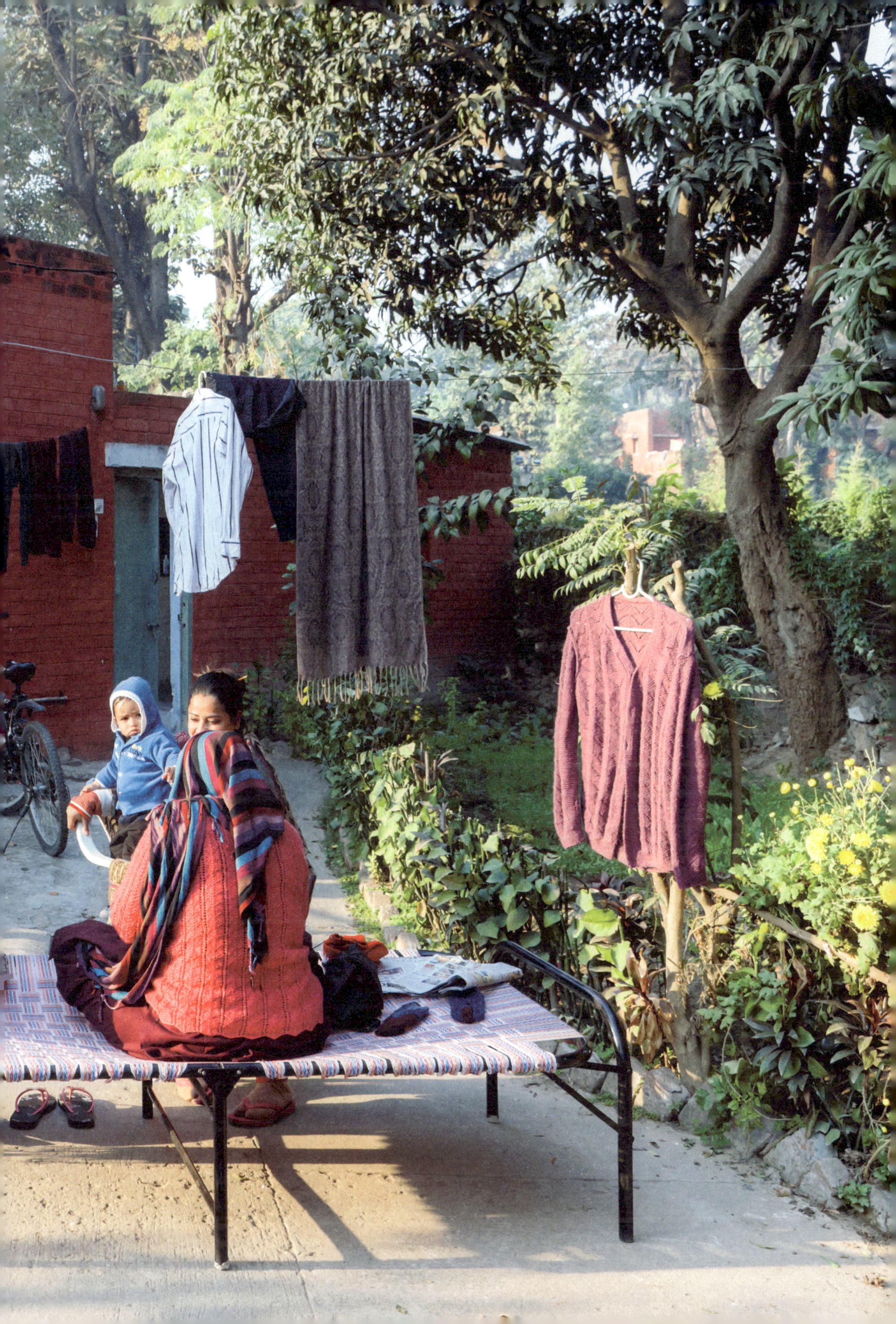

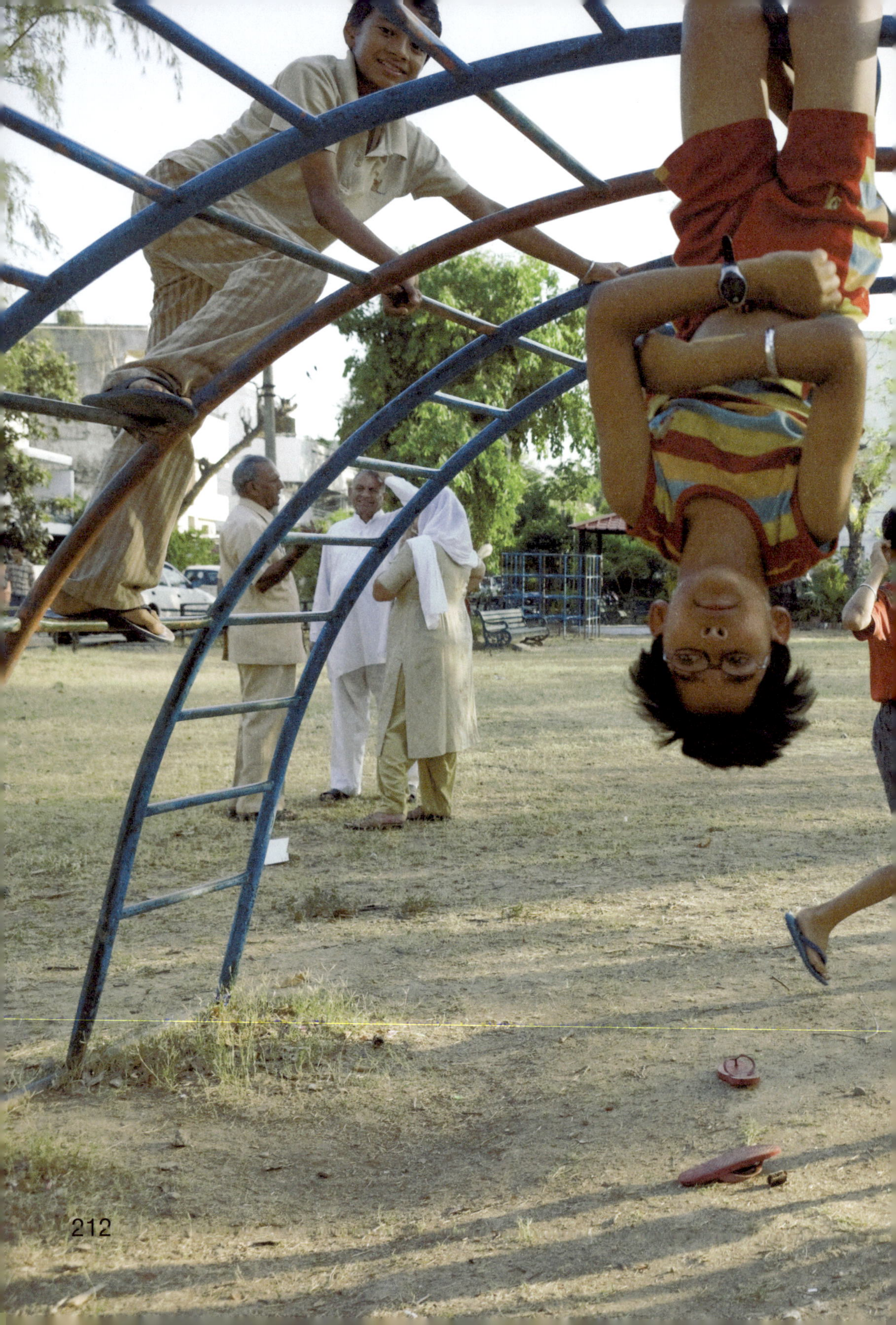

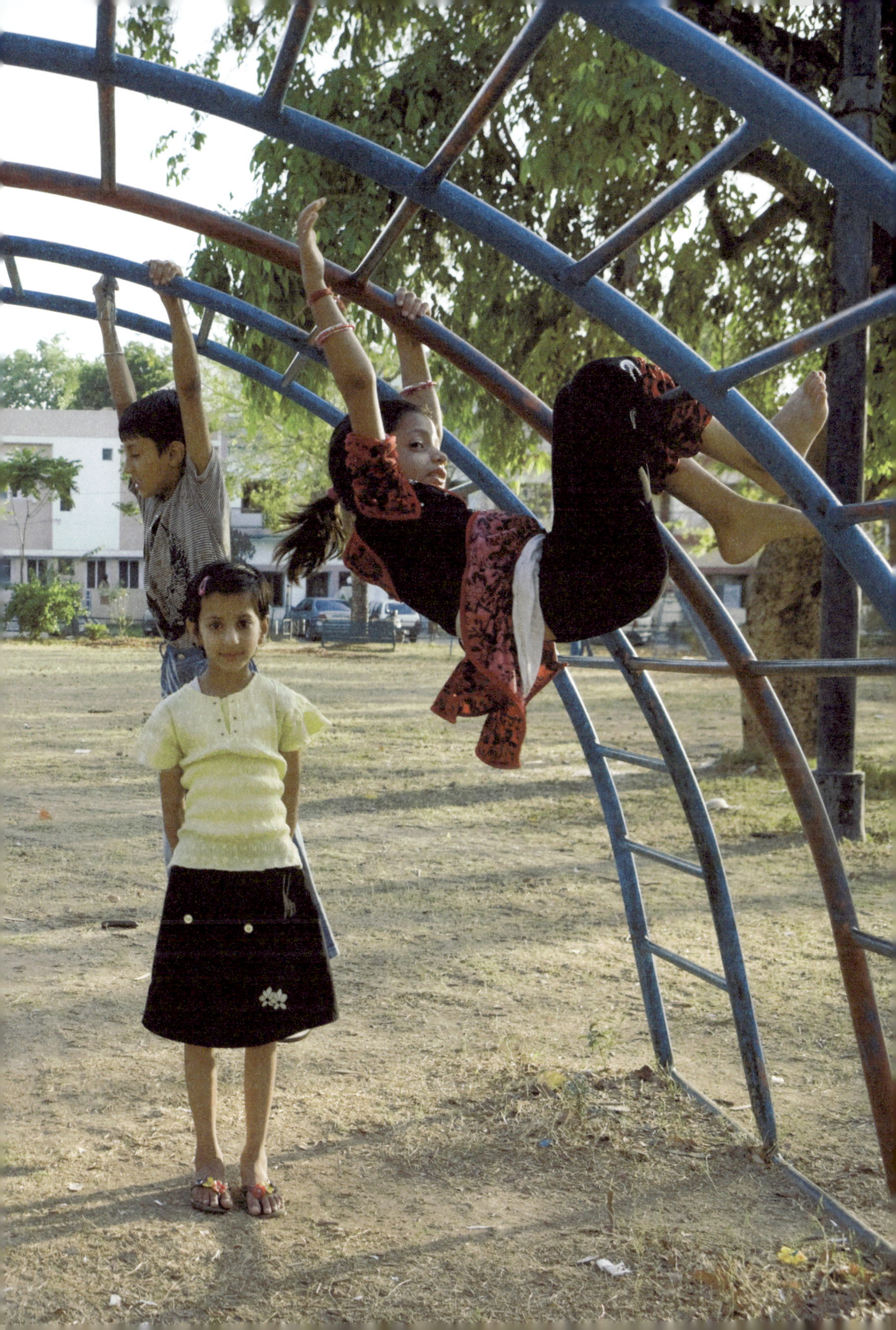

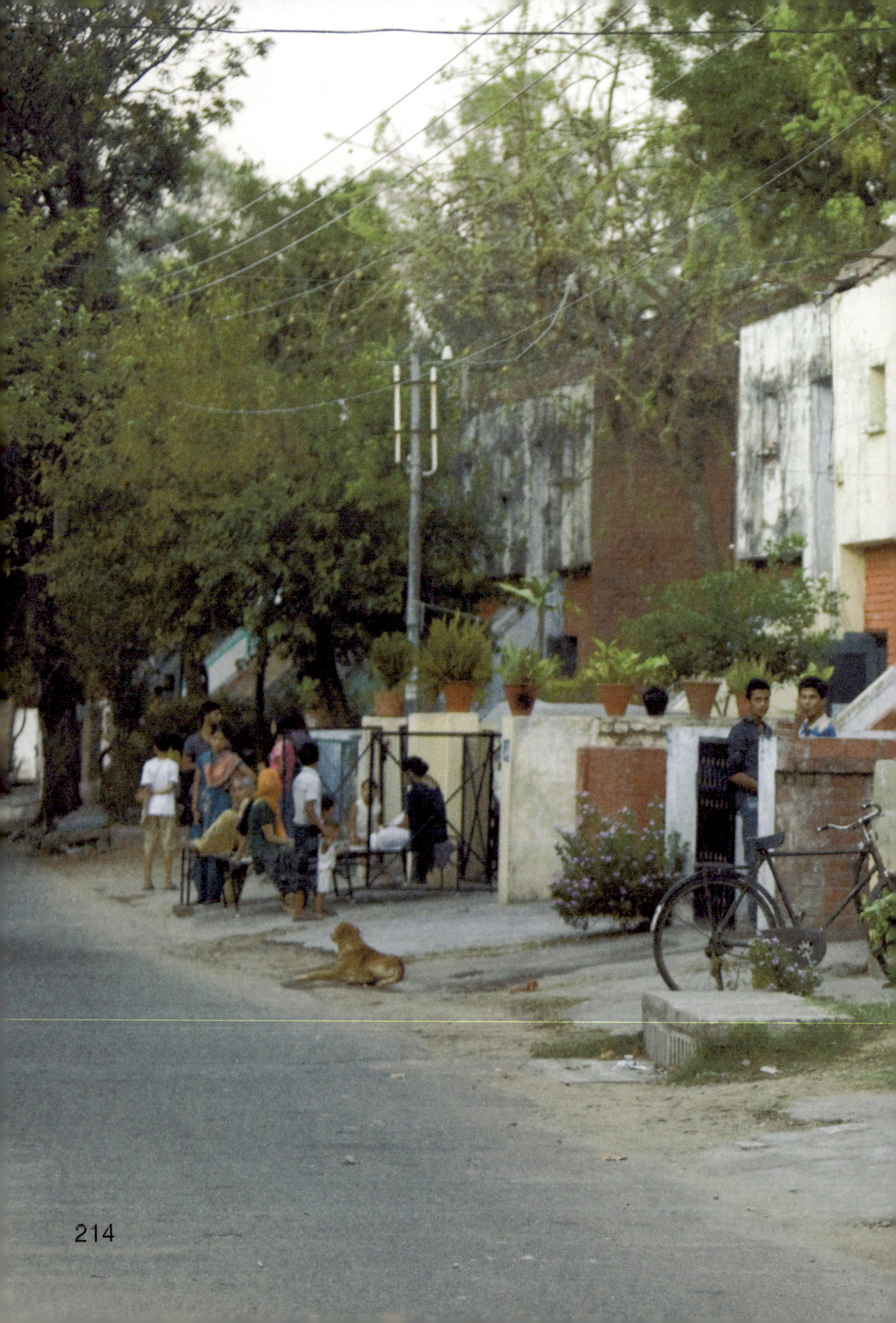

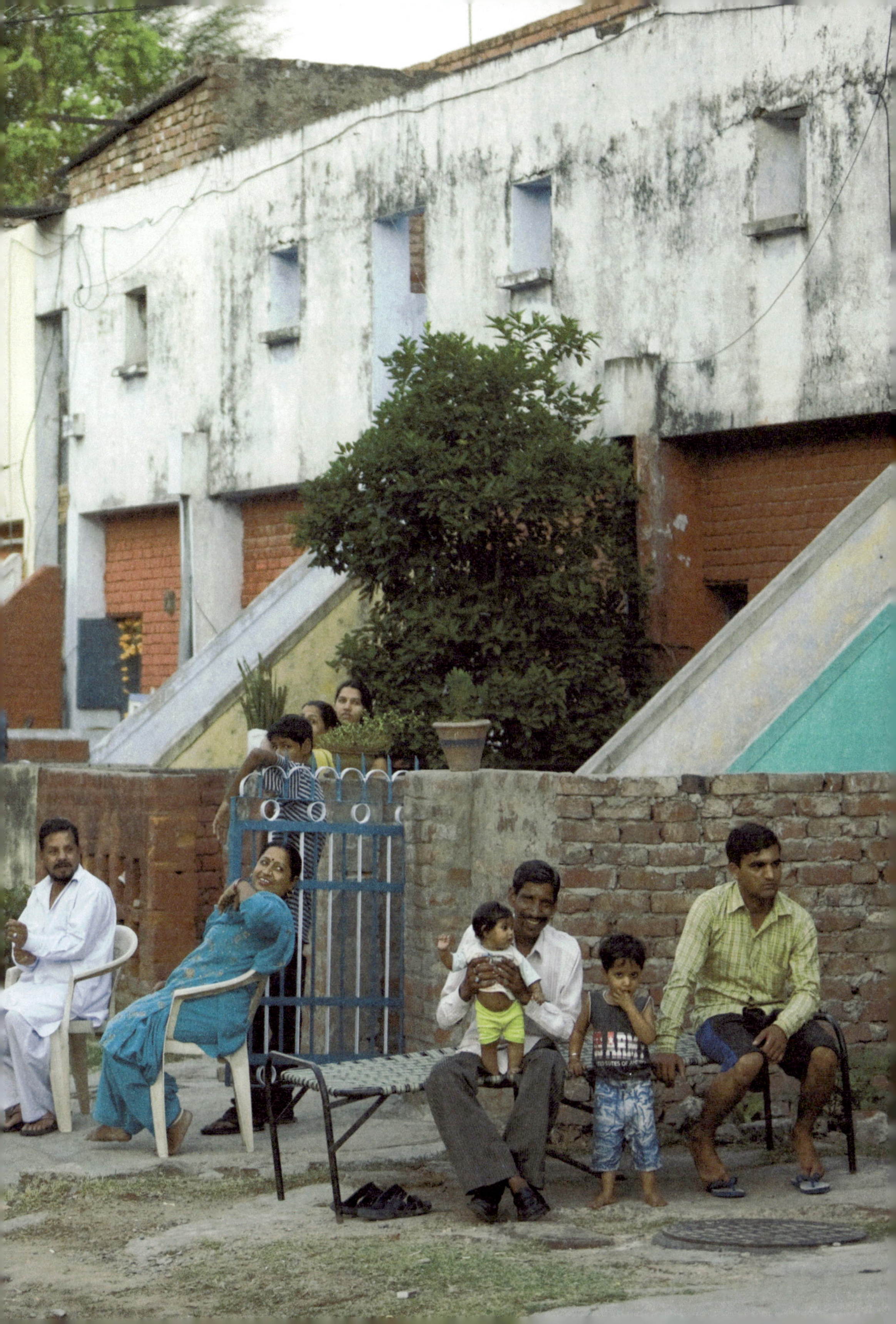

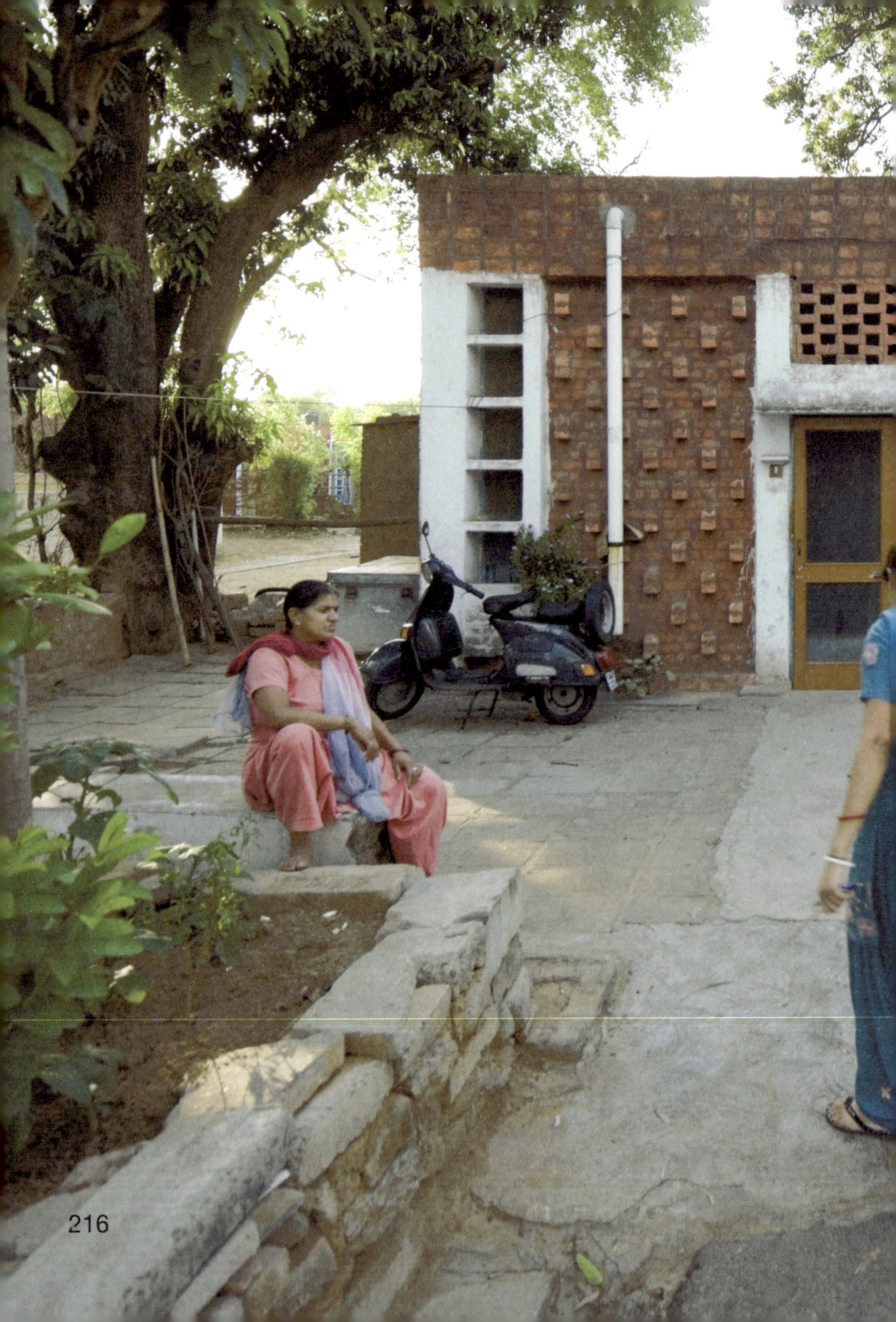

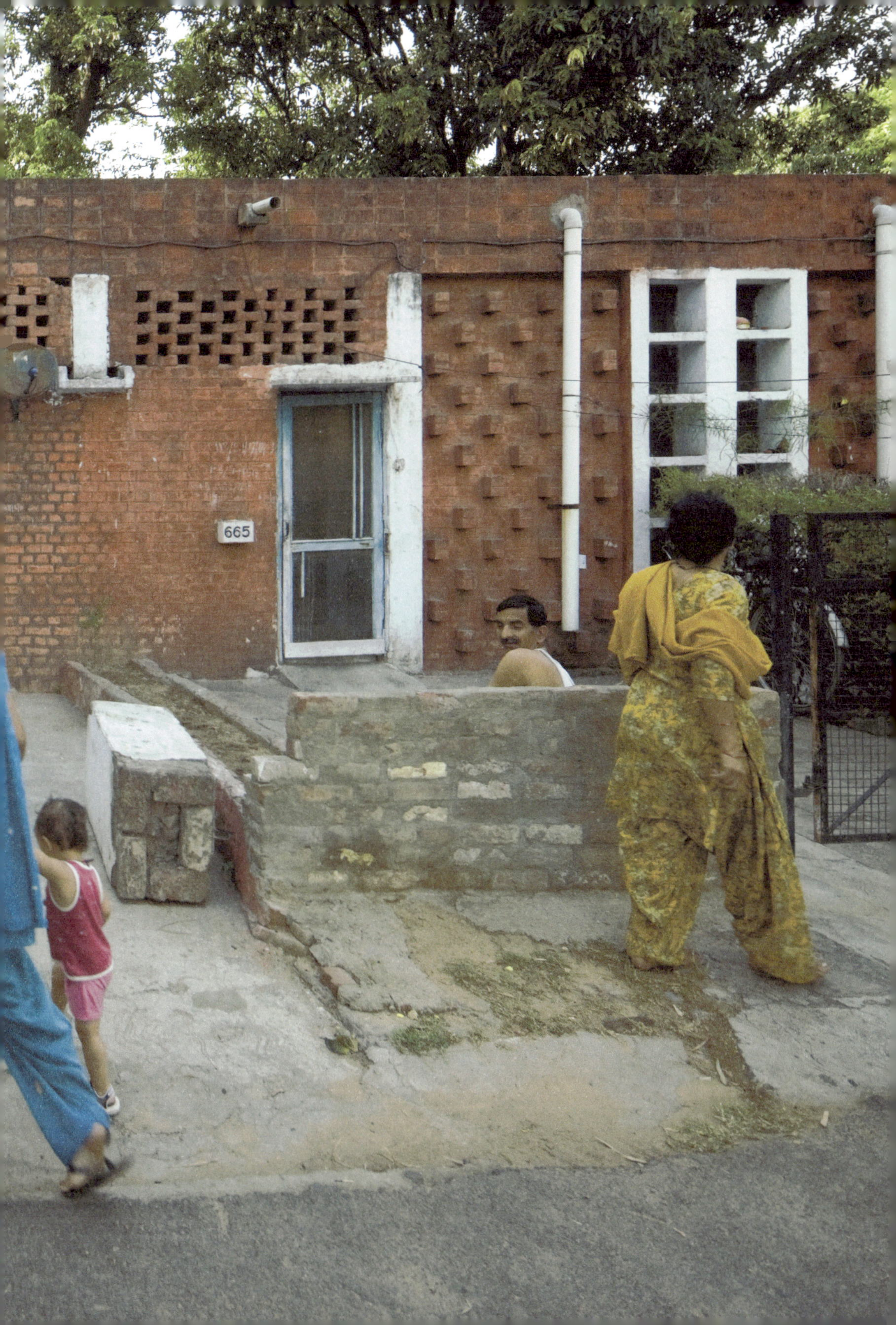
665

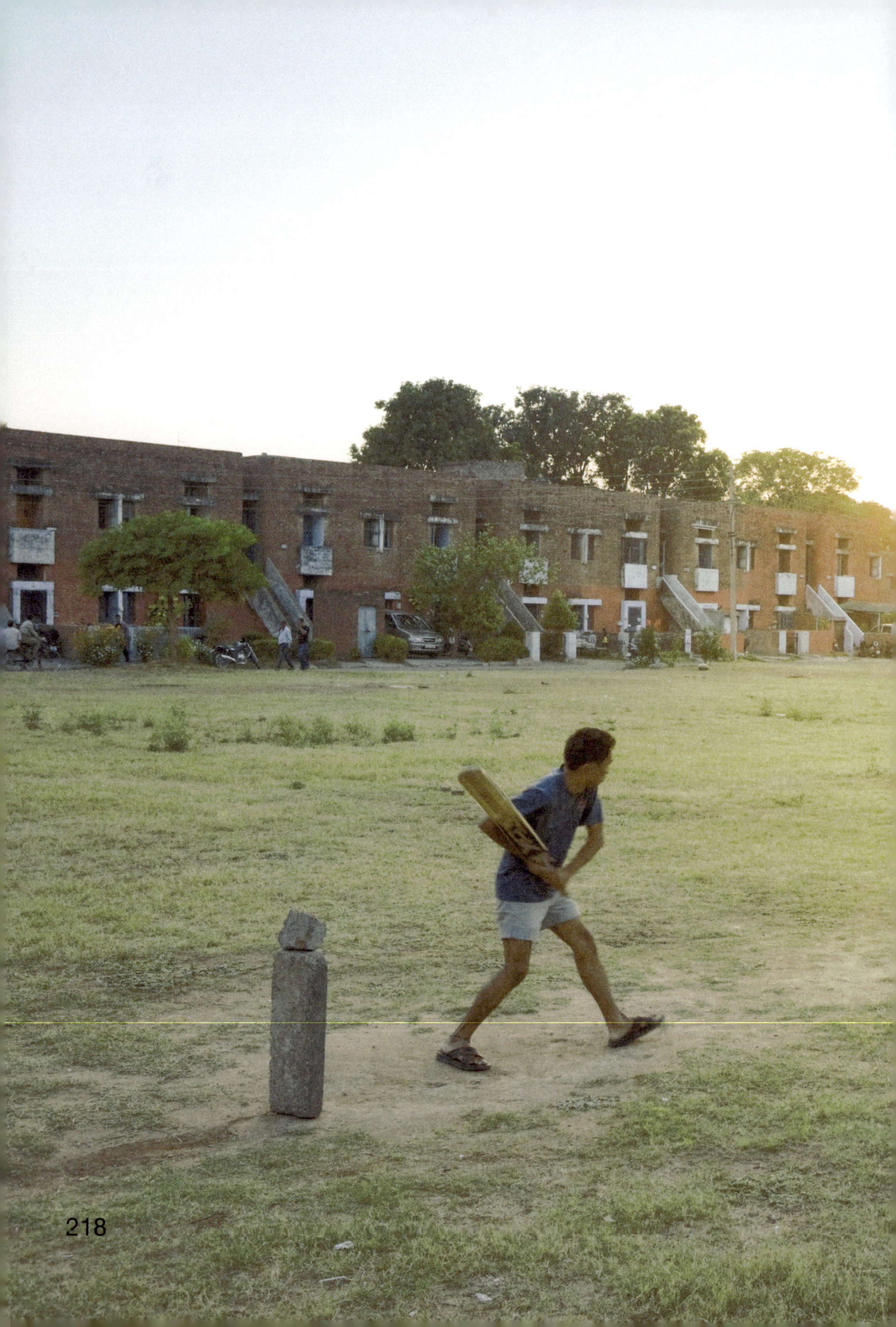

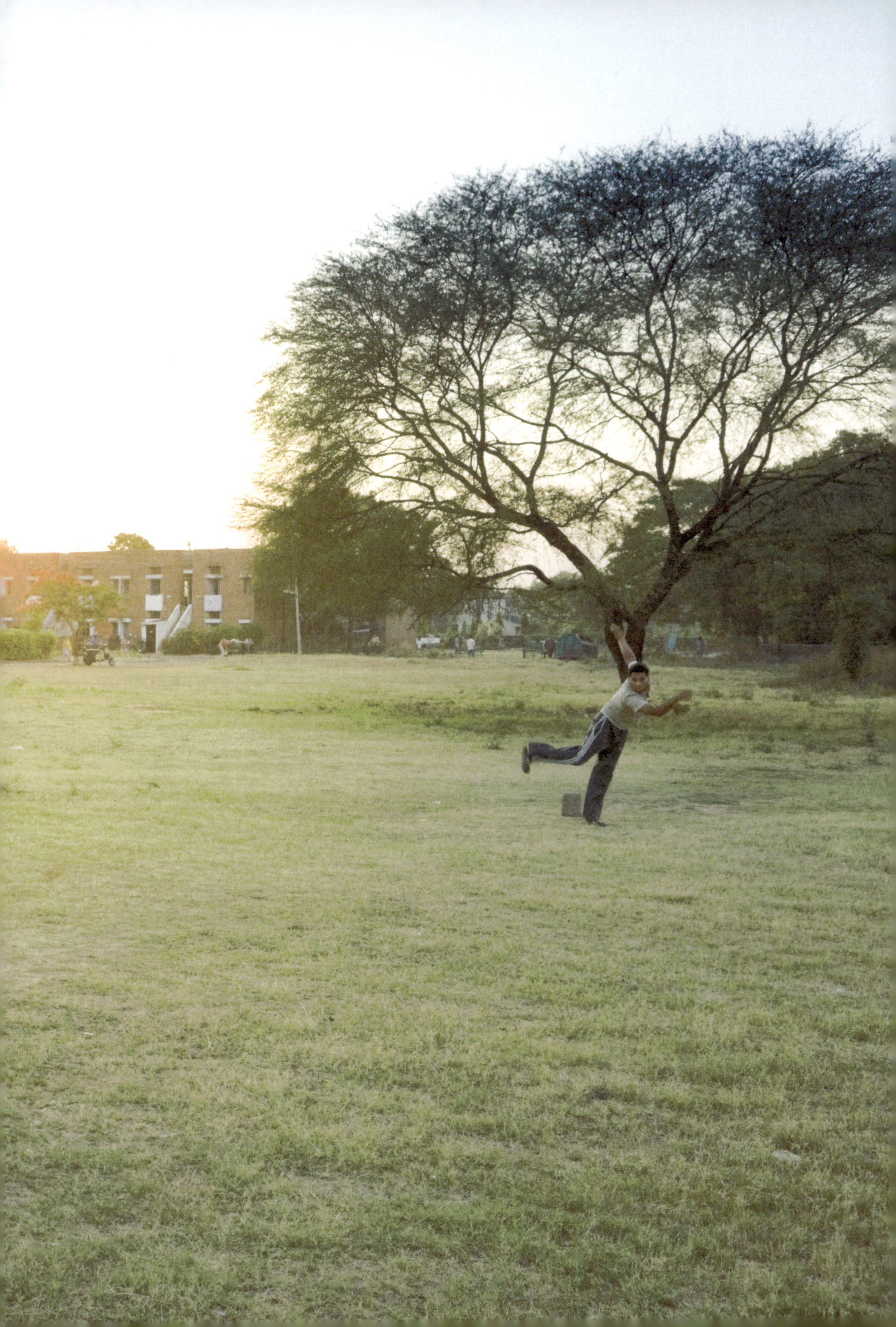

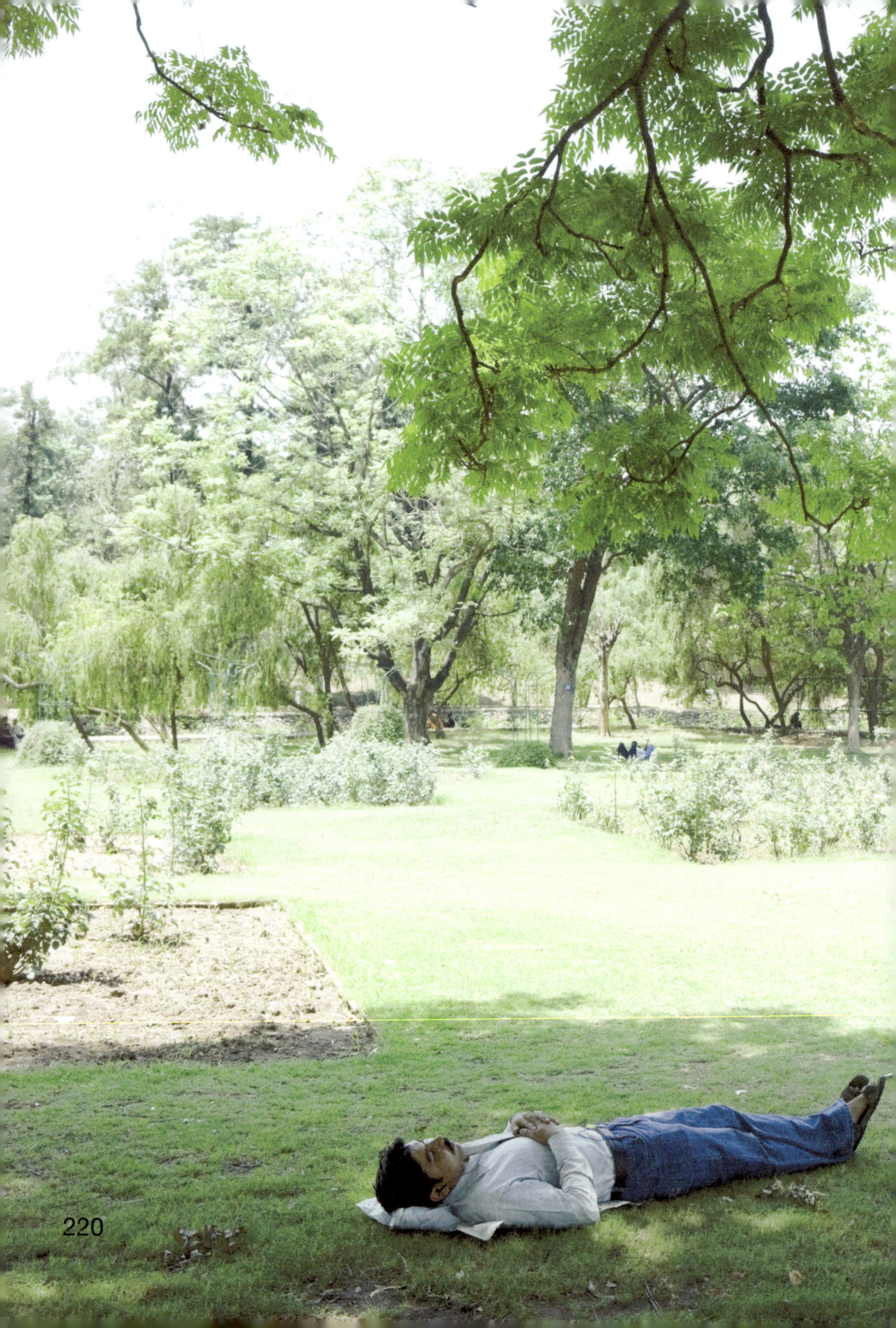

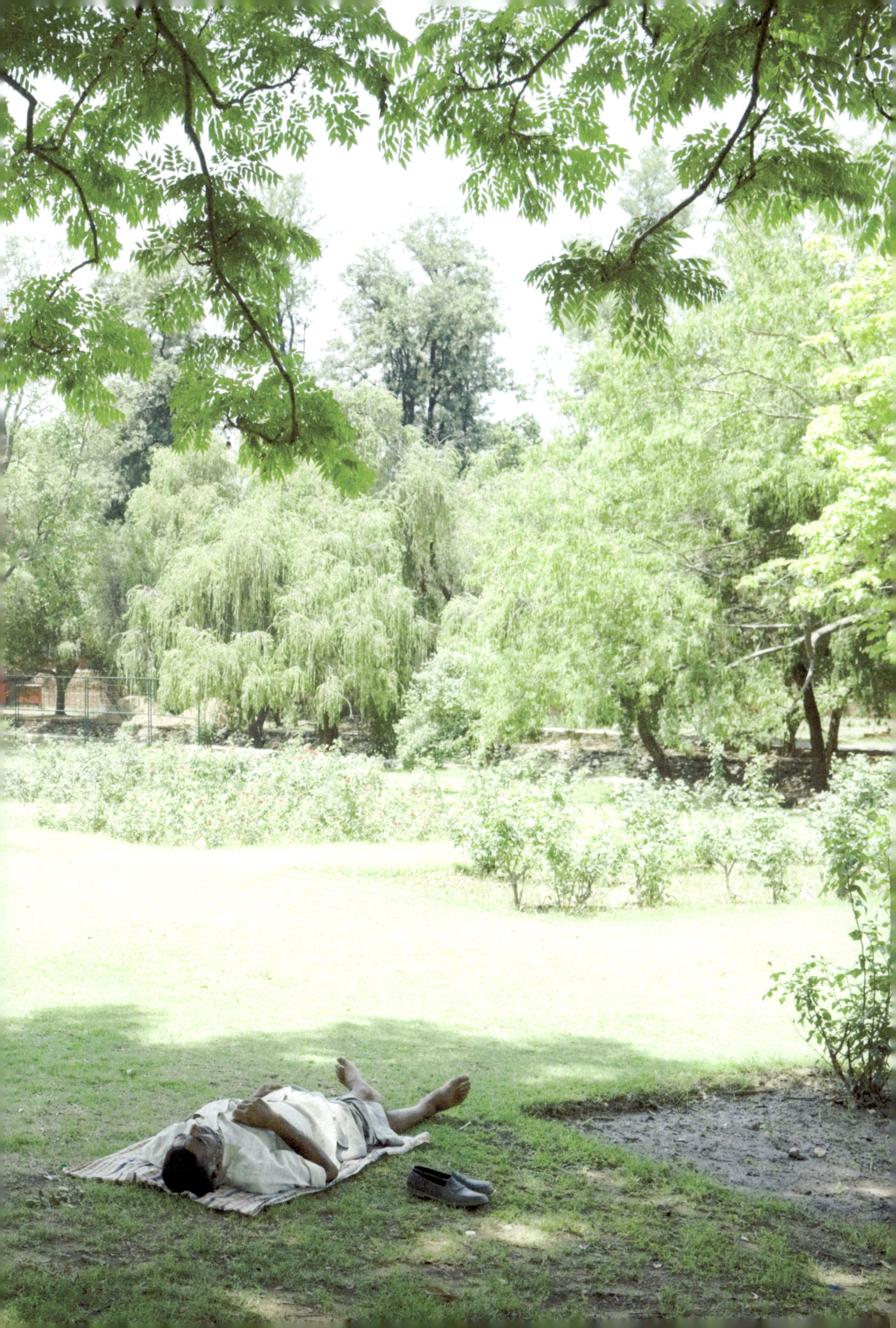

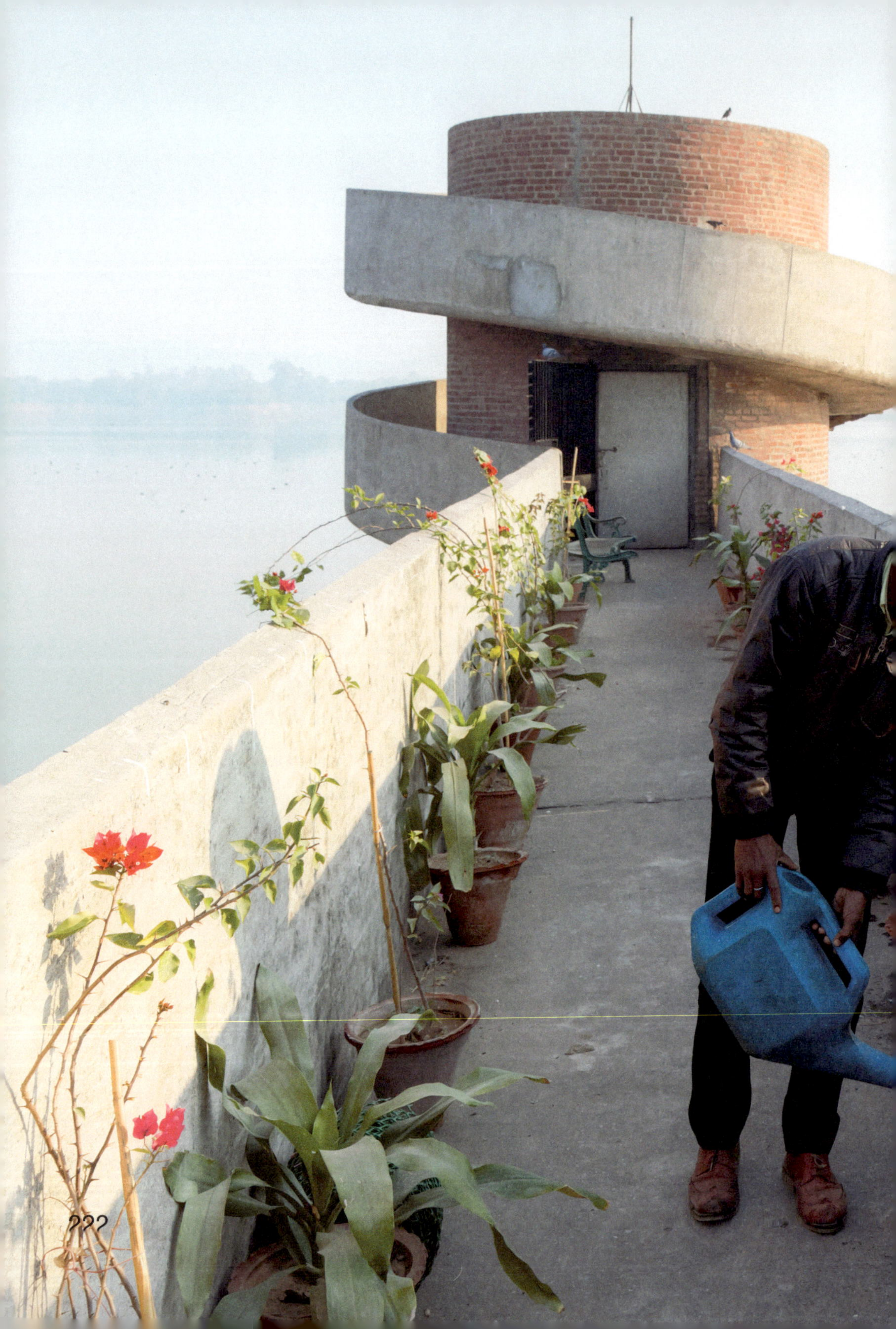

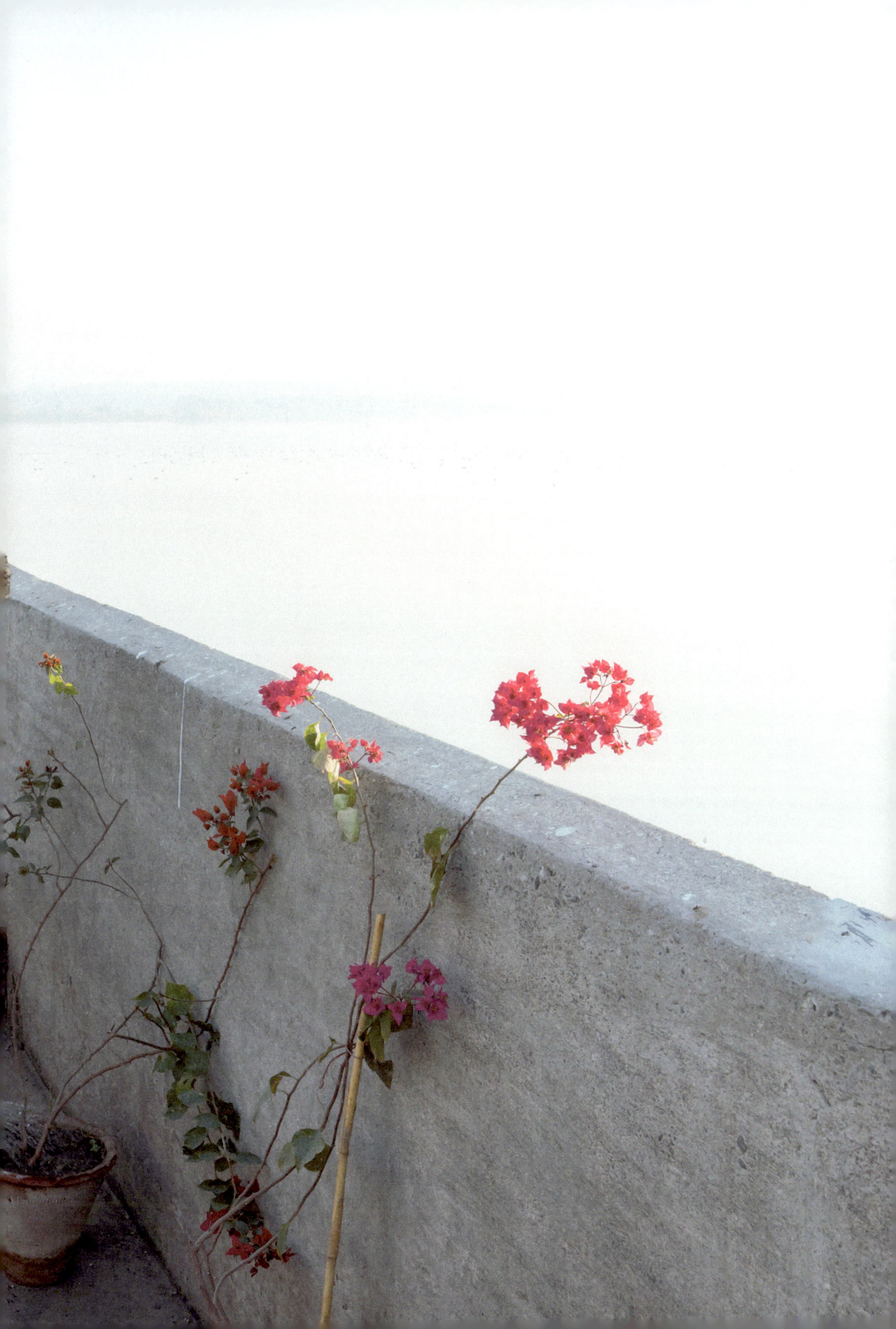

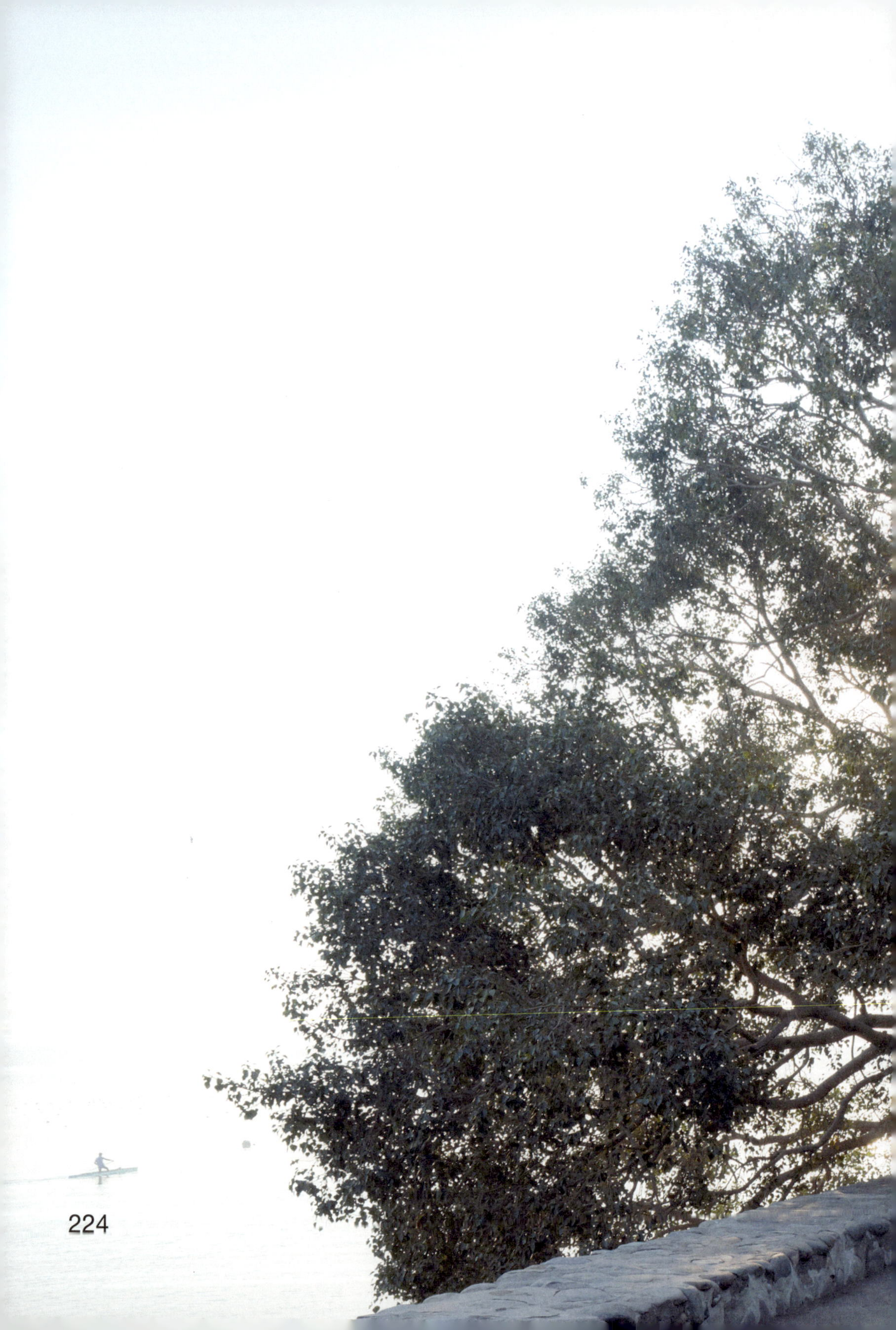

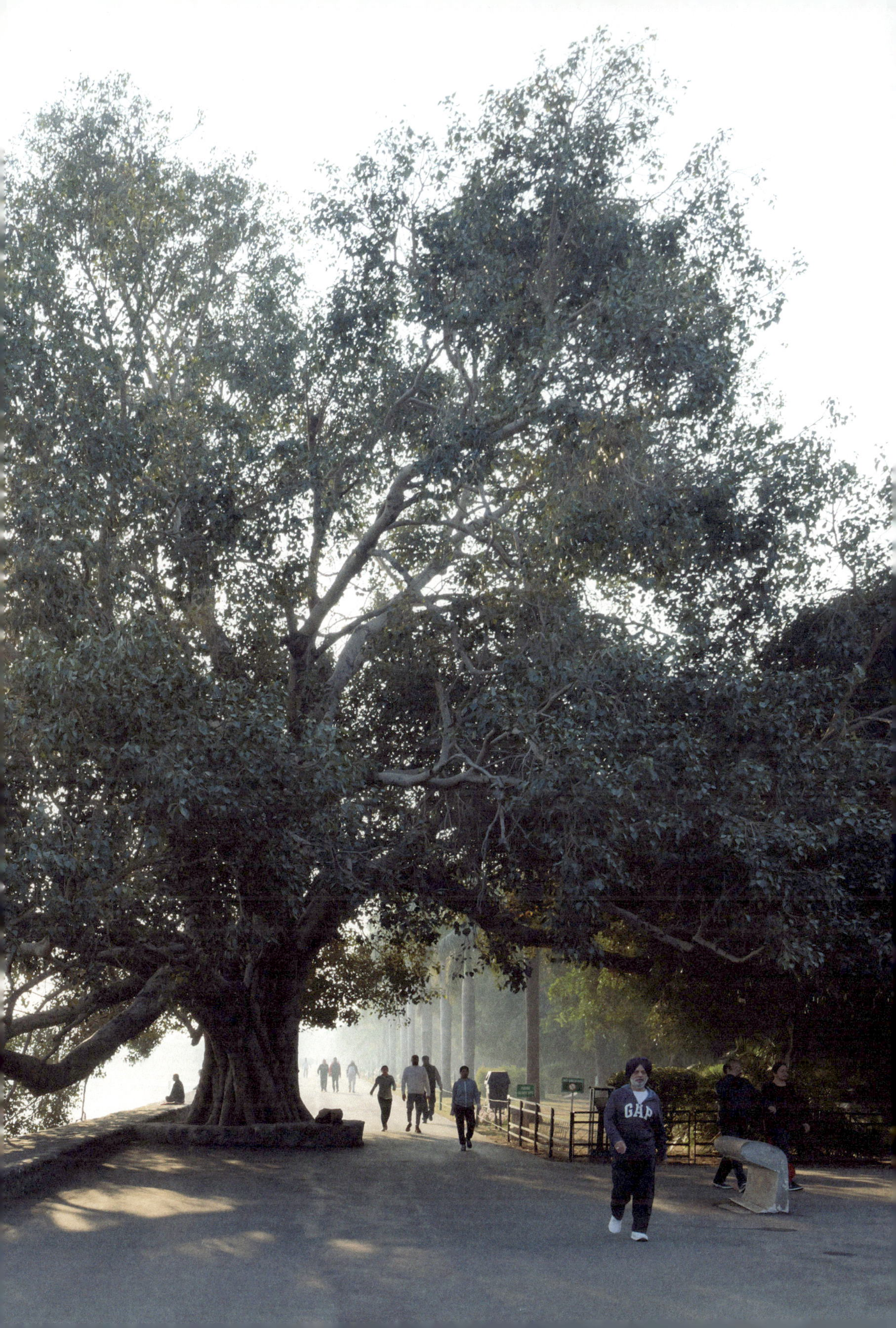
GAP

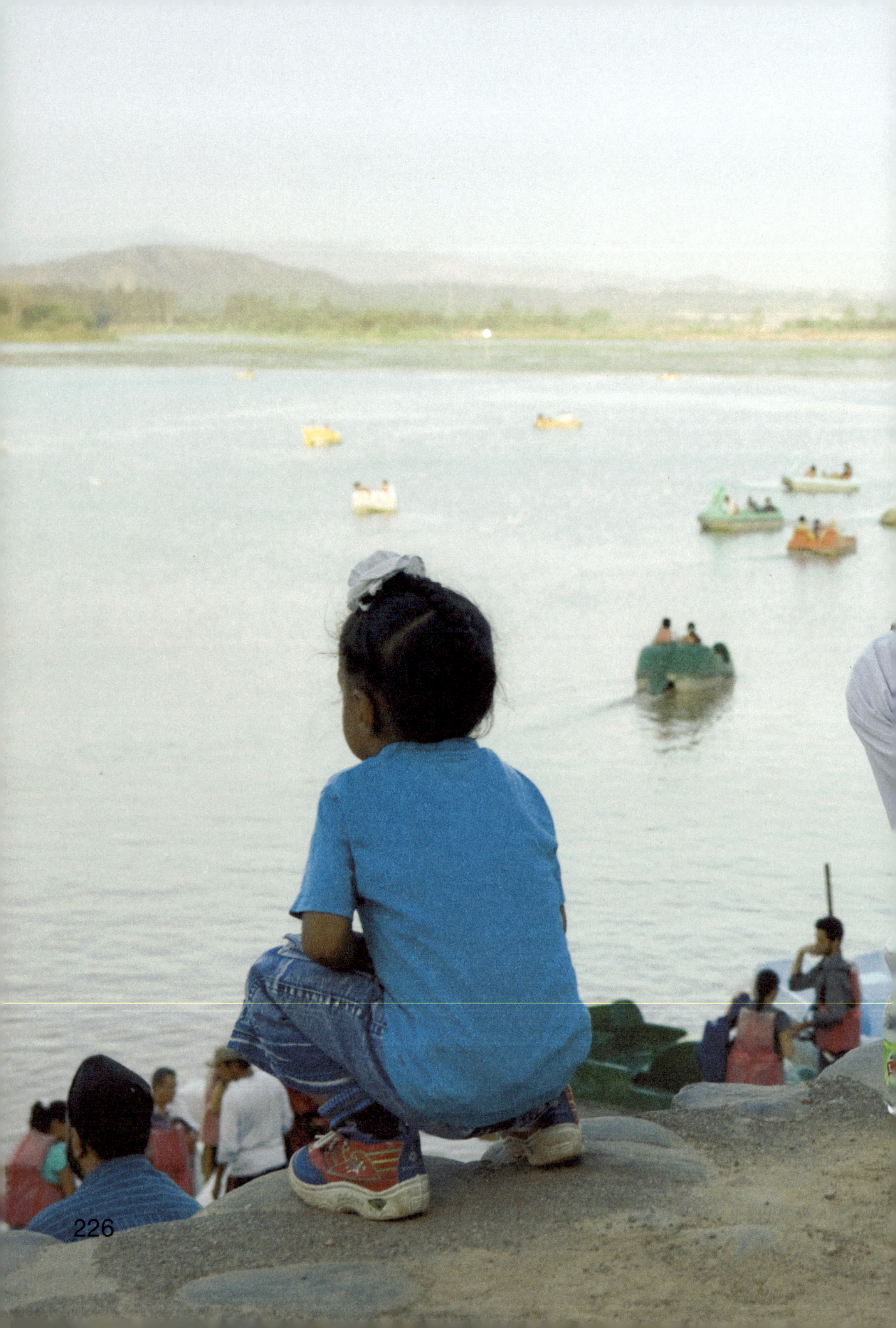

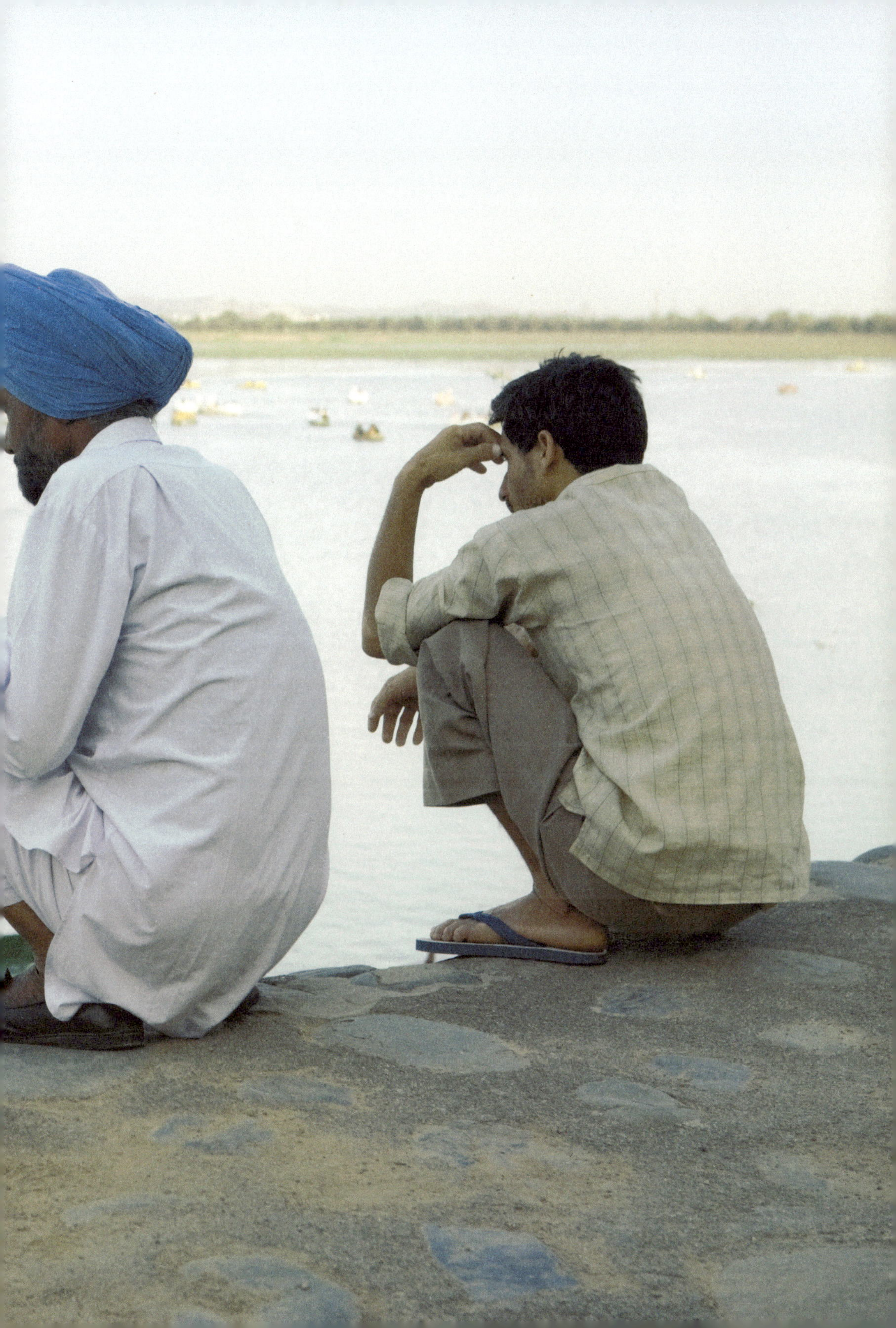

Monuments to Modernity*

Martino Stierli

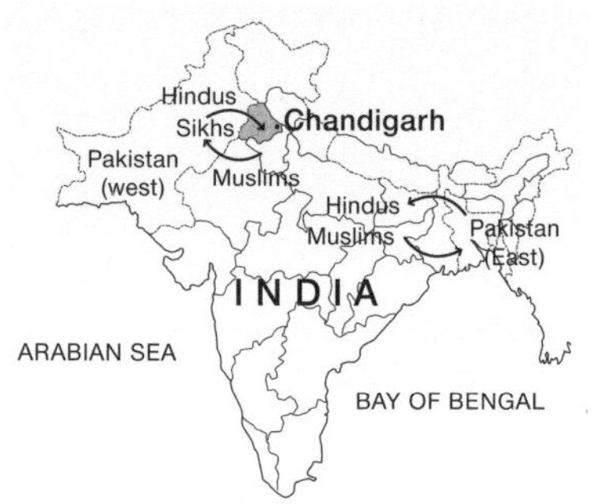

Map showing the 1947 separation of India and Pakistan, and the location of Chandigarh in the Indian state of Punjab (1)

Chandigarh: Building Utopia

Chandigarh may only be the capital of a comparatively small federal state in northwestern India, but its foundation was so intrinsically linked to the independence of the new nation from British rule in 1947 that it served as a strong symbol for the newly gained sovereignty. In the political process preceding independence, the British successfully campaigned for dividing the territory of their former colony into two separate states: Hindu-dominated India and what was to become the Islamic Republic of Pakistan. What was, among other things, intended as a measure to grant the religious minority a certain degree of self-rule led to a fiercely fought civil war that killed hundreds of thousands and displaced millions. The newly drawn border between the two newly established nations resulting from these violent events ran right through the former province of Punjab. Its historical capital, Lahore, found itself on Pakistani territory, leaving the Indian half of the province and new state of Punjab without a political and functional center. From the very beginning, Prime Minister Jawaharlal Nehru and his recently established central government in New Delhi realized that this situation presented a unique chance for the new nation to manifest its self-confidence and economic, cultural, and political aspirations, and the foundation of the new Punjabi capital of Chandigarh was to be the site where these hopes and ambitions were to become concrete symbols, national promise materialized in built form.

Despite its peripheral situation Chandigarh was very much an operation on a grand scale steered from above in the service of national interests. Nothing epitomizes this top-down politics more clearly than the very myth associated with the city's founding, according to which the two Indian officials Prem N. Thapar and P. L. Varma decided on its location on a plain at the foot of the Himalaya Mountains while flying over the site in an airplane, basing their choice quite literally on an abstract bird's-eye view that was detached from the realities of everyday Indian life.[1] This attitude was reflected in the choice of the American city planner Albert Mayer and of the Pole Matthew Nowicki as the designated chief architect as well. When the latter died in a plane crash in August 1950, Varma and Thapar traveled to Europe to find a replacement, whom they found in Jane Drew and Maxwell Fry, a British couple who had gained an international reputation in tropical architecture thanks to their earlier experience in Africa and Asia. The two architects proposed a collaboration with Le Corbusier, at that time one of the most prominent architects alive, who was then completing his Unité d'Habitation at Marseille, which counts among the most seminal modern experiments in collective residential housing. Despite his initial hesitations, Le Corbusier soon realized a unique opportunity was being offered to him to implement some of the utopian ideas on urbanism he had been developing since the early twenties, starting with his proposal of a Contemporary City of Three Million Inhabitants

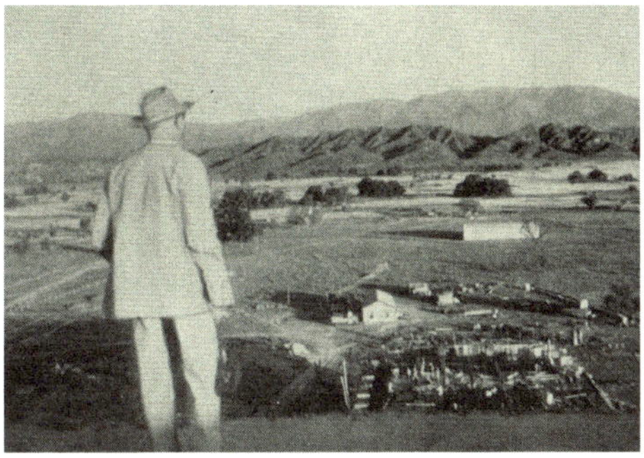

Le Corbusier on the roof of the Secretariat building surveying the site of the future capitol complex (2)

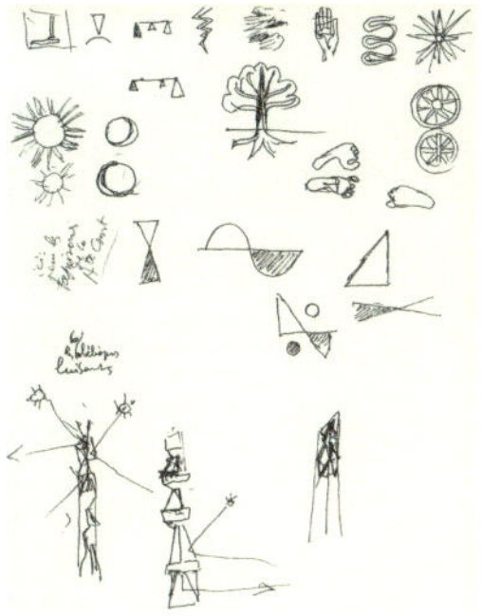

Sketches of Le Corbusier's symbols for the buildings in the capitol complex (3)

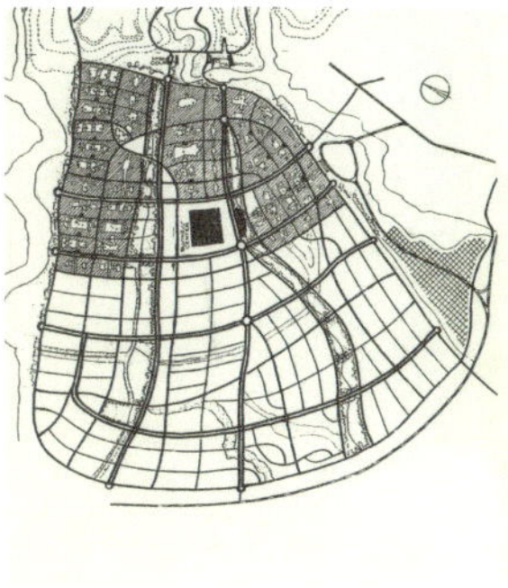

Master plan for Chandigarh by architect Albert Mayer with the capitol complex at the upper edge of the city, c. 1950 (4)

(Ville contemporaine de trois millions d'habitants) of 1922 and its application in the so-called Plan Voisin, in which he proposed to tear down large parts of the historic fabric of Paris and replace it by a rationalist scheme. The team of architects responsible for the project was completed with the addition of Le Corbusier's cousin and former collaborator Pierre Jeanneret, and a contract was signed with the Indian government shortly before Christmas of 1950. As part of the fulfillment of the provisions, Jeanneret, Drew, and Fry moved to Chandigarh the following year in order to plan and supervise the works on site, while Le Corbusier kept his base in his Paris studio. If the Indian government had taken care to entrust the ambitious endeavor of building a state capital to some of the most prominent international exponents of contemporary architecture, it proved equally authoritative in only allowing young Indians to complement the design team, which by November 1951 had grown to roughly thirty architects and draftsmen. Prominently among them were Balkrishna V. Doshi, Aditya Prakash and the eminent structural engineer Mahendra Raj. This system was clearly aimed at national emancipation: Chandigarh was meant not only to produce a powerful symbol of a new and progressive India, but also to constitute a workshop in which a transfer of architectural knowledge from the international elite to an emerging domestic caste of architects would take place. Modern architecture was to play a key role in a fundamental transformation of traditional Indian society, and Chandigarh would serve as the stage upon which this development was set in motion.

Albert Mayer had left a more or less fully elaborated plan for a city of 150,000 that was to be extended in a second phase to half a million inhabitants. Nearly all the major parameters set by this original plan were taken over in principle by the new team in charge, in particular the subdivision of the terrain into individual sectors, the situation of the representative government buildings in a separate area outside the actual settlement, and the construction of a business center. Unlike the curved streets in the tradition of the Garden City movement in the initial scheme, Le Corbusier opted for an orthogonal grid in the rationalist tradition, at the same time modifying the surface area of the individual sectors to 800 × 1200 m. In addition to the sectorial subdivision, Le Corbusier introduced his system of street hierarchies according to his seven V's theory first elaborated for the planning of Bogotá.[2] This system, which separated the individual means of traffic according to their respective speeds, was later adapted to include an eighth V for bicycles, which, despite its prime importance in Indian everyday life, had not been provided for initially.[3] Chandigarh was the most consistent realization of the urbanistic principles of the Congrès Internationaux d'Architecture Moderne (CIAM) and the so-called *Charte d'Athènes,* or Athens Charter.[4] Following

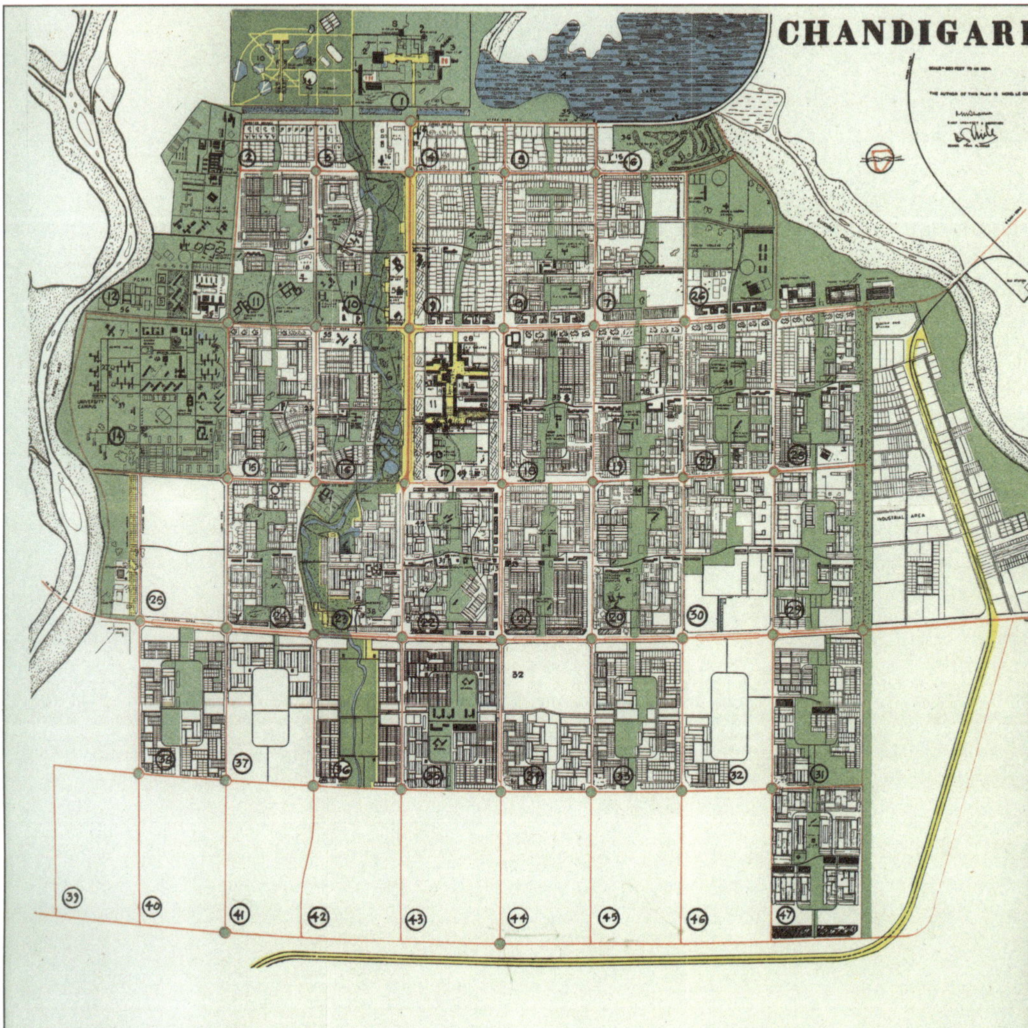

Map of Chandigarh according to Le Corbusier's scheme indicating the capitol complex at the upper edge and the numbered individual sectors of the plan, c. 1952 (5)

its tenets, the individual sectors of the city were to be segregated according to the four essential functions of dwelling, work, recreation, and circulation. Sir Edwin Lutyens' plan for the new Indian capital at New Delhi dating from the early twentieth century was another important point of reference for the elaboration of the plan,[5] as was the nineteenth-century tradition of Hausmannian French city planning with its strong bias for broad representational axes. Moreover, Chandigarh's spread-out plan owes much to Le Corbusier's quasi-cultic infatuation with speed and the automobile, and his excessively elaborated system of roads must be considered a monumental celebration of this ideology rather than an answer to functional considerations or even local needs.[6] At the same time, the plan, with its clearly distinguishable head (the capitol area) and the organic layout of the body of the city, came to resemble an anthropomorphic model.

The first few years of the realization of the ambitious project were focused on implementing the

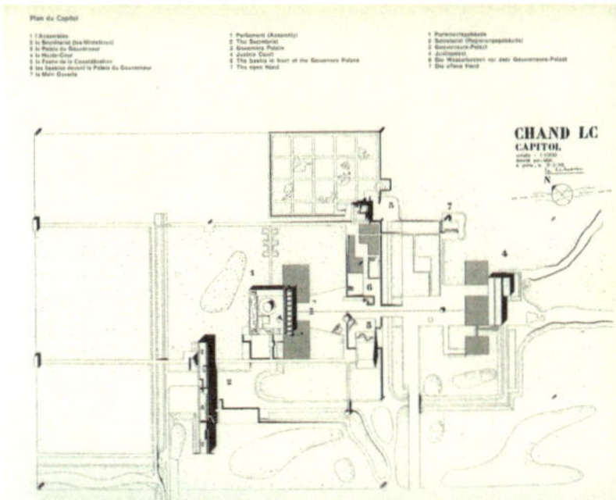

Plan of the capitol complex by Le Corbusier, 1956 (6)

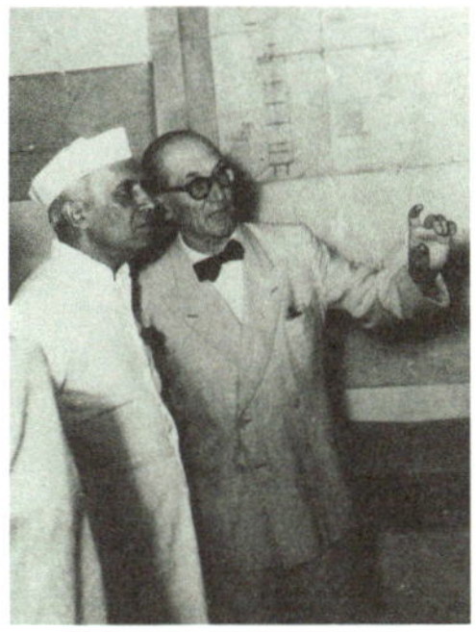

Le Corbusier explaining the High Court drawings to Prime Minister Jawaharlal Nehru, 1952 (7)

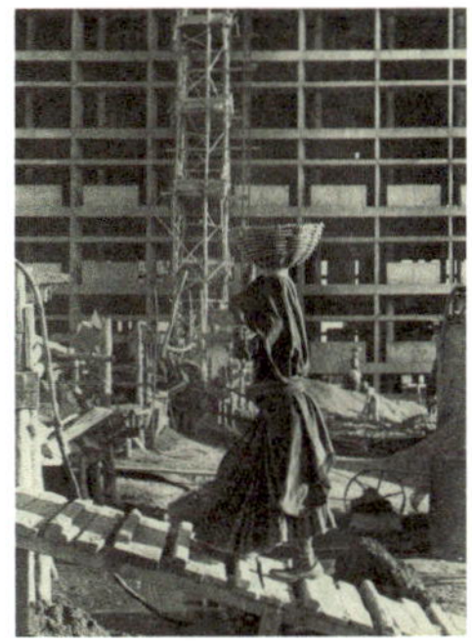

An Indian woman working on the construction site in front of the Secretariat building under construction (8)

plan, on public housing, and on the capitol area with its representative buildings. The city was officially dedicated on November 7, 1953, and the High Court was inaugurated in March 1955 as the first of the iconic government buildings. Whereas the bulk of the buildings resulted in fairly non-descript, primarily functional structures, the representative buildings in the capitol area that were designed by Le Corbusier himself constituted not only the climax of his work as a designer, but one of the finest ensembles of modernist architecture ever built. The central plaza of the capitol district is surrounded by the buildings for the main powers of government, namely the Main Court, the bicameral Parliament building, and the so-called Secretariat building housing the executive offices of the ministries. While Le Corbusier's initial proposal had foreseen a representative palace for the state's prime minister, Nehru blocked its construction, deeming individual representation at this scale undemocratic.[7] Characteristic of all the realized buildings is a certain sense of crude materiality, with most of them exposing rough concrete façades leading to what has been called a monumentalization of the archaic and the vernacular.[8] The exposed concrete surfaces are treated artistically, forming patterns and ornaments, which Le Corbusier explicitly refers to in his writings.[9] While one may consider this celebration of the brute and the unrefined as the ultimate break with the abstract aesthetics and white elegance of the International Style, its resurgence in Brasília only a few years later could be seen as its re-enthronement.[10] In Chandigarh, the material ruggedness is balanced by the sculptural appearance of the buildings, which vaguely reference the classical and the regional vocabulary of monumental architecture. Indeed, it has been argued that Le Corbusier's buildings in Chandigarh "revitalized the modern concept of monumental architecture."[11] While the High Court displays a series of arcades reminiscent of the classical language of architecture, the motif seems equally indebted to natural ventilation systems employed in Mogul palace architecture such as the Red Fort in Delhi, which Le Corbusier, Jane Drew, and Maxwell Fry had visited together in the early phase of their collaboration.[12] In turn, the hyperbolic form of the Parliament's House of Commons may be traced back to an Indian cooling tower Le Corbusier had seen from the air in 1951.[13] If such forms underscore the architect's interest in traditional, vernacular forms, the reference to more classical forms of monumentality is equally present in the capitol complex. While the latter appears to be the result of a unique and highly original design process, these buildings in fact "participate in the great theme of Chandigarh: the old architectural and urbanistic metaphors of rule are appropriated and transformed by the new political establishment."[14] The capitol therefore expresses not only traditional gestures of power but also the ideology of the new state, its embrace of progress and its optimistic belief in the creativity of its people.

Chandigarh was criticized at an early stage for its poor adaptation to the realities of everyday Indian city life and to prevailing cultural conditions.[15] The over-dimensioned circulation system principally oriented towards a fully automobilized society in particular has repeatedly been cited as one of the main flaws of the plan given that, even sixty years after its completion, the vast majority of people continue to rely primarily on bicycles, rickshaws or simply their own feet. Chandigarh has also failed to provide dwellings for the poor despite the design of fourteen different housing types meant to accommodate every income class. As a consequence of a restrictive land policy imposed by the government, the city was soon faced with a dramatic housing shortage, leaving a considerable percentage of its inhabitants without proper living quarters. Chandigarh has in recent years grown to the size of roughly one million people, thus doubling the originally projected number of inhabitants, while the Chandigarh Capital Region comes to roughly 3.4 million permanent residents. Furthermore, Le Corbusier's scheme has hardly managed to care for hawkers and itinerate traders, who are not only characteristic of Indian street life but also immensely important for the country's domestic economy.[16] The monofunctional character of the business center located in Sector 17 of the plan has been spectacularly ineffective in attracting civic or public life and appears empty and uninhabited after businesses have closed, in stark contrast to the incessant bustle of traditional Indian cities with their typical mix of living and working. Due to the fact that the situation has hardly changed up to the present, Le Corbusier's enthusiastic celebration of a bright future based on technological development seems outdated in an era of globalization that relies more than ever before on an economic gap between North and South and in a world that has painfully become aware of the ecological threats of unhindered technological progress. However, Le Corbusier's plan should be considered against the conditions upon which it was originally elaborated. In light of India's move to independence and its strong need for a powerful symbol epitomizing the hopes and expectations of a bright future, the architect's utopian scheme seemed indeed more than adequate. Both the political leaders and their architect saw Chandigarh not as a means to enforce the cultural and ideological values of the past but, quite to the contrary, as a monumental statement towards a radically different, more democratic and affluent future. As Prime Minister Nehru famously voiced in his speech on the occasion of the official dedication of the city in 1953, Chandigarh was to be "the first large expression of our creative genius, flowering on our newly earned freedom, ...unfettered by traditions of the past,...reaching beyond the existing encumbrances of old towns and old tradition"; in fact, it was to become the "temple of new India."[17]

The uncritical way in which Le Corbusier embraced political power to realize his urbanistic and social vision may indeed seem problematic in retrospect, but he perfectly adapted to the role of a compliant executor of the new authority's need to represent itself and its ambitious progressive program in monumental built form.

Brasília: A Vision of Progress

If Chandigarh's existence is owed to the alliance of an energetic leader figure with an extraordinary team of architects, Brasília's foundation equally relied on the seemingly undeviating will of a single visionary and his firm instinct for the seductive power of architectural imagery. When Juscelino Kubitschek, the governor of the Brazilian state of Minas Gerais, was elected President of the Republic in 1955, he knew that he had just one five-year term in order to turn his campaign slogan "Fifty years of progress in five" from promise to fact. It was in the short period of his presidency from 1956 to 1961 that the long-time dream of a new Brazilian capital became manifest. Other countries had given themselves a new capital in earlier periods, but Brasília was the

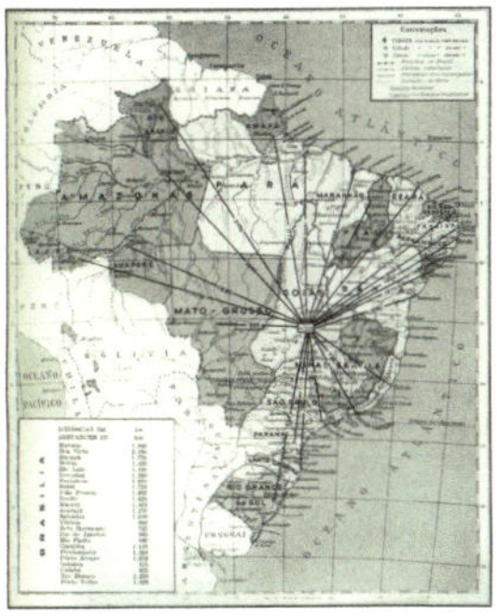

Map indicating the location of Brasília with distances to the Brazilian state capitals (9)

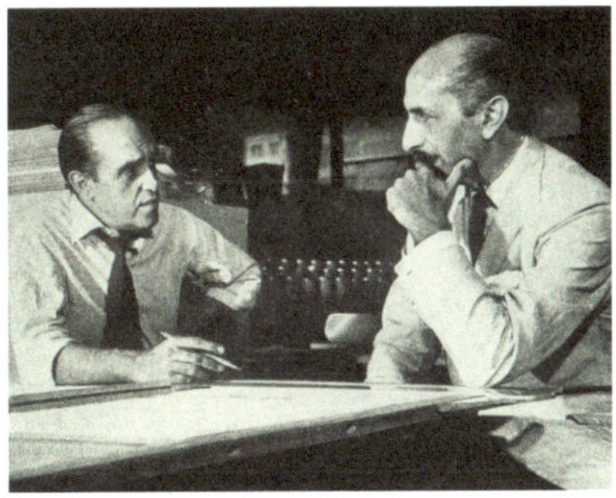

Architects Lúcio Costa and Oscar Niemeyer discussing their plans and designs for Brasília, c. 1958 (10)

first opportunity for architects to construct an entire city according to the tenets of modern architecture. In its beginning, it was, just like Chandigarh, more of a symbol of a strong belief in the future than a real functional city. As in all capitals, the main architectural challenge lay in representing national power in monumental form. Modern architects had for a long time rejected traditional monumentality as an empty gesture of the theatricality of nineteenth-century historicist architecture, but both Chandigarh and Brasília served as a unique – and indeed inevitable – opportunity to come to terms with a concept of modern monumentality and national representation.

The dream of a national capital free of any symbolic associations with the Portuguese colonial regime had haunted the Brazilian people since the end of the eighteenth century.[18] In 1822 a Brazilian delegate coined the name of the prospective capital that was to be situated in the largely unexplored – yet by no means uninhabited – interior of the vast national territory, and in 1891 the newly approved constitution of the republic explicitly called for the creation of a federal district on the central plateau. In the following decades, several commissions were set up by the central government in order to present recommendations as to the specific location of the future capital, but only after a new law had been passed in 1953 was its site finally chosen, in April 1955. When shortly afterwards Kubitschek gained the presidency with only one third of the popular vote, the foundation of a new national capital became his prime political goal in which he invested all his energy and influence to create irreversible facts during his term of office. Rio, the country's historic government center, was increasingly faced with population pressure, a shortage of housing, and limited possibilities for future expansion due to its topography.[19] Furthermore, Rio was notorious for its inefficient bureaucracy, and it held the stigma of a colonial past. On the other hand, a number of positive expectations were associated with the founding of Brasília. It would form, so it was hoped, a "neutral" territory in the service of the whole nation rather than reinforcing the traditional colonial dominance of the coastal area – while paradoxically continuing the project of interior colonization at the expense of the indigenous peoples who had been inhabiting these lands for millenia.[20] In this respect, the foundation of Brasília was seen as a catalyst for the interior colonization and strengthening of the vast Brazilian hinterland, and as a measure against its ceaseless depopulation.[21]

When the newly elected president set out to make his ambitious plan a reality, he asked the architect Oscar Niemeyer for advice, whom he had known and esteemed since his time as mayor of Belo Horizonte in the early 1940s. The selection of a master plan was determined through an open competition, while Niemeyer himself was charged with designing the majority

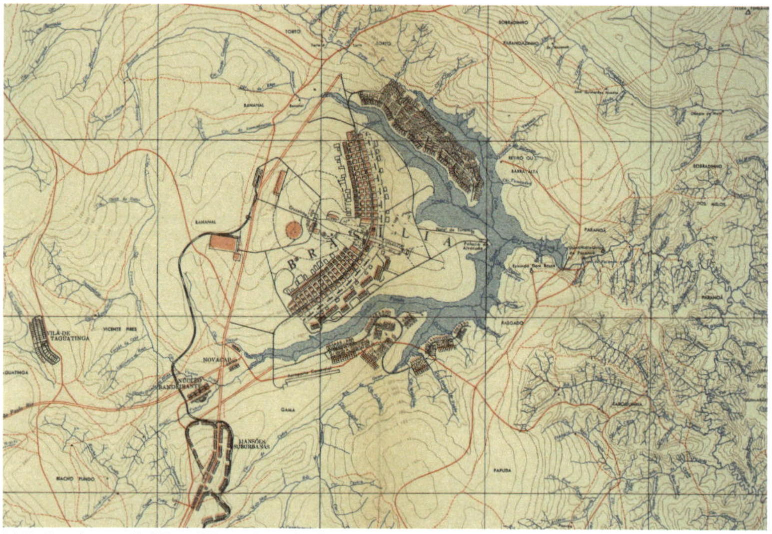

Lúcio Costa's so-called Plano Piloto scheme for Brasília's city center in its topographical situation, 1957 (11)

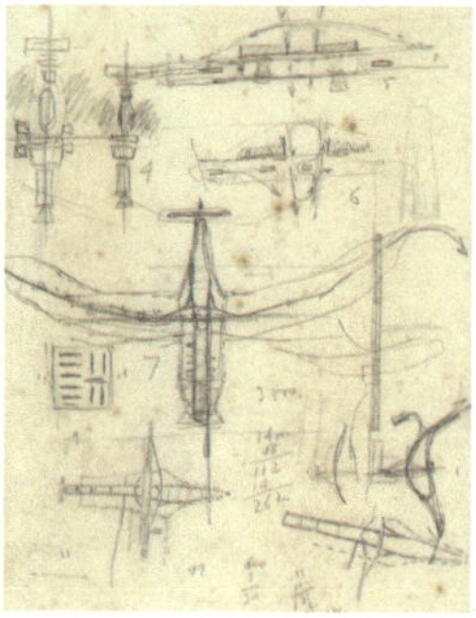

Draft design by Lúcio Costa for the so-called Plano Piloto, 1957 (12)

of the representative government buildings of the new capital. In August of 1956 the national congress created the Companhia Urbanizadora da Nova Capital (NOVACAP), which announced the competition for a city of 500,000 inhabitants among all of the country's licensed architects one month later. In March 1957 Lúcio Costa emerged as the winner. When the city was officially inaugurated on April 21, 1960, it seemed hardly possible that the new capital had started from a simple design only three years earlier. The first task had been to build roads and railways to the inaccessible site of the new capital, and to provide for an airport. This infrastructure was the prerequisite for the arrival of the necessary building materials and manpower. Afterwards, things moved very fast: In October 1957 Brasília's first school opened, in June of 1958 Niemeyer set up his permanent headquarters in the city, and in September of the same year, the first house was completed. The initial drive was somewhat lost after Kubitschek's retirement from office in 1961 as both of his short-term successors were less than enthusiastic about bringing the plan to a successful end. The situation changed with the military coup of 1964, when the new leaders reanimated the project with full force. Norma Evenson has argued convincingly that Brasília's strong monumental emphasis "accorded well with the military fondness for ceremony and nationalist symbols."[22] Despite its political ambiguity, Brasília has become an international landmark of modernist urbanism, and in 1987 the city was selected as one of the first protected monuments of the twentieth century to be added to the UNESCO World Heritage list.

The main feature of Lúcio Costa's master plan consisted in two monumental axes intersecting at right angles. While this cross plan relates back to urban planning models in ancient Greece or Rome, the Christian iconography is explicit, furthering the implicit colonial symbolism of the undertaking. Costa's masterplan represented a decisively different concept than the gridiron scheme implemented at Chandigarh. With respect to the specific situation of the future city between the arms of an artificial lake, one of the axes forms a curve so as to fit the plan inside the given topographical situation. This feature gave the plan the characteristic appearance of an airplane, a powerful symbol of progress, which Costa evoked by calling his project "Plano Piloto" or Pilot Plan. While the East-West axis with its ample mall is reserved for the representative government and administrative buildings,

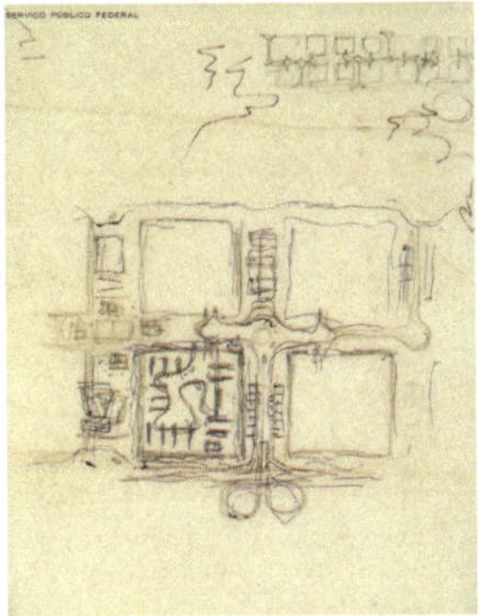

Sketch of a neighborhood unit by Lúcio Costa, 1957 (13)

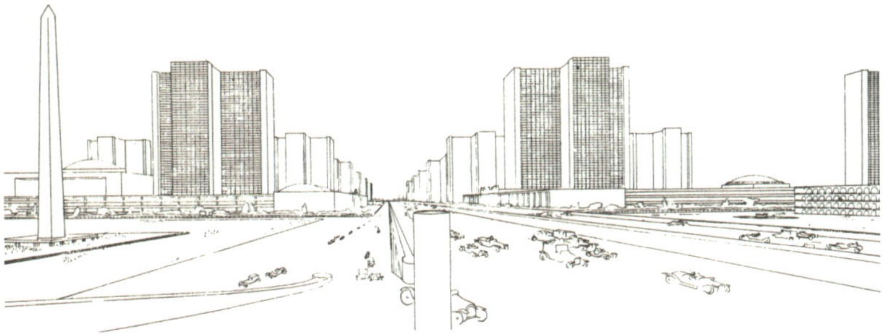

Le Corbusier's design for a Contemporary City of Three Million Inhabitants, 1922 (14)

the curving North-South axis is taken up by a major urban highway. Along this corridor the so-called residential *superquadras,* or superblocks, are aligned on both sides. These individual units measure 280 × 280 m each and are thus substantially larger than regular city blocks (hence the name). They are all lined with a twenty-meter band of trees and bushes, giving the city a pronouncedly green aspect. Each of the superblocks holds eight to eleven residential slabs (of usually six stories) arranged at right angles, as well as an elementary school.[23] Where the two main axes intersect in a monumental traffic interchange, Costa envisioned a platform for an amusement center consisting of theaters, cinemas, restaurants, and the like. Extending eastward on the government axis, he planned (in succession towards the lakefront) a cultural district, a cathedral, the ministries, and finally, as the architectural, symbolic, and political climax of the scheme, the triangular expanse of the Plaza of the Three Powers with the most representative monumental structures: the Parliament, Alvorada Palace, i.e., the presidential residence, the Supreme Court, and Planalto Palace, housing the executive headquarters. Although this axis resembles conventional compositions in the tradition of the École des Beaux-Arts, the architectural vocabulary employed is a clear statement in favor of the modernist International Style. On the other side of the intersection of the two principal axes and extending westward, Costa proposed a large mall with the television tower, a sports center, the zoological and botanical gardens, as well as a number of additional amenities. As in the case of Chandigarh, the Plano Piloto was inspired by the doctrine of the "functional city" as elaborated by the Congrès Internationaux d'Architecture Moderne (CIAM), and indeed the urbanistic visions of Le Corbusier form a major point of reference for Costa's plan. This is evidenced not only in the functional differentiation, but also in the monumentalization of automobile traffic, the use of *pilotis* (or piers, in the sense of reinforced concrete stilts employed to raise a structure off the earth) in all residential buildings to keep the ground open, the concentration of dwellings in dense housing units, or the combination of metropolitan urban life with a suburban setting in an extensive park-like situation. The indebtedness to Le Corbusier manifests itself in the architectural imagery as well. Thus, the two-dimensional upside-down arches of Alvorada Palace seem directly inspired by the parabolic arches of the initial designs for the Parliament at Chandigarh.[24]

Costa's plan was treated with great respect and translated into reality as he designed it for the most part. Not unlike at Chandigarh, the abstract nature of the modernist concept was somewhat moderated by the use of conventional construction techniques, i.e., predominantly poured-in-place concrete structural framing with brick infill panels rather than precast concrete elements. Almost all of the buildings in Brasília

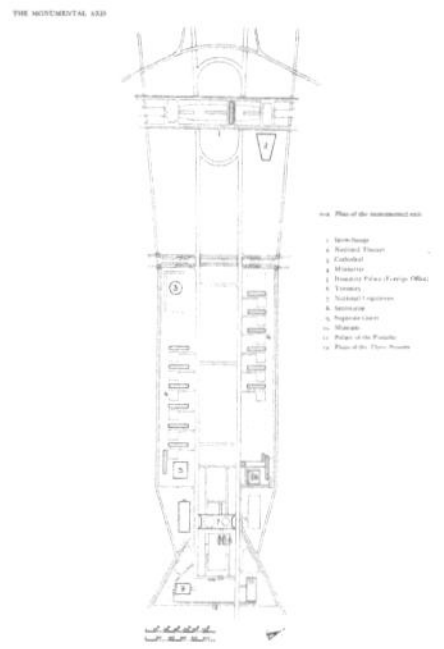

Lúcio Costa's plan of Brasília's monumental axis, c. 1957 (15)

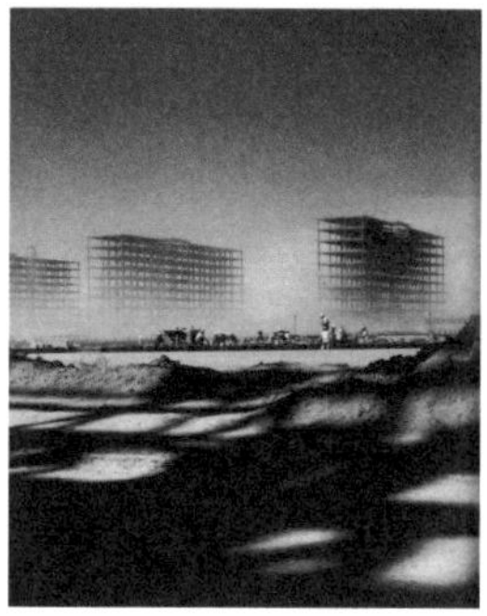

The Ministries' buildings along Brasília's monumental axis under construction, c. 1959 (16)

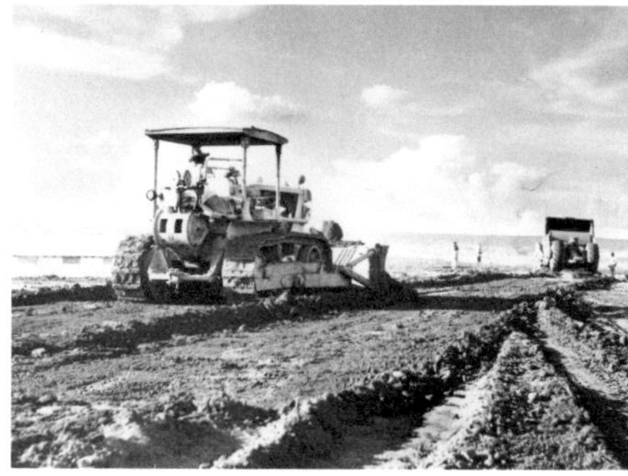

Preparation works on the site of the future Brazilian capital, c. 1957 (17)

corresponded to a small number of standardized types. Whereas all the government ministries along the central mall were designed according to a single scheme, i.e., a ten-story rectilinear slab framed in steel with the principal façades sheathed in glass and end walls faced in ceramic tile, housing was executed in six-story structures for the most part. The residential slabs are characterized by their differentiation between a usually open, fully glassed front façade and a rear façade covered by various screening devices made of open brickwork or concrete elements. Contrary to Chandigarh, where such ornamental components primarily helped regulate indoor temperatures, in Brasília they served mainly to hide the service balconies that were apparently considered unworthy of open display. Furthermore, external sun-breakers were used only scarcely, and privately accessible open spaces were hardly provided for. The lack of consideration for climate conditions has repeatedly been subject to critique.

While Brasília's urbanistic scheme was based on the Costa plan, it was Niemeyer who was chiefly responsible for the design of the major building types and monuments of the new capital. The famous Brazilian architect was not only involved in the blueprints of some of the housing, but also in such structures as the National Theater or the Cathedral with its tentlike roof and characteristic circular plan of roughly sixty meters in diameter. Needless to say, Niemeyer's architectural ambitions were focused primarily on the government axis and the problem of monumental representation in a modernist idiom. Alvorada Palace (1957) was conceived basically as a glass pavilion screened by the peculiarly curving supports mentioned above, a scheme Niemeyer was to adopt and vary with a number of additional structures in the capitol complex such as the Supreme Court (1958–60) or Planalto Palace, housing the presidential offices (1958–60), while the sequence of arches at Itamarati Palace (1962), the home of the Foreign Ministry, which anticipates some of the most iconic buildings of Philip Johnson of the following years, seems to echo more directly the High Court building at Chandigarh. Niemeyer, very much in the manner of another hero of modern architecture, Mies van der Rohe, expressed architectural sophistication by using luxurious materials such as white marble and black granite. The National Congress (1958) is perhaps Brasília's most dramatic architectural gesture. The building is defined, again, by a low pavilion-like structure with a cantilevering flat roof resting on elegant columns upon which two spherical calottes, representing the two chambers of the national parliament, are placed symmetrically, one of them inverted so as to form a colossal bowl. The well-balanced composition is completed by two slender curtain-walled office slabs resembling the U.N. Headquarters building on the East River in New York.

One of the most critical aspects of the transformation of an abstract urbanistic concept into a real city was Brasília's failure to accommodate for the traditional Brazilian ways of life as well as for the less affluent and the poor, a situation quite similar to that at Chandigarh.[25] Equally problematic was the treatment of the land as *tabula rasa* even though the Karajá people had been living here for generations, and a delegation of whom were invited to a Catholic mass celebrated in 1957 to commemorate the foundation of the construction site of the city. While in the Punjabi capital this part of the population was absorbed by undefined urban intermediary zones and thus made invisible, Costa's initial plan did not provide guidelines for further expansion of the city. This flaw quickly resulted in the unplanned construction of satellite towns outside the Plano Piloto area for the working class, whose everyday commute in turn led to dramatic traffic problems. Although attempts were made to regulate the further development of these satellites, Brasília has been characterized from early on by a sharp contrast between the rigid monumental center and the seemingly chaotic urban sprawl surrounding it. Commenting on the problematic social topography of the two cities, the architectural historian Alan Colquhoun remarked, "Chandigarh and Brasília are both middle-class cities from which lower-paid workers, necessary for the cities' economies, are excluded. In Chandigarh... such workers are allowed to squat in the interstices of the city; in Brasília, they are banished to unplanned satellite towns from which they commute daily to work."[26] The number of inhabitants of the central area was soon dwarfed by the surrounding fringe settlements, a process that continues to the present day and is symptomatic of an unbroken global trend toward urbanization and the growth of megalopolises, particularly in developing and emerging nations. This asymmetric development of center and periphery is reflected in a number of striking figures. While in 1964 Brazil's Federal District counted roughly 270,000 inhabitants, a third of whom lived in the Plano Piloto area, the city's metropolitan area in 2022 had reached 4.3 million inhabitants. Of the roughly 3 million living within the confines of the Federal District, just over 200,000 people actually dwelt in the originally planned area, or roughly the same number as in 1970. Reality has after all caught up with utopia, and Brasília has in many ways become a mirror of a global urban situation. Nevertheless, it remains, just like Chandigarh, a powerful monument to the modernist ideal of building a society upon an architectural base.

A Legacy

With the foundation of Chandigarh and Brasília dating back more than 60 years, these monuments built to the ideology of progress appear today like urbanistic fossils of a distant past. However, both cities have turned out to be not merely ossified museifications of their initial grand utopias but, despite their persistent problems and flaws, fairly successful examples of living with modernity. Furthermore, both cities offer a number of characteristics that render them relevant within the contemporary discourse on architecture and urbanism. In order to sum up the significance of Chandigarh and Brasília today, I would like to briefly discuss a few of these aspects.

It has been argued repeatedly that the visions for the city as well as their implementation by Juscelino Kubitschek, Oscar Niemeyer and Lúcio Costa on the one hand, and Jawaharlal Nehru, Le Corbusier, and his colleagues on the other were much more related to the grand urbanistic endeavors of absolutist regimes of past centuries than to the contemporary situation of urban planning at the beginning of the twenty-first century. At the same time Chandigarh and Brasília were perhaps only the two most prominent in a number of similar undertakings with equally (post-)colonial implications. Pakistan started to build its new capital Islamabad in the sixties according to the vision of the Greek architect Constantinos Doxiadis, while the Japanese architect Kenzo Tange took charge of the construction of Abuja, the new Nigerian capital, as late as 1976. That planned capitals have their own history is evidenced by such diverse examples as Karlsruhe, Saint Petersburg, Washington, DC, New Delhi, or Canberra.

While it cannot be contested that the building of an entire city on an alleged *tabula rasa* as proposed by the Brazilian and Indian examples would hardly be possible within the cultural climate of the post-industrialized democratic Western nations of today, the situation looks much less clear with regard to the contemporary urban hotspots in the Middle and Far East.

A striking characteristic of the image of modernity put forward by the architects of both Chandigarh and Brasília is their predilection for ornamental surfaces and layers. If more recent architecture has been characterized by a considerable revival of ornamental tendencies not least triggered by the new possibilities of Computer-Aided Architectural Design (CAAD), and if several key practitioners of the field of contemporary architecture have claimed to have been first in challenging and overcoming the alleged "taboo" set up by the Viennese architect and theoretician Adolf Loos in his seminal 1908 essay on "Ornament and Crime," Chandigarh and Brasília both belie ornament's supposedly novel status in contemporary architecture. A more historically conscious analysis of the problem would reveal that the "taboo" was already seriously questioned by the thirties in a number of prominent figures and instances. Planar ornamentation resurfaced powerfully in fifties architecture, from where it made its way into the visual repertoire of the Brazilian and Punjabi capitals. At least in Chandigarh, the ornamental screens on the façades of the buildings help air circulation and thus serve climatic needs; they are not merely applications for the sake of aesthetics but rather important tools for the functioning of the structures. Contemporary architectural research has attempted to dissolve the boundaries between construction and ornamental decoration (in the sense of an appliqué) by developing the concept of "structural ornament." As it turns out, such a questioning of seemingly rigid and mutually exclusive categories may already be found in the ornamental experimentations in Chandigarh and Brasília.

The intermediary position of Chandigarh and Brasília between a strong commitment to abstract rigidity and its creative – and at times subversive – appropriation by the people is nowhere better epitomized than in the handling of seriality and modularity. Both concepts are omnipresent, perhaps more so in Brasília than in Chandigarh, and seem to make a strong statement for a Fordist idea of architectural production based on rationalization, standardization, and prefabrication. However, as suggested by the history of the construction of the two cities, such modernist production techniques were hardly applied consistently, and construction relied heavily on more conventional building methods. The strong presence of modularity in the architectural imagery of the two cities (and in particular Brasília) appears to be more the representation of an abstract ideal than the consequence of an actual building process. Rather than questioning the utopian character of the two cities, it is actually being enforced: Brasília – like Chandigarh – was built according to an image of the city of the future, and its iconic architecture was to present a vision of a prospective, fully rationalized construction economy. Meanwhile Iwan Baan's photographs affirm that the Fordist ideal put forward by the architectural imagery has been appropriated and humanized by the inhabitants. It has not become an all-dominating, even intimidating symbol of state power or suppression but, quite to the contrary, a receptive backdrop upon which the play of everyday life is continuously being re-enacted. The technological and bureaucratic sublime has been consumed long ago by everyday life, by the actions and the performance of the inhabitants. They have customized their cities for their own needs and ways of life, and through their actions have reworked modern architecture, including its problematic aspects, for successfully living with modernity.

* Author's note: The following essay was written in 2010 and reflects the then state of research. It appears here with only minor edits to consider some more recent avenues of research.
1 Chandigarh became the capital of two Indian states after Haryana seceded from Punjab in 1966. As a union territory, it is administered directly by India's central government. 2 See Le Corbusier, *Oeuvre complète 1946–1952,* vol. 5, ed. W. Boesiger (Zurich: Girsberger, 1953), 42–7.
3 Le Corbusier apparently only hesitantly accepted this fact by claiming somewhat mysteriously that the bicycle was introduced into India only after his plan had been developed and by calling the "two wheelers" the enemy of the automobile that "must not occupy the same roadway." Le Corbusier, *Oeuvre complète 1957–65,* vol. 7, ed. W. Boesiger (Zurich: Les Editions d'Architecture, 1965), 68. 4 See CIAM-France, *La charte d'Athènes, avec un cours liminaire de Jean Giraudoux* (Paris: Plon, 1943). 5 See Le Corbusier, *Oeuvre complète 1952–1957,* vol. 6, ed. W. Boesiger (Zurich: Editions Girsberger, 1957), 52. 6 See Stanislaus von Moos, "The Politics of the Open Hand: Notes on Le Corbusier and Nehru at Chandigarh," *The Open Hand: Essays on Le Corbusier,* ed. Russell Walden (Cambridge, Mass. and London: MIT Press, 1977), 422–3. 7 See von Moos 1977 (n. 6), 437.
8 See Stanislaus von Moos, "Vers une 'Grille ChaBra': Notes on the Exhibition," *Twilight of the Plan: Chandigarh and Brasilia,* ed. Maristella Casciato and Stanislaus von Moos (Mendrisio: Mendrisio Academy Press, 2007), 38.
9 See for example Le Corbusier 1957 (n. 5), 72. 10 For a more detailed discussion of the use and symbolic meaning of concrete in post-Independence architecture in India, see Martino Stierli, "The Politics of Concrete: Industry, Craft, and Labor in the Modern Architecture of South Asia," in Martino Stierli, Anoma Pieris, and Sean Anderson (eds.), *The Project of Independence: Architectures of Decolonization in South Asia, 1947–1985* (New York: MoMA, 2022), 9–34. 11 Norma Evenson, *Two Brazilian Capitals: Architecture and Urbanism in Rio de Janeiro and Brasília* (New Haven and London: Yale University Press, 1973), 203. 12 See Maxwell Fry, "Le Corbusier at Chandigarh," Walden 1977 (n. 6), 357. 13 See Jean-Louis Cohen, *Le Corbusier 1887–1965. Die Lyrik der Architektur um Maschinenzeitalter* (Cologne: Taschen, 2004), 79. Cohen also points to smokehouses in Le Corbusier's native Jura region where farmers used to cure their ham and which had impressed the young architect in his youth. 14 Von Moos 1977 (n. 6), 428. 15 For a critical appraisal of Chandigarh written roughly twenty years after its inception, see Madhu Sarin, "Chandigarh as a Place to Live in" (1974), Walden 1977 (n. 6), 374–411. 16 The Indian architect Aditya Prakash would try to accommodate this kind of informal street life in his unbuilt Linear City proposal. See Vikramaditya Prakash, *One Continuous Line: Art, Architecture and Urbanism of Aditya Prakash* (Ahmedabad: Mapin 2019), 164–171. 17 Quoted in von Moos 1977 (n. 6), 440. 18 For a detailed account of the prehistory as well as the construction of Brasília, see Norma Evenson, *Two Brazilian Capitals: Architecture and Urbanism in Rio de Janeiro and Brasília* (New Haven and London: Yale University Press, 1973); see also Paul Claval et al., *Brasilia. L'Épanouissement d'une capitale* (Paris: Picard, 2006). 19 See Evenson 1973 (n. 1), 115. 20 See in this context Paulo Tavares, "Brasília: Colonial Capital," October 2020, https://www.e-flux.com/architecture/the-settler-colonial-present/351834/braslia-colonial-capital/. 21 See for example J. O. de Meira Penna's contribution in the official brochure on the building of the new capital issued by the Cultural Division of the Ministry of Foreign Relations, "Brasilien baut Brasilia," J. O. de Meira Penna and Lúcio Costa, *Brasilia* (Rio de Janeiro: Divisão Cultural do Ministerio das Relações Exteriores, 1959). 22 See Evenson (n. 1), 165. 23 See in this respect Farès El-Dahdah (ed.), *Lucio Costa: Brasilia's Superquadra* (Munich: Prestel, 2005). 24 See Stanislaus von Moos, *Le Corbusier: Elements of a Synthesis,* revised and expanded edition (Rotterdam: 010 Publishers, 2009), 253. Norma Evenson, in contrast, has emphasized Niemeyer's relative autonomy from Le Corbusier's example by the time of his designs for Brasília; see Evenson 1973 (n. 1), 204. 25 For a thorough appraisal of Brasília from a sociological-anthropological point of view, see James Holston, *The Modernist City: An Anthropological Critique of Brasília* (Chicago and London: University of Chicago Press, 1989).
26 Alan Colquhoun, *Modern Architecture* (Oxford: Oxford University Press, 2002), 216–7.

Authors' Biographies

Iwan Baan (*1975) is a Dutch photographer based between Amsterdam and the U.S., known primarily for images that narrate the life and interactions that occur within architecture. With no formal training in architecture, Baan's photographs reflect the questions and perspectives of the everyday individuals who give meaning and context to the architecture and spaces that surround us. His artistic approach has given matters of architecture an approachable and accessible voice. In 2012, he received the Golden Lion at the Venice Biennale for his work on the Torre David in Caracas, Venezuela, gaining him further international acclaim. Architects turn to Baan to give their work a sense of place and narrative within their environments.

Cees Nooteboom (*1933) debuted in 1955 with the novel *Philip en de anderen* (Philip and the Others) and has since built up an imposing oeuvre of novels, poetry, short stories and travelogues. As one of the greatest and most innovative contemporary Dutch writers, he is the recipient of the prestigious P.C. Hooft Prize and the Prijs der Nederlandse Letteren for his extensive oeuvre. An internationally renowned, well-traveled individual, his work has been translated into over twenty languages and he has won numerous awards, including the American Pegasus Prize, the European Aristeion Prize and the Formentor Literature Prize 2020. Nooteboom has received honorary doctorates from various universities, including the Freie Universität Berlin and University College London.

Martino Stierli (*1974) is The Philip Johnson Chief Curator of Architecture and Design at the Museum of Modern Art, New York. He is the author of *Montage and the Metropolis: Architecture, Modernity and the Representation of Space* (Yale University Press, 2018) and *Las Vegas in the Rearview Mirror: The City in Theory, Photography, and Film* (Getty Research Institute, 2013). He has organized and co-curated exhibitions on a variety of topics, including the international traveling exhibition *Las Vegas Studio: Images from the Archives of Robert Venturi and Denise Scott Brown.* At MoMA, he curated, among various others, the exhibitions *Toward a Concrete Utopia: Architecture in Yugoslavia, 1948–1980* (with Vladimir Kulić), and *The Project of Independence: Architectures of Decolonization in South Asia, 1947–1985* (with Anoma Pieris and Sean Anderson).

Credits

Iwan Baan
BRASILIA – CHANDIGARH
Living with Modernity

An initiative by Lars Müller

Contributors: Cees Nooteboom, Martino Stierli
Design: Integral Lars Müller
Translation of Cees Nooteboom's essay: Laura Watkinson
Copyediting: John O'Toole
Lithography: Ast & Jakob, Vetsch AG, Köniz, Switzerland
Paper: Munken Lynx, 150 g/m², 1.13
Printing and binding: Graspo, Zlín, the Czech Republic

Lars Müller Publishers
Baden, Switzerland
www.lars-muller-publishers.com

ISBN 978-3-03778-750-2

Printed in the Czech Republic

Acknowledgments

We have decided to reprint this book due to the continuing interest in the title. The two city visions have not lost their appeal. In view of the current urban planning discourse, however, they are somewhat outdated. We express our thanks to Surinder Bahga and Sanyam Bahga for their valuable contacts and reliable knowledge of local conditions in Chandigarh. For help and advice during the preparation and realization of this project, we are indebted to Stephan Ast, Cristina Casagrande, Leonardo Finotti, Joseph Grima, Günther Vogt and Alexander Scherrer. We thank Cees Nooteboom and Martino Stierli for their texts, which have not diminished in validity nor in impact.
— Lars Müller and Iwan Baan

I would like to thank all those who have helped to make this book a reality: Adalberto Vilela, who opened all the doors that needed to be opened in Brasília, and Joana França, who negotiated the city streets and back alleys. Surinder Bahga and his son, Sanyam Bahga, who for many years have greeted Le Corbusier aficionados coming to Chandigarh and know every sector of the city. Caroline James, whose research helped me get my bearings in both places. Joost Elffers and Andreas Landshoff, for ingraining in me a love for making books. And finally Lars Müller, for trusting me on this journey.
— Iwan Baan